Microsoft

Microsoft Word
Step by Step
(Microsoft 365 and Office 2021)

Joan Lambert

© **Microsoft Word Step by Step (Microsoft 365 and Office 2021)**
Published with the authorization of Microsoft Corporation by:
Pearson Education, Inc.

Copyright © 2023 by Pearson Education Inc.

ISBN-13: 978-0-13-752272-9
ISBN-10: 0-13-752272-X

Library of Congress Control Number: 2023935870

1 2023

Trademarks

Warning and Disclaimer

Special Sales

For information about buying this title in bulk quantities, or for special sales opportunities (which may include electronic versions; custom cover designs; and content particular to your business, training goals, marketing focus, or branding interests), please contact our corporate sales department at corpsales@pearsoned.com or (800) 382-3419.

For government sales inquiries, please contact governmentsales@pearsoned.com.

For questions about sales outside the U.S., please contact intlcs@pearson.com.

Editor-in-Chief
Brett Bartow

Executive Editor
Loretta Yates

Development Editor
Songlin Qiu

Managing Editor
Sandra Schroeder

Senior Project Editor
Tracey Croom

Project Editor/Copy Editor
Dan Foster

Indexer
Valerie Haynes Perry

Proofreader
Scout Festa

Technical Editor
Laura Acklen

Editorial Assistant
Cindy Teeters

Cover Designer
Twist Creative, Seattle

Compositor
Danielle Foster

Figure Credits
Chapter 6, Green bamboo: Qi Feng/123RF, Defocus abstract background of the sunshine: Icak Dwi Anggraeni/Shutterstock, Rainbow Birthday: AnnieSpratt/Shutterstock, Beautiful dog: RAGHAVENDRA SINGH RD/Shutterstock, Blue flower: Md Shihab Mia/Shutterstock, Google Map: Google LLC. Chapter 7, Two elephants in a zoo: Heiko Kueverling/Shutterstock, Cornucopia horn of plenty: Dan Kosmayer/Shutterstock, Chicken on white background: Dew_gdragon/Shutterstock. Chapter 9, Clouds: paul prescott/Shutterstock. Chapter 10, Bamboo branches: Elnur/Shutterstock.

Contents

Part 1: Get started with Microsoft Word 365

1   Word basics

Part 2: Create professional documents

Part 3: Enhance document content

Part 4: Review and finalize documents

Part 5: Use advanced Word functions

Acknowledgments

Every book represents the combined efforts of many individuals. First and foremost, I must extend my deep appreciation to Paul McFedries for jumping into the void to contribute to many chapters of this edition of the book. Paul is the author of several books in the *Step by Step* series. We've worked together on a few, although we've never met in person.

At Pearson, I'm thankful to Loretta Yates for the continuing opportunity to be part of this series, to Charvi Arora and Malobika Chakraborty for keeping things on track, and to Tracey Croom for overseeing the production process.

Laura Acklen performed the technical review of this book, helping us to catch some of the many changes Microsoft rolled out to Word between the time we started and the time we finished creating this content. I'm sure there will be more by the time this book reaches your hands! Please use the feedback mechanism described in the Introduction to let us know about any issues you find.

It was a pleasure to work once again with the production team of Dan Foster (copy editor and absolutely priceless backup developmental editor and technical reviewer), Danielle Foster (compositor and graphics processor), Valerie Haynes Perry (indexer), and Scout Festa (proofreader). They are consummate professionals, and I become a better author each time I work with them.

As always, many thanks and all my love to my divine daughter, Trinity Preppernau.

About the author

Joan Lambert is a certified expert in accessibility, training, Adobe InDesign, Intuit QuickBooks, Dynamics, Windows Server technologies, and many Microsoft applications and systems including Access, Excel, OneNote, Outlook, PowerPoint, SharePoint, Windows, and Word. A former small business owner and recovering workaholic, she has worked for over 36 years with Microsoft and Microsoft technologies and for over 26 years in the training and certification industry.

As a member of the Pearson VUE Accessibility team since 2022, Joan has gained a new perspective on computer interactions and the importance of providing equitable access to technology and content. Through her books, Joan enjoys helping people gain confidence and increase their productivity. She has written more than 50 books about Windows, Office, and SharePoint technologies, including dozens of *Step by Step* books and five generations of Microsoft Office Specialist certification study guides. Students who use the *GO! with Microsoft Office* textbook products from Pearson may overhear her cheerfully demonstrating Office features in the videos that accompany the series.

A native of the Pacific Northwest, Joan has had the good fortune to live in many parts of the world—including Germany, New Zealand, Sweden, and Denmark—and many of our United States. She currently resides with her family—one daughter, two dogs, two cats, and five chickens—in the Beehive State, where she enjoys the majestic mountain views, mostly blue skies, and occasional snowstorm.

Introduction

Welcome! This *Step by Step* book has been designed so you can read it from the beginning to learn about Microsoft Word 365 (or Word 2021) and then build your skills as you learn to perform increasingly specialized procedures. Or, if you prefer, you can jump in wherever you need guidance for performing tasks. The how-to steps are delivered crisply and concisely—just the facts. You'll also find informative graphics that support the instructional content.

Who this book is for

Microsoft Word Step by Step (Microsoft 365 and Office 2021) is designed for use as a learning and reference resource by people who want to use Word to create and edit documents, and who want to make use of the many features that help users achieve an attractive and professional result. The book content is designed to be useful for people who are upgrading from earlier versions of Word and for people who are discovering Word for the first time.

The *Step by Step* approach

This book's coverage is divided into parts representing general Word skill sets. Each part is divided into chapters representing skill set areas, and each chapter is divided into topics that group related skills. Each topic includes expository information followed by generic procedures. At the end of the chapter, you'll find a series of practice tasks that you can complete on your own by using the skills taught in the chapter. You can use the practice files available from this book's website to work through the practice tasks, or you can use your own files.

Features and conventions

This book has been designed to lead you step by step through tasks you're likely to want to perform in Word. The topics are all self-contained, so you can start at the beginning and work your way through all the procedures or reference them independently. If you have worked with a previous version of Word, or if you complete all the exercises and later need help remembering how to perform a procedure, the following features of this book will help you locate specific information:

- **Detailed table of contents** Browse the listing of the topics, sections, and sidebars within each chapter.

- **Chapter thumb tabs and running heads** Identify the pages of each chapter by the thumb tabs on the book pages' open fore edge. Find a specific chapter by number or title by looking at the running heads at the top of even-numbered (verso) pages.

- **Topic-specific running heads** Within a chapter, quickly locate the topic you want by looking at the running heads at the top of odd-numbered (recto) pages.

- **Practice tasks page tabs** Easily locate the practice tasks at the end of each chapter by looking for the full-page stripe on the book's fore edge.

- **Detailed index** Look up coverage of specific tasks and features in the index at the back of the book.

You can save time when reading this book by understanding how the *Step by Step* series provides procedural instructions and auxiliary information and identifies on-screen and physical elements that you interact with. The following table lists content formatting conventions used in this book.

Convention	Meaning
TIP	This reader aid provides a helpful hint or shortcut to simplify a task.
IMPORTANT	This reader aid alerts you to a common problem or provides information necessary to successfully complete a procedure.
SEE ALSO	This reader aid directs you to more information about a topic in this book or elsewhere.
1. Numbered steps 2. 3.	Numbered steps guide you through generic procedures in each topic and hands-on practice tasks at the end of each chapter.
■ Bulleted lists	Bulleted lists indicate single-step procedures and sets of multiple alternative procedures.
Interface objects	In procedures and practice tasks, semibold black text indicates on-screen elements that you should select (click or tap).
User input	Light semibold formatting identifies specific information that you should enter when completing procedures or practice tasks.
Ctrl+P	A plus sign between two keys indicates that you must select those keys at the same time. For example, "press **Ctrl+P**" directs you to hold down the **Ctrl** key while you press the **P** key.
Emphasis and *URLs*	In expository text, italic formatting identifies web addresses and words or phrases we want to emphasize.

Download the practice files

Before you can complete the practice tasks in this book, you must download the book's practice files to your computer from:

MicrosoftPressStore.com/Word365SBS/downloads

Follow the instructions on the webpage.

> ⚠ **IMPORTANT** Word and other Microsoft 365 apps are not available from this book's website. You should install Word 365 from the Microsoft 365 desktop app or from *www.microsoft.com/microsoft-365*, or install Word 2021, before working through the procedures and practice tasks in this book.

You can open the files that are supplied for the practice tasks and save the finished versions of each file. If you want to repeat practice tasks later, you can download the original practice files again.

> 🔍 **SEE ALSO** For information about opening and saving files, see "Open and move around in documents" in Chapter 2, "Create and manage documents."

The following table lists the files available for use while working through the practice tasks in this book.

Chapter	Folder	File
Part 1: Get started with Microsoft Word		
1: Word basics	Word365SBS\Ch01	None
2: Create and manage documents	Word365SBS\Ch02	DisplayViews.docx EditProperties.docx NavigateFiles.docx
3: Enter and edit text	Word365SBS\Ch03	EditText.docx FindText.docx ImportText.docx ResearchText.docx
Part 2: Create professional documents		
4: Modify the structure and appearance of text	Word365SBS\Ch04	ApplyStyles.docx ChangeTheme.docx CreateLists.docx FormatCharacters.docx FormatParagraphs.docx StructureContent.docx
5: Organize information in columns and tables	Word365SBS\Ch05	AddColumns.docx CreateTabbedLists.docx CreateTables.docx FormatTables.docx

Chapter	Folder	File
6: Add simple graphic elements	Word365SBS\Ch06	AddInformation.docx Bamboo1.jpg EditPictures.docx InsertClippings.docx InsertIcons.docx InsertPictures.docx
Part 3: Enhance document content		
7: Insert and modify diagrams and 3D models	Word365SBS\Ch07	Astronaut.glb Chickens.jpg Create3DModels.docx CreateDiagrams.docx CreatePictograms.docx Fish.jpg Globe.glb ModifyDiagrams.docx Penguins.jpg Tiger.jpg
8: Insert and modify charts	Word365SBS\Ch08	CreateCharts.docx FormatCharts.docx ModifyCharts.docx Temperatures.xlsx
9: Format document elements	Word365SBS\Ch09	AddWatermarks.docx Clouds.jpg InsertBuildingBlocks.docx InsertHeadersFooters.docx Logo.jpeg
10: Organize and arrange content	Word365SBS\Ch10	ArrangeObjects.docx Bamboo1.jpg Bamboo2.jpg ControlLayout.docx ReorganizeOutlines.docx

Chapter	Folder	File
Part 4: Review and finalize documents		
11: Collaborate on documents	Word365SBS\Ch11	ControlChanges.docx MergeDocs1.docx MergeDocs2.docx ReviewComments.docx TrackChanges.docx
12: Finalize and distribute documents	Word365SBS\Ch12	ControlLayout.docx CorrectErrors.docx PrepareDocument.docx PreviewPages.docx PrintDocument.docx
Part 5: Use advanced Word functions		
13: Reference content and content sources	Word365SBS\Ch13	CompileBibliography.docx CreateIndexes.docx CreateTOC.docx DisplayFields.docx InsertBookmarks.docx InsertFootnotes.docx
14: Merge data with documents and labels	Word365SBS\Ch14	CreateEnvelopes.docx CustomerList.csv CustomerList.xlsx InsertFields.docx PolicyholdersList.xlsx RefineData.docx StartMerge.docx
15: Create custom document elements	Word365SBS\Ch15	ChangeTheme.docx CreateBuildingBlocks.docx CreateStyles.docx CreateTemplates.docx CreateThemes.docx
16: Customize options and the user interface	Word365SBS\Ch16	None

E-book edition

If you're reading the e-book edition of this book, you can do the following:

- Search the full text

- Print

- Copy and paste

You can purchase and download the e-book edition from the Microsoft Press Store at:

MicrosoftPressStore.com/Word365SBS/detail

Get support and give feedback

We've made every effort to ensure the accuracy of this book and its companion content. We welcome your feedback.

Errata and support

If you discover an error, please submit it to us at:

MicrosoftPressStore.com/Word365SBS/errata

We'll investigate all reported issues, update downloadable content if appropriate, and incorporate necessary changes into future editions of this book.

For additional book support and information, please visit:

MicrosoftPressStore.com/Support

For assistance with Microsoft software and hardware, visit the Microsoft Support site at:

support.microsoft.com

Stay in touch

Let's keep the conversation going! We're on Twitter at *twitter.com/MicrosoftPress.*

Adapt exercise steps

This book contains many images of the Word user interface elements (such as the ribbon and the app window) that you'll work with while performing tasks in Word 365 on a Windows computer. Unless we're demonstrating an alternative view of content, the screenshots shown in this book were captured on a horizontally oriented display at a screen resolution of 1920 × 1080 and a magnification of 100 percent. If your settings are different, the ribbon on your screen might not look the same as the one shown in this book. As a result, exercise instructions that involve the ribbon might require a little adaptation.

Simple procedural instructions use this format:

- On the **Insert** tab, in the **Illustrations** group, select the **Chart** button.

If the command is in a list, our instructions use this format:

- On the **Home** tab, in the **Editing** group, select the **Find** arrow and then, in the **Find** list, select **Go To**.

If differences between your display settings and ours cause a button to appear differently on your screen than it does in this book, you can easily adapt the steps to locate the command. First select the specified tab, and then locate the specified group. If a group has been collapsed into a group list or under a group button, select the list or button to display the group's commands. If you can't immediately identify the button you want, point to likely candidates to display their names in ScreenTips.

Multistep procedural instructions use this format:

1. To select the paragraph that you want to format in columns, triple-click the paragraph.

2. On the **Layout** tab, in the **Page Setup** group, select the **Columns** button to display a menu of column layout options.

3. On the **Columns** menu, select **Three**.

On subsequent instances of instructions that require you to follow the same process, the instructions might be simplified in this format because the working location has already been established:

1. Select the paragraph that you want to format in columns.

2. On the **Columns** menu, select **Three**.

The instructions in this book assume that you're selecting on-screen content and user interface elements on your computer by clicking (with a mouse, touchpad, or other hardware device) or tapping a touchpad or the screen (with your finger or a stylus). Instructions refer to Word user interface elements that you click or tap on the screen as *buttons*, and to physical buttons that you press on a keyboard as *keys*, to conform to the standard terminology used in documentation for these products.

When the instructions tell you to enter information, you can do so by typing on a connected external keyboard, tapping an on-screen keyboard, or even speaking aloud, depending on your computer setup and your personal preferences.

Pearson's Commitment to Diversity, Equity, and Inclusion

Pearson is dedicated to creating bias-free content that reflects the diversity of all learners. We embrace the many dimensions of diversity, including but not limited to race, ethnicity, gender, socioeconomic status, ability, age, sexual orientation, and religious or political beliefs.

Education is a powerful force for equity and change in our world. It has the potential to deliver opportunities that improve lives and enable economic mobility. As we work with authors to create content for every product and service, we acknowledge our responsibility to demonstrate inclusivity and incorporate diverse scholarship so that everyone can achieve their potential through learning. As the world's leading learning company, we have a duty to help drive change and live up to our purpose to help more people create a better life for themselves and to create a better world.

Our ambition is to purposefully contribute to a world where:

- Everyone has an equitable and lifelong opportunity to succeed through learning.
- Our educational products and services are inclusive and represent the rich diversity of learners.
- Our educational content accurately reflects the histories and experiences of the learners we serve.
- Our educational content prompts deeper discussions with learners and motivates them to expand their own learning (and worldview).

While we work hard to present unbiased content, we want to hear from you about any concerns or needs with this Pearson product so that we can investigate and address them.

Please contact us with concerns about any potential bias at https://www.pearson.com/report-bias.html.

Part 1

Get started with Microsoft Word 365

Word basics

1

When you use a computer app to create, edit, and format text documents, you're performing a task known as *word processing*. Word 365 is one of the most sophisticated word-processing apps available. You can use Word to efficiently create a wide range of business and personal documents, from a simple letter to a complex report. Word includes many desktop publishing features that you can use to enhance the appearance of documents so that they are visually appealing and easy to read.

The elements that control the appearance of Word and the way you interact with it while you create documents are collectively referred to as the *user interface*. Some user interface elements, such as the color scheme, are cosmetic. Others, such as toolbars, menus, and buttons, are functional. The default Word configuration and functionality is based on the way that most people work with the app. You can modify cosmetic and functional user interface elements to suit your preferences and working style.

This chapter guides you through procedures related to starting Word, working in the Word user interface, discovering new features, managing Microsoft 365 app settings, getting help, and sending feedback to the Microsoft Word team.

In this chapter

- Start Word
- Work in the Word user interface
- Manage Microsoft 365 app settings
- Get help and provide feedback

Start Word

You can start Word 365 from the Start menu app list or tile area, the Start screen, or the taskbar search box. You might also have a shortcut to Word on your desktop or on the Windows taskbar.

When you start Word without opening a specific document, the Word Home page appears. The Home page is a simplified hybrid of the Open and New pages of the Backstage view. It displays file templates and recent files that you might want to reopen. If you're using Word as part of a Microsoft 365 subscription, the Home page displays files from all the Word instances linked to your account.

The Word Home page

> ✓ **TIP** You can turn off the appearance of the Home page (also called the Start screen) if you want to go directly to a new, blank document. For information, see "Change default Word options" in Chapter 16, "Customize options and the user interface."

To start Word by opening a document

- In File Explorer, double-click the document.

- In Microsoft Outlook, double-click a document attached to an email message.

> ✓ **TIP** By default, Word opens documents from online sources in Protected View, which prevents editing and printing of the documents. To turn off Protected View, select Enable Editing on the information bar below the ribbon.

To start Word without opening a document

1. Select the Start button, and then select **All apps**.

2. In the app list, select any index letter to display the alphabet index, and then select **W** to scroll the app list to the apps starting with that letter.

3. Scroll the list if necessary, and then select **Word** to start the app.

Work in the Word user interface

The Word user interface provides intuitive access to all the tools you need to develop sophisticated documents tailored to the needs of your audience. You can use Word 365 to do the following:

- Create professional-looking documents that incorporate impressive graphics.

- Review document content for spelling, grammar, and punctuation issues; consistent and audience-appropriate writing style; clarity, conciseness, inclusiveness, and other attributes that you select.

- Give documents a consistent look by applying styles and themes that control the font, size, color, and effects of text and the page background.

- Store and reuse preformatted elements such as cover pages and sidebars.

- Create personalized mailings to multiple recipients without repetitive typing.

- Track reference information and compile tables of contents, indexes, and bibliographies.

- Find quotes, information sources, and images to support your document content.

- Coauthor documents with team members.

- Safeguard documents by controlling who can make changes and the types of changes that can be made, and by removing personal and confidential information.

When you're working with a document, it's displayed in an app window that contains all the tools you need to add and format content.

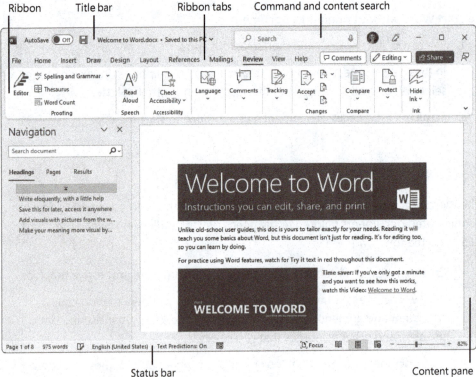

A typical document displayed in Word

Identify app window elements

The Word app window contains the elements described in this section. Commands for tasks you perform often are readily available, and even those you might use only infrequently are easy to find.

Title bar

Located at the top of the app window, the title bar displays the name of the active file and provides tools for managing the app window and content. If the file is stored online in Microsoft OneDrive or Microsoft SharePoint, a menu adjacent to the file name provides a place to edit the file name and access the storage location and version history.

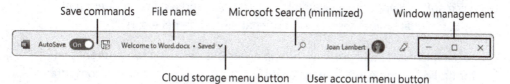

The title bar elements differ based on the file storage location

The three window-management buttons at the right end of the title bar serve the same functions in all Microsoft 365 apps. You control the display of the ribbon by selecting commands on the Ribbon Display Options menu, temporarily hide the app window by selecting the Minimize button, adjust the size of the window by selecting the Restore Down/Maximize button, and close the active document or exit the app by selecting the Close button.

> **SEE ALSO** For information about different methods of closing documents and exiting Word, see "Save and close documents" in Chapter 2, "Create and manage documents."

About Microsoft 365 apps

Word 365 is part of the Microsoft 365 suite of apps, which also includes Microsoft Access, Calendar, Excel, Forms, Lists, Loop, OneDrive, OneNote, Outlook, People, PowerPoint, SharePoint, Sway, Teams, To Do, and many others. (For a full list, visit *microsoft.com/microsoft-365/products-apps-services*.) Some of these are desktop apps that run on your computer, some are web apps that run in a browser, and some, such as Word, have both desktop and online versions. The core Microsoft 365 apps—Word, Excel, Outlook, PowerPoint, OneDrive, SharePoint, and Teams—are designed to work together to provide highly efficient methods of getting things done.

Microsoft 365 apps are available by subscription and receive frequent feature updates, quality updates, and security patches when necessary.

Some Microsoft 365 apps have multiple versions designed for different platforms. For example, you can install different versions of Word on a computer, a smartphone, and a tablet; you can also work in a version of Word hosted entirely online. Although the core purpose of an app remains the same regardless of the platform on which it runs, the available functionality and the way you interact with the app might differ.

Microsoft 365 has subscription options designed for individual home and business users, students, families, small businesses, midsize businesses, enterprises, government agencies, academic institutions, and nonprofits; in other words, whatever your needs may be, there's a subscription option for you! Many of the subscription options include licensing for the desktop apps and the online apps and permit each user to install the desktop apps on up to five devices, including Windows computers, Mac computers, Windows tablets, Android tablets, iPads, and smartphones.

If you have Word as part of a Microsoft 365 subscription and are working on a document stored in a Microsoft SharePoint document library or Microsoft OneDrive folder, you'll also have access to Word Online. You can review and edit documents in Word Online, which runs directly in your web browser instead of as an app installed on your computer. Online apps are installed in the online environment in which you're working and are not part of the desktop version that you install directly on your computer.

SEE ALSO For information about connecting to OneDrive and SharePoint sites, see "Manage Microsoft 365 app settings" later in this chapter.

Word Online displays the contents of a document very much like the desktop app does, and offers a limited subset of the commands and content formatting options available in the full desktop app. If you're working with a document in Word Online and find that you need more functionality than is available, and you have the full version of Word installed on your computer, you can select Open In Word to open the document in the full desktop app.

The ribbon of commands

Below the title bar, most commands for working with a Word document are available from the *ribbon* so you can work efficiently with the app. The ribbon is divided into tabs; each tab displays groups of commands. There are two types of tabs:

- **Standard ribbon tabs**   These tabs are available regardless of the content you're working with. The Home tab, which is active by default, contains the most frequently used commands. Other standard tabs contain commands specific to the type of action you want to perform, such as Insert, Draw, and Design.

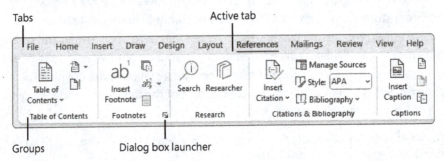

Elements of the ribbon

> ![check] **TIP**   The available ribbon tabs and the appearance of commands on the ribbon might differ from what is shown in this book, based on the apps installed on your computer, the Word settings and window size, the screen settings, and whether your computer has a touchscreen. For more information, see the sidebar "Adapt procedures for your environment" later in this section.

- **Object-specific tool tabs**   When a graphic element such as a picture, table, or chart is selected in a document, one or more *tool tabs* appear at the right end of the ribbon to make commands related to that specific object easily accessible. Tool tabs are available only when the relevant object is selected. They are differentiated from the standard tabs by name and color, and are always located to the right of the standard tabs.

A typical tool tab

> **TIP** Some older commands no longer appear as buttons on the ribbon but are still available in Word. You can make these commands available by adding them to the Quick Access Toolbar or the ribbon. For more information, see "Customize the Quick Access Toolbar" and "Customize the ribbon" in Chapter 16.

On each tab, buttons representing commands are organized into named groups. You can point to any button to display a ScreenTip with the command name, its keyboard shortcut (if it has one), and a description of its function.

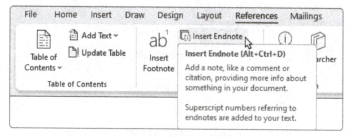

ScreenTips provide helpful information about commands

> **TIP** You can control the display of ScreenTips and of feature descriptions in ScreenTips. For more information, see "Change default Word options" in Chapter 16.

Some buttons include an arrow, which might be integrated with or separate from the button. To determine whether a button and its arrow are integrated, point to the button to activate it. If both the button and its arrow are shaded, selecting the button displays options for refining the action of the button. If only the button or arrow is shaded when you point to it, selecting the button carries out its default action or applies the current default formatting. Selecting the arrow and then an action carries out the action. Selecting the arrow and then a formatting option applies the formatting and sets it as the default for the button.

Buttons with separate and integrated arrows

When a formatting option includes several choices, they're often displayed in a gallery of images, called *thumbnails*, that provide a visual representation of each choice. When you point to a thumbnail in a gallery, the Live Preview feature shows you what the active content will look like if you select the thumbnail to apply the associated formatting. When a gallery contains more thumbnails than can be shown in the available ribbon space, you can display more content by selecting one of the scroll arrows or the More button located on the right edge of the gallery.

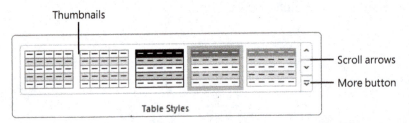

You can scroll gallery content or expand it as a pane

Related but less common commands are not represented as buttons in a group. Instead, they're available in a dialog or pane, which you open by selecting the dialog launcher located in the lower-right corner of the group. (Three of the images shown earlier in this chapter include dialog box launchers. In the fourth image in this chapter, a dialog box launcher is labeled.)

> **TIP** To the right of the groups on the ribbon is the Collapse The Ribbon button, which is shaped like a chevron. For more information, see "Work with the ribbon and status bar," later in this topic.

The Backstage view of Word

Commands related to managing Word and documents (rather than document content) are gathered together in the Backstage view, which you display by selecting the File tab located at the left end of the ribbon. Commands available in the Backstage view are organized on named pages, which you display by selecting the page tabs in the left pane. You redisplay the document and the ribbon by selecting the Back arrow located above the page tabs.

Manage files and app settings on various pages of the Backstage view

If all the page tabs don't fit vertically in the left pane because of the window size or screen resolution, "More" appears at the bottom of the left pane. Selecting the More button displays a menu of the hidden page tabs.

Accessing hidden pages

Collaboration tools

In most versions of Word 365, the Comments, Editing status, Share, and Feedback
buttons appear below the window-management commands, at the right end of the
ribbon. (This might vary in Enterprise subscriptions and new releases.)

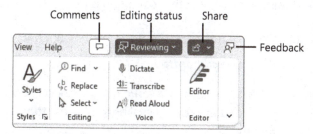

The available collaboration tools vary by file storage location

The Comments button opens the Comments pane, in which you can easily create,
review, respond to, and manage comments. This functionality is also available on the
Review tab.

The Editing Status button indicates (and allows you to change) the read/write and
change-tracking status of the document. The button displays Editing when Track
Changes is off, Reviewing when Track Changes is on, or Viewing when the file is in
read-only mode. To change the settings, select the button and then the new setting.
You can control the change-tracking settings from the Review tab and the read-write
setting from the Backstage view. Grouping the settings together here simplifies things
quite a bit.

Selecting the Share button displays the Share, Copy Link, and Manage Access commands. Select the Share command to create an email message that contains a link to
or copy of the file, or Copy Link if you want to insert a link to the file into a chat message or existing email. The Manage Access command provides insight into the people
who currently have read or edit access to the file.

 SEE ALSO For information about the Feedback button, see "Get help and provide
feedback" later in this chapter.

Status bar

Across the bottom of the Word window, the *status bar* displays information about the current document and provides access to certain Word functions. You can choose which statistics and tools appear on the status bar. Some items, such as Document Updates Available, appear on the status bar only when that condition is true.

The left end of the Word status bar displays document information and tools

At the right end of the status bar in the Word, Excel, and PowerPoint app windows are the View Shortcuts toolbar, the Zoom slider, and the Zoom Level button. These tools provide convenient methods for adjusting the display of file content.

Change the on-screen display of file content from the right end of the status bar

> **SEE ALSO** On a touchscreen device, the appearance of the buttons on the View Shortcuts toolbar changes depending on whether you're in Mouse mode or Touch mode. For more information, see the next section, "Work with the ribbon and status bar." For information about changing the content view, see "Display different views of documents" in Chapter 2.

Work with the ribbon and status bar

The goal of the ribbon is to make working with document content as intuitive as possible. The ribbon is dynamic, meaning that as its width changes, its buttons adapt to the available space. As a result, a button might be large or small, it might or might not have a label, or it might even change to a list entry.

At 1600 pixels wide, all button labels are visible

If you make the app window narrower (and decrease the horizontal space available to the ribbon), small button labels disappear, and entire groups of buttons might hide under one button that represents the entire group. Selecting the group button displays a list of the commands available in that group.

At 1200 pixels wide, command labels disappear, and groups collapse under buttons

When the ribbon becomes too narrow to display all the groups, a scroll arrow appears at its right end. Selecting the scroll arrow displays the hidden groups.

In narrow windows, scroll to display additional group buttons

The width of the ribbon depends on these three factors:

- **App window width** Maximizing the app window provides the most space for the ribbon.

- **Screen resolution** Screen resolution is the size of your screen display expressed as pixels wide × pixels high. The greater the screen resolution, the greater the amount of information that will fit on one screen. Your screen resolution options are dependent on the display adapter installed in your computer, and on your monitor. Common screen resolutions range from 800 × 600 to 2560 × 1440 (and some are larger). The greater the number of pixels wide (the first number), the greater the number of buttons that can be shown on the ribbon.

- **The magnification of your screen display** If you change the screen magnification setting in Windows, text and user interface elements are larger and therefore more legible, but fewer elements fit on the screen.

Adapt procedures for your environment

This book contains many images of the Word ribbon, app window, and other user interface elements that you'll work with while performing tasks in Word on a Windows computer. Depending on your screen resolution, window width, or other installed apps, the Word ribbon on your screen might look different from what's shown in this book. As a result, exercise instructions that involve the ribbon might require a little adaptation.

Simple procedural instructions use this format:

- On the **Insert** tab, in the **Illustrations** group, select the **Chart** button.

If the command is in a list, instructions use this format:

- On the **Home** tab, in the **Editing** group, select the **Find** arrow and then, in the **Find** list, select **Go To**.

A procedure that has multiple simple methods of completion uses this format:

- On the Quick Access Toolbar, select **Save**.

- In the left pane of the Backstage view, select **Save**.

- Press **Ctrl+S**.

If differences between your display settings and ours cause a button to appear differently on your screen than it does in this book, you can easily adapt the steps to locate the command. First select the specified tab, and then locate the specified group. If a group has been collapsed into a group list or under a group button, select the list or button to display the group's commands. If you can't immediately identify the button you want, point to likely candidates to display their names in ScreenTips.

Multistep procedural instructions use this format:

1. To select the paragraph that you want to format in columns, triple-click the paragraph.

2. On the **Layout** tab, in the **Page Setup** group, select the **Columns** button to display a menu of column layout options.

3. On the **Columns** menu, select **Three**.

On subsequent instances of instructions that require you to follow the same process, the instructions might be simplified in this format because the working location has already been established:

1. Select the paragraph that you want to format in columns.

2. On the **Columns** menu, select **Three**.

The instructions in this book assume that you're interacting with on-screen elements on your computer by selecting or clicking them with a mouse, or on a touchpad or other hardware device. If you're using a different method—for example, if your computer has a touchscreen interface and you're tapping the screen (with your finger or a stylus)—substitute the applicable tapping action when the book directs you to select a user interface element.

Instructions in this book refer to user interface elements that you select on the screen as *buttons*, and to physical buttons that you press on a keyboard as *keys*, to conform to the standard terminology used in documentation for these products.

When the instructions tell you to enter information, you can do so by typing on a connected external keyboard, tapping an on-screen keyboard, or even speaking aloud, depending on your computer setup and your personal preferences.

You can hide the ribbon completely if you don't need access to any of its buttons or hide it so that only its tabs are visible. (This is a good way to gain vertical space when working on a smaller screen.) Then you can temporarily redisplay the ribbon to select a button, or permanently redisplay it if you need to select several buttons.

If you're working on a touchscreen device, you can turn on Touch mode, which provides more room between elements of the ribbon, Navigation pane, and status bar. (It doesn't affect the layout of dialogs or panes.) The extra space is intended to lessen the possibility of accidentally tapping the wrong button with your finger. The same commands are available in Touch mode as in Mouse mode (the standard desktop app user interface), but they're sometimes hidden under group buttons.

Mouse mode (left) vs Touch mode (right)

The command for switching between Touch mode and Mouse mode is hidden away, presumably because it isn't one that you would use often. Fortunately, it's quickly available from the Microsoft Search box. Switching any one of the desktop Microsoft 365 apps (Access, Excel, Outlook, PowerPoint, or Word) to Touch mode turns it on in all of them.

To maximize the app window

- Select the **Maximize** button.

- Double-click the title bar.

- Drag the borders of a non-maximized window.

- Drag the window to the top of the screen. (When the pointer touches the top of the screen, the dragged window maximizes.)

To change the screen resolution

1. Do either of the following to open the Display pane of the System settings page:

   - Right-click or long-press (tap and hold) the Windows desktop, and then select **Display settings**.

   - Enter screen resolution in Windows Search, and then in the search results, select **Change the resolution of the display**.

2. In the **Scale and layout** section of the **Display** pane, in the **Screen resolution** list, select the screen resolution you want. Windows displays a preview of the selected screen resolution.

3. If you like the change, select **Keep changes** in the message box that appears. If you don't like the change, select **Revert** or wait for the screen resolution to automatically revert to the previous setting.

To change the magnification

1. Do either of the following to open the Display pane of the System settings page:

   - Right-click the Windows desktop, and then select **Display settings**.

   - Enter screen resolution in Windows Search, and then in the search results, select **Change the resolution of the display**.

2. In the **Scale and layout** section of the **Display** pane, in the **Scale** list, do either of the following:

   - Select the standard scaling option you want.

   - Select **Custom scaling** and enter a custom scaling size from 100 percent to 500 percent.

To completely hide the ribbon

1. In the lower-right corner of the ribbon, select the **Ribbon Layout Options** button.

The new full-screen mode provides the largest work area

2. On the **Ribbon Layout Options** menu, select **More options** and then **Full-screen mode**.

> ✓ **TIP** Select the ellipsis (...) near the upper-right corner of the full-screen app window to temporarily redisplay the ribbon, select the Ribbon Layout Options button, and then select either Show Tabs Only or Always Show Ribbon to restore it.

To display only the ribbon tabs

-   With the full ribbon showing, double-click any tab name.

-   In the lower-right corner of the ribbon, select the **Ribbon Layout Options** button, and then select **Show tabs only**.

-   Press **Ctrl+F1**.

To temporarily redisplay the ribbon

-   Select any tab name to display the tab until you select a command or click or tap away from the ribbon.

To permanently redisplay the ribbon

- With only the ribbon tabs showing, double-click any tab name.

- Select any tab name, select the **Ribbon Layout Options** button, and then select **Always show Ribbon**.

- Press **Ctrl+F1**.

To optimize the ribbon for touch interaction

1. If the Microsoft Search box is not visible on the title bar, do either of the following to activate it:

   - Select the **Search** icon on the title bar.

   - Press **Alt+Q**.

2. In the **Microsoft Search** box, enter touch.

3. In the **Actions** list, select **Touch/Mouse Mode** and then **Touch**.

To specify the items that appear on the status bar

1. Right-click the status bar (at the bottom of the Word window) to display the Customize Status Bar menu.

Customize Status Bar		
Formatted Page Number	1	
Section	1	
✓ Page Number	Page 1 of 1	
Vertical Page Position	1"	
Line Number	1	
Column	1	
✓ Word Count	0 words	
Character Count (with spaces)	0 characters	
✓ Spelling and Grammar Check	No Errors	
Language	English (United States)	
✓ Label		
✓ Signatures	Off	
Information Management Policy	Off	

Permissions		Off
Track Changes		Off
Text Predictions		Text Predictions: On
Caps Lock		Off
Overtype		Insert
Selection Mode		
✓ Macro Recording		Not Recording
✓ Accessibility Checker		Accessibility: Good to go
✓ Upload Status		
✓ Document Updates Available		
✓ Focus		
✓ View Shortcuts		
✓ Zoom Slider		
✓ Zoom		80%

A check mark indicates each active status bar tool

2. Click or tap to activate or deactivate a status bar indicator or tool. The change is implemented immediately. The menu remains open to permit multiple selections.

3. When you finish, click or tap away from the menu to close it.

Discover new features

To go along with the name change from Office 365, many new features have been incorporated into the Microsoft 365 apps since the previous edition of this book. Experienced Word users would probably like to know about the following changes:

- The user interface does not display the Quick Access Toolbar by default. You can display it above or below the ribbon and add controls to it from the Customize Quick Access Toolbar menu, the Options dialog, or the ribbon just as before.

TIP You might find that you work more efficiently if you organize the commands you use frequently on the Quick Access Toolbar and then display it below the ribbon, directly above the workspace. For more information, see "Display and customize the Quick Access Toolbar" in Chapter 16.

- The Save command that was previously on the Quick Access Toolbar is now located at the left end of the title bar along with the new AutoSave toggle. AutoSave is available only for files that are in cloud storage.

- Also for cloud-stored files, you can rename or move a file while editing it, display its version history, and display, compare, and restore previous file versions from the title bar.

- In the center of the title bar, the Microsoft Search feature provides easy access to file content, app features, Help articles, and previously edited files. Type a search term into the search box.

- If your computer has an internal microphone or you've connected an external microphone or headset to the computer, select the microphone at the right end of the Microsoft Search box, wait for the Listening prompt, and then speak the search term.

- Also available with a microphone or headset, if you prefer speaking to typing you can enter content into files by using the Dictate feature that's available from the Home tab.

- When you dock multiple panes on the right side of the app window—for example, the Styles pane and the Alt Text pane, or even the Navigation pane—they arrange themselves on tabs, taking up only the space of one pane.

- In the Backstage view, if all the page tabs don't fit vertically in the left pane because of the window size or screen resolution, "More" appears at the bottom of the left pane. Selecting the More button displays a menu of the hidden page tabs.

- An extensive library of professional-quality images and icons is available from the Insert Pictures menu. The Online Pictures feature provides easy access to thousands of Creative Commons-licensed images that you can browse by category or locate by search term.

- A new Focus mode displays document content against a black background with none of the app interface visible. You can turn on Focus mode from the status bar, Review tab, or View tab, and turn it off by pressing the Esc key.

- Many accessibility features have been incorporated into the apps.

  - The Accessibility Checker runs by default in the background.

  - An Accessibility command on the status bar provides immediate feedback as to the accessibility of your document and easy access to the Accessibility Pane, which displays the Accessibility Checker's findings and suggested solutions.

  - Alt text is automatically added to pictures that you insert into documents. (You can, and should, review and refine the automatically generated alt text.)

  - Accessibility tools are available from a new Accessibility group on the Review tab. From here, you can check the document accessibility, open the Alt Text pane, open the Navigation pane, turn on Focus mode, and quickly access accessibility-related options in the Word Options dialog.

IMPORTANT Accessibility is frequently associated with the availability of content to people with disabilities such as limited vision or hearing loss, or to people who use assistive technologies such as screen readers, screen magnifiers, or braille displays. In fact, a website or document that is designed for accessibility is easier for *all* people to navigate and comprehend, regardless of the method they use to access the content.

continues

- You can increase the space between commands on the ribbon, menus, and the status bar to make it easier to access the right command when working on a touch-enabled device such as a tablet.

- The ribbon display options now support the display of the whole ribbon, only the tabs, or a full-screen display that entirely hides the ribbon.

- The Help tab provides access to information and training resources and links to contact Microsoft Support, provide feedback about features you like and don't like, and suggest features you'd like to see in future releases. You can also access the release notes for each recent release of Word.

Each new release of Word, particularly through the frequent Microsoft 365 channel, has new features, fixes, or just improvements. As with the certainty of death and taxes, the one thing we know is that we don't know what we don't know! Most people who use a new version of a product try to accomplish things the same way they did in the old version, but this might be more work than necessary. If you're a seasoned Word user, review the ribbon tabs, Backstage view pages, and Word Options dialog for any new or modified features that will simplify the tasks you perform and support your productivity.

Manage Microsoft 365 app settings

You access app settings from the Backstage view—specifically, from the Account page and the Word Options dialog.

The Account page of the Backstage view in Word displays information about your installation of Word (and other Microsoft 365 apps) and the resources you connect to. This information includes:

- Your Microsoft account and links to manage it.

- The current app window background and theme.

- Storage locations and services (such as OneDrive and SharePoint) to which Word is connected.

- Your subscription information and links to manage the subscription.

- The installed version and build number, update options, and links to information about Word and recent updates.

Account information in Word

Microsoft account options

If you use Microsoft 365, Skype, OneDrive, Xbox Live, or Outlook.com, you already have a Microsoft account. (Microsoft account credentials are also used by many non-Microsoft products and websites.) If you don't already have a Microsoft account, you can register any existing account as a Microsoft account, sign up for a free Outlook.com or Hotmail.com account and register that as a Microsoft account, or create an alias for an Outlook.com account and register the alias.

TIP Many apps and websites authenticate transactions by using Microsoft account credentials. For that reason, it's a good idea to register a personal account that you control, rather than a business account that your employer controls, as your Microsoft account. That way, you won't risk losing access if you leave the company.

You can personalize the appearance of your Microsoft 365 app windows by choosing a color scheme, called a *theme*. There are five theme options, which at the time of writing are still referred to in the user interface as Office themes:

- **Dark Gray** Displays the title bar and ribbon tabs in dark gray, and the ribbon commands, status bar, and Backstage view in light gray.

- **Black** Displays the title bar, ribbon tabs, ribbon commands, and status bar in black and dark gray.

- **White** Displays the title bar, ribbon tabs, and ribbon commands in white, and the status bar in the app-specific color.

- **Use System Setting** Coordinates the Microsoft 365 desktop app window settings with the Windows theme settings.

- **Colorful** Displays the title bar and ribbon tabs in a color specific to the app (such as blue for Word and green for Excel), and the ribbon commands, status bar, and Backstage view in light gray.

You can also choose a *background*. which is a subtle design that appears in the title bar area of the Backstage view. (In previous versions of the desktop apps, it appeared in the title bar of the app window, regardless of the active tab.) There are 14 different backgrounds to choose from—Calligraphy, Circles and Stripes, Circuit, Clouds, Doodle Circles, Doodle Diamonds, Geometry, Lunchbox, School Supplies, Spring, Stars, Straws, Tree Rings, and Underwater. If you prefer to not clutter up the title bar, you can choose not to have a background.

From the Connected Services area of the page, you can connect Word to SharePoint sites and OneDrive storage locations to access the files you store there. You must already have an account with one of these services to connect Word to it.

Until you connect to storage locations, they aren't available to you from within Word. For example, when inserting a picture onto a page, you'll have the option to insert a locally stored picture or to search online for a picture. After you connect to your SharePoint or OneDrive accounts, you can also insert pictures stored in those locations.

The changes you make on the Account page apply to all the Microsoft 365 desktop apps installed on all the computers associated with your account. For example, changing the background in Word on one computer also changes it in Outlook on any other computer on which you sign in to Microsoft 365 desktop apps with the same account.

Some of the settings on the Account page are also available in the Word Options dialog, which you open from the Backstage view. This dialog also contains hundreds of options for controlling the way Word works. Chapter 16 provides in-depth coverage of these options. It's a good idea to familiarize yourself with the dialog content so you know what you can modify.

To display your Microsoft account settings

1. With Word running, select the **File** tab to display the Backstage view.

2. In the left pane of the Backstage view, select **Account**.

To manage your Microsoft account settings and connection

1. Display the **Account** page of the Backstage view.

2. In the **User Information** area, select **Sign out** or **Switch account** to begin the selected process.

To change the app window background for all Microsoft 365 desktop apps

■ On the **Account** page, in the **Office Background** list, point to any background to display a live preview in the app window, and then select the background you want.

To change the app window color theme for all Microsoft 365 desktop apps

■ On the **Account** page, in the **Office Theme** list, select **Colorful**, **Dark Gray**, **Black**, or **White**.

To connect to a cloud storage location

1. Display the **Account** page of the Backstage view.

2. At the bottom of the **Connected Services** area, select **Add a service**, **Storage**, and then the specific service you want to add.

Add a service ˅	
Storage Store your documents in the cloud and get to them from almost anywhere >	Box Citrix ShareFile Egnyte OneDrive OneDrive for Business

Connect to personal and business cloud storage locations

To manage your Microsoft 365 subscription

1. On the **Account** page, in the **Product Information** area, select **Manage Account** to display the sign-in page for your Microsoft 365 management interface.

2. Provide your account credentials and sign in to access your options.

To manage Microsoft 365 desktop app updates

- On the **Account** page, select **Update Options**, and then select the action you want to take.

Install available updates from the Backstage view before the automatic installation occurs

To open the Word Options dialog

- In the left pane of the Backstage view, select **Options**.

> **SEE ALSO** For more information about the Word Options dialog, see Chapter 16.

Get help and provide feedback

Word 365 puts help at your fingertips, quite literally, and also makes it easy for you to express your opinions and make requests about app features.

You can get information about a specific topic or command, or locate a person or file, by using the Microsoft Search feature that is conveniently located in the center of the title bar.

🔍 style|	✕

Actions

A̅A̅	Text Styles	
ⅯA	Style Set	>
A⁵	Apply Styles	
A̷	Text Styles	>

Find in Document

🗎	"style" 11 results

Get Help

⑦	Customize or create new styles - Microsoft Support
⑦	Change the color or style of a chart in Office - Microsoft Support
⑦	Get Help on "style"

Media

🖼	"style" - pictures, icons, illustrations...
🔍	More search results for "style"

The easy path to help in any Microsoft 365 desktop app

The Help tab provides access to app information and training resources and ways to contact the Microsoft Support team or submit feedback about your experience using Word. You can browse general information about Word, and find links to additional training resources, in the Help pane.

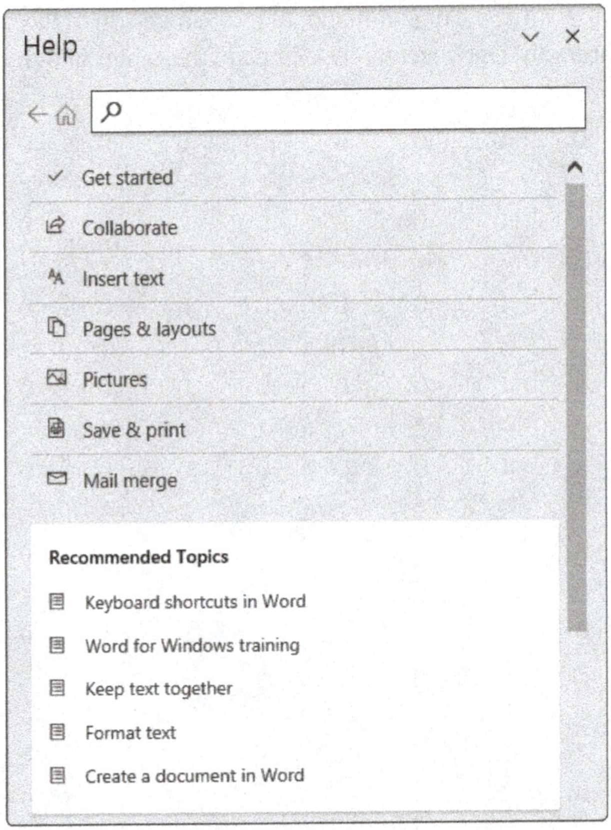

Help	∨ ✕
← ⌂	🔍

✓ Get started

↪ Collaborate

ᴬA Insert text

🗐 Pages & layouts

🖼 Pictures

📄 Save & print

✉ Mail merge

Recommended Topics

📋 Keyboard shortcuts in Word

📋 Word for Windows training

📋 Keep text together

📋 Format text

📋 Create a document in Word

The Help pane displays online content from a variety of resources

✅ **TIP** Most Word Help content is stored online and is available to you only when you have an internet connection.

1

As you use Word and find things that work or don't work for you, you can provide feedback directly to Microsoft from within the program. You can review and vote for existing feature requests and add your own requests. This functionality has been available to early reviewers in the past but is now available to all Microsoft 365 desktop app users.

Send feedback and feature requests

To use the Microsoft Search feature

1. Do one of the following to activate the search box:

   - On the title bar, click or tap in the **Search** box when it's maximized.
   - On the title bar, select the **Search** icon when the search box is minimized.
   - Press **Alt+Q**.

2. In the search box that appears, do either of the following to display a list of related commands and links to online resources, contacts, and files:

   - Enter a search term by typing or tapping.
   - Select the microphone icon (requires a connected audio input device) and then when the search box displays "Listening..." speak your search term or question.

To display the Help pane

- Press **F1**.
- On the **Help** tab, in the **Help** group, select **Help**.

To display the Feedback page of the Backstage view

- At the right end of the ribbon, select the **Feedback** button.

Formerly labeled with a smiley face but still in the same location

- On the **Help** tab, in the **Help** group, select **Feedback**.
- Select the **File** tab to display the Backstage view, and then select the **Feedback** tab.

To send positive or negative feedback about a Word feature

1. If you want to include a screenshot of something specific with your feedback, display it on the screen before proceeding.

2. Display the **Feedback** page of the Backstage view.

3. Select either **Send a Smile** or **Send a Frown** to open a feedback pane.

Send detailed feedback to the Microsoft Word team

4. In the message box, enter your feedback. Be as specific as possible; if you're reporting a problem, detail the steps that led to the problem.

5. If you want to submit a screenshot of the current app window, select the **Include screenshot** checkbox.

6. If you want Microsoft to follow up with you on your query, select the **You can contact me about this feedback** checkbox and then enter your email address.

7. Select **Submit** to send your feedback.

To suggest changes to Word

1. Display the **Feedback** page, and then select **Send a Suggestion** to go to the online feedback forum for the app you're working in.

2. In the **Filters** list on the right, under **Categories**, select categories related to your idea to filter the existing ideas.

3. If an existing idea is the suggestion you want to make, vote for it by selecting **Vote** (the upward-pointing arrow) to the left of the idea title.

4. If your idea hasn't already been suggested, select **Post a new idea**, enter a detailed yet succinct description of your idea, enter your email address (for Microsoft's use only), and then select **Post idea**.

Key points

- Word has many user interface features in common with other Microsoft 365 desktop apps.

- You can change the appearance and functionality of the Word user interface. Changes to the color scheme or app header image affect all Microsoft 365 desktop apps on all computers linked to your user account.

- Information and training is available from the Help tab of the ribbon. Help content is stored online, so it's not available to you when your computer or device is offline.

- You can send feedback and feature requests to the Microsoft Word team, and review and vote for requests that other people have made.

Practice tasks

No practice files are necessary to complete the practice tasks in this chapter.

Start Word

Perform the following tasks:

1. Use one of the procedures described in this chapter to start Word.

2. When the Word Home page appears, press the **Esc** key (or press **Enter** with the Blank Document template selected) to create a new blank document.

Work in the Word user interface

Start Word, create a new blank document, maximize the app window, and then perform the following tasks:

1. On each tab of the ribbon, do the following:

    -   Review the available groups and commands.

    -   Display the ScreenTip of any command you're not familiar with. Notice the different levels of detail in the ScreenTips.

    -   If a group has a dialog launcher in its lower-right corner, select it to display the associated dialog or pane.

2. Change the width of the app window and notice the effect it has on the ribbon. When the window is narrow, locate a group button and select it to display the commands.

3. Maximize the app window. Hide the ribbon entirely and notice the change in the app window. Redisplay the ribbon tabs (but not the commands). Temporarily display the ribbon commands, and then click or tap away from the ribbon to close it.

4. Use any of the procedures described in this chapter to permanently redisplay the ribbon tabs and commands.

5. Display the status bar shortcut menu and identify the tools and statistics that are currently displayed on the status bar. Add any indicators to the status bar that will be useful to you.

6. Keep the document open in Word for use in the next set of practice tasks.

Manage Microsoft 365 app settings

With a new blank document open in Word, perform the following tasks:

1. Display the **Account** page of the Backstage view and review the information available there.

2. Expand the **Office Background** list. Point to each background to display a live preview of it. Then select the background you want to apply.

3. Apply each of the themes and consider its merits. Then apply the theme you like best.

> ✅ **TIP** Depending on the theme you apply, your interface colors may be different from the interface shown in the screenshots in this book, but the functionality will be the same.

4. Review the services to which Word is currently connected. Expand the **Add a service** menu and point to each of the menu items to display the available services. Connect to any of these that you want to use.

5. Select the **Update Options** button and note whether updates are currently available to install.

> ✅ **TIP** When updates are available, the update process takes from 1 to 5 minutes and requires that you exit all the Microsoft 365 desktop apps. (Don't forget to save any work in progress.) If updates are available, apply them after you finish the practice tasks in this chapter.

6. On the **Update Options** menu, select **View Updates** to display the *What's New* webpage in your default browser. Review the information on this page to learn about any new features that interest you.

7. Return to Word and open the **Word Options** dialog.

8. Explore each page of the dialog. Notice the sections and the settings in each section. Note the settings that apply only to the current file.

9. Review the settings on the **General** page and modify them as necessary to fit the way you work. Then close the dialog.

10. Close the document without saving changes.

Get help and provide feedback

Start Word, create a new blank document, and then perform the following tasks:

1. Using the Microsoft Search feature or Help pane, locate information about inserting 3D models into documents. Then research any other topics that interest you.

2. From the Backstage view, display the **Feedback** page and review the options available there.

3. Select **Send a Suggestion** to go to the Word online feedback forum. Review the feature requests that have already been made. If you find a feature request that would be particularly helpful to you, vote for it.

4. Close the webpage and return to the **Feedback** page of the Word Backstage view.

5. If you've already found a feature that you like or dislike, display that feature or an example of it, and use the **Send a Smile** or **Send a Frown** command to send feedback that includes a screenshot.

Create and manage documents

Using Microsoft Word, you can create many different types of documents, for many different purposes. Word is widely used in schools, businesses, and many kinds of organizations to create letters, newsletters, reports, résumés, and other documents that contain text. Word provides a lot of flexibility in document design, so you can also create documents that contain images and content that doesn't fit a standard sheet of paper, such as mailing labels, trifold brochures, greeting cards, business cards, certificates, and signs.

You can open and work with documents from a variety of locations. Word introduces methods of quickly accessing documents from multiple computers that can save you time and conserve storage space. When working in a Word document, you can display different views of the content and the document structure, and use different methods to move around within the document. You can also display and modify document properties, such as the name of the document author and any keywords that apply to the document.

This chapter guides you through procedures related to creating documents, opening and moving around in documents, displaying different views of documents, displaying and editing file properties, and saving and closing documents.

In this chapter

- Create documents
- Open and move around in documents
- Display different views of documents
- Display and edit file properties
- Save and close documents

Create documents

All documents are based on *templates*. Even when you create a "blank" document, that document is based on the default Normal template in Word. You can create a blank document of the default file type or create a document with a predefined design, such as one of the other templates provided with Word. Each non-blank template incorporates specific design elements such as fonts and colors. Most non-blank templates also include typical information that you can modify or build on to create a useful document.

When you start Word, the app displays the Home page that gives you options for opening an existing file or creating a new one. In the New section, you see several templates, including **Blank document**, which creates a new, empty document based on the Normal template. In the Home page, you can select **More templates** to open the New page of the Backstage view.

The Home page appears by default but can be disabled

> ✓ **TIP** The document templates available in Word include standard templates that have been available for many years and featured templates that change occasionally. The templates on the New page of the Backstage view in your installation of Word might be different from those shown in images in this book.

If you're already working in Word, you can create a new document from the New page of the Backstage view. The same templates and search options are available from both the Home page and the New page.

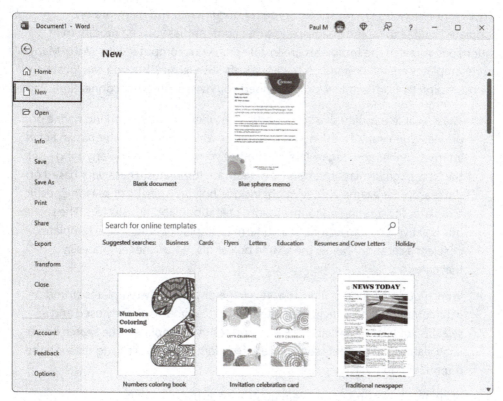

Word provides document templates for a wide variety of purposes

If you create custom templates and save them in your Custom Office Templates folder, Featured and Personal links appear below the search box on the New page. You can select these links to switch between viewing app-supplied templates on the Featured page and your custom templates on the Personal page.

> **SEE ALSO** For information about creating custom templates, see "Create and attach templates" in Chapter 15, "Create custom document elements."

You can start with a blank document that contains one page. You can then add content, apply structure and design elements, and make any necessary configuration changes.

New blank documents are based on the built-in Normal template by default. You can save time by basing your document on a content template and then customizing the content provided in the template to meet your needs.

Most Word templates are for specific types of documents, and many are pre-populated with text, tables, images, and other content that you can modify to fit your needs. A few of the templates are installed on your computer with Word. Many more templates are maintained on the Microsoft 365 website, but you can locate and use them directly from within Word (provided you have an internet connection).

- The available templates vary depending on whether you're working online or offline. When you're working online (that is, when your computer has an active internet connection, regardless of whether you're using it to do anything else), the New page displays thumbnails of featured templates. These vary based on the season; for example, they might include holiday-specific or season-specific templates for creating announcements, invitations, and newsletters. The search box is active; you can enter a search term to display related online templates, or select a category below the search box to display online templates in that category.

- When you're working offline, the New page displays only templates stored on your computer. These include any templates that you've already used and a selection of letter, newsletter, report, and résumé templates. The search box is unavailable; you can only search the offline templates by scrolling through the thumbnails on the New page.

Word document templates contain elements such as the following:

- **Formatting**   Most templates contain formatting, which in addition to styles can include page-layout settings, backgrounds, and themes. A template that contains only formatting defines the look of the document; you add your own content.

- **Text**   Templates can also contain text that you customize for your own purposes. For example, if you base a new document on an agenda template from the Microsoft 365 website, the text of the agenda is already in place; all you have to do is customize it. Sometimes, a document based on a template displays formatted text placeholders surrounded by square brackets—for example, [Company Name]—instead of actual text. You replace a placeholder with your own text by selecting the placeholder and then typing the replacement. If you don't need a placeholder, you can delete it.

2

- **Graphics, tables, charts, and diagrams** Templates can contain ready-made graphic elements, either for use as is or as placeholders for elements tailored to the specific document.

- **Building blocks** Some templates make custom building blocks, such as headers and footers or a cover page, available for use with a particular type of document. They might also include AutoText, such as contact information or standard copyright or privacy policies.

> **SEE ALSO** For information about working with building blocks, see "Insert preformatted document parts" in Chapter 9, "Format document elements," and "Create custom building blocks" in Chapter 15.

- **Custom tabs, commands, and macros** Sophisticated templates might include custom ribbon tabs or toolbars with commands and macros specific to the purposes of the template. A *macro* is a recorded series of commands that helps a user perform a process with minimal effort. The topic of macros is beyond the scope of this book; for information, refer to Word Help.

> **TIP** Current Word template files have one of two file name extensions, depending on their content. Those that contain macros have the .dotm file name extension; those that don't contain macros have the .dotx extension.

When you base a new document on a template, that template is *attached* to the document. The styles defined in the attached template appear in the Styles pane so that you can quickly apply them to any content you add to the document. You can change the document template by attaching a different one.

> **SEE ALSO** For information about attaching templates to existing documents, see "Create and attach templates" in Chapter 15.

To create a new blank document

1. Start Word.

   Word automatically creates a blank document and displays the Home page of the Backstage view.

2. Press the **Esc** key to close the Backstage view.

Or

1. If Word is already running, select the **File** tab to display the Backstage view.

2. Do either of the following:

   - In the **New** section at the top of the Home page of the Backstage view, select the **Blank document** thumbnail.

   - In the left pane of the Backstage view, select **New**. Then on the **New** page of the Backstage view, select the **Blank document** thumbnail.

To preview design templates

1. Display the **New** page of the Backstage view.

2. On the **New** page, scroll through the pane to view the design templates that were installed with Word.

3. Select any thumbnail to open a preview window that displays a sample document page. Then do any of the following:

   - To create a document based on the template that is active in the preview window, select the **Create** button.

   - To view the next or previous template, select the arrow to the right or left of the preview window.

   - To close the preview window without creating a document, select the **Close** button in the upper-right corner of the preview window or click or tap outside the preview window.

When you select a template thumbnail, Word displays a preview of the template

2

To create a document based on an installed template

1. Display the **New** page of the Backstage view.

2. Scroll through the pane to locate the design you want to use.

3. Double-click the thumbnail to create the document.

To create a document based on an online template

1. Display the **New** page of the Backstage view.

2. Do either of the following to display templates related to a specific topic:

   - In the search box, enter a term related to the template content or design you're looking for, and then select the **Search** button or press **Enter**.

   - Below the search box, select one of the suggested searches.

3. Scroll through the pane to locate a design that fits your needs.

4. Double-click any thumbnail to create a file based on the template.

To clear a template search

- To the left of the search box, select **Back**.

Open and move around in documents

In addition to templates, the Home page displays documents you've worked in recently, documents you've pinned to the page so they're always available, and documents other people have shared with you.

Open existing documents

If the document you want to open appears on the Home page, you can open it directly from there. Otherwise, you can open documents stored locally on your computer or in a remote storage location such as a Microsoft OneDrive folder or a Microsoft SharePoint document library, either from within Word or from the document storage location.

> ✅ **TIP** If you receive a Word document as an attachment to an email message, you can open the attached document and start Word, if it isn't already running, from within Outlook, or you can preview the document content directly in the Outlook Reading pane without starting Word.

> ⚠️ **IMPORTANT** Never open a Word document attached to an email message if you do not know the sender because malicious users can embed malware within Word files. Even if you know the sender, if you weren't expecting the Word document, it's best to check with the sender to make sure the file was sent legitimately (and not, say, by a malicious user having hijacked or spoofed that person's email). For more information, see the sidebar "Open documents in Protected View" later in this chapter.

The Open page includes all the locations you've linked to from Microsoft 365 apps

The Open page displays only documents saved in the Word-specific file formats (.docx and .doc) and templates created for those standards. For more information about file formats, see "Save and close documents" later in this chapter.

The Recent list in the right pane of the Open page provides quick access to the documents you've worked with recently. The Recent list includes locally stored documents and documents that you've worked with while signed in with your current account on any computer, tablet, or other device, if the documents are stored in a shared location. This is one of the tremendous benefits of the Microsoft 365 subscription model and the cloud storage that comes with it: you can be up and running on a new computer in minutes, without having to move files or configure settings and preferences. If you use multiple computers, you can use this very convenient feature to seamlessly transition between computers without having to transport files (on a USB flash drive or hard drive) or maintain multiple copies of files in different locations.

> **SEE ALSO** For more information about Microsoft 365 apps, see the sidebar "About Microsoft 365 Apps" in Chapter 1, "Word basics."

To ensure that you can find a specific document quickly regardless of whether you've worked with it recently, you can pin it to your document list. On the Open page, pinned files appear in the Pinned section at the top of the list and are indicated by a thumbtack. On the Home page, they appear on the Pinned tab.

To open a recent document

1. Start Word.

2. On the **Home** page, in the **Recent** list, select the file name of the file you want to open.

Or

1. With Word running, select the **File** tab to display the Backstage view.

2. In the left pane of the Backstage view, select **Open** to display the Open page.

3. With **Recent** selected at the top of the left pane of the Open page, scroll through the file list in the right pane if necessary to locate the document you want to open. Then select the file name to open it.

Open documents in Protected View

When you open a document from an online location (such as a cloud storage location or email message) or from a location that has been deemed unsafe, Word opens the file in Protected View, with most editing functions disabled. This prevents any malicious code from gaining access to your computer. If you're uncertain about the origin of a file that you're opening, you can choose to open the file in Protected View.

In Protected View, the title bar displays *[Read-Only]* to the right of the file name, and a yellow banner at the top of the content pane provides information about why the file has been opened in Protected View. If you know that the document is from a safe location or sender, and you want to edit the file content, you can choose to enable editing. If you don't intend to modify the file content, you can hide the banner by selecting the Close button (the X) at its right end.

If you want to open documents from a specific online storage folder without going into Protected View, you can add that folder (and its subfolders, if you want) to your Trusted Locations list. For information about trusted locations and other Trust Center settings, see "Manage add-ins and security options" in Chapter 16, "Customize options and the user interface."

To pin a document to the Recent file list

1. Display the **Recent** list on the **Open** page of the Backstage view.

2. If necessary, scroll through the list to locate the file you want to pin.

3. Point to the file name, and then select the **Pin** button that appears to the right of the file name to add the file to the Pinned area at the top of the Recent list on the Open page and to the Pinned tab on the Home page.

To open any existing document from within Word

1. Do either of the following to display the **Open** page of the Backstage view:

   - Start Word, and then select **Open**.

   - With Word running, display the Backstage view, and then select **Open**.

2. In the location list, select the local or network storage location where the file is stored.

3. Navigate to the file storage folder you want by using one of the following methods:

- In the right pane, select **Folders**. Then select pinned or recently accessed folders until you reach the folder you want.

- In the left pane, select **Browse** to display the Open dialog. Then select folders in the **Navigation** pane, double-click folders in the file pane, or enter the folder location in the **Address** bar.

4. Double-click the document you want to open.

> **TIP** In the Open dialog, selecting a file name and then selecting the Open arrow displays a list of alternative ways to open the selected document. To look through a document without making any inadvertent changes, you can open the document as read-only, open a copy of the document, or open it in Protected View. You can also open the document in a web browser. In the event of a computer crash or other similar incident, you can instruct the app to open the document and try to repair any damage.

Open and edit PDF files in Word

A useful feature of Word is the ability to open PDF files and edit them by using all the standard Word features. When you finish, you can save the file as a document or as a PDF.

To open a PDF file in Word, do either of the following:

- In File Explorer, right-click or long-press (tap and hold) the PDF file, select **Open with**, and then select **Word**. If you don't see Word in the list of apps, select **Choose another app**, select **Word**, and then select **Just once**.

- In Word, display the **Open** page of the Backstage view, navigate to the file location, select the file, and then select **Open**. (In the Open dialog, PDF files fall into the category of Word Documents.)

Word converts the file to an editable Word document. If the file contains complicated formatting and layout, the Word version of the document might not be a perfect replica of the PDF, but most simple files convert cleanly.

To open a file directly from a OneDrive storage site

1. In your web browser, navigate to the OneDrive folder.

2. Browse to and select the file you want to open.

3. If prompted to do so, enter the Microsoft account credentials associated with your OneDrive, and then select **Sign in**.

Or

1. In File Explorer, navigate to the OneDrive folder.

2. Browse to and double-click the file you want to open.

3. If prompted to do so, enter the Microsoft account credentials associated with your OneDrive, and then select **Sign in**.

Move around in documents

If you open a document that is too long or too wide to fit in the content pane, you can bring off-screen content into view without changing the location of the cursor by using the vertical and horizontal scroll bars. The scroll bars appear only when the document is longer or wider than the content pane. To remove distractions, the scroll bars and pointer fade from sight when you're not using the mouse. You can make them reappear by moving the mouse.

You can also move around in a document by moving the cursor. You can place the cursor in a specific location by clicking or tapping there, or you can move the cursor different distances and in different directions and by pressing keyboard keys.

The cursor location is displayed on the status bar. By default, the status bar displays the page the cursor is on, but you can also display the cursor's location by section, line number, and column, and in inches from the top of the page.

> **SEE ALSO** For information about displaying information on the status bar, see "Work with the ribbon and status bar" in Chapter 1.

In a long document, you might want to move quickly among elements of a certain type—for example, from heading to heading, from page to page, or from graphic to graphic. You can do this from the Navigation pane.

In the Navigation pane, you can move to the next object of a specific type

> **SEE ALSO** For information about working in the Navigation pane, see "Display different views of documents," later in this chapter. For information about using the Navigation pane to search for specific content in a document, see "Find and replace text" in Chapter 3, "Enter and edit text."

A greater variety of browsing options is available from the Go To tab of the Find and Replace dialog. From this tab, you can locate pages, sections, lines, bookmarks, comments, footnotes, endnotes, fields, tables, graphics, equations, objects, or headings. You can jump directly to a specific object if you know its position within the sequence of that type of object in the document (for example, if it is the fifth equation), move forward or backward a specific number of objects, or browse from one object to the next.

From the Go To tab of the Find and Replace dialog, you can move to a specific object

To change the area of a document that is displayed in the content pane

- On the vertical scroll bar, do any of the following:

  - Click or tap the scroll arrows to move up or down one line.

  - Click or tap above or below the scroll box to move up or down by the height of one screen.

  - Drag the scroll box on the scroll bar to display the part of the document corresponding to the location of the scroll box. For example, dragging the scroll box to the middle of the scroll bar displays the middle of the document.

- On the horizontal scroll bar, do any of the following to move side to side:

  - Click or tap the scroll arrows.

  - Click or tap to the left or right of the scroll box.

  - Drag the scroll box on the scroll bar to display the part of the document corresponding to the location of the scroll box.

To move the cursor by using the keyboard keys

- Move the cursor by pressing the key or key combination described in the following table.

To move the cursor	Press
Left one character	Left Arrow
Right one character	Right Arrow
Up one line	Up Arrow
Down one line	Down Arrow
Left one word	Ctrl+Left Arrow
Right one word	Ctrl+Right Arrow
Up one paragraph	Ctrl+Up Arrow
Down one paragraph	Ctrl+Down Arrow
To the beginning of the current line	Home
To the end of the current line	End
To the beginning of the document	Ctrl+Home
To the end of the document	Ctrl+End

To the beginning of the previous page	Ctrl+Page Up
To the beginning of the next page	Ctrl+Page Down
Up one screen	Page Up
Down one screen	Page Down

To show or hide the Navigation pane in a document

- On the **View** tab, in the **Show** group, select the **Navigation Pane** checkbox.

To browse by object from the Navigation pane

- Open the **Navigation** pane, and then do any of the following:

  - At the top of the **Navigation** pane, select **Headings**. Then select any heading to move directly to that location in the document.

  - At the top of the **Navigation** pane, select **Pages**. Then select any thumbnail to move directly to that page of the document.

  - At the right end of the search box, select the arrow. In the **Find** list, select the type of object you want to browse by. Then select the **Next** and **Previous** arrows to move among those objects.

To display the Go To tab of the Find and Replace dialog

- On the **Home** tab, in the **Editing** group, select the **Find** arrow, and then **Go To**.

- In the **Navigation** pane, select the **Search** arrow, and then in the **Search for more things** list, select **Go To**.

- Press **Ctrl+G**.

To browse by object from the Go To What list

1. Display the **Go To** tab of the Find and Replace dialog.

2. In the **Go to what** list, select the type of object you want to search for. Then do any of the following:

   - Select the **Next** button to move to the next object of that type.

   - Select the **Previous** button to move to the previous object of that type.

- In the text box (the name of which varies depending on what you select in the **Go to what** list), enter either of the following, and then select the **Go To** button:

  - Enter a number identifying the position of the object within the total objects of that type in the document. (For example, if you select **Footnote** in the **Go to what** list, enter 4 to move to the fourth footnote in the document.)

  - Enter + (plus sign) or – (minus sign) and then a number to move forward or backward by that many objects of the selected type.

Display different views of documents

You can display a document in different views that provide different types of information and make it easier to interact with specific document elements. For a closer look at the document content, you can increase the magnification of the content pane. If you want a high-level view of the content—for example, to quickly review all the pages of a document for length—you can decrease the magnification and view multiple pages at the same time.

Word has five views in which you can create, organize, and preview documents. Each view is suited to a specific purpose. The views are:

- **Print Layout**   This view displays a document on the screen the way it will look when printed. You can review elements such as margins, page breaks, headers and footers, and watermarks. This is the default view and the view you'll use most frequently (or perhaps the only view you'll use) when developing content.

- **Read Mode**   This view displays as much document content as will fit on the screen at a comfortable size for reading. In this view, the ribbon is replaced by one toolbar at the top of the screen with buttons for searching and navigating in the document. You can display comments, but you can't edit the document in this view.

- **Web Layout**   This view displays the document the way it will look when viewed in a web browser so that you can review the way that text wraps to fit the window and the positioning of graphics. Web Layout view also displays page backgrounds and effects.

- **Outline**   This view displays the structure of a document as nested levels of headings and body text and provides tools for viewing and changing the hierarchy.

> **SEE ALSO** For information about displaying and modifying a document in Outline view, see "Reorganize document outlines" in Chapter 10, "Organize and arrange content."

2

- **Draft** This view displays the content of a document with a simplified layout so that you can quickly enter and edit text. Draft view doesn't display images or layout elements such as headers and footers.

You manage the display of views and of window elements from the View tab of the ribbon. Three of the views are also available from the View Shortcuts toolbar near the right end of the status bar.

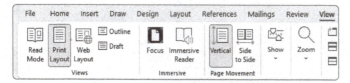

In the Views group on the View tab, the active view is shaded

While you're developing a document in Print Layout view, the content pane displays the content of the document you're working in. Each page is represented at the size specified in the document layout settings, with margins and other white space represented as they will appear when the document is printed. As you scroll through a multipage document, spaces appear between the pages. If you want to fit more content on the screen, you can hide the white space between pages and the margin content—including page headers and footers if the document has them—at the top and bottom of each page.

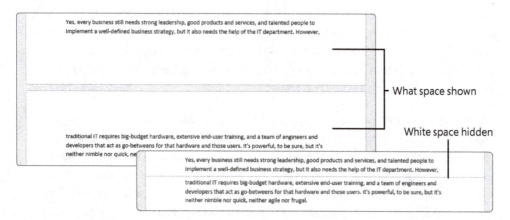

The bottom of one page and the top of the next page with and without white space

When working in Outline view or Draft view, you can display the paragraph style of each paragraph in the left margin, in an area called the style area pane. (It's not a pane, though; it's just a marginal area of the page.) By default, the style area pane width is set to zero inches wide, so it is effectively closed. If you want to display it, you can increase the width.

Style area pane set to 1" width

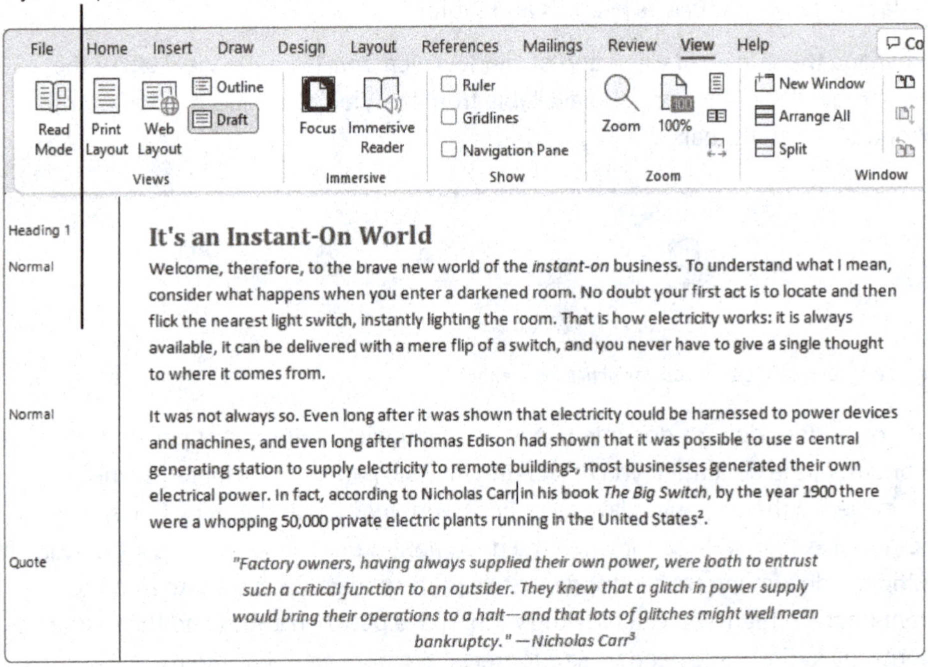

The style area pane is available only in Draft view and Outline view

If your document uses styles to control the appearance and hierarchy of the content, you can display the headings in the Navigation pane and styles in the style area pane so that you can more quickly access and work with styles and styled content. You can also use the Navigation pane to display and move among page thumbnails or search results, as described in the previous topic.

Word has many other task-specific panes in which you can, for example, display Clipboard content, research terminology, review spelling, and format graphics. These panes usually appear to the right or left of the content pane and span its full height. Some of them can float within or outside the Word window or be docked to other sides of the window. Other chapters discuss these panes in the context of their functionality. Regardless of the purpose of the pane, however, you use the same methods to resize or move it.

2

You can change the space available for document content and app window elements by resizing the window, adjusting the relative sizes of the panes, or collapsing or hiding the ribbon. You can entirely hide not only the ribbon content but also the ribbon tabs and the app window title bar.

> **SEE ALSO** For information about hiding, collapsing, and displaying the ribbon, see "Work with the ribbon and status bar" in Chapter 1.

When you want to focus on the layout of a document, you can display rulers and gridlines to help you position and align elements. You can also adjust the magnification of the content area by using the tools available in the Zoom group on the View tab and at the right end of the status bar.

Change the content area magnification by using either the Zoom slider or the Zoom dialog

> **SEE ALSO** For information about controlling paragraph formatting from the ruler, see "Apply paragraph formatting" in Chapter 4, "Modify the structure and appearance of text."

If you want to work with different parts of a document at the same time, you can open the same document in a second window and scroll through each window separately, or you can split the current window into two panes and scroll through each pane independently.

You're not limited to working with one document at a time. You can quickly switch among multiple open documents. If you want to compare or work with the content of multiple documents, you can simplify the process by displaying the documents next to each other.

A feature that can be invaluable when you're fine-tuning the layout of a document in Word is the display of nonprinting characters (such as tabs, paragraph marks, and section breaks) that control the layout of your document. You can control the display of these characters for each window.

To switch among views of a document

- On the **View** tab, in the **Views** group, select the view you want.

- On the **View Shortcuts** section of the status bar, select the view button you want.

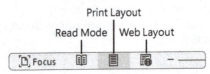
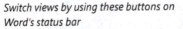

Switch views by using these buttons on Word's status bar

To hide or display the top and bottom page margins in Print Layout view

1. Point to the page break indicator between the end of one page and the start of the next page.

   - When the margins are displayed, including the page headers and footers, a gap between the pages indicates the page break.

   - When the margins are hidden, a horizontal line indicates the page break.

2. When the pointer changes to a representation of the page break with two arrows pointing away from the break when the margins are hidden or toward the break when the margins are displayed), double-click.

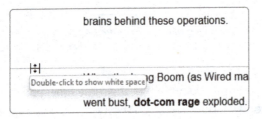

Point to the break between any two pages and then double-click

To show or hide the Navigation pane

- On the **View** tab, in the **Show** group, select or clear the **Navigation Pane** checkbox.

To adjust the size of the Navigation pane

- Point to the right border of the **Navigation** pane. When the pointer changes to a double-headed arrow, drag to the right or left.

> **TIP** The Navigation pane is available in all views except Read Mode. When you adjust the width of the Navigation pane, the pane content changes accordingly. For example, the Navigation pane displays fewer page thumbnails in a narrow pane and more page thumbnails in a wide pane.

To display the style area pane in Draft view or Outline view

1. In the Backstage view, select the **Options** page tab to open the Word Options dialog.

2. In the **Word Options** dialog, select the **Advanced** page tab.

3. On the **Advanced** page, scroll to the **Display** area (about halfway down the page) and change the **Style area pane width in Draft and Outline views** setting to any number greater than 0. Then select **OK**.

To resize the style area pane in Draft view or Outline view

1. Point to the right border of the style area pane.

2. When the pointer changes to a double-headed arrow, drag the border to the left or right.

To change the magnification of document content

1. Do either of the following to open the Zoom dialog:

   - On the **View** tab, in the **Zoom** group, select **Zoom**.

   - At the right end of the status bar, select the **Zoom Level** button.

2. In the **Zoom** dialog, select a **Zoom to** option or enter a specific percentage in the **Percent** box, and then select **OK**.

Or

- In the zoom controls at the right end of the status bar, do any of the following:

  - Drag the slider to the left to decrease the magnification or to the right to increase the magnification.

  - At the left end of the slider, select the **Zoom Out** button to decrease the magnification in 10-percent increments.

  - At the right end of the slider, select the **Zoom In** button to increase the magnification in 10-percent increments.

To display or hide rulers or gridlines in a document

- On the **View** tab, in the **Show** group, do either of the following:

  - Select or clear the **Ruler** checkbox.

  - Select or clear the **Gridlines** checkbox.

> 🔍 **SEE ALSO** For information about controlling document gridlines, see "Arrange objects on a page" in Chapter 10.

To display or hide nonprinting characters and formatting marks in a document

- On the **Home** tab, in the **Paragraph** group, select the **Show/Hide ¶** button.

- Press **Ctrl+*** (asterisk).

> ✅ **TIP** When entering an asterisk (*) on a standard keyboard rather than a numeric keypad, you must hold down the Shift key and then press the number 8 to enter an asterisk. So, in effect, you are pressing Ctrl+Shift+8.

To open a second window displaying the current document

- On the **View** tab, in the **Window** group, select **New Window**.

To split a window into two panes

- On the **View** tab, in the **Window** group, select **Split**.

To display a different open document

- On the **View** tab, in the **Window** group, select **Switch Windows**, and then select the file you want to view.

- Point to the **Word** icon on the Windows taskbar, and then select the thumbnail of the document you want to display.

To display multiple open documents at the same time

- On the **View** tab, in the **Window** group, select **Arrange All**.

Display and edit file properties

Properties are file attributes or settings, such as the file name, size, creation date, author, and read-only status. Some properties exist to provide information to computer operating systems and apps. You can display properties within the content of a document (for example, you can display the page number on the document pages). Word automatically tracks some of the file properties for you, and you can set others.

You can examine the properties attached to a file from the Info page of the Backstage view.

Properties ˅	
Size	53.0KB
Pages	4
Words	851
Total Editing Time	125 Minutes
Title	When the long boom t...
Tags	Add a tag
Comments	Add comments

Related Dates

Last Modified	Today, 1:01 PM
Created	Today, 10:56 AM
Last Printed	

Related People

Author	PM Paul McFedries
	Add an author
Last Modified By	PM Paul McFedries

Some of the properties stored with a typical Word document

You can change or remove basic properties in the default Properties list or expand the list to make more properties available. You can also display the Properties dialog to access even more properties.

To display file properties

1. Display the **Info** page of the Backstage view. The Properties section in the right pane displays the standard properties associated with the document.

2. At the bottom of the **Properties** section, select **Show All Properties** to expand the section.

3. At the top of the **Properties** section, select **Properties**, and then select **Advanced Properties** to open the Properties dialog.

To edit file properties

1. In the **Properties** section of the **Info** page, select the value for the property you want to edit to activate the content box.

2. Enter or replace the property value, and then press **Enter**.

Or

- In the **Properties** dialog, do either of the following:

    - On the **Summary** tab, select the box to the right of the property you want to modify, and then enter or replace the property value.

    - On the **Custom** tab, select the property you want to modify in the **Name** list, and then enter or replace the property value in the **Value** box.

Save and close documents

When you save a document in Word, it is saved in the default .docx file format, but you can also select a different format from many other choices. For example, if you plan to distribute the document electronically to people who use a different word-processing program, you can choose a compatible format, or if you want to protect the document content, you can save it as a PDF file.

Manually save documents

You save a document the first time by selecting the Save button on the title bar or by displaying the Backstage view and then selecting Save As. Both actions open the Save As page, where you can select a storage location.

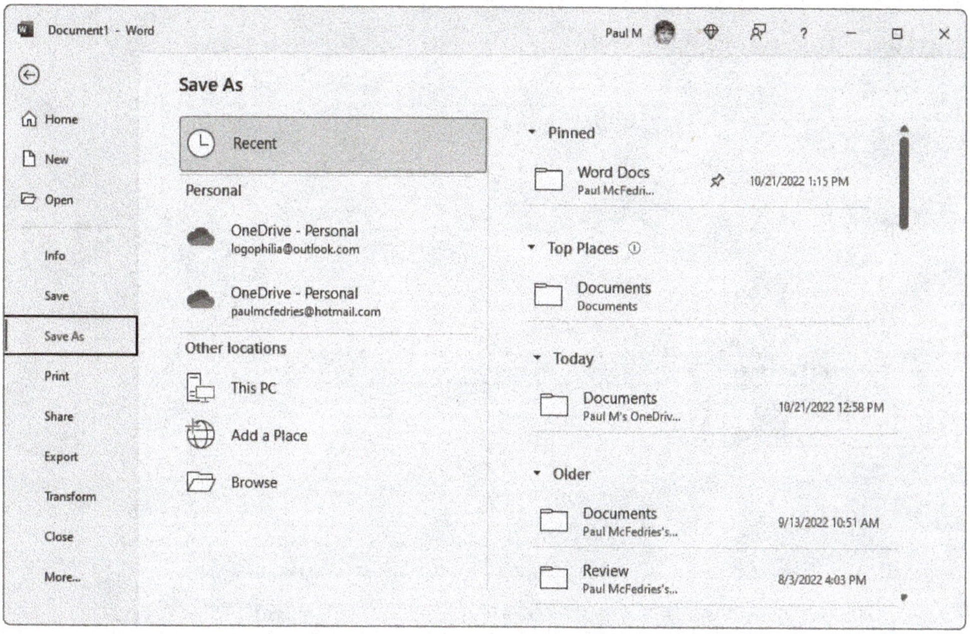

Save your document in an online location to access it from anywhere

You can save the document in a folder on your computer or, if you have an internet connection, in a folder on your OneDrive. If your company uses SharePoint, you can add a SharePoint site so that it is available from the location list on the Save As page, just like any other folder.

SEE ALSO For information about OneDrive, see the sidebar "Save files to OneDrive" later in this chapter.

Selecting Browse at the bottom of the left pane displays the Save As dialog, in which you assign a name to the document and specify the folder in which you want to save it.

The Save As dialog shows other files of the same type that are saved in the current folder

> **TIP** If you want to create a new folder in which to store the document, select New Folder on the Save As dialog toolbar.

After you save a document for the first time, you save changes by selecting the Save button on the title bar. A new version of the document then overwrites the previous version.

To save a document for the first time

1. Select the **File** tab to display the Backstage view.

2. In the left pane of the Backstage view, select **Save As**.

3. On the Save As page of the Backstage view, select a storage location, and then select a recently accessed folder in the right pane, or select **Browse**.

4. In the **Save As** dialog, browse to the folder you want to save the document in.

5. In the **File name** box, enter a name for the document.

6. If you want to save the document in a format other than the one shown in the Save As Type box, select the **Save as type** arrow and then select the file format you want.

7. In the **Save As** dialog, select **Save**.

To add a cloud storage location

1. On the **Save As** page of the Backstage view, select **Add a Place**.

2. In the **Add a Place** list, select a place, such as **OneDrive**.

3. In the **Add a service** dialog, enter the email address you use to sign in to the cloud storage service, and then select **Next**.

4. In the **Sign in** dialog, enter the password associated with the account, and then select **Sign In** to add the cloud storage location associated with that account to the Places list.

To save a copy of a document

1. Display the **Save As** page of the Backstage view.

2. Save the document with a different name in the same location or with any name in a different location. (You can't store two documents with the same name in the same folder.)

To save a document without changing its name or location

- On the title bar, select the **Save** button.

- In the Backstage view, select **Save**.

- Press **Ctrl+S**.

2

Save files to OneDrive

When you save a document to OneDrive, you and other people with whom you share the document can work on it by using a local installation of Word or by using Word Online, which is available in the OneDrive environment. If you're new to the world of OneDrive, here's a quick tutorial to help you get started.

OneDrive is a cloud-based storage solution. The purpose of OneDrive is to provide a single place for you to store and access all your files. Although this might seem like a simple concept, it provides major value for people who use Word or other Microsoft 365 Apps on multiple devices, including Windows computers, Mac computers, iPads and other tablets, and Windows, iPhone, and Android smartphones.

For example, you can create a document on your desktop computer at work, edit it on your laptop at home, and review it on your smartphone while you're waiting for your lunch to be served at a restaurant. If you use the full suite of Microsoft 365 Apps within your organization, you can even present the document in a Microsoft Teams meeting from your tablet PC, all while the document is stored in the same central location.

There are currently two types of OneDrive—one for personal use and one for business use:

- **OneDrive**   This *personal* OneDrive storage site is provided free with every Microsoft account. Each OneDrive is linked to a specific account.

- **OneDrive for Business**   An *organizational* OneDrive storage site is provided with every business-level Microsoft 365 subscription license. These storage locations are part of an organization's Microsoft 365 online infrastructure.

You might have both types of OneDrive available to you. If you do, you can connect to both from within Word (or any Microsoft 365 app).

In this book, the personal and organizational versions are referred to generically as *OneDrive* sites.

To make OneDrive a realistic one-stop storage solution, Microsoft has chosen to support the storage of very large files (up to 10 gigabytes [GB] each) and to provide a significant amount of storage—from 5 GB to 1 terabyte (TB) per user, depending on your account type.

By default, documents that you store on your OneDrive site are password-protected and available only to you. You can share specific files or folders with other people by sending a personalized invitation or a generic link that allows recipients to view or edit files. You can access documents stored on your OneDrive in several ways:

- From within Word when opening or saving a file.

- Through File Explorer, when you synchronize your OneDrive site contents with the computer.

- Through a web browser. Personal OneDrive sites are available at *https://onedrive.live.com*; organizational OneDrive for Business sites have addresses linked to your Microsoft 365 business account, such as *https://contoso-my.sharepoint.com/personal/joan_contoso_com*.

Because OneDrive and OneDrive for Business file storage locations are easy to add to any version of Word, OneDrive is a simple and useful cloud storage option.

Automatically save documents

Word automatically saves new versions of documents stored on SharePoint or OneDrive; these files have an AutoSave button on the title bar that you can use to toggle the function off and on.

When the AutoSave function is turned on:

- If you're working in a new, unnamed file, the app saves a temporary copy of the file to your default storage location.

- If you're working in a previously saved file, the app saves a copy of the file to the location in which you opened or last saved it.

You can turn off the automatic file-saving function if you prefer to save changes manually (although this is not advisable).

To toggle AutoSave on or off

- In the title bar, select the AutoSave button.

> **SEE ALSO** For information about working with document versions, see "Compare and combine documents" in Chapter 11, "Collaborate on documents." For information about configuring other Word options, see "Change default Word options" in Chapter 16.

Save documents in other formats

Word uses file formats based on a markup language called *Extensible Markup Language* or, more commonly, *XML*. These file formats, called the *Microsoft Office Open XML Formats*, were introduced with Microsoft Office 2007.

Word offers a selection of file formats intended to provide specific benefits. Each file format has a file name extension that identifies the file type to the system. The file formats and file name extensions for Word files include the following:

- Word Document (.docx)

- Word Macro-Enabled Document (.docm)

- Word Template (.dotx)

- Word Macro-Enabled Template (.dotm)

- Word XML Document (.xml)

Older Word document types and other file types not specific to Word, such as text files, webpages, PDF files, and XPS files, are available from the Save As dialog.

Save a document in any of these file formats

The default file format for files created in Word is the .docx format, which provides the following benefits over the previous default .doc file format:

- **Decreased file size**   Files are compressed when saved, decreasing the amount of disk space and bandwidth needed to store and transmit files.

- **Simpler retrieval and editing of content**   XML files can be opened in text-editing apps such as Notepad.

- **Increased security**   Personal data can be located and removed from the document, and files can't store macros. (The .docm file format is designed for documents that contain macros.)

If you want to save a Word document in a format that can be opened by the widest variety of programs (including text editors that are installed with most operating systems), use one of these two formats:

- **Rich Text Format (*.rtf)**   This format preserves the document's formatting.
- **Plain Text (*.txt)**   This format preserves only the document's text.

If you want people to be able to view a document exactly as it appears on your screen, use one of these two formats:

- **PDF (*.pdf)** This format is preferred by commercial printing facilities. Recipients can display the file in the Microsoft Edge browser or the free Microsoft Reader or Adobe Reader apps and can display and edit the file in Word or Adobe Acrobat.

- **XPS (*.xps)** This format precisely renders all fonts, images, and colors. Recipients can display the file in the free Windows XPS Viewer app.

> **TIP** Another way to create a PDF file or XPS file is by selecting that option when sending the document by email. For more information, see "Print and send documents" in Chapter 12, "Finalize and distribute documents."

The PDF (Portable Document Format) and XPS (XML Paper Specification) formats are designed to deliver documents as electronic representations of the way they appear when printed. Both types of files can easily be sent by email to many recipients and can be made available on a webpage for downloading by anyone who wants them. However, the files are no longer Word documents. A PDF file can be converted to the editable Word format; an XPS file, however, cannot be opened, viewed, or edited in Word.

Create a PDF file from all or part of a document

When you save a Word document in PDF or XPS format, you can optimize the file size of the document for your intended distribution method—the larger Standard file size is better for printing, whereas the Minimum file size is suitable for online publishing.

Maintain compatibility with earlier versions of Word

Word 2003 and earlier versions of Word used the .doc file format. You can open .doc files in Word 365, but some modern Word features will be unavailable.

When you open a file created in Word 2010 or an earlier version of Word, the title bar displays *[Compatibility Mode]* to the right of the document name. You can work in Compatibility mode, or you can convert the document to the current format by selecting the Convert button on the Info page of the Backstage view, or by saving a copy of the document with Word Document (*.docx) as the file type.

If you work with people who are using a version of Word earlier than Word 2007, you can save your documents in a format that they will be able to use by choosing the *Word 97-2003* file format in the Save As Type list, or they can install the free Microsoft Office Compatibility Pack for Word, Excel, and PowerPoint File Formats from the Microsoft Download Center (located at *download.microsoft.com*). The Compatibility Pack doesn't provide additional functionality in the older versions of the apps, but it does enable users of those earlier versions to open current documents, workbooks, and presentations.

To save all or part of a document in PDF format

1. Open the **Save As** dialog.

2. In the **Save as type** list, select **PDF**. The dialog content changes to provide additional options.

3. If you want to create a PDF file that has a smaller file size (but lower quality), select **Minimum size (publishing online)**.

4. To modify any of the default settings, select the **Options** button, do any of the following, and then select **OK**:

    - Specify the pages to include in the file.

    - Include or exclude comments and tracked changes.

    - Include or exclude nonprinting elements such as bookmarks and properties.

    - Select compliance, font embedding, and encryption options.

5. If you don't want to automatically open the new PDF file in your default PDF viewer, clear the **Open file after publishing** checkbox.

6. In the **Save As** dialog, select **Save**.

Close documents

Every time you open a document, a new instance of Word starts. When you close the file, you can exit that instance of Word. If you have only one document open, you can close the file and exit Word, or you can close the file but leave Word running.

To close a document

- At the right end of the title bar, select the **Close** button to close the document and the Word window.

- Display the Backstage view, and then select **Close** to close the document without exiting Word.

- On the Windows taskbar, point to the Word button to display thumbnails of all open documents. Point to the thumbnail of the document you want to close, and then select the **Close** button that appears in its upper-right corner.

Key points

- You can create simple and complex Word documents by starting with a template.

- You can open more than one Word document, and you can view more than one document at a time, but only one document can be active at a time.

- You can move the cursor by clicking or tapping in the text or by pressing keys and keyboard shortcuts.

- Information about a Word document is saved with the document as file properties that are available from the Info page of the Backstage view and from the document's Properties dialog. Some properties are created and managed by Word, and others are customizable.

- Word 365 documents use the.docx file format. When you save a Word document, you specify its location on the Save As page of the Backstage view, and its name and file format in the Save As dialog. You can save a Word document as a different file type if necessary.

- You can display a variety of views of documents, depending on your needs as you create the document and the purpose for which you are creating it.

Chapter 2

Practice tasks

Before you can complete these tasks, you must copy the book's practice files to your computer. The practice files for these tasks are in the **Word365SBS\Ch02** folder. You can save the task results in the same folder.

The Introduction includes a complete list of practice files and download instructions.

Create documents

Perform the following tasks:

1. Start Word and create a new, blank document.

2. Display the available templates for new documents. Scroll through the list of featured templates and note the types of documents you can create from them.

3. Search for a template that's related to something you're interested in. For example, you could use a search term such as food, school, children, or customers.

4. Preview a template from the search results. If the template preview includes multiple images, preview each of those by selecting the arrows below the image.

5. Without closing the preview window, preview the next or previous template by selecting the arrows to the sides of the preview window.

6. From the preview window, create a document based on the currently displayed template. Notice that the unsaved blank document remains open.

7. Close the blank document without saving it. Leave the template-based document open for use in a later set of practice tasks.

Open and move around in documents

In Word, perform the following tasks:

1. Display the **Open** page of the **Backstage** view.

2. If there are files in the **Recent** list, notice the groups they're divided into, their file storage locations, and whether any are pinned to the list.

3. From the **Open** page, browse to the practice files folder, and open the **NavigateFiles** document.

4. In the second line of the document title, click or tap at the right end of the paragraph to position the cursor.

5. Use a keyboard method to move the cursor to the beginning of the line.

6. Use a keyboard method to move the cursor to the beginning of the word *Regulations*.

7. Use a keyboard method to move the cursor to the end of the document.

8. Use the scroll bar to move to the middle of the document.

9. Use the scroll bar to change the view of the document by one screen.

10. Open the **Navigation** pane.

11. In the **Navigation** pane, select the *Landscaping* heading to move the cursor directly to the selected heading.

12. At the top of the **Navigation** pane, select **Pages**. On the **Pages** page, scroll through the thumbnails to review the amount of visible detail, and then select the thumbnail for page **5** to move the cursor directly to the top of the selected page.

13. At the right end of the **Navigation** pane title bar, select the **Close** button (the X) to close the pane.

14. On the **Open** page of the Backstage view, pin the **NavigateFiles** document to the **Recent** list.

15. Close the document without saving it.

Display different views of documents

Open the **DisplayViews** document in Word, and then perform the following tasks:

1. If the document is not already in Print Layout view, display it in that view.

2. Switch to Web Layout view and scroll through the document to the end. Notice that the lines break differently and that there are no longer any page breaks.

3. Move the cursor back to the beginning of the document, and switch to Read Mode view.

4. On the Read Mode toolbar, select **Tools** to review the commands on the menu, and then select **View** to review the commands on that menu. Then, on the **View** menu, select **Edit Document** to return to Print Layout view.

5. In Print Layout view, hide the white space between pages. Scroll through the document and notice the change in the page lengths when the white space is hidden.

6. Open the **Navigation** pane and display the document headings. Adjust the pane width to the minimum necessary to display the headings.

7. Close the **Navigation** pane.

8. In the **Word Options** dialog, set the width of the style area pane to 2". Then select **OK** to return to the document.

9. Display the document in Draft view. Notice that the style area pane is visible along the left side of the document, but it is wider than necessary.

10. Drag the style area pane's right border to the left until it takes up about half the original amount of space.

11. Display the document in Print Layout view, and use any method described in this chapter to change the magnification to **75%**.

12. Split the window into two panes, position the cursor in the top pane, and then change the magnification to **100%**. Notice that only the active pane changes. Then remove the split.

13. Use commands on the **View** tab to arrange the **DisplayViews** document and the document you created in the first set of practice tasks side by side on the screen.

14. In the **DisplayViews** document, display the gridlines. Notice that they appear in both open documents.

15. Switch to the document you created in the first set of practice tasks. Display the rulers. Notice the effect of this action in the other open document.

16. Save and close both documents.

Display and edit file properties

Open the **EditProperties** document in Word, and then perform the following tasks:

1. On the **Info** page of the Backstage view, do the following:

    - Review the information in the **Properties** list. Notice the types of information that have been saved with the document.

    - Point to each of the property values and notice the values that you can edit.

    - Set the **Title** property to Welcome to Word.

2. Expand the **Properties** list to display all properties, and then do the following:

    - Notice the additional properties that were not previously visible. (If necessary, select **Show Fewer Properties** to switch back to the original list for comparison purposes.)

    - Point to the **Manager** and **Author** property values and notice that Check Names and Address Books buttons appear. Experiment with adding a Manager property from your address book.

3. Select the **Properties** header, and then display the advanced properties. In the **EditProperties Properties** dialog, do the following:

    - Compare the properties on the **Summary** tab with those in the **Properties** list. Notice the properties that you added in steps 1 and 2.

    - In the **Author** box, enter your name.

    - In the **Keywords** box, enter Word 365 new features.

    - Review the information on the **General**, **Statistics**, **Contents**, and **Custom** tabs. Notice the information that is available only in the Properties dialog.

    - Select **OK**.

4. Verify that the information you entered in the **Properties** dialog appears in the **Properties** list. If it doesn't, save, close, and reopen the document to update the properties.

Save and close documents

In Word, perform the following tasks:

1. Save a copy of the **EditProperties** document in the practice file folder as MyDocument. Close the document and this instance of Word.

2. Close the document you created in the first task without exiting Word.

3. Close the remaining open documents and exit Word.

Enter and edit text

Word is a word-processing app designed primarily for working with text. This can be text that you enter yourself or text that you import from another file.

After you've entered or imported text into a document, you can select and edit the text as needed. For example, you can select a word, a sentence, a line, or a paragraph. You can select one of these elements at a time, or you can select several at the same time. These words, sentences, lines, or paragraphs can be adjacent (that is, next to each other in your document) or non-adjacent (that is, in different areas of the document). You can also select all the content in a document at the same time.

Word makes it easy to find and replace text—for example, if you realize you made a mistake and want to locate and fix each instance of the error. Word also includes a wide array of reference and research tools.

This chapter guides you through procedures related to entering and importing text; selecting, moving, copying, and deleting text; finding and replacing text; and using reference and research tools.

In this chapter

- Enter and import text
- Select, move, copy, and delete text
- Find and replace text
- Use reference and research tools

Enter and import text

Entering new text in a document is straightforward. A vertical, blinking cursor shows where the next character you enter will appear. When you begin entering text, any existing text to the right of the cursor moves to make room for the new text. When the cursor reaches the right margin, the word you're entering moves to the next line.

> **TIP** If a wavy line appears under a word or phrase, Word is flagging a possible error. For information about proofing errors, see "Locate and correct text errors" in Chapter 12, "Finalize and distribute documents."

If the text you want to add to the document already exists in another document, you can import it. Importing one or more documents is a quick way to assemble the content of multiple files into one document. For example, suppose you want to compile eight departmental reports into a single company report. It would be tedious to open each report, select and copy the text, and then paste it into the company report document. Instead, you can have Word import the text from those documents in one operation.

If you prefer, you can dictate text into your document rather than typing it. You can tell Word the text that you want to enter and the punctuation you want to use. Then, when you have the content in the document, you can make any necessary corrections. This feature works best when you have a headset with a microphone that enables Word to hear you clearly.

To enter text by typing

1. Click or tap to position the cursor where you want to add your text, and then begin typing.

2. Press the **Enter** key at the end of each paragraph to begin a new paragraph.

To import text from another document

1. In the target document, position the cursor where you want to insert the text.

> **TIP** It isn't necessary to open the source document to complete this operation.

2. On the **Insert** tab, in the **Text** group, select the **Object** arrow (not the button), and then select **Text from File** to open the Insert File dialog.

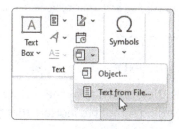

Use the Text From File command to import text from another document

3. Browse to the file that contains the text you want to insert, select the file, and then select the **Insert** button to import the text into your document.

To import text from multiple documents

1. In the target document, position the cursor where you want to insert text.

2. On the **Insert** tab, in the **Text** group, select the **Object** arrow (not the button), and then select **Text from File**.

3. In the **Insert File** dialog, open the folder that contains the files you want to insert.

4. Select the files:

    •   If the files containing the text you want to import are listed together, select the first file. Then, while pressing the **Shift** key, select the last file. All the files will be selected.

    •   If the files are not listed together, select the first file. Then, while pressing the **Ctrl** key, select each additional file.

5. Select the **Insert** button. The content of each file you selected will be added to the target document.

To dictate text into a document

> ⚠️ **IMPORTANT** You must have a Microsoft 365 subscription and a microphone to use this feature.

1. Position the cursor where you want to insert the text.

2. On the **Home** tab, in the **Voice** group, select **Dictate** to display the Dictate toolbar. The Dictate icon displays a red Recording symbol to indicate that the Dictate feature is listening for your voice input.

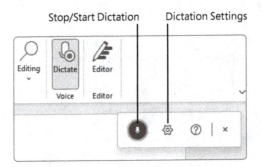

Control dictation from the Dictate toolbar

3. To change the dictation language or the microphone, select **Dictation Settings** to open the Dictation Settings dialog, make your changes, and then select **Save**.

4. Begin speaking slowly and clearly. Word enters the text in the document as you speak. If you need to pause (for example, to talk to someone without recording that conversation), select **Stop Dictation**, and then select **Start Dictation** when you're ready to resume.

5. Enter punctuation marks by saying any of the following:

- Period
- Comma
- Question mark
- Exclamation point
- Exclamation mark
- New line
- New paragraph

- Semicolon
- Colon
- Open quote
- Close quote
- Open quotes
- Close quotes

Select, move, copy, and delete text

You'll rarely write a perfect document that requires no editing. You'll almost always want to add or remove a word or two, change a phrase, or move text from one place to another. Or you might want to edit a document that you created for one purpose so that you can use it for a different purpose. You can edit a document as you create it, or you can write it first and then revise it.

It's easy to modify a few characters, but if you want to edit more than that efficiently, you need to know how to select text. Selected text appears highlighted on the screen.

> **TIP** Many instructional materials incorrectly refer to *selecting* text as *highlighting* text, which is misleading. To highlight text is to apply the Highlight character format.

You can select content by using the mouse, using the keyboard, tapping, or combining multiple selection tools. Some methods of selecting use an area of the document's left margin called the *selection area*. When the mouse pointer is in the selection area, it changes to an arrow that points toward the upper-right corner of the page.

Day of the Living Dead

We can't stop the march of technology, but we need to halt the iPod pedestrian, cycle, and driver zombies. —Edmund King, president, British Automobile Association

I first realized a zombie apocalypse was upon us when I read about Email 'n Walk, an iPhone app that turns on the phone's camera while you compose email. To take a picture to use as an attachment, right? Oh no, that would be *so* last year. The idea, as the app's name implies, is to let you read or compose messages and walk at the same time, all the while remaining "safe" because the camera lets you see what's happening on the other side of your phone.

Select an entire line of text with just one click or tap

> **TIP** When you select content, Word displays the Mini Toolbar, from which you can quickly format the selection or perform other actions, depending on the type of content you select. For information about applying formatting from the Mini Toolbar, see Chapter 4, "Modify the structure and appearance of text." For information about turning off the display of the Mini Toolbar, see "Change default Word options" in Chapter 16, "Customize options and the user interface."

You can move or copy selected text within a document or between documents by using these methods:

- Drag a selection from one location to another. This method is easiest to use when you can display the original location and destination on the screen at the same time. (You can create a copy by holding down the Ctrl key while dragging.)

- Cut or copy the text from the original location to the Clipboard, and then paste it from the Clipboard into the new location. There are multiple methods for cutting, copying, and pasting text. No matter which method you use, when you cut text, Word removes it from its original location. When you copy text, Word leaves the original text intact.

The Clipboard is a temporary storage area shared by the Microsoft 365 apps. You can display items that have been cut or copied to the Clipboard in the Clipboard pane.

The Clipboard stores items that have been cut or copied from any Microsoft 365 app

You can cut and copy content to the Clipboard and paste the most recent item from the Clipboard without displaying the Clipboard pane. If you want to work with items other than the most recent, you can display the Clipboard pane and then do so.

If you make a change to a document and then realize that you made a mistake, you can easily reverse—or *undo*—one or more recent changes. You can redo changes that you've undone or repeat your most recent action elsewhere in the document.

Besides moving and copying text, you can also delete it. The easiest way to do this is by pressing either the Delete key or the Backspace key on the keyboard. However, when you delete text by using one of these keys, the text is not saved to the Clipboard, and you can't paste it elsewhere.

To select text

- To select adjacent words, lines, or paragraphs, click (or tap) and drag through the text.

- Position the cursor at the beginning of the text you want to select, and then do any of the following:

  - To select one character at a time, hold down the **Shift** key and then press the **Left Arrow** or **Right Arrow** key.

  - To select one word at a time, hold down the **Shift** and **Ctrl** keys and then press the **Left Arrow** or **Right Arrow** key.

  - To select one line at a time, hold down the **Shift** key and then press the **Up Arrow** or **Down Arrow** key.

  - To select any amount of adjacent content, hold down the **Shift** key and then click or tap at the end of the content that you want to select.

- To select a word, double-click anywhere in the word. Word selects the word and the space immediately after the word but not any punctuation after the word.

- To select a sentence, hold down the **Ctrl** key and click or tap anywhere in the sentence. Word selects all the characters in the sentence, from the first character through the space following the ending punctuation mark.

> ⚠️ **IMPORTANT** You cannot select a sentence by using this technique if other text is already selected. This activates the non-adjacent multi-selection functionality described in a bullet point below.

- To select a line, click or tap in the selection area to the left of the line.

- To select a paragraph, do either of the following:

  - Triple-click anywhere in the paragraph.

  - Double-click in the selection area to the left of the paragraph.

  Word selects the text of the paragraph and the paragraph mark.

> **TIP** Paragraph marks are nonprinting characters that are usually hidden. For information about displaying nonprinting characters, see "Display different views of documents" in Chapter 2, "Create and manage documents."

- To select non-adjacent words, lines, or paragraphs, select the first text segment and then hold down the **Ctrl** key while selecting the next text segment.

- To select all the content in a document, text box, shape, or other text container, do either of the following:

  - Triple-click in the selection area.

  - Press **Ctrl+A**.

To release a selection

- Click or tap anywhere in the window other than the selection area.

To cut text to the Clipboard

- Select the text, and then do any of the following:

  - On the **Home** tab, in the **Clipboard** group, select the **Cut** button.

  - Right-click the selection, and then select **Cut**.

  - Press **Ctrl+X**.

To copy text to the Clipboard

- Select the text, and then do any of the following:

  - On the **Home** tab, in the **Clipboard** group, select the **Copy** button.

  - Right-click the selection, and then select **Copy**.

  - Press **Ctrl+C**.

To paste the most recent item from the Clipboard

- Position the cursor where you want to insert the text, and then do either of the following:

  - On the **Home** tab, in the **Clipboard** group, select the **Paste** button.

  - Press **Ctrl+V**.

- Right-click where you want to insert the text, and then in the **Paste Options** section of the menu, select a paste option.

To move text

- Cut the text from the original location, and then paste it into the new location.

- Select the text, and then drag it to the new location.

To copy text from one location to another

- Copy the text from the original location, and then paste it into the new location.

- Select the text, hold down the **Ctrl** key, and then drag the text to the new location.

> **TIP** To drag selected text, point to it, hold down the mouse button and move the pointer to the insertion location (indicated by a thick vertical line), and then release the mouse button.

To display the Clipboard pane

- On the **Home** tab, select the **Clipboard** dialog launcher.

To manage cut and copied items in the Clipboard pane

- To paste an individual item at the cursor, select the item, or point to the item, select the arrow that appears, and then select **Paste**.

- To paste all the items stored on the Clipboard at the same location, select **Paste All** at the top of the Clipboard pane.

- To remove an item from the Clipboard, point to the item in the Clipboard pane, select the arrow that appears, and then select **Delete**.

- To remove all items from the Clipboard, select **Clear All** at the top of the Clipboard pane.

Paste options

Selecting the Paste arrow on the Home tab displays the Paste menu of options for controlling the way Word inserts content that you paste into a document. The available options vary depending on the type of content that you have cut or copied to the Clipboard. For example, when pasting text, the Paste menu includes buttons for keeping source formatting, merging formatting, or pasting only the text.

Word offers several different methods of pasting content

Pointing to a button on the Paste menu displays a preview of how the source content will look if you use that option to paste it at the current location.

In addition to these buttons, the Paste menu includes Paste Special and Set Default Paste options.

3

Selecting Paste Special opens a dialog in which you can choose from additional options.

The Paste Special dialog offers several options for pasting text

Selecting Set Default Paste on the Paste Options menu displays the Advanced page of the Word Options dialog. In the Cut, Copy, And Paste section of this page, you can set default paste options. For more information, see Chapter 16.

To control the behavior of the Clipboard pane

- At the bottom of the pane, select **Options**, and then select the display option you want.

Show Office Clipboard Automatically

Show Office Clipboard When Ctrl+C Pressed Twice

Collect Without Showing Office Clipboard

✓ Show Office Clipboard Icon on Taskbar

✓ Show Status Near Taskbar When Copying

Options

The Clipboard pane display options

To undo your last editing action

- On the **Home** tab, select the **Undo** button.

- Press **Ctrl+Z**.

To undo two or more actions

- On the **Home** tab, in the **Undo** list, select the first action you want to undo. Word reverts that action and all those that follow.

- Press **Ctrl+Z** multiple times until the actions are undone.

To delete only one or a few characters

1. Position the cursor immediately to the left of the text you want to delete.

2. Press the **Delete** key once for each character you want to delete.

Or

1. Position the cursor immediately to the right of the text you want to delete.

2. Press the **Backspace** key once for each character you want to delete.

To delete any amount of text

1. Select the text you want to delete.

2. Press the **Delete** key or the **Backspace** key.

Find and replace text

One way to ensure that the text in your documents is consistent and accurate is to use the Find feature to search for and review every occurrence of a particular word or phrase. For example, if you're responsible for advertising a trademarked product, you can search your marketing materials to check that every occurrence of the product's name is correctly identified as a trademark.

You can use the search box at the top of the Navigation pane to locate all instances of a specific word, phrase, or formatting mark in the current document. When you enter characters in the search box at the top of the pane, Word highlights all occurrences of those characters in the document and displays them on the Results page of the Navigation pane. When you point to a search result on the Results page, a ScreenTip displays the number of the page on which that result appears and the name of the heading preceding the search result. Select a search result in the pane to move directly to that location in the document or select the Next and Previous arrows to move between results.

> 🔍 **SEE ALSO** For more information about working with the Navigation pane, see Chapter 2.

Navigation	▾ ✕
firewall	✕ ⌄

3 results   ⌃ ⌄

Headings   Pages   **Results**

of select networking components (e.g., host **firewalls**).

premises and so reside behind the corporate **firewall**, while public clouds are "out there" on the

have been known to penetrate corporate **firewalls**, and of course there is always the risk of

[Page 19] Myth #5: Private Clouds are Secure, Public Clouds are Insecure

The Results page of the Navigation pane displays each instance of the search term in context

> ✓ **TIP** From the Results page of the Navigation pane, you can continue editing your document as you normally would while still having access to all the search results.

If you want to be more specific about the text you're looking for—for example, if you want to look for occurrences that match the exact capitalization of your search term—you can do so from the Find tab of the Find and Replace dialog.

Narrow search results by specifying search options

If you want to substitute a specific word or phrase for another, you can use the Replace function. As on the Find tab, the Replace tab contains options you can use to carry out more complicated replacement operations. Note that the settings in the Search Options area apply to the search term and not to its replacement.

Easily correct errors and inconsistencies by using the Replace feature

You can evaluate and decide whether to replace individual instances of the search term, or you can replace all occurrences of the search term in the document at the same time.

To display the Results page of the Navigation pane

- On the **Home** tab, in the **Editing** group, select the **Find** button.

- On the **View** tab, in the **Show** group, select the **Navigation Pane** checkbox and then, near the top of the **Navigation** pane, select **Results**.

- Press **Ctrl+F.**

To search for text

- On the **Results** page of the **Navigation** pane, enter the text you want to find in the search box.

To find a search result in the document

1. On the **Results** page of the **Navigation** pane, point to a search result to display a ScreenTip with the number of the page on which that result appears and the name of the heading that precedes that search result.

2. Select the search result to move directly to that location in the document.

To display the Find tab of the Find And Replace dialog

- In the **Navigation** pane, select the **Search for more things** arrow at the right end of the search box, and then select **Advanced Find**.

- On the **Home** tab, in the **Editing** group, select the **Find** arrow, and then select **Advanced Find**.

To conduct a more specific search

1. Display the **Find** tab of the **Find and Replace** dialog.

2. Select **More** in the lower-left corner of the dialog to display additional search options.

3. Do either of the following:

   - In the **Find what** box, enter the text you want to search for.

   - Select **Special**, and then select the symbol or formatting symbol you want to locate.

4. Modify your search by selecting any of the following options in the expanded dialog:

   • Guide the direction of the search by selecting **Down, Up**, or **All** from the **Search** list.

   • Locate only text that matches the capitalization of the search term by selecting the **Match case** checkbox.

   • Exclude occurrences of the search term that appear within other words by selecting the **Find whole words only** checkbox. (For example, if you're searching for the word *pan*, selecting this checkbox prevents Word from listing search results such as *pane*, *span*, *repanel*, and so on.)

   • Find two similar words, such as *effect* and *affect*, by selecting the **Use wildcards** checkbox and then including one or more wildcard characters in the search term.

   > **TIP** The two most common wildcard characters are ?, which represents any single character in this location in the Find What text, and *, which represents any number of characters in this location in the Find What text. For a list of the available wildcards, select the Use Wildcards checkbox and then select the Special button.

   • Find occurrences of the search text that sound the same but are spelled differently, such as *there* and *their*, by selecting the **Sounds like** checkbox.

   • Find occurrences of a particular word in any form, such as *try*, *tries*, and *tried*, by selecting the **Find all word forms** checkbox.

   • Locate formatting, such as bold, or special characters, such as tabs, by selecting them from the **Format** or **Special** list.

   • Locate words with the same beginning as the search term by selecting the **Match prefix** checkbox.

   • Locate words with the same ending as the search term by selecting the **Match suffix** checkbox.

   • Locate words with different hyphenation or spacing by selecting the **Ignore punctuation characters** or **Ignore white-space characters** checkbox.

5. Select the **Find Next** button to find the next instance of the search term in the document.

> **TIP** Conduct a more specific search directly from the Navigation pane by selecting the Search For More Things arrow at the right end of the search box and then selecting Options. The Find Options dialog opens, where you can select many of these same settings while continuing to use the Results page of the Navigation pane to conduct your search.

To display the Replace tab of the Find And Replace dialog

- If the **Find and Replace** dialog is already open, select the **Replace** tab.

- If the **Navigation** pane is open, select the **Search for more things** arrow at the right end of the search box, and then select **Replace**.

- On the **Home** tab, in the **Editing** group, select the **Replace** button.

- Press **Ctrl+H**.

To replace text

1. Display the **Replace** tab of the **Find and Replace** dialog.

2. In the **Find what** box, enter the text you want to replace.

> **TIP** Select the More button in the lower-left corner to expand the dialog to display the Search Options area, which contains additional search options.

3. In the **Replace with** box, enter the replacement text.

4. Do one of the following:

   - Select **Replace** to find the next occurrence of the text in the **Find what** box, replace it with the text in the **Replace with** box, and move to the next occurrence.

   - Select **Replace All** to replace all occurrences of the text in the **Find what** box with the text in the **Replace with** box.

   > **TIP** Before selecting Replace All, ensure that the replacement is clearly defined. For example, if you want to change *trip* to *journey*, be sure to tell Word to find only the whole word *trip*; otherwise, the word *triple*, for example, could become *journeyle*.

   - Select **Find Next** to find the first occurrence of the text in the **Find what** box or to leave the selected occurrence as it is and locate the next one.

Use reference and research tools

Language is often contextual. That is, you use different words and phrases in a marketing brochure than you would in a letter requesting immediate payment of an invoice or in an informal memo about a social gathering after work. To help ensure that you use the words that best convey your meaning in any given context, you can look up definitions, synonyms, and antonyms of words from within a document by using Word's built-in reference tools. You can also use the selected word as a jumping-off point for further research.

You can display definitions of words in the Search pane. By default, this pane displays dictionary definitions and articles from online sources.

The Search pane displays information about the selected word

You can also install free dictionaries from the Microsoft Office Store. After you install a dictionary, you can display synonyms and definitions in the Thesaurus pane whether you're online or offline.

Installing a dictionary makes definitions available at any time

Install Office tools

A dictionary isn't the only tool, or *app*, that you can install. There are many other useful apps available for Word and other Office apps, including fax services, maps, newsfeeds, and social connectors.

To locate apps that are available for Word:

1. On the **Insert** tab, in the **Add-ins** group, select **Get Add-ins** to display the Store tab of the Office Add-ins dialog.

2. Browse the available apps or use the search box to search for a specific app.

3. Select **Add** to install the add-in.

To display and remove your installed add-ins:

1. To display a list of the add-in apps you've installed, on the **Insert** tab, in the **Add-ins** group, select **My Add-ins**.

2. To remove an add-in app, right-click or long-press (tap and hold) it on the **My Add-ins** page of the **Office Add-ins** dialog, select **Remove**, and then select **Remove** again to confirm the removal.

Sometimes it's difficult to think of the best word to use in a specific situation. You can display a list of synonyms (words that have the same meaning) and usually an antonym (a word that has the opposite meaning) from the shortcut menu that appears when you right-click a selected word. You can display a more comprehensive list of synonyms in the Thesaurus pane. Select any synonym in the Thesaurus pane to display the synonyms and definition of that word, until you find the word that best suits your needs.

You can use the Microsoft Translator tool to translate words, phrases, or even entire documents into other languages. When you translate a word or phrase, Word displays the translation and associated tools in the Translator pane. When you translate a document, Word creates a new document.

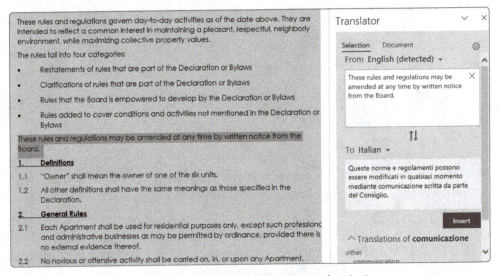

Using the Mini Translator is the quickest way to obtain the translation of a selection

You can translate from and to many languages, including Arabic, Chinese, French, German, Greek, Hebrew, Italian, Japanese, Korean, Polish, Portuguese, Russian, Spanish, and Swedish. You set which languages you want to use in the Translation Language Options dialog.

Display document statistics

Word displays information about the size of a document at the left end of the status bar. To show the number of words in only part of the document, such as a few paragraphs, simply select that part. You can review more statistics and specify the content to include in the statistics in the Word Count dialog. To open it, select the Word Count indicator on the status bar or the Word Count button in the Proofing group on the Review tab.

3

In addition to counting pages and words, Word counts characters, paragraphs, and lines

To display the definition of a word while online

1. Select the word that you want to define.

2. Open the **Search** pane by doing either of the following:

   - On the **References** tab, in the **Research** group, select **Search**

   - Right-click the selected word and then select **Search "*term*"**, where *term* is the selected word.

To add a dictionary

1. On the **Insert** tab, in the **Add-ins** group, select **Get Add-ins** to display the Store tab of the Office Add-ins dialog.

2. In the search box in the dialog, enter dictionary to display a list of available dictionaries.

3. Select the dictionary you want to install. The dialog displays information about the dictionary.

4. Select the **Back** button to display the list of available dictionaries again, and then select the **Add** button to install the one you want. A pane with the added dictionary's name opens on the right.

To display synonyms for a word

- Right-click the word, and then select **Synonyms**.

To display synonyms, antonyms, and the definition of a word

- Right-click the word, select **Synonyms**, and then on the submenu, select **Thesaurus**.
- Select the word. Then do either of the following:
  - On the **Review** tab, in the **Proofing** group, select the **Thesaurus** button.
  - Press **Shift+F7**.

To replace a word with a synonym

- Display the list of synonyms, and then select the synonym you want to use.
- Display the **Thesaurus** pane, point to the synonym you want to use, select the arrow that appears, and then select **Insert**.

To change the languages used by the Translator tool

1. On the **Review** tab, in the **Language** group, select **Translate**, and then select **Translator Preferences** to display the Translator pane.

2. In the **Translator** pane, from the **Selection** or **Document** page, do the following:
   - In the **From** list, select the original language.
   - In the **To** list, select the translation language.

To translate text within Word

1. Select the word or phrase you want to translate.

2. On the **Review** tab, in the **Language** group, select **Translate**, and then select **Translate Selection** to open the Translator pane.

3. The **From** and **To** boxes display the currently selected original and translation languages. If either language is incorrect, you can change it.

4. If you want to replace the selected text with the translation, select **Insert**.

To translate a word or phrase that does not appear in the text of a document

1. In the **Translate** pane, in the **From** box, enter the word or phrase you want to translate.

2. Microsoft Translator automatically detects the language. If the detected language is incorrect, in the **From** list, select the original language of the text you want to translate.

3. In the **To** list, select the language to which the text should be translated.

4. If you want to insert the translated text at the location of your cursor, select **Insert**.

To translate an entire document

1. Open the document you want to translate in Word.

2. On the **Review** tab, in the **Language** group, select **Translate**, and then select **Translate Document**.

3. On the Document page of the Translator pane, confirm or change the From and To languages, and then select **Translate**. Word creates a translation of the document in a new file.

Key points

- You can enter text into a document by typing, speaking, or importing it from another file.

- You can drag text from one location in a document to another, or between documents.

- You can cut or copy text and paste it elsewhere in the same document or in a different document. Cut and copied text is stopped on the Clipboard.

- You can search for text and formatting and use wildcards and special characters to enhance your search. Similarly, you can find each occurrence of a word or phrase and replace it with another.

- Word has many reference checkboxes that simplify the process of creating and refining content from within your document.

Practice tasks

Before you can complete these tasks, you must copy the book's practice files to your computer. The practice files for these tasks are in the **Word365SBS\Ch03** folder. You can save the results of the tasks in the same folder.

The Introduction includes a complete list of practice files and download instructions.

Enter and import text

Start Word, and then perform the following tasks:

1. Create a new document based on the blank document template.

2. With the cursor at the beginning of the new document, enter Parks Appreciation Day, and then create a new paragraph.

3. Enter Help beautify our city by participating in the annual cleanup of Log Drift Park, Swamp Creek Park, and Tall Tree Park. Volunteers will receive a free T-shirt and barbeque lunch. Bring your own gardening tools and gloves and be ready to have fun!

4. Create a new paragraph, and then enter The Park Service Committee is coordinating group participation in this event. If you are interested in spending time outdoors with family and friends while improving the quality of our parks, contact Nancy Anderson by email at nancy@adventure-works.com.

5. Create a new paragraph, and with the cursor in the first blank line, insert the text from the **ImportText** file from the practice file folder.

6. Save the document as EnterText and close it.

Select, move, copy, and delete text

Open the **EditText** document in Print Layout view, display formatting marks, and then perform the following tasks:

1. Press **Ctrl+*** to turn on and off the display of formatting marks and hidden text. In the second bullet point under **Project Goals**, delete the word *natural*.

2. In the third bullet point, use the arrow keys to select the words *and motivate* and the following space, and then delete the selection.

3. In the fourth bullet point, select the word *Forge*, and then replace it by entering **Build**. Notice that you don't have to enter a space after *Build*; Word inserts the space for you.

4. In the middle of page 1, use the selection area to select the entire first bullet point after *Questions for Team Leaders*.

5. Copy the selection to the Clipboard.

6. At the bottom of page 1, click or tap to the left of *What* in the first bullet point after *Questions for Department Reps*. Then, in the **Clipboard** group, expand the **Paste Options** menu. Notice that, because you're pasting a list item into a list, two of the three available buttons have list-related icons.

7. Point to each of the **Paste Options** buttons to review how the source text will look with that paste option implemented.

8. Select the **Merge List** button to paste the copied bullet point into the second list and retain its formatting.

9. On page 2, in the *Set Up Team* section, select the entire paragraph that begins with *Explain the position's responsibilities*.

10. Cut the selection, and then paste it before the preceding paragraph to switch the order of the two paragraphs.

11. In the **Undo** list, point to the third action (**Paste Merge List**). Notice that the text at the bottom of the list indicates that three actions will be undone if you select this action.

12. In the **Undo** list, select **Paste Merge List** to undo the previous cut-and-paste operation and the pasting of the copied text.

13. In the *Pre-Plan Project* section, select the *If some employee input* paragraph.

14. Drag the paragraph to the left of the word *If* at the beginning of the preceding bullet point to switch the order of the bullet points.

15. Release the selection and move the cursor to the end of the paragraph.

16. Delete the paragraph mark to merge the two bullet points. Add a space to separate the two sentences.

17. If you prefer not to show formatting symbols, turn them off.

18. Save and close the document.

Find and replace text

Open the **FindText** document in Print Layout view, and then perform the following tasks:

1. With the cursor at the beginning of the document, open the **Results** page of the **Navigation** pane.

2. Enter Board in the search box.

3. Select the **Next** button (the downward-pointing triangle under the search box) to move through the first few search results.

4. Scroll through the document to show other highlighted results. Notice that on page **2**, in section **4**, Word has highlighted the *board* portion of *skateboards*. You need to restrict the search to the whole word *Board*.

5. Open the **Find Options** dialog.

6. Select the **Match case** and **Find whole words only** checkboxes, and then select **OK**.

7. Enter Board in the search box again and scroll through the list of results. Notice that the word *skateboards* is no longer highlighted.

8. Move the cursor to the beginning of the document.

9. Open the **Find and Replace** dialog with the **Replace** tab active. Notice that the Find What box retains the entry from the previous search.

10. Display the **Search Options** area. Notice that the Match Case and Find Whole Words Only checkboxes are still selected.

11. In the **Search Options** area, ensure that **Down** is selected in the **Search** list. Then select **Less** to hide the **Search Options** area.

12. Enter Association Board in the **Replace with** box and select **Find Next** to have Word highlight the first occurrence of *Board*.

13. Select **Replace** to have Word replace the selected occurrence of *Board* with *Association Board* and then find the next occurrence.

14. Select **Replace All**. Word tells you how many replacements it made from the starting point forward.

15. Close the **Find and Replace** dialog.

16. Close the **Navigation** pane.

17. Save and close the document.

Use reference and research tools

> ⚠️ **IMPORTANT** You must have an active internet connection to complete the following tasks.

Open the **ResearchText** document in Print Layout view, and perform the following tasks:

1. In the second line of the first paragraph, select the word *acclaimed*.

2. Display a definition of the word *acclaimed* in the **Search** pane.

3. Display a list of synonyms for the word *acclaimed* in the **Thesaurus** pane.

4. Scroll through the list of synonyms. Notice that an antonym appears at the bottom of the list.

5. In the synonym list, select a synonym of *acclaimed* to replace the word in the search box at the top of the pane.

6. From the synonym list, replace the word *acclaimed* in the document with one of its synonyms.

7. Close the open panes.

8. In the first line of the first paragraph, select the word *mistake*, and then display the **Translator** pane.

9. Translate the word *mistake* to French.

10. Replace *mistake* with the word *erreur*.

11. Close the **Translator** pane.

12. Translate the entire document to German.

13. Save and close the document.

Part 2

Create professional documents

Modify the structure and appearance of text

Documents contain text that conveys information to readers, but the appearance of the document content also conveys a message. You can provide structure and meaning by formatting the text in various ways. Word 365 provides a variety of simple-to-use tools that you can use to apply sophisticated formatting and create a navigational structure.

In a short document or one that doesn't require a complex navigational structure, you can easily format words and paragraphs so that key points stand out and the structure of your document is clear. You can achieve dramatic flair by applying predefined WordArt text effects. To keep the appearance of documents and other Microsoft 365 files consistent, you can format document elements by applying predefined sets of formatting called *styles*. In addition, you can change the fonts, colors, and effects throughout a document with one click by applying a theme.

This chapter guides you through procedures related to applying character and paragraph formatting, structuring content manually, creating and modifying lists, applying styles to text, and changing a document's theme.

In this chapter

- Apply paragraph formatting
- Structure content manually
- Apply character formatting
- Create and modify lists
- Apply built-in styles to text
- Change the document theme

Apply paragraph formatting

You create a paragraph by entering text and then pressing the Enter key. A paragraph can contain one word, one sentence, or multiple sentences. Every paragraph ends with a paragraph mark, which looks like a backward P (¶). Paragraph marks and other structural characters (such as spaces, line breaks, and tabs) are usually hidden, but you can display them. Sometimes displaying these hidden characters makes it easier to accomplish a task or understand a structural problem.

> **SEE ALSO** For information about working with hidden structural characters, see "Structure content manually," later in this chapter.

You can change the look of a paragraph by changing its indentation, alignment, and line spacing, in addition to the space before and after it. You can also put borders around it and shade its background. Collectively, the settings you use to vary the look of a paragraph are called *paragraph formatting*.

You can modify a paragraph's left and right edge alignment and vertical spacing by using tools on the Home tab of the ribbon or in the Paragraph dialog, and its left and right indents from the Home tab, the Layout tab, the Paragraph dialog, or the horizontal ruler. The ruler is often hidden to provide more space for the document content.

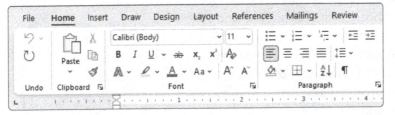

The left indent can be changed from the Home tab, the Layout tab, or the ruler

If you modify a paragraph and aren't happy with the changes, you can restore the original paragraph and character settings by clearing the formatting to reset the paragraph to its base style.

> **SEE ALSO** For information about styles, see "Apply built-in styles to text" later in this chapter.

When you want to make several adjustments to the alignment, indentation, and spacing of selected paragraphs, it's sometimes quicker to make changes in the Paragraph dialog than to select buttons and drag markers.

Indent and spacing settings in the Paragraph dialog

Configure alignment

The alignment settings control the horizontal position of the paragraph text between the page margins. There are four alignment options:

- **Align Left**   This is the default paragraph alignment. It sets the left end of each line of the paragraph at the left page margin or left indent. It results in a straight left edge and a ragged right edge.

- **Align Right**   This option sets the right end of each line of the paragraph at the right page margin or right indent. It results in a straight right edge and a ragged left edge.

- **Center** This option centers each line of the paragraph between the left and right page margins or indents. It results in ragged left and right edges.

- **Justify** This option adjusts the spacing between words so that the left end of each line of the paragraph is at the left page margin or indent, and the right end of each line of the paragraph (other than the last line) is at the right margin or indent. It results in straight left and right edges.

The icons on the alignment buttons on the ribbon depict the effect of each alignment option.

To open the Paragraph dialog

- On the **Home** tab or the **Layout** tab, in the **Paragraph** group, select the **Paragraph Settings** dialog launcher.

- On the **Home** tab, in the **Paragraph** group, select the **Line and Paragraph Spacing** button and then **Line Spacing Options**.

To set paragraph alignment

- Position the cursor anywhere in the paragraph or select all the paragraphs you want to adjust. Then do either of the following:

  - On the **Home** tab, in the **Paragraph** group, select the **Align Left**, **Center**, **Align Right**, or **Justify** button.

  - Open the **Paragraph** dialog. On the **Indents and Spacing** tab, in the **General** area, select **Left**, **Centered**, **Right**, or **Justified** in the **Alignment** list.

Configure vertical spacing

Paragraphs have two types of vertical spacing:

- **Paragraph spacing** This is the space between paragraphs, defined by setting the space before and after each paragraph. This space is usually measured in *points*.

- **Line spacing** This is the space between the lines within a paragraph, defined by setting the height of the lines either in relation to the height of the text (single, double, or a specific number of lines) or by specifying a minimum or exact point measurement.

The default line spacing for documents created in Word 365 is 1.15 lines. Changing the line spacing alters the appearance and readability of the text in the paragraph and the amount of space it occupies on the page.

> *The line spacing of this left-aligned paragraph is set to Single (1 line).* A paragraph can contain one word, one sentence, or multiple sentences. You can change the look of a paragraph by changing its indentation, alignment, and line spacing, as well as the space before and after it. You can also put borders around it and shade its background. Collectively, the settings you use to vary the look of a paragraph are called *paragraph formatting*.
>
> *The line spacing of this justified paragraph is set to Double (2 lines).* A paragraph can contain one word, one sentence, or multiple sentences. You can change the look of a paragraph by changing its indentation, alignment, and line spacing, as well as the space before and after it. You can also put borders around it and shade its background. Collectively, the settings you use to vary the look of a paragraph are called *paragraph formatting*.

The effect of changing line spacing

You can set the paragraph and line spacing for individual paragraphs and for paragraph styles. You can quickly adjust the spacing of most content in a document by selecting an option from the Paragraph Spacing menu on the Design tab. (Although the menu is named Paragraph Spacing, the menu options control both paragraph spacing and line spacing.) These options, which are named by effect rather than by specific measurements, work by modifying the spacing of the Normal paragraph style and any other styles that depend on the Normal style for their spacing. (In standard templates, most other styles are based on the Normal style.) The Paragraph Spacing options modify the Normal style in only the current document and do not affect other documents.

The following table describes the effect of each Paragraph Spacing option on the paragraph and line spacing settings.

Paragraph spacing option	Before paragraph	After paragraph	Line spacing
Default	Controlled by style set	Controlled by style set	Controlled by style set
No Paragraph Space	0 points	0 points	1 line
Compact	0 points	4 points	1 line
Tight	0 points	6 points	1.15 lines
Open	0 points	10 points	1.15 lines
Relaxed	0 points	6 points	1.5 lines
Double	0 points	8 points	2 lines

To quickly adjust the vertical spacing before, after, and within all paragraphs in a document

1. On the **Design** tab, in the **Document Formatting** group, select **Paragraph Spacing** to display the Paragraph Spacing menu.

Each paragraph spacing option controls space around and within the paragraph

2. Select the option you want to apply to all the paragraphs in the document.

To adjust the spacing between paragraphs

1. Select all the paragraphs you want to adjust.

2. On the **Layout** tab, in the **Paragraph** group, adjust the **Spacing Before** and **Spacing After** settings.

Spacing is measured in points

To adjust spacing between the lines of paragraphs

- Position the cursor anywhere in the paragraph or select all the paragraphs you want to adjust. Do either of the following:

  - To make a quick adjustment to the selected paragraphs, on the **Home** tab, in the **Paragraph** group, select the **Line and Paragraph Spacing** button, and then select any of the line-spacing commands on the menu.

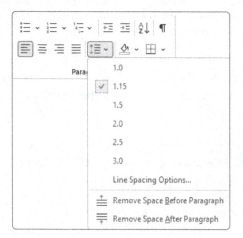

You can choose from preset internal line-spacing options or adjust paragraph spacing

> **TIP** You can also adjust the space before and after selected paragraphs from the Line And Paragraph Spacing menu. Selecting one of the last two options adds or removes a preset amount of space between the selected paragraphs.

  - To make a more-specific adjustment, open the **Paragraph** dialog. Then, on the **Indents and Spacing** tab, in the **Spacing** area, make the adjustments you want to the paragraph spacing, and then select **OK**.

Configure indents

In Word, you don't define the width of paragraphs and the length of pages by defin-ing the area occupied by the text. Instead, you define the size of the white space—the left, right, top, and bottom margins—around the text.

> ⊘ **SEE ALSO** For information about setting margins, see "Preview and adjust page layout" in Chapter 12, "Finalize and distribute documents." For information about sections, see "Control what appears on each page" in the same chapter.

Although the left and right margins are set for a whole document or for a section of a document, you can vary the position of a paragraph between the margins by indent-ing the left or right edge of the paragraph.

A paragraph indent is the space from the page margin to the text. You can change the left indent by selecting buttons on the Home tab, or you can set the indents directly on the ruler. Three indent markers are always present on the ruler:

- **Left Indent**   This defines the outermost left edge of each line of the paragraph.

- **Right Indent**   This defines the outermost right edge of each line of the paragraph.

- **First Line Indent**   This defines the starting point of the first line of the paragraph.

The ruler indicates the space between the left and right page margins in a lighter color than the space outside of the page margins.

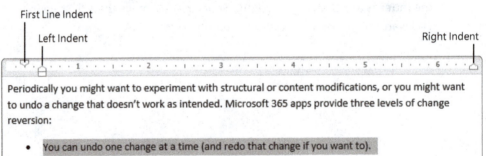

The indent markers on the ruler

The default setting for the Left Indent and First Line Indent markers is 0.0", which aligns with the left page margin. The default setting for the Right Indent marker is the distance from the left margin to the right margin. For example, if the page size is set to 8.5 inches wide and the left and right margins are set to 1.0 inch, the default Right Indent marker is at 6.5 inches.

You can arrange the Left Indent and First Line Indent markers to create a hanging indent or a first line indent. Hanging indents are most commonly used for bulleted and numbered lists, in which the bullets or numbers are indented less than the main text (essentially, they are *out*dented). First line indents are frequently used to distinguish the beginning of each subsequent paragraph in documents that consist of many consecutive paragraphs of text. Both types of indents are set by using the First Line Indent marker on the ruler.

> **TIP** The First Line Indent marker is linked to the Left Indent marker. Moving the Left Indent marker also moves the First Line Indent marker to maintain the first line indent distance. You can move the First Line Indent marker independently of the Left Indent marker to change the first line indent distance.

To display the ruler

- On the **View** tab, in the **Show** group, select the **Ruler** checkbox.

> **TIP** In this book, we show measurements in inches. If you want to change the measurement units that Word uses, open the Word Options dialog. On the Advanced page, in the Display area, select the units you want in the Show Measurements In Units Of list. Then select OK.

To indent or outdent the left edge of a paragraph

- Position the cursor anywhere in the paragraph or select all the paragraphs you want to adjust. Then do any of the following:

  - On the **Home** tab, in the **Paragraph** group, select the **Increase Indent** or **Decrease Indent** button to move the left edge of the paragraph in 0.25 inch increments.

    > **TIP** You cannot increase or decrease the indent beyond the margins by using the Increase Indent and Decrease Indent buttons. If you need to extend an indent beyond the margins, you can do so by setting negative indentation measurements in the Paragraph dialog.

- Open the **Paragraph** dialog. Then, on the **Indents and Spacing** tab, in the **Indentation** area, set the indent in the **Left** box, and then select **OK**.

- On the ruler, drag the **Left Indent** marker to the ruler measurement at which you want to position the left edge of the body of the paragraph.

To create a hanging indent or first line indent

1. Position the cursor anywhere in the paragraph or select all the paragraphs you want to adjust.

2. Open the **Paragraph** dialog. Then, on the **Indents and Spacing** tab, in the **Indents** area, select **First line** or **Hanging** in the **Special** box.

3. In the **By** box, set the amount of the indent, and then select **OK**.

Or

1. Set the left indent of the paragraph body.

2. On the ruler, drag the **First Line Indent** marker to the ruler measurement at which you want to begin the first line of the paragraph.

To indent or outdent the right edge of a paragraph

- Position the cursor anywhere in the paragraph or select all the paragraphs you want to adjust. Then do either of the following:

  - On the ruler, drag the **Right Indent** marker to the ruler measurement at which you want to set the maximum right edge of the paragraph.

  - Open the **Paragraph** dialog. Then, on the **Indents and Spacing** tab, in the **Indentation** area, set the right indent in the **Right** box, and then select **OK**.

> **TIP** Unless the paragraph alignment is justified, the right edge of the paragraph will be ragged, but no line will extend beyond the right indent or outdent.

Configure paragraph borders and shading

To make a paragraph really stand out, you might want to put a border around it or shade its background. (For real drama, you can do both.) Select a predefined border from the Borders menu or design a custom border in the Borders And Shading dialog.

You can customize many aspects of the border

After you select the style, color, width, and location of the border, you can select Options to specify its distance from the text.

Structure content manually

At times, it's necessary to manually position text within a paragraph. You can do this by using two different hidden characters: line breaks and tabs. These characters are visible only when the option to show paragraph marks and formatting symbols is turned on.

These hidden characters have distinctive appearances:

- A line break character looks like a bent left-pointing arrow (↵)

- A tab character looks like a right-pointing arrow (→)

You can use a line break, also known as a *soft return*, to wrap a line of a paragraph in a specific location without ending the paragraph. You might use this technique to display only specific text on a line or to break a line before a word that would otherwise be hyphenated.

> **TIP** Inserting a line break does not start a new paragraph, so when you apply paragraph formatting to a line of text that ends with a line break, the formatting is applied to the entire paragraph, not only to that line.

> **SEE ALSO** For information about page and section breaks, see "Control what appears on each page" in Chapter 12.

A tab stop defines the space between two document elements. For example, you can separate numbers from list items, or columns of text, by using tabs. You can then set tab stops that define the location and alignment of the tabbed text.

| Left tab | Center tab | Decimal tab | Right tab |

We·coordinate·many·types·of·cruises,·including·the·following:¶

Traditional	→	Formal·atmosphere	→	$1599.99	→	Worldwide	→	5%·off·now!¶
Freestyle	→	Casual·atmosphere	→	$1299.99	→	Worldwide	→	15%·off·now!¶
Weekend	→	Quick·getaways	→	$999.00	→	Domestic·only	→	Call·now!¶

You can align text in different ways by using tabs

You can align lines of text in different locations across the page by using tab stops. The easiest way to set tab stops is directly on the horizontal ruler. By default, Word sets left-aligned tab stops every half inch (1.27 centimeters). These default tab stops aren't shown on the ruler. To set a custom tab stop, start by selecting the Tab button (located at the intersection of the vertical and horizontal rulers) until the type of tab stop you want appears.

4

Tab setting options

You have the following tab options:

- **Left tab**   Aligns the left end of the text with the tab stop.

- **Center tab**   Aligns the center of the text with the tab stop.

- **Right tab**   Aligns the right end of the text with the tab stop.

- **Decimal tab**   Aligns the decimal point in the text (usually a numeric value) with the tab stop.

- **Bar tab**   Draws a vertical line at the position of the tab stop.

If you find it too difficult to position tab stops on the ruler, you can set, clear, align, and format tab stops from the Tabs dialog.

You can specify the alignment and tab leader for each tab

You might also work from this dialog if you want to use tab leaders—visible marks such as dots or dashes connecting the text before the tab with the text after it. For example, tab leaders are useful in a table of contents to carry the eye from the text to the page number.

When you insert tab characters, the text to the right of the tab character aligns on the tab stop according to its type. For example, if you set a center tab stop, pressing the Tab key moves the text so that its center aligns with the tab stop.

To display or hide paragraph marks and other structural characters

- On the **Home** tab, in the **Paragraph** group, select the **Show/Hide ¶** button.

- Press **Ctrl+Shift+8 (Ctrl+*)**.

To insert a line break (soft return)

- Position the cursor where you want to break the line. Then do either of the following:

  - On the **Layout** tab, in the **Page Setup** group, select **Breaks** and then **Text Wrapping**.

  - Press **Shift+Enter**.

To insert a tab character

- Position the cursor where you want to add the tab character, and then press the **Tab** key.

To open the Tabs dialog

1. Select any portion of one or more paragraphs that you want to manage tab stops for.

2. Open the **Paragraph** dialog.

3. In the lower-left corner of the **Indents and Spacing** tab, select the **Tabs** button.

To align a tab and set a tab stop

1. Select any portion of one or more paragraphs that you want to set the tab stop for.

2. Display the ruler, if it isn't shown, by selecting the **Ruler** checkbox in the **Show** group on the **View** tab.

3. Select the **Tab** button at the left end of the ruler to cycle through the tab stop alignments, in this order:

- Left

- Center

- Right

- Decimal

- Bar

4. When the **Tab** button shows the alignment you want, select the ruler at the point where you want to set the tab.

> **TIP** When you manually align a tab and set a tab stop, Word removes any default tab stops to the left of the one you set. (It doesn't remove any manually set tab stops.)

Or

1. Open the **Tabs** dialog.

2. In the **Tab stop position** box, enter the position for the new tab stop.

3. In the **Alignment** and **Leader** areas, set the options you want for this tab stop.

4. Select **Set** to set the tab, and then select **OK**.

To change the position of an existing custom tab stop

- Drag the tab marker on the ruler to the left or right.

- Open the **Tabs** dialog. In the **Tab stop position** list, select the tab stop you want to change. Select the **Clear** button to clear the existing tab stop. Enter the replacement tab stop position in the **Tab stop position** box, select **Set**, and then select **OK**.

To remove a custom tab stop

- Drag the tab marker away from the ruler.

- In the **Tabs** dialog, select the custom tab stop in the **Tab stop position** list, select **Clear**, and then select **OK**.

Apply character formatting

The appearance of your document helps convey not only the document's message but also information about the document's creator: you. A neatly organized document that contains consistently formatted content and appropriate graphic elements, and that doesn't contain spelling or grammatical errors, invokes greater confidence in your ability to provide any product or service.

Earlier in this chapter, you learned about methods of applying formatting to paragraphs. This topic covers methods of formatting the text of a document. Formatting that you apply to text is referred to as *character formatting*.

In Word documents, you can apply three types of character formatting:

- Individual character formats including font, font size, font color, bold, italic, underline, strikethrough, subscript, superscript, and highlight color

- Artistic text effects that incorporate character outline and fill colors

- Preformatted styles associated with the document template, many of which not only affect the appearance of the text but also convey structural information (such as titles and headings)

When you enter text in a document, it is displayed in a specific font. By default, the font used for text in a new blank document is 11-point Calibri; however, you can change the font of any text element at any time. The available fonts vary from one computer to another, depending on the apps installed. Common fonts include Arial, Verdana, and Times New Roman.

You can vary the look of a font by changing the following attributes:

- **Size** Almost every font has a range of sizes you can select from. (Sometimes you can set additional sizes beyond those listed.) The font size is measured in points, from the top of the ascenders (the letter parts that go up, like the left line of the letter *h*) to the bottom of the descenders (the letter parts that drop down, like the left line of the letter *p*). A point is approximately 1/72 of an inch (about 0.04 centimeters).

- **Style**   Almost every font has a range of font styles. The most common are regular (or plain), italic, bold, and bold italic.

- **Effects**   Fonts can be enhanced by applying effects, such as underlining, small capital letters (small caps), or shadows.

- **Character spacing**   You can alter the spacing between characters by pushing them apart or squeezing them together.

Although some attributes might cancel each other out, they are usually cumulative. For example, you might use a bold font style in various sizes and colors to make words stand out in a newsletter.

You apply character formatting from three locations:

- **Mini Toolbar**   Several common formatting buttons are available on the Mini Toolbar that appears temporarily when you select text.

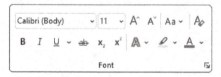

The Mini Toolbar appears temporarily when you select text, becomes transparent when you move the pointer away from the selected text, and disappears if not used

- **Font group on the Home tab**   This group includes buttons for changing the font and most of the font attributes you're likely to use.

The most common font formatting commands are available on the Home tab

- **Font dialog**   Less commonly applied attributes such as small caps and special underlining are available from the Font dialog.

Less-common font and character attributes can be set in the Font dialog

In addition to applying character formatting to change the look of characters, you can apply predefined text effects (sometimes referred to as *WordArt*) to a selection to add more zing. The available effects match the current theme colors.

You can apply any predefined effect in the gallery or define a custom effect

These effects are somewhat dramatic, so you'll probably want to restrict their use to document titles and similar elements to which you want to draw particular attention.

To change the font of selected text

- On the **Mini Toolbar** or in the **Font** group on the **Home** tab, in the **Font** list, select the font you want to apply.

To change the font size of selected text

- Do any of the following on the **Mini Toolbar** or in the **Font** group on the **Home** tab:

  - In the **Font Size** list, select the font size you want to apply.

  - In the **Font Size** box, enter the font size you want to apply (even a size that doesn't appear in the list). Then press the **Enter** key.

  - To increase the font size in set increments, select the **Increase Font Size** button or press **Ctrl+>**.

  - To decrease the font size in set increments, select the **Decrease Font Size** button or press **Ctrl+<**.

To format selected text as bold, italic, or underlined

- On the **Mini Toolbar**, select the **Bold**, **Italic**, or **Underline** button.

- On the **Home** tab, in the **Font** group, select the **Bold**, **Italic**, or **Underline** button.

- Press **Ctrl+B** to format the text as bold.

- Press **Ctrl+I** to format the text as italic.

- Press **Ctrl+U** to underline the text.

> **TIP** To quickly apply a different underline style to selected text, select the Underline arrow (the arrow to the right of the Underline button in the Font group on the Home tab), and then in the list, select the underline style you want to apply. The Underline arrow is not available from the Mini Toolbar.

To cross out selected text by drawing a line through it

- On the **Home** tab, in the **Font** group, select the **Strikethrough** button.

To format selected characters as superscript or subscript

- On the **Home** tab, in the **Font** group, do either of the following:

  - Select the **Subscript** button to decrease the size of the selected characters and shift them to the bottom of the line.

  - Select the **Superscript** button to decrease the size of the selected characters and shift them to the top of the line.

> ✓ **TIP** Word automatically applies superscript formatting to characters in specific combinations, such as 1st, 2nd, 3rd, and 4th. If you don't want the superscript formatting, press Ctrl+Z or select the Undo button immediately after the format is applied; select the text and press Ctrl+Spacebar to clear extra formatting from the base style; or select the text and then clear the Superscript style in the Font group on the Home tab.

To apply artistic effects to selected text

- On the **Home** tab, in the **Font** group, select the **Text Effects and Typography** button, and then do either of the following:

  - In the **Text Effects and Typography** gallery, select the preformatted effect combination that you want to apply.

  - On the **Text Effects and Typography** menu, select **Outline**, **Shadow**, **Reflection**, **Glow**, **Number Styles**, **Ligatures**, or **Stylistic Sets**. Then make selections on the submenus to apply and modify those effects.

To change the font color of selected text

1. On the **Home** tab, in the **Font** group, select the **Font Color** arrow (not the button) to display the **Font Color** menu.

2. In the **Theme Colors** or **Standard Colors** palette, select a color swatch to apply that color to the selected text.

> ✓ **TIP** To apply the Font Color button's current color, you can simply select the button (not its arrow). If you want to apply a color that is not shown in the Theme Colors or Standard Colors palette, select More Colors. In the Colors dialog, select the color you want in the honeycomb palette on the Standard page, select the color gradient, or enter values for a color on the Custom page.

To change the case of selected text

- On the **Home** tab, in the **Font** group, select the **Change Case** button and then select **Sentence case**, **lowercase**, **UPPERCASE**, **Capitalize Each Word**, or **tOGGLE cASE**.

- Press **Shift+F3** repeatedly to cycle through the standard case options (Sentence case, UPPERCASE, lowercase, and Capitalize Each Word).

> ⚠ **IMPORTANT** The case options vary based on the selected text. If the selection ends in a period, Word does not include the Capitalize Each Word option in the rotation. If the selection does not end in a period, Word does not include Sentence case in the rotation.

4

Character formatting and case considerations

The way you use character formatting in a document can influence the document's visual impact on your readers. Used judiciously, character formatting can make a plain document look attractive and professional, but excessive use can make it look amateurish and detract from the message. For example, using too many fonts in the same document is a mark of inexperience, so don't use more than two or three.

Bear in mind that lowercase letters tend to recede, so using all uppercase (capital) letters can be useful for titles and headings or for certain kinds of emphasis. However, large blocks of uppercase letters are tiring to the eye.

TIP Where do the terms *uppercase* and *lowercase* come from? Until the advent of computers, individual characters made of lead were assembled to form the words that would appear on a printed page. The characters were stored alphabetically in cabinet cases, with the capital letters in the upper case and the small letters in the lower case.

To highlight text

- Select the text you want to highlight, and then do either of the following:

  - On the **Mini Toolbar**, or in the **Font** group on the **Home** tab, select the **Text Highlight Color** button to apply the default highlight color.

  - On the **Mini Toolbar**, or in the **Font** group on the **Home** tab, select the **Text Highlight Color** arrow, and then select a color swatch to apply the selected highlight color and change the default highlight color.

Or

1. Without first selecting text, do either of the following:

   - Select the **Text Highlight Color** button to select the default highlight color.

   - Select the **Text Highlight Color** arrow and then select a color swatch to select that highlight color.

2. When the pointer changes to a highlighter, drag it across one or more sections of text to apply the highlight.

3. Select the **Text Highlight Color** button or press the **Esc** key to deactivate the highlighter.

To copy formatting to other text

1. Select anywhere in the text that has the formatting you want to copy.

2. On the **Home** tab, in the **Clipboard** group, do either of the following:

   - If you want to apply the formatting to only one target, select **Format Painter** once.

   - If you want to apply the formatting to multiple targets, double-click **Format Painter**.

3. When the pointer changes to a paintbrush, select or drag across the text you want to apply the copied formatting to.

4. If you activated the Format Painter for multiple targets, repeat step 3 until you finish applying the formatting. Then select the **Format Painter** button once or press the **Esc** key to deactivate the tool.

To repeat the previous formatting command

- Select the text to which you want to apply the repeated formatting. Then do either of the following to repeat the previous formatting command:

   - On the **Quick Access Toolbar**, select the **Repeat** button.

   - Press **Ctrl+Y**.

To open the Font dialog

- On the **Home** tab, in the **Font** group, select the **Font** dialog launcher.

- Press **Ctrl+Shift+F**.

Format the first letter of a paragraph as a drop cap

Many books, magazines, and reports begin the first paragraph of a section or chapter by using an enlarged, decorative capital letter. Called a dropped capital, or simply a *drop cap*, this effect can be an easy way to give a document a finished, professional look. When you format a paragraph to start with a drop cap, Word inserts the first letter of the paragraph in a text box and formats its height and font in accordance with the Drop Cap options.

W ith the Room Planner, you'll never make a design mistake again. Created by acclaimed interior designers to simplify the redecorating process, this planning tool incorporates elements of color, dimension, and style to guide your project. It includes a furniture location guide; room grid; drawing tools; and miniature furniture, rugs, accessories, and color swatches that match our large in-store selection. Here's how to use the planner to create the room of your dreams!

By default, a drop-cap letter is the height of three lines of text

Word 365 has two basic drop-cap styles:

- **Dropped** The letter is embedded in the original paragraph.

- **In margin** The letter occupies its own column, and the remaining paragraph text is moved to the right.

To format the first letter of a paragraph as a drop cap:

1. Click anywhere in the paragraph.

2. On the **Insert** tab, in the **Text** group, select the **Drop Cap** button and then select the drop-cap style you want to apply.

To change the font, height, or distance between the drop cap and the paragraph text, select Drop Cap Options on the Drop Cap menu, and then select the options you want in the Drop Cap dialog.

If you want to apply the drop-cap format to more than the first letter of the paragraph, add the drop cap to the paragraph, click to the right of the letter in the text box, and enter the rest of the word or text that you want to make stand out. If you do this, don't forget to delete the word from the beginning of the paragraph!

4

To remove character formatting

- Select the text you want to clear the formatting from. Then do any of the following:

  - Press **Ctrl+Spacebar** to remove manually applied formatting (but not styles).

  - On the **Home** tab, in the **Font** group, select the **Clear All Formatting** button to remove all styles and formatting other than highlighting from selected text.

    > ⚠️ **IMPORTANT** If you select an entire paragraph, the Clear All Formatting command will clear character and paragraph formatting from the paragraph and reset it to the default paragraph style.

  - On the **Home** tab, in the **Font** group, select the **Text Highlight Color** arrow and then, on the menu, select **No Color** to remove highlighting.

To change the character spacing

1. Select the text you want to change.

2. Open the **Font** dialog, and then select the **Advanced** tab to display character spacing and typographic features.

3. In the **Spacing** list, select **Expanded** or **Condensed**.

4. In the adjacent **By** box, set the number of points you want to expand or condense the character spacing.

5. In the **Font** dialog, select **OK**.

Create and modify lists

Lists are paragraphs that start with a character—usually a number or bullet—and are formatted with a hanging indent so the character stands out on the left end of each list item. Fortunately, Word takes care of formatting lists for you. You simply indicate the type of list you want to create.

When the order of items is not important—for example, for a list of people or supplies—a bulleted list is the best choice. When the order is important—for example, for the steps in a procedure—you should create a numbered list.

You can format an existing set of paragraphs as a list or create the list as you enter text into the document. After you create a list, you can modify, format, and customize the list as follows:

- You can move items around in a list, insert new items, or delete unwanted items. If the list is numbered, Word automatically updates the numbers.

- You can modify the indentation of the list. You can change both the overall indentation of the list and the relationship of the first line to the other lines.

- For a bulleted list, you can sort list items alphabetically in ascending or descending order, change the bullet symbol, or define a custom bullet (even a picture bullet).

- For a numbered list, you can change the number style to use different punctuation, roman numerals, or letters, or define a custom style, and you can specify the starting number.

To format a new bulleted or numbered list as you enter content

- With the cursor at the position in the document where you want to start the list, do either of the following:

  - To start a new bulleted list, enter * (an asterisk) at the beginning of a paragraph, and then press the **Spacebar** or the **Tab** key before entering the list item text.

  - To start a new numbered list, enter 1. (the number 1 followed by a period) at the beginning of a paragraph, and then press the **Spacebar** or the **Tab** key before entering the list item text.

  When you start a list in this fashion, Word automatically formats the text as a bulleted or numbered list.

  When you press Enter to start a new item, Word continues the formatting to the new paragraph. Typing text and pressing Enter adds subsequent bulleted or numbered items. To end the list, press Enter twice; or select the Bullets arrow or Numbering arrow in the Paragraph group on the Home tab, and then in the gallery, select None.

> ✓ **TIP** If you want to start a paragraph with an asterisk or number but don't want to format the paragraph as a bulleted or numbered list, select the AutoCorrect Options button that appears after Word changes the formatting, and then in the list, select the appropriate Undo option. Alternatively, select the Undo button on the Quick Access Toolbar or press Ctrl+Z.

To convert paragraphs to bulleted or numbered list items

1. Select the paragraphs that you want to convert to list items.

2. On the **Home** tab, in the **Paragraph** group, do either of the following:

   - Select the **Bullets** button to convert the selection to a bulleted list.

   - Select the **Numbering** button to convert the selection to a numbered list.

To create a list with multiple levels

1. Start creating a bulleted or numbered list.

2. When you want the next list item to be at a different level, do either of the following:

   - To create the next item one level lower (indented more), press the **Tab** key at the beginning of that paragraph before you enter the lower-level list item text.

   - To create the next item one level higher (indented less), press **Shift+Tab** at the beginning of the paragraph before you enter the higher-level list item text.

   In the case of a bulleted list, Word changes the bullet character for each item level. In the case of a numbered list, Word changes the type of numbering used, based on a predefined numbering scheme.

> **TIP** For a multilevel list, you can change the numbering pattern or bullets by selecting the Multilevel List button in the Paragraph group on the Home tab and then selecting the pattern you want, or you can define a custom pattern by selecting Define New Multilevel List.

To modify the indentation of a list

- Select the list items whose indentation you want to change, and do any of the following:

   - On the **Home** tab, in the **Paragraph** group, select the **Increase Indent** button to move the list items to the right.

   - In the **Paragraph** group, select the **Decrease Indent** button to move the list items to the left.

   - Display the ruler and drag the indent markers to the left or right.

> **TIP** You can adjust the space between the bullets and their text by dragging only the Hanging Indent marker.

> **SEE ALSO** For information about paragraph indentation, see "Apply paragraph formatting" earlier in this chapter.

4

To sort bulleted list items alphabetically

1. Select the bulleted list items whose sort order you want to change.

2. On the **Home** tab, in the **Paragraph** group, select the **Sort** button to open the Sort Text dialog.

3. In the **Sort by** area, select **Ascending** or **Descending**. Then select **OK**.

To change the bullet symbol

1. Select the bulleted list whose bullet symbol you want to change.

2. On the **Home** tab, in the **Paragraph** group, select the **Bullets** arrow.

3. In the **Bullets** gallery, select the new symbol you want to use to replace the bullet character that begins each item in the selected list.

To define a custom bullet

1. In the **Bullets** gallery, select **Define New Bullet**.

2. In the **Define New Bullet** dialog, select the **Symbol**, **Picture**, or **Font** button, and then select from the wide range of options.

3. Select **OK** to apply the new bullet style to the list.

To change the number style

1. Select the numbered list whose number style you want to change.

2. On the **Home** tab, in the **Paragraph** group, select the **Numbering** arrow to display the Numbering gallery.

3. Choose a different style to apply it to the number that begins each item in the selected list.

To define a custom number style

1. In the **Numbering** gallery, select **Define New Number Format**.

2. In the **Define New Number Format** dialog, do either of the following:

    -   Change the selections in the **Number Style**, **Number Format**, or **Alignment** boxes.

    -   Select the **Font** button, and then select from the wide range of options.

3. Select **OK** to apply the new numbering style to the list.

To start a list or part of a list at a predefined number

1. Place the cursor within an existing list, in the list paragraph whose number you want to set.

2. Do either of the following to open the Set Numbering Value dialog:

    -   Right-click or long-press (tap and hold) the number, and then on the short-cut menu, select **Set Numbering Value**.

    -   Display the **Numbering** gallery, and then select **Set Numbering Value**.

3. In the **Set Numbering Value** dialog, do either of the following to permit custom numbering:

    -   Select **Start new list**.

    -   Select **Continue from previous list**, and then select the **Advance value (skip numbers)** checkbox.

4. In the **Set value to** box, enter the number you want to assign to the list item. Then select **OK**.

You can start or restart a numbered list at any number

Format text as you type

The Word list capabilities are only one example of the app's ability to intuit how you want to format an element based on what you type. You can learn more about these and other AutoFormatting options by exploring the AutoCorrect dialog, which you open from the Proofing page of the Word Options dialog.

The AutoFormat As You Type page shows the options Word implements by default, including bulleted and numbered lists.

You can select and clear options to control automatic formatting behavior

One interesting option in this dialog is Border Lines. When this checkbox is selected, typing three consecutive hyphens (---) or three consecutive under-scores (___) and pressing Enter draws a single line across the page. Typing three consecutive equal signs (===) and pressing Enter draws a double line. Typing three consecutive tildes (~~~) and pressing Enter draws a zigzag line.

Apply built-in styles to text

You don't have to know much about character and paragraph formatting to format your documents in ways that will make them easier to read and more professional looking. With a couple of mouse clicks or screen taps, you can easily change the look of words, phrases, and paragraphs by using styles. Heading styles are important to the accessibility of a document; they create a structure (the document outline) that is reflected in the Navigation pane and table of contents, and is also perceptible to screen readers and other assistive technology.

> **SEE ALSO** For information about tables of contents, see "Create and modify tables of contents" in Chapter 13, "Reference content and content sources."

Apply styles

Styles are classified as character styles, which control character formatting (such as font, size, and color); paragraph styles, which control paragraph formatting (such as line spacing and outline level); or linked styles, which control both character and paragraph formatting. Heading styles are a common type of linked style.

Styles are stored in the template that is attached to a document. New, blank documents are based on the Normal template. The Normal template includes a standard selection of styles that fit the basic needs of most documents. These styles include nine heading levels, various text styles including those for multiple levels of bulleted and numbered lists, index and table of contents entry styles, and many specialized styles such as those for hyperlinks, quotations, placeholders, captions, and other elements.

By default, the most common predefined styles are available in the Styles gallery on the Home tab. You can add styles to the gallery or remove those that you don't often use.

The Styles gallery in a new, blank document based on the Normal template

Styles stored in a template are usually based on the Normal style and use only the default body and heading fonts associated with the document's theme, so they all go together well. For this reason, formatting document content by using styles produces a harmonious effect. After you apply named styles, you can easily change the look of an entire document by switching to a different style set that contains styles with the same names but different formatting.

> **SEE ALSO** For information about document theme elements, see "Change the document theme," later in this chapter.

Style sets are available from the Document Formatting gallery on the Design tab.

Pointing to a style set in the gallery displays a live preview of the effects of applying that style set to the entire document

> **TIP** Style sets provide a quick and easy way to change the look of an existing document. You can also modify style definitions by changing the template on which the document is based. For more information about styles and templates, see "Create and modify styles" and "Create and attach templates" in Chapter 15, "Create custom document elements."

To open the Styles pane

- On the **Home** tab, select the **Styles** dialog launcher.

The Styles pane displays a simple list or formatted previews of style names

> **TIP** If the Styles pane floats above the page, you can drag it by its title bar to the right or left edge of the app window to dock it.

To change which styles are displayed in the Styles pane

1. Open the **Styles** pane, and then select **Options**.

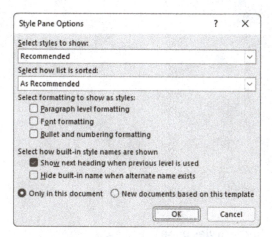

To make it easier to find specific styles, sort the list alphabetically

2. In the **Style Pane Options** dialog, do any of the following, and then select **OK**:

    -   In the **Select styles to show** list, select one of the following:

        -   **Recommended** Displays styles that are tagged in the template as recommended for use

        -   **In use** Displays styles that are applied to content in the current document

        -   **In current document** Displays styles that are in the template that is attached to the current document

        -   **All styles** Displays built-in styles, styles that are in the attached template, and styles that were brought into the document from other templates

    -   In the **Select how list is sorted** list, select **Alphabetical**, **As Recommended**, **Font**, **Based on**, or **By type**.

    -   In the **Select formatting to show as styles** area, select each checkbox for which you want to display variations from named styles.

    -   In the **Select how built-in style names are shown** area, select the checkbox for each option you want to turn on.

*Displaying paragraph-level and font formatting
exposes deviations from style definitions*

To display or hide style previews in the Styles pane

- Open the **Styles** pane, and then select or clear the **Show Preview** checkbox.

To add a style to the Styles gallery

- In the **Styles** pane, point to the style, select the arrow that appears, and then select **Add to Style Gallery**.

To remove a style from the Styles gallery

- In the **Styles** pane, point to the style, select the arrow that appears, and then select **Remove from Style Gallery**.

- In the **Styles** gallery, right-click the style, and then select **Remove from Style Gallery**.

To apply a built-in style

1. Select the text or paragraph to which you want to apply the style.

> **TIP** If the style you want to apply is a paragraph style, you can position the cursor anywhere in the paragraph. If the style you want to apply is a character style, you must select the text.

2. In the **Styles** gallery on the **Home** tab, or in the Styles pane, select the style you want to apply.

To change the style set

1. On the **Design** tab, in the **Document Formatting** group, select the **More** button to display all the style sets (if necessary).

2. Point to any style set to preview its effect on the document.

3. Select the style set you want to apply.

Manage outline levels

Styles can be used for multiple purposes: to change the appearance of the content, to build a document outline, or to tag content as a certain type so that you can easily locate it.

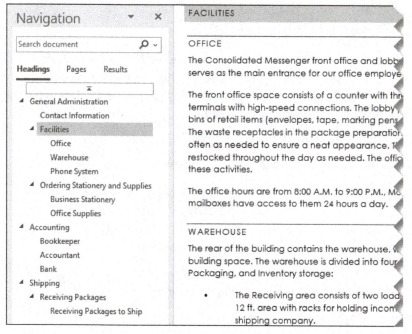

Heading styles define a document's outline

Each paragraph style has an associated Outline Level setting. Outline levels include Body Text and Level 1 through Level 9. Most documents use only body text and the first three or four outline levels.

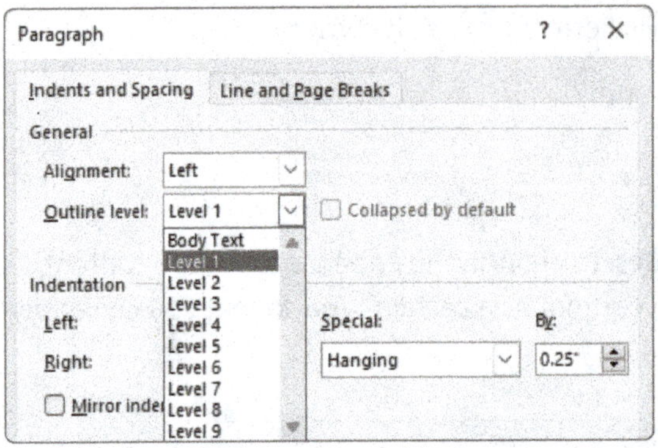

Most documents use only two to four of the outline levels

Paragraphs that have the Level 1 through Level 9 outline levels become part of the hierarchical structure of the document. They appear as headings in the Navigation pane and act as handles for the content that appears below them in the hierarchy. You can collapse and expand the content below each heading and move entire sections of content by dragging the headings in the Navigation pane.

To display the document outline in the Navigation pane

- In the Navigation pane, select **Headings** to display the document structure.

> **TIP** Only headings that are styled by using document heading styles, or other styles that have outline levels applied, appear in the Navigation pane.

To expand or collapse the outline in the Navigation pane

- In the Navigation pane, do either of the following:

  - If there is a white triangle to the left of a heading, select it to expand that heading to show its subheadings.

  - If there is a downward-angled black triangle to the left of a heading, select it to collapse the subheadings under that heading.

> **TIP** If there is no triangle next to a heading, that heading does not have subheadings.

To expand or collapse sections in the document

■ In a document that contains styles, point to a heading to display a triangle to its left. Then do either of the following:

• If the triangle points down and to the right, the content within the document section governed by the heading is visible. Select the triangle to hide the content below the heading.

• If the triangle points to the right, the content within the document section is hidden. Select the triangle to display the hidden document content.

4

Change the document theme

Every document you create is based on a template, and the look of the template is controlled by a theme. The *theme* is a combination of coordinated colors, fonts, and effects that visually convey a certain tone. To change the look of a document, you can apply a different theme from the Themes gallery.

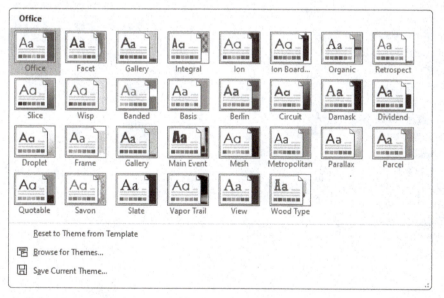

The default installation of Word 365 offers 30 themes to choose from

Each theme has a built-in font set and color set, and an associated effect style.

- Each font set includes two font definitions: one for headings and one for body text. In some font sets, the heading and body fonts are the same.

- Each color in a color set has a specific role in the formatting of styled elements. For example, the first color in each set is applied to the Title and Intense Reference styles, and different shades of the third color are applied to the Subtitle, Heading 1, and Heading 2 styles.

If you like the background elements of a theme but not the colors or fonts, you can mix and match theme elements.

Word 365 offers thousands of different combinations for creating a custom theme that meets your exact needs

> **SEE ALSO** For information about creating custom themes, see "Create and manage custom themes" in Chapter 15.

> **TIP** In addition to colors and fonts, you can control the subtler design elements associated with a theme, such as paragraph spacing and visual effects.

If you create a combination of theme elements that you would like to use with other documents, you can save the combination as a new theme. By saving the theme in the default Document Themes folder, you make the theme available in the Themes gallery. However, you don't have to store custom themes in the Document Themes folder; you can store them anywhere on your hard disk, on removable media, or in a network location.

4

> **TIP** The default Document Themes folder is stored within your user profile. On a default freestanding installation, the folder is located at C:\Users\<*user name*>\ AppData\Roaming\Microsoft\Templates\Document Themes. In a corporate environment with managed computer configurations, the user profile folder might be located elsewhere.

By default, Word applies the Office theme to all new, blank documents. In Word 365, the Office theme uses a primarily blue palette, the Calibri font for body text, and Calibri Light for headings. If you plan to frequently use a theme other than the Office theme, you can make that the default theme.

> **TIP** If multiple people create corporate documents for your company, you can ensure that everyone's documents have a common look and feel by assembling a custom theme and making it available to everyone. Use theme elements that reflect your corporate colors, fonts, and visual style, and then save the theme to a central location or send the theme file by email and instruct your colleagues to save it to the default Document Themes folder.

To apply a built-in theme to a document

- On the **Design** tab, in the **Document Formatting** group, select the **Themes** button, and then select the theme you want to apply.

> **TIP** If you have manually applied formatting to document content, the theme does not override the manual formatting. To ensure that all document elements are controlled by the theme, select Reset To The Default Style Set on the Document Formatting menu.

To change theme elements in a document

- On the **Design** tab, in the **Document Formatting** group, do any of the following:

  - Select **Colors** (the ScreenTip says *Theme Colors*), and then select the color set you want to apply.

  - Select **Fonts** (the ScreenTip says *Theme Fonts*), and then select the font set you want to apply.

  - Select **Effects** (the ScreenTip says *Theme Effects*), and then select the effect style you want to apply.

To save a custom theme

1. Apply a base theme, and then modify the theme colors, fonts, and effects as you want them.

2. On the **Design** tab, in the **Document Formatting** group, select **Themes**.

3. At the bottom of the **Themes** menu, select **Save Current Theme** to display the contents of the Document Themes folder in the **Save Current Theme** dialog.

4. Accept the theme name that is in the **File name** box or replace the suggested name with one that's more descriptive. Then select **Save**.

To apply a custom theme

1. Display the **Themes** menu. If you have created a custom theme, the Themes menu now includes a Custom area that contains your theme.

2. Select the theme to apply it to the document.

To change the default theme

1. In the document, apply the theme you want to use as the default theme.

2. On the **Design** tab, in the **Document Formatting** group, select **Set as Default**.

To apply a theme from a nonstandard location

1. On the **Design** tab, in the **Document Formatting** group, select **Themes**.

2. At the bottom of the **Themes** menu, select **Browse for Themes**.

3. In the **Choose Theme or Themed Document** dialog, browse to the theme you want to apply, and then select **Open**.

To find the location of your Document Themes folder

1. On the **Design** tab, in the **Document Formatting** group, select **Themes**.

2. At the bottom of the **Themes** menu, select **Save Current Theme**.

3. In the **Save Current Theme** dialog, select the folder icon at the left end of the address bar to display the full path to the Document Themes folder.

To delete a custom theme

- Open File Explorer, browse to the **Document Themes** folder, and delete the theme file.

- In Word, display the **Themes** menu, right-click the custom theme, and then select **Delete**.

Note that the second method removes the theme choice from the gallery but does not remove the theme file from the Document Themes folder.

Key points

- You can format many aspects of a paragraph, including its indentation, alignment, internal line spacing, preceding and following space, border, and background. Within a paragraph, you can control the content structure by using hidden line breaks and tabs, and the appearance of the content by changing the size, color, style, effects, and spacing of the text.

- You can apply paragraph and character formatting manually, or you can format multiple elements of a paragraph, and control the outline level of the content, by using styles.

- You can change the formatting applied by all the styles within a document by changing the document theme or any individual element of the theme, such as the theme colors, theme fonts, or theme effects.

- To make a set of items or instructions stand out from the surrounding text, you can format it as an ordered (numbered) or unordered (bulleted) list.

Practice tasks

Before you can complete these tasks, you must copy the book's practice files to your computer. The practice files for these tasks are in the **Word365SBS\Ch04** folder. You can save the results of the tasks in the same folder.

The book's Introduction includes a complete list of practice files and download instructions.

Apply paragraph formatting

Open the **FormatParagraphs** document, display formatting marks, and then perform the following tasks:

1. Display the rulers and adjust the zoom level to display most or all of the paragraphs in the document.

2. Select the first two paragraphs (*Welcome!* and the next paragraph) and center them between the margins.

3. Select the second paragraph (*We would like...*) and apply a first-line indent.

4. Select the third paragraph (*Please take a few...*). Format the paragraph so its edges are flush against the left and right margins. Then indent the paragraph by a half inch on the left and on the right.

5. Indent the *Be careful* paragraph by 0.25 inches.

6. Simultaneously select the *Pillows, Blankets, Towels, Limousine winery tour,* and *In-home massage* paragraphs. Change the paragraph spacing to remove the space after the paragraphs.

7. At the top of the document, apply an outside border to the *Please take a few minutes* paragraph.

8. Save and close the document.

Structure content manually

Open the **StructureContent** document, display formatting marks, and then perform the following tasks:

1. Display the rulers and adjust the zoom level to display most or all of the paragraphs in the document.

2. In the second paragraph (*We would like...*), insert a line break immediately after the comma and space that follow the word *cottage*.

3. Select the *Pillows, Blankets, Towels,* and *Dish towels* paragraphs. Insert a left tab stop at the 2-inch mark and clear any tab stops to the left of that location.

4. In the *Pillows* paragraph, replace the space before the word *There* with a tab marker. Repeat the process to insert tabs in each of the next three paragraphs. The part of each paragraph that follows the colon is now aligned at the 2-inch mark, producing more space than you need.

5. Select the four paragraphs containing tabs. Change the left tab stop from the 2-inch mark to the **1.25**-inch mark. Then, on the ruler, drag the **Hanging Indent** marker to the tab stop at the **1.25**-inch mark (the Left Indent marker moves with it) to cause the second line of the paragraphs to start in the same location as the first line. Finally, press the **Home** key to release the selection so you can review the results.

6. At the bottom of the document, select the three paragraphs containing dollar amounts. Set a **Decimal Tab** stop at the 3-inch mark. Then replace the space to the left of each dollar sign with a tab to align the prices on the decimal points.

7. Hide the formatting marks to better display the results of your work.

8. Save and close the document.

Apply character formatting

Open the **FormatCharacters** document, and then perform the following tasks:

1. In the second bullet point, underline the word *natural*. Then repeat the formatting command to underline the word *all* in the fourth bullet point.

2. In the fourth bullet point, select anywhere in the word *across*. Apply a thick underline to the word in a way that also assigns the **Thick underline** format to the **Underline** button. Then apply the thick underline to the word *departments*.

3. Apply bold formatting to the *Employee Orientation* heading.

4. Copy the formatting, and then paint it onto the *Guidelines* subtitle to make the subtitle a heading.

5. Select the *Guidelines* heading, and apply the following formatting:

   - Change the font to **Impact**.

   - Set the font size to **20** points.

   - Apply the **Small caps** font effect.

   - Expand the character spacing by **10** points.

6. Change the font color of the words *Employee Orientation* to **Green, Accent 6**.

7. Select the *Community Service Committee* heading, and apply the following formatting:

   - Outline the letters in the same color you applied to *Employee Orientation*.

   - Apply an **Offset Diagonal Bottom Left** outer shadow. Change the shadow color to **Green, Accent 6, Darker 50%**.

   - Fill the letters with the **Green, Accent 6** color, and then change the text outline to **Green, Accent 6, Darker 25%**.

   You have now applied three text effects to the selected text by using three shades of the same green.

8. In the first bullet point, select the phrase *the concept of service* and apply a **Bright Green** highlight.

9. In the fifth bullet point, select the words *brainstorming*, *planning*, and *leadership*, and simultaneously change the case of all the letters to uppercase.

10. Save and close the document.

Create and modify lists

Open the **CreateLists** document, display formatting marks and rulers, and then perform the following tasks:

1. Select the first four paragraphs below *The rules fall into four categories*. Format the selected paragraphs as a bulleted list. Then change the bullet character for the four list items to the one composed of four diamonds.

2. Select the two paragraphs below the *Definitions* heading. Format the selected paragraphs as a numbered list.

3. Select the first four paragraphs below the *General Rules* heading. Format the paragraphs as a second numbered list. Ensure that the new list starts with the number 1.

4. Format the next three paragraphs as a bulleted list. (Notice that Word uses the bullet symbol you specified earlier.) Indent the bulleted list as a subset of the preceding numbered list item.

5. Format the remaining three paragraphs as a numbered list. Ensure that the list numbering continues from the previous numbered list.

6. Locate the *No large dogs* numbered list item. Create a new second-level numbered list item (**a**) from the text that begins with the word *Seeing*. Then create a second item (**b**) and enter The Board reserves the right to make exceptions to this rule.

7. Create a third list item (**c**). Promote the new list item to a first-level item, and enter All pets must reside within their Owners' Apartments. Notice that the *General Rules* list is now organized hierarchically.

8. Sort the three bulleted list items in ascending alphabetical order.

9. Save and close the document.

Apply built-in styles to text

Open the **ApplyStyles** document in Print Layout view, and then perform the following tasks:

1. Scroll through the document to review its content. Notice that the document begins with a centered title and subtitle, and there are several headings throughout.

2. Display the Navigation pane. Notice that the Headings page of the pane does not reflect the headings in the document because the headings are formatted with manually applied formatting instead of styles.

3. Open the Styles pane and dock it to the right edge of the app window.

4. Set the zoom level of the page to fit the page content between the Navigation pane and the Styles pane.

5. Apply the **Title** style to the document title, *All About Bamboo*.

6. Apply the **Subtitle** style to the *Information Sheet* paragraph.

7. Apply the **Heading 1** style to the first bold heading, *Moving to a New Home*. Notice that the heading appears in the Navigation pane.

8. Hide the content that follows the heading. Then redisplay it.

9. Apply the **Heading 1** style to *Staying Healthy*. Then repeat the formatting to apply the same style to *Keeping Bugs at Bay*.

10. Scroll the page so that both underlined headings are visible. Select the *Mites* and *Mealy Bugs* headings. Then simultaneously apply the **Heading 2** style to both selections.

11. Configure the Styles pane to display all styles, in alphabetical order.

12. Move to the beginning of the document.

13. In the first paragraph of the document, select the company name *Wide World Importers*, and apply the **Intense Reference** style.

14. In the second paragraph, near the end of the first sentence, select the word *clumping*, and apply the **Emphasis** style. Then, at the end of the sentence, apply the same style to the word *running*.

15. Close the Navigation pane and the Styles pane. Then configure the view setting to display both pages of the document in the window.

16. Apply the **Basic (Elegant)** style set to the document. Change the view to **Page Width** and notice the changes to the styled content.

17. Save and close the document.

Change the document theme

Open the **ChangeTheme** document, and then perform the following tasks:

1. Apply the **Facet** theme to the document.

2. Change the theme colors to the **Orange** color scheme.

3. Change the theme fonts to the **Georgia** theme set.

4. Save the modified theme in the default folder as a custom theme named *My Theme*. Verify that the custom theme is available on the **Themes** menu.

5. Save and close the document.

Organize information in columns and tables

In Word documents, text is most commonly presented in paragraph form. To make certain types of information more legible, you can arrange it in two or more columns or display it in a table. For example, flowing text in multiple columns is a common practice in newsletters, flyers, and brochures, whereas presenting information in tables is common in reports.

When you need to present facts and figures in a document, using columns or tables is often more efficient than describing the data in a paragraph, particularly when the data consists of numeric values. You can display small amounts of data in simple columns separated by tabs, which creates a *tabbed list*. Larger amounts of data and data that is more complex are better presented in table form—that is, in a structure of rows and columns, frequently with row and column headings. Tables make data easier to read and understand.

This chapter guides you through procedures related to presenting information in columns and tables, creating tabbed lists, and formatting tables.

In this chapter

- Present information in columns
- Create tabbed lists
- Present information in tables
- Format tables

Present information in columns

By default, Word displays text in one column that spans the width of the page between the left and right margins. If you prefer, however, you can specify that text be displayed in two, three, or more columns to create layouts like those used in newspapers and magazines.

Simple Room Design

With the Room Planner, you'll never make a design mistake again. Created by acclaimed interior designers to simplify the redecorating process, this planning tool incorporates elements of color, dimension, and style to guide your project. It includes a furniture location guide; room grid; drawing tools; and miniature furniture, rugs, accessories, and color swatches that match our large in-store selection. Here's how to use the planner to create the room of your dreams!

Look at how your home is decorated and note the things you like and dislike. Pay special attention to the color scheme and to how each room "feels" to you. Is it inviting? Does it feel comfortable? Does it relax you or does it invigorate you?

Focus on the room(s) you would most like to change. Brainstorm all the things you would change in that room if you could. Don't give a thought to any financial considerations; just let your imagination go wild! It might be helpful to write down all the negatives and positives. You don't need to come up with solutions all at once. Just be clear on what you like and what you hate about that room.

love, and the rest will fall into place.

Take your Room Planner home and get to work! Adjust the planner so that it models the room dimensions. Don't forget to place the windows and doors. Arrange the furniture placeholders to mirror how your room is currently set up. Add the current colors, too.

This is where the fun begins! Start changing things around a bit. Move the furniture, add different colors, and watch the room come together! Here's where you can tell if that rich red rug you saw in the showroom enhances or overwhelms your room. What about that overstuffed chair that caught your eye? Place a

design for a day or two. Then review it again. Does it still look perfect, or is something not quite right? You might need to "live" with the new plan for a few days, especially if you've made big changes. When everything feels just right to you, you're ready for the next big step!

Come back to the store. Look again at the pieces you liked during your last visit and see if you still love them. If you're not quite sure, go back to your planner for a little more tweaking. If you are sure, look around the store one more time to see if anything else catches your eye. Then make your purchases. You're almost there!

NOTE: If you decided to

You can format text to flow in columns

Columns can be divided by empty space or by vertical lines. When you format text to flow in columns, the text fills the first column on each page and then moves to the top of the next column. When all the columns on one page are full, the text moves to the next page. You can manually adjust the text flow within columns and across pages so it looks the way you want.

> **IMPORTANT** Assistive devices such as screen readers do not always correctly process text that is arranged in columns. Consider the limitations of these devices if you want your document to meet accessibility requirements.

The Columns gallery in the Page Setup group on the Layout tab displays several standard options for dividing text into columns. You can choose one, two, or three columns of equal width or two columns of unequal width.

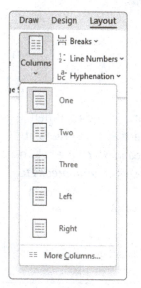

The Columns gallery displays the predefined column options

If the standard options don't suit your needs, choose More Columns. This opens the Columns dialog, where you can specify the number and width of columns. The number of columns is limited by the width and margins of the page. Each column must be at least a half inch (or 0.27 centimeter) wide.

For more options, you can open the Columns dialog

You can format an entire document or a section of a document in columns. When you select a section of text and format it in columns, Word inserts *section breaks* at the beginning and end of the selected text to delineate the area in which the columnar formatting is applied. Within the columnar text, you can insert *column breaks* to specify where you want to end one column and start another. Section and column breaks are visible when you display hidden formatting marks in the document.

> **SEE ALSO** For information about formatting marks, see "Display different views of documents" in Chapter 2, "Create and manage documents."

> **TIP** You can format the content within a specific section of a document independently of other sections. For example, you can place a wide table in its own section and change the page orientation of that section to landscape to accommodate the wider table. For more information about sections, see "Control what appears on each page" in Chapter 12, "Finalize and distribute documents."

You apply character and paragraph formatting to columnar text in the same way you do to any other text. Here are some formatting tips for columnar text:

- When presenting text in columns, justify the paragraphs to give the page a clean and organized appearance. When you justify text, Word adjusts the spacing between words to align all the paragraphs in the document with both the left and right margins.

Justify text in columns for a clean look

SEE ALSO For information about justifying paragraphs, see "Apply paragraph formatting" in Chapter 4, "Modify the structure and appearance of text."

- You can reduce the column widths, minimizing the space between columns. That way, you can fit more text on the page. You can choose to change the column widths in the entire section, in the entire document, or from the current cursor location to the end of the document.

> **TIP** Selecting the Line Between checkbox in the Columns dialog inserts a vertical line between columns. This can more clearly denote the separation of the columns, which is especially helpful if you have reduced the space between columns to fit more content on a page.

Look at how your home is decorated and note the things you like and dislike. Pay special attention to the color scheme and to how each room "feels" to you. Is it inviting? Does it feel comfortable? Does it relax you or does it invigorate you?

Focus on the room(s) you would most like to change. Brainstorm all the things you would change in that room if you could. Don't give a thought to any financial considerations; just let your imagination go wild! It might be helpful to write down all the negatives and positives. You don't need to come up with solutions all at once. Just be clear on what you like and what you hate about that room.

to place the windows and doors. Arrange the furniture placeholders to mirror how your room is currently set up. Add the current colors, too.

This is where the fun begins! Start changing things around a bit. Move the furniture, add different colors, and watch the room come together! Here's where you can tell if that rich red rug you saw in the showroom enhances or overwhelms your room. What about that overstuffed chair that caught your eye? Place a furniture or accessory shape, and then color it. Does it look great or is it too jarring? Change the color... does that help? Don't forget about the walls. Try

Come back to the store. Look again at the pieces you liked during your last visit and see if you still love them. If you're not quite sure, go back to your planner for a little more tweaking. If you are sure, look around the store one more time to see if anything else catches your eye. Then make your purchases. You're almost there!

NOTE: If you decided to paint your room, do that before your new pieces are delivered. You'll want to start enjoying your new room as soon as your purchases arrive.

After a few weeks, ask yourself whether the room is as great as you thought it would be. Does it achieve the look and feel you

Wider columns display more content and generally look neater on the page

- To reduce the amount of white space within a line, you can set up Word to hyphenate the text and break longer words into syllables.

When hyphenating a document, you can specify whether you want to allow stacked hyphens at the ends of consecutive lines of a paragraph

- To emphasize a certain portion of the text, you can indent it in the column.

> tweaking. If you are sure, look around the store one more time to see if anything else catches your eye. Then make your purchases. You're almost there!
>
> NOTE: If you decided to paint your room, do that before your new pieces are delivered. You'll want to start enjoying your new room as soon as your purchases arrive.
>
> After a few weeks, ask yourself whether the room is as great as you thought it would be. Does it achieve the look and feel you were after? You have 30 days to

You can change the indentation of individual paragraphs within a column

- You can manually break columns. When you break a column, the text after the break moves to the top of the next column. You might manually break a column to even out the text along the bottom of the page or if you just want certain text to appear at the top of the next column.

> Visit· our· showroom· and· purchase· a· Room· Planner.· While· you're· there,· look· around· and· see· what· really· appeals· to· you.· Sometimes· entire· rooms· are· designed· around·just·one·or·two·special· pieces,·so·don't·be·afraid·to·fall· in· love· with· something· that· doesn't· seem· to· fit· into· your· overall· scheme.· Go· with· what· you·love,·and·the·rest·will·fall· into·place.¶
>
> ·············· Column Break···············
>
> and· then· color· it.· Does· it· look· great· or· is· it· too· jarring?· Change· the· color…· does· that· help?· Don't· forget· about· the· walls.· Try· different· colors· to· see· the· effect· on· the· room· overall.¶
>
> When·you're·sure·you·have·the· right· look· and· feel,· take· a· break.· Put· the· planner· away· and·sleep·on·your·design·for·a· day· or· two.· Then· review· it· again.·Does·it·still·look·perfect,· or·is·something·not·quite·right?· You· might· need· to· "live"· with·
>
> purchases·arrive.¶
>
> After·a·few·weeks,·ask·yourself· whether·the·room·is·as·great·as· you·thought·it·would·be.·Does· it·achieve·the·look·and·feel·you· were· after?· You· have· 30· days· to·fall·in·love·with·our·furniture· and· accessories,· so· if· you· are· disappointed· in· any· way,· you· can· return· undamaged· pieces· for· just· a· nominal· restocking· charge.¶
>
> If·you're·not·sure·you·made·the· right· choices· and· don't· know· which· way· to· turn,· arrange· to·

Manually break columns to even out the text at the end of a page

To lay out text in columns

> ✓ **TIP** To make columns easier to work with, display formatting marks and the ruler before you begin.

1. Do either of the following:

   - To format only a section of the document, select the paragraphs that you want to display in columns.

   - To format the entire document with the same number of columns, position the cursor anywhere in the document—you don't have to select the text.

2. On the **Layout** tab, in the **Page Setup** group, select **Columns**.

3. In the **Columns** gallery, do either of the following:

   - Select one of the thumbnails to flow the selected text into that column configuration.

   - At the bottom of the gallery, select **More Columns** to display the **Columns** dialog. Make the adjustments you want, and then select **OK**.

To justify column text

- Select the columns you want to align. Then do either of the following:

  - On the **Home** tab, in the **Paragraph** group, select the **Justify** button.

  - Press **Ctrl+J**.

> 🔍 **SEE ALSO** For more information about keyboard shortcuts, see the appendix, "Keyboard shortcuts," at the end of this book.

To resize columns

1. Position the cursor anywhere in the columnar text.

2. On the **Layout** tab, at the bottom of the **Columns** gallery, select **More Columns** to open the Columns dialog.

3. In the **Width** box for any of the columns, enter or select a new width. The Width measurements for the other columns change to match, and the width of all the columns changes. The columns in the Preview thumbnail reflect the new settings.

4. When the column width is changed to your satisfaction, select **OK**.

Or

1. Position the cursor anywhere in the columnar text.

2. On the horizontal ruler, drag the margins to expand or contract the columns to the width you want.

> **TIP** To display the rulers, select the Ruler checkbox in the Show group on the View tab.

To hyphenate document content

- On the **Layout** tab, in the **Page Setup** group, select the **Hyphenation** button, and then select **Automatic** to hyphenate the text of the document.

To change the indentation of a paragraph in a column

1. Position the cursor anywhere in the paragraph you want to indent.

2. To change the left indentation, do any of the following on the horizontal ruler:

   - Drag the column's **First Line Indent** marker to the right to indent only the first line of the paragraph.

   - Drag the column's **Hanging Indent** marker to the right to indent all but the first line of the paragraph.

   - Drag the column's **Left Indent** marker to the right to indent all lines of the paragraph.

3. To change the right indentation of all lines of a paragraph, drag the column's **Right Indent** marker to the left.

To insert a column break

1. Position the cursor at the beginning of the line you want to flow to the next column.

2. In the **Page Setup** group of the **Layout** tab, select **Breaks**, and then select **Column** to insert a column break. The text that follows the column break moves to the top of the next column.

5

Create tabbed lists

If you have a relatively small amount of data to present, you might choose to display it in a tabbed list. A tabbed list arranges text in simple columns separated by tabs.

If some text items in the list are longer than others, the columns might not line up at first. You can align the text within the columns by using left, right, centered, or decimal tab stops.

Consultation·Fee·Schedule¶		
Location →	**Discount·Applies** →	**Hourly·Rate¶**
In·home →	No →	$50.00¶
Phone →	Yes →	$35.00¶
In·store →	Yes →	$40.00¶

One way to present a small amount of data is to convert the data to a tabbed list

> **SEE ALSO** For more information about setting tab stops, see "Structure content manually" in Chapter 4.

When entering text in a tabbed list, many inexperienced Word users simply press the Tab key multiple times to align the columns of the list with the default tab stops. This approach offers no control over the column widths, however. In addition, if you change the text between two tabs, you might inadvertently misalign the next section of text. To be able to fine-tune the columns, you must set custom tab stops rather than relying on the default ones.

When setting up a tabbed list, you first enter the text, pressing Tab only once between the items that you want to appear in separate columns. Then you apply any necessary formatting, such as bold formatting, so you can accurately set the column width. You can also adjust the spacing of the list—for example, to make it single-spaced. To set the list apart from the rest of the document, you can indent it. Finally, you can set custom tab stops—left (the default), right, centered, or decimal—to align the text in each column. By setting the tabs in order from left to right, you can check the alignment of the text within each column as you go.

> ✓ **TIP** It's more efficient to make all character and paragraph formatting changes to the text before setting tab stops. Otherwise, you might have to adjust the tab stops after applying the formatting.

To create a tabbed list

1. Open a document to which you want to add a tabbed list, and display formatting marks and the rulers.

2. Position the cursor in the document where you want to create the tabbed list, enter the text that you want to appear in the top line of the left column, and press **Tab**.

3. Enter the text you want to appear in the top line of the second column, and press **Tab**.

4. Repeat this action for each additional column you want to create. After you enter the text for the top line in the final column, press **Enter**.

5. Add more lines to the list by entering your content and pressing the **Tab** key to move to the next column or the **Enter** key to move to the next row.

6. When you've finished creating the list, select the entire list.

7. Set the custom tab stops you want for the list.

To format column headings for a tabbed list

1. Select the first line of the tabbed list.

2. Do either of the following:

   - On the **Mini Toolbar** that appears, or in the **Font** group on the **Home** tab, select the **Bold**, **Italic**, or **Underline** button, or select the **Font Color** arrow and then the color you want to apply.

   - Press **Ctrl+B** to apply bold, **Ctrl+I** to apply italic, or **Ctrl+U** to apply underlining.

To indent a tabbed list

1. Select all the lines of the tabbed list, including the headings.

2. On the **Layout** tab, in the **Paragraph** group, in the **Indent** area, enter or select a value in the **Left** box.

5

To change the alignment of a column

1. Select all the lines of the tabbed list.

2. On the horizontal ruler, double-click any tab marker to open the **Tabs** dialog.

3. In the **Tab stop position** box, select the tab stop you want to change and then, in the **Alignment** area, select the alignment you want.

4. In the **Tabs** dialog, select **OK**.

Present information in tables

A *table* is a structure of vertical columns and horizontal rows. Each column and each row can be identified by a heading, although some tables have only column headings or only row headings. The box at the junction of each column and row is a *cell* in which you can store data (text or numeric information). A table is an excellent way to present structured information; it makes it easy to compare information in various categories.

You can create tables in a Word document in the following ways:

- To create a blank table of up to 10 columns and eight rows, you can display the Insert Table gallery and menu. The gallery is a grid that represents columns and rows of cells. When you point to a cell in the grid, Word outlines the cells that would be included in a table created by selecting that cell and displays a live preview of the prospective table. Selecting a cell in the grid inserts an empty table the width of the text column. The table has the number of rows and columns you indicated in the grid, with each row one line high and all the columns of an equal width.

- To create a more customized empty table, use the Insert Table dialog. Here, you can specify the number of columns and rows and the width of the table and its columns.

- To manually create an empty table, use the Draw Table feature, available from the Insert Table menu. When you select this option, the cursor shape changes to a pencil, which you use to draw cells directly in the Word document to create a table. Word snaps the drawn cells to a grid for uniform sizing and spacing of the rows and columns. You can adjust these manually.

> **TIP** When drawing a table, you can display the rulers or gridlines to help guide you in placing the lines. For more information about rulers, see "Display different views of documents" in Chapter 2. For information about controlling document gridlines, see "Arrange objects on a page" in Chapter 10, "Organize and arrange content."

> **IMPORTANT** Assistive devices such as screen readers can usually access content in tables that are created by using the Insert Table command but not in manually drawn tables. Consider the limitations of these devices if you want your document to meet accessibility requirements.

5

- To present data that already exists in the document (either as regular text or as a tabbed list) as a table, you can use the Convert Text To Table feature. When you do, Word prompts you to specify the number of columns; whether the column width should be fixed or if AutoFit settings should apply; and whether columns should correlate to paragraph marks, commas, tabs, or some other character.

- You can insert an existing table from a recently edited document by selecting the table in the From File area at the bottom of the Insert Table menu.

A table appears in a document as a set of cells, usually delineated by borders or gridlines. Each cell contains an end-of-cell marker, and each row ends with an end-of-row marker. You can move and position the cursor in the table by pressing the Tab key or the arrow keys or by clicking or tapping in a table cell.

> **TIP** In some Quick Tables, borders and gridlines are turned off. For more information about Quick Tables, see the sidebar "Quick Tables" in the next topic.

> **TIP** There are two separate Word elements named *gridlines*: *document gridlines* and *table gridlines*. Both can be used in association with tables. From the Show group on the View tab, you can display the *document gridlines*, which you can use to position content on the page. From the Table group on the Layout tab, you can display the *table gridlines*, which define the cells of a table.

Insert spreadsheet content into a document

In addition to inserting a table, you can insert a Microsoft Excel spreadsheet in your Word document. To do so, select Excel Spreadsheet on the Insert Table menu. Then enter the data you want in the spreadsheet window that appears in the document. You can use Excel features such as formulas to create or manipulate the data, and the results will appear in your Word document.

When you insert an Excel spreadsheet into your document and activate it, the Excel ribbon temporarily replaces the Word ribbon

Inserting Excel spreadsheet content into your document doesn't create a Word table. Rather, it creates a snapshot of the Excel content. You cannot work with the content in Word or use any of the table tools discussed in this chapter. You can, however, format the data in the spreadsheet window by using various Excel tools and features. To access the spreadsheet for editing, double-click it.

When you point to a table, a move handle appears in its upper-left corner and a size handle in its lower-right corner. When the cursor is in a table, two Table Tools tabs—Table Design and Layout—appear on the ribbon.

A table has its own controls and tool tabs

> **TIP** The end-of-cell markers and end-of-row markers are identical in appearance and are visible only when you display formatting marks in the document. The move handle and size handle appear only in Print Layout view and Web Layout view.

After you create a table in Word, you can enter data (such as text, numbers, or graphics) into the table cells. You can format the data in a table as you would any other text in Word, changing the font, aligning the text, and so on. You can also sort data in a table. For example, in a table that has the column headings *Name, Address, Postal Code,* and *Phone Number,* you can sort on any one of those columns to arrange the information in alphabetical or numerical order.

When you want to perform calculations on numbers in a Word table, you can create a formula by using the tools in the Formula dialog.

To use a function other than SUM in the Formula dialog, you select the function you want in the Paste Function list. You can use built-in functions to perform several calculations, including averaging (AVERAGE) a set of values, counting (COUNT) the number of values in a column or row, or finding the maximum (MAX) or minimum (MIN) value in a series of cells.

You can create a formula to calculate a value in a table

Although formulas commonly refer to the cells above or to the left of the active cell, you can also use the contents of specified cells in formulas by entering the cell address in the parentheses following the function name. The *cell address* is a combination of the column letter and the row number. For example, A1 is the cell at the intersection of the first column and the first row.

A series of cells in a row can be addressed as a range consisting of the first cell and the last cell separated by a colon, such as A1:D1. For example, the formula *=SUM(A1:D1)* totals the values in row 1 of columns A through D. A series of cells in a column can be addressed in the same way. For example, the formula *=SUM(A1:A4)* totals the values in column A of rows 1 through 4. You can also use constants in formulas.

You can modify a table's structure in many ways, including the following:

- **Insert rows or columns**   You can insert a row or column with just one step. Adding multiple rows and columns is also very easy.

- **Insert cells**   You can insert cells in a Word table. When you do, you must specify the direction in which adjacent cells should move to accommodate the new cells.

- **Resize an entire table**   You can easily make a table larger or smaller, maintaining its original aspect ratio if you want.

- **Resize a single column or row**   You can drag to resize a single column or row. For finer control, you can use the commands in the Cell Size group on the Layout tab.

- **Merge and split cells**   You can merge cells so they span multiple columns or rows. For example, to enter a title for a table in the table's first row, you could merge the cells in that row to create one merged cell that spans the table's width. You could then enter the title in the merged cell. For added flair, you could even center the title. In addition to merging multiple cells to create a single cell, you can split a single cell to create multiple cells. When you do, you must specify the number of columns and rows into which you want to split the cell.

- **Delete table elements** You can delete table elements, including cells, columns, rows, and the entire table, from the Mini Toolbar or the Layout tab.

To quickly create a table of up to 10 columns and 10 rows

1. Position the cursor where you want to insert the table.

2. On the **Insert** tab, in the **Tables** group, select **Table**.

3. In the **Insert Table** gallery, point to (don't select) a cell in the gallery to preview the effect of creating the table in the document.

The intended table dimensions (expressed as columns x rows) are shown in the gallery header

4. Select a cell to create a blank table consisting of the selected number of columns and rows.

> **TIP** Move a table by using the same techniques you would use to move text or pictures in Word. For more information, see "Move, copy, and delete text" in Chapter 3, "Enter and edit text."

To create a custom table

1. Position the cursor where you want to insert the table.

2. On the **Insert Table** menu, select **Insert Table** to open the Insert Table dialog.

Create a custom table from the
Insert Table dialog

3. In the **Table size** area, enter or select the number of columns and the number of rows you want the table to have.

4. In the **AutoFit behavior** area, do any of the following, and then select **OK**:

    - Select **Fixed column width**, and then specify a standard width for the table columns.

    - Select **AutoFit to contents** to size the table columns to fit their contents. The width of the resulting table can be less than the width of the page.

    - Select **AutoFit to window** to create a table that fits within the page margins and is divided into columns of equal size.

To draw a table

1. On the **Insert Table** menu, select **Draw Table**. The cursor changes to a pencil.

2. In the document, point to the location where you want the upper-left corner of the table to be, and then click or tap to start the table.

3. Move the cursor to the location where you want the lower-right corner of the table to be, and then click or tap to complete the table footprint. If there is text within the footprint of the table, it moves to accommodate the table.

4. Point to the table borders and then select + to create columns and rows.

5. When you finish adding columns and rows, press the **Esc** key to turn off the table-drawing function.

To enter data in a table

1. Position the cursor in the cell in which you want to enter data.

2. Enter the data.

3. Continue entering data in cells, pressing the **Tab** key or the arrow keys to move from cell to cell.

To navigate within a table

- With the cursor in a table cell, do either of the following:

  - Press the **Tab** key or the arrow keys to move the cursor to the next cell in the row, or from the last cell of a row to the first cell of the next row.

  - Press **Shift+Tab** to move the cursor to the previous cell.

To convert a tabbed list to a table

1. Select the tabbed list.

2. On the **Insert** tab, in the **Tables** group, select **Table**, and then select **Convert Text to Table**.

Convert Text to Table	?	×
Table size		
Number of columns:	3	
Number of rows:	4	
AutoFit behavior		
● Fixed column width:	Auto	
○ AutoFit to contents		
○ AutoFit to window		
Separate text at		
○ Paragraphs	○ Commas	
● Tabs	○ Other:	-
	OK	Cancel

Cleanly convert content separated by any single character to a table

3. In the **Convert Text to Table** dialog, verify that the **Number of columns** box displays the number of columns you want, and then select **OK**.

> ✓ **TIP** Conversely, you can convert a table to regular text by selecting the table and selecting Convert To Text in the Data group on the Layout tab.

Other table layout options

You can control many aspects of a table in the Table Properties dialog, which you display by selecting the Properties button in the Table group on the Layout tab.

You can control many aspects of a table

The Table Properties dialog contains the following tabs:

- **Table** On the Table tab, you can specify the width of the table and the way it interacts with the surrounding text. You can also access border and shading options, including those for the internal margins of table cells.

- **Row** On the Row tab, you can specify the height of the selected rows, whether rows can break across pages (when the table is wider than the page), and whether the header row is repeated at the top of each page when a table spans more than one page. Note that the Repeat As Header Row option applies to the entire table rather than the selected row. This option is available only when the cursor is in the top row of the table. Selecting this option helps readers of a document more easily interpret data in multi-page tables. It also allows assistive devices such as screen readers to correctly interpret the table contents.

- **Column** On the Column tab, you can set the width of each column.

- **Cell** On the Cell tab, you can set the width of selected cells and the vertical alignment of text within them. Select the Options button on this tab to set the internal margins and text wrapping of individual cells.

- **Alt Text** On the Alt Text tab, you can enter text that describes the table. Alt text might appear when a table can't be displayed on the page or when the document is read aloud by an assistive device. Including alt text or a table caption improves the accessibility of the table.

You can also control cell width, alignment, and margins by using the settings in the Cell Size and Alignment groups on the Layout tab.

5

To add calculations to a table cell

1. Position the cursor in the cell to which you want to add a calculation.

2. On the **Layout** tab, in the **Data** group, select **Formula** to open the Formula dialog.

3. If the rows above the selected cell contain numeric data, the **Formula** box contains a simple formula for adding the numbers in the rows above the cell. To apply a different formula, delete the existing formula and choose a different formula from the **Paste function** list.

4. Verify that the parentheses following the function name include the correct cells, and then select **OK**.

To update a calculation in a table

- In the cell that contains a calculation you want to update, right-click or long-press (tap and hold) the formula results and select **Update Field**.

To align text in a table cell

1. Select the cell or cells that you want to align.

2. On the **Layout** tab, in the **Alignment** group, select an alignment button to align the text in the cell.

To sort data in a table

1. Position the cursor anywhere in the table.

2. On the **Layout** tab, in the **Data** group, select **Sort**.

3. In the **Sort** dialog, do the following, and then select **OK**:

   a. In the **Sort by** area, select the primary column by which you want to sort the content, the content type (**Text**, **Number**, or **Date**) if necessary to set the correct numeric sorting order, and **Ascending** or **Descending**.

   b. In the **Then by** area, select and configure up to two additional nested sorting criteria.

To select table cells

- To select a single cell, double-click in the cell.

- To select multiple cells, select the first cell you want to select, and then do either of the following:

  - To select adjacent cells, hold down the **Shift** key, and select the last cell you want to select. The first cell, the last cell, and all the cells in between will be selected.

  - To select non-adjacent cells, hold down the **Ctrl** key, and select each additional cell you want to select. All these cells will be selected.

To select table columns

- To select a single column, point to the top of the column. When the cursor changes to a downward-pointing arrow, click or tap to select the column.

- To select multiple columns, when the cursor changes to a downward-pointing arrow, click or tap to select the first column. Then do either of the following:

  - To select adjacent columns, hold down the **Shift** key, and then click or tap to select the last column.

  - To select non-adjacent columns, hold down the **Ctrl** key, and then click tap to select each additional column.

To select table rows

- To select a single row, point to the left edge of the row. When the cursor changes to an upward-pointing arrow, click or tap to select the row.

- To select multiple rows, when the cursor changes to an upward-pointing arrow, click or tap to select the first row. Then do either of the following:

  - To select adjacent rows, hold down the **Shift** key, and then click or tap to select the last row.

  - To select non-adjacent rows, hold down the **Ctrl** key, and then click or tap to select each additional row.

5

To select a table

- Point to the table to display the move handle in the upper-left corner, and then select the move handle.

To resize a table column

- Point to the right border of the column you want to resize. When the cursor changes to a vertical line with arrows on each side, select and drag the border to the left or right to make the column narrower or wider.

- Double-click the right border of a column to adjust the width so that it is as narrow as possible while accommodating the contents of the column.

- Position the cursor in the column you want to resize. Then, on the **Layout** tab, in the **Cell Size** group, change the **Width** setting.

To resize a table row

- Point to the bottom border of the row you want to resize. When the cursor changes to a horizontal line with arrows on each side, drag the border up or down to make the row shorter or taller.

- Position the cursor in the row you want to resize. Then, on the **Layout** tab, in the **Cell Size** group, change the **Height** setting.

To resize a table

1. Point to the table.

2. Select the size handle that appears in the lower-right corner of the table and drag it inward to make the table smaller or outward to make it larger.

 TIP To maintain the table's original aspect ratio, hold down the Shift key as you drag.

To insert a table column

1. Point to the top of the table where you want to insert a column. A gray insertion indicator with a plus sign appears.

2. Point to the plus sign. Then, when it turns blue, select it to insert a column where indicated.

To insert multiple table columns

■ Adjacent to the location where you want to insert the new columns, select one existing column for each of the number of columns you want to insert in the table. For example, to insert two columns, select two existing columns. Then do either of the following:

- On the **Mini Toolbar** that appears, select **Insert**, and then select **Insert Left** or **Insert Right**.

- On the **Layout** tab, in the **Rows & Columns** group, select **Insert Left** or **Insert Right**.

To insert one table row

■ To insert a row at the end of a table, position the cursor in the last cell of the last row, and then press **Tab** to create a new row with the same formatting as the previous row.

Or

1. Point to the left of the table where you want to insert a row. A gray insertion indicator with a plus sign appears.

2. Point to the plus sign. When it turns blue, click or tap it to insert a row where indicated.

To insert multiple table rows

■ Adjacent to the location where you want to insert the new rows, select one existing row for each of the number of rows you want to insert in the table. For example, to insert three rows, select three existing rows. Then do either of the following:

- On the **Mini Toolbar** that appears, select **Insert**, and then select **Insert Above** or **Insert Below**.

- On the **Layout** tab, in the **Rows & Columns** group, select **Insert Above** or **Insert Below**.

To insert table cells

1. Adjacent to the location where you want to insert the new cells, select one existing cell for each of the number of cells you want to insert. For example, to insert four cells, select four existing cells.

2. Select the **Rows & Columns** dialog launcher on the **Layout** tab to open the Insert Cells dialog.

Insert Cells   ?   X

○ Shift cells right
● Shift cells down
○ Insert entire row
○ Insert entire column

OK   Cancel

When inserting less than a full row or column, you must specify the movement of the surrounding cells

3. Specify the direction to move adjacent cells to accommodate the new cells, and then select **OK**.

To merge table cells

1. Select the cells you want to merge.

2. On the **Layout** tab, in the **Merge** group, select **Merge Cells** to combine the selected cells into one cell.

To split table cells

1. Select or place the cursor in the cell or cells you want to split.

2. On the **Layout** tab, in the **Merge** group, select **Split Cells**.

3. In the **Split Cells** dialog, enter or select the number of columns and the number of rows you want to create from the selected cell or cells, and then select **OK**.

Split Cells   ?   X

Number of columns: 2
Number of rows: 1

☑ Merge cells before split

OK   Cancel

Specify the number of columns and rows into which you want to split the selected cell or cells

To delete table elements

- Select one or more cells, columns, or rows that you want to delete. Then do either of the following:

    - On the **Mini Toolbar** that appears, select **Delete**, and then select **Delete Cells**, **Delete Columns**, or **Delete Rows**.

    - On the **Layout** tab, in the **Rows & Columns** group, select **Delete** and choose from the same set of options.

To delete a table

1. Position the cursor anywhere in the table.

2. On the **Mini Toolbar** or on the **Layout** tab, in the **Rows & Columns** group, select **Delete**.

Format tables

Manually formatting a table to best convey its data can be a process of trial and error. With Word, you can quickly get started by applying one of the table styles available in the Table Styles gallery on the Table Design tab. The table styles include a variety of borders, colors, and other attributes that give the table a very professional appearance.

In Word, the Table Styles gallery is divided into sections for plain tables, grid tables, and list tables

The Table Styles gallery includes three categories of styles:

- **Plain Tables**   These have very little formatting.

- **Grid Tables**   These include vertical separators between columns and horizontal separators between rows.

Item	Repair Type	Quantity	Cost in $
Elastomeric Decks	Resurface	400 sq. ft.	1,600
Wood Decks	Replace	1,200 sq. ft.	6,500
Building Exterior	Repaint	9,000 sq. ft.	9,000
Roof	Reseal	5,000 sq. ft.	2,700
Entry Doors	Repaint	4	600
Carpet	Replace	150 sq. yds.	4,500
Intercom	Replace	1	2,500
Garage Door Opener	Replace	1	2,000
Steel Doors	Repaint	10	750
Exterior Trim	Repaint	800 ft.	4,500
Elevator Hydraulics	Replace	1	55,000
Fire Alarm System	Replace	1	3,000
TOTAL			92,650

An example of a simple grid table

- **List Tables**   These do not include vertical column separators.

If you want to control the appearance of a table more precisely, you can use the commands on the Table Design and Layout tabs for tables to format the table elements. For example, you can do the following:

- Apply formatting to emphasize the header row and total row.

Item	Repair Type	Quantity	Cost in $
Elastomeric Decks	Resurface	400 sq. ft.	1,600
Wood Decks	Replace	1,200 sq. ft.	6,500
Building Exterior	Repaint	9,000 sq. ft.	9,000
Roof	Reseal	5,000 sq. ft.	2,700
Entry Doors	Repaint	4	600
Carpet	Replace	150 sq. yds.	4,500
Intercom	Replace	1	2,500
Garage Door Opener	Replace	1	2,000
Steel Doors	Repaint	10	750
Exterior Trim	Repaint	800 ft.	4,500
Elevator Hydraulics	Replace	1	55,000
Fire Alarm System	Replace	1	3,000
TOTAL			**92,650**

Apply special formatting to emphasize the header and total rows

■ Apply formatting to emphasize the first and last columns.

Item	Repair Type	Quantity	Cost in $
Elastomeric Decks	Resurface	400 sq. ft.	1,600
Wood Decks	Replace	1,200 sq. ft.	6,500
Building Exterior	Repaint	9,000 sq. ft.	9,000
Roof	Reseal	5,000 sq. ft.	2,700
Entry Doors	Repaint	4	600
Carpet	Replace	150 sq. yds.	4,500
Intercom	Replace	1	2,500
Garage Door Opener	Replace	1	2,000
Steel Doors	Repaint	10	750
Exterior Trim	Repaint	800 ft.	4,500
Elevator Hydraulics	Replace	1	55,000
Fire Alarm System	Replace	1	3,000
TOTAL			92,650

Apply special formatting to emphasize the first and last columns in the table

■ Apply formatting to the rows or columns so they appear banded.

Item	Repair Type	Quantity	Cost in $
Elastomeric Decks	Resurface	400 sq. ft.	1,600
Wood Decks	Replace	1,200 sq. ft.	6,500
Building Exterior	Repaint	9,000 sq. ft.	9,000
Roof	Reseal	5,000 sq. ft.	2,700
Entry Doors	Repaint	4	600
Carpet	Replace	150 sq. yds.	4,500
Intercom	Replace	1	2,500
Garage Door Opener	Replace	1	2,000
Steel Doors	Repaint	10	750
Exterior Trim	Repaint	800 ft.	4,500
Elevator Hydraulics	Replace	1	55,000
Fire Alarm System	Replace	1	3,000
TOTAL			92,650

Applying banding can help to differentiate the text in each row or column

5

- Apply a border to a cell, row, column, or table.

Item	Repair Type	Quantity	Cost in $
Elastomeric Decks	Resurface	400 sq. ft.	1,600
Wood Decks	Replace	1,200 sq. ft.	6,500
Building Exterior	Repaint	9,000 sq. ft.	9,000
Roof	Reseal	5,000 sq. ft.	2,700
Entry Doors	Repaint	4	600
Carpet	Replace	150 sq. yds.	4,500
Intercom	Replace	1	2,500
Garage Door Opener	Replace	1	2,000
Steel Doors	Repaint	10	750
Exterior Trim	Repaint	800 ft.	4,500
Elevator Hydraulics	Replace	1	55,000
Fire Alarm System	Replace	1	3,000
TOTAL			**92,650**

A heavy border applied to a row

- Change the shading of a cell, row, or column.

Item	Repair Type	Quantity	Cost in $
Elastomeric Decks	Resurface	400 sq. ft.	1,600
Wood Decks	Replace	1,200 sq. ft.	6,500
Building Exterior	Repaint	9,000 sq. ft.	9,000
Roof	Reseal	5,000 sq. ft.	2,700
Entry Doors	Repaint	4	600
Carpet	Replace	150 sq. yds.	4,500
Intercom	Replace	1	2,500
Garage Door Opener	Replace	1	2,000
Steel Doors	Repaint	10	750
Exterior Trim	Repaint	800 ft.	4,500
Elevator Hydraulics	Replace	1	55,000
Fire Alarm System	Replace	1	3,000
TOTAL			**92,650**

Set off specific content by using unique shading

You can apply character formatting—for example, making text bold or changing the font color—to the text in tables just as you would to regular text: by selecting buttons on the Mini Toolbar and in the Font, Paragraph, and Styles groups on the Home tab.

> **TIP** If the first row of your table has several long headings that make it difficult to fit the table on one page, you can turn the headings sideways. Select the heading row and select the Text Direction button in the Alignment group on the Layout tab.

To apply a table style to a table

1. Position the cursor anywhere in the table.

2. On the **Design** tab, in the **Table Styles** group, select the **More** button to expand the gallery of available table styles.

3. Scroll through the gallery and preview styles that you like.

4. Select a thumbnail to format the table to match the thumbnail. The selected thumbnail moves to the visible row of the Table Style gallery on the ribbon.

To apply special formatting to the header or total row

1. Position the cursor anywhere in the table.

2. In the **Table Style Options** group, select the **Header Row** or **Total Row** checkbox.

> **TIP** When you choose options in the Table Style Options group, the thumbnails in the Table Styles gallery are updated to reflect your selections.

To apply special formatting to the first or last column

1. Position the cursor anywhere in the table.

2. In the **Table Style Options** group, select the **First Column** or **Last Column** checkbox.

To apply banding to table rows or columns

1. Position the cursor anywhere in the table.

2. In the **Table Style Options** group, select the **Banded Rows** or **Banded Columns** checkbox.

To add a border to a table element

1. Select the cell, row, or column to which you want to add a border, or select the whole table.

2. On the **Design** tab, in the **Borders** group, in the **Line Weight** list, select a border thickness.

3. In the **Borders** group, in the **Borders** list, select the border option you want.

To change the background color of a table element

1. In the table, select the cell, row, or column to which you want to add a background color.

2. In the **Table Styles** group, in the **Shading** list, select a color swatch.

Quick Tables

In addition to inserting empty tables, you can insert any of the available Quick Tables, which are predefined tables of formatted data that you can replace with your own information. Built-in Quick Tables include a variety of calendars and simple tables.

Double Table

The Greek alphabet

Letter name	Uppercase	Lowercase	Letter name	Uppercase	Lowercase
Alpha	A	α	Nu	N	ν
Beta	B	β	Xi	Ξ	ξ
Gamma	Γ	γ	Omicron	O	o
Delta	Δ	δ	Pi	Π	π
Epsilon	E	ε	Rho	P	ρ
Zeta	Z	ζ	Sigma	Σ	σ
Eta	H	η	Tau	T	τ

Matrix

City or Town	Point A	Point B	Point C	Point D	Point E
Point A	—				
Point B	87	—			
Point C	64	56	—		
Point D	37	32	91	—	
Point E	93	35	54	43	—

Tabular List

ITEM	NEEDED
Books	1
Magazines	3
Notebooks	1
Paper pads	1
Pens	3
Pencils	2
Highlighter	2 colors
Scissors	1 pair

With Subheads 1

Save Selection to Quick Tables Gallery...

The predefined Quick Tables can be a convenient starting point

To insert a Quick Table

1. On the **Insert** tab, in the **Tables** group, select **Table**. Then select **Quick Tables** to expand the Quick Tables gallery.

2. Scroll through the gallery to review the available table types, and then select the one you want.

3. Modify content and apply formatting to tailor the Quick Table to your needs.

You can also save a modified Quick Table, or any customized table, to the Quick Tables gallery. Saving a table saves both the table structure and the table content to the gallery. You can then easily insert an identical table into any document.

To save a table to the Quick Tables gallery

1. Select the table.

2. On the **Insert** tab, in the **Tables** group, select **Table**, select **Quick Tables**, and then select **Save Selection to Quick Tables Gallery**.

3. In the **Create New Building Block** dialog, assign a name to the table, and then select **OK**.

4. When you exit Word, you'll be prompted to save the Building Blocks template. Select the **Save** button to ensure that the table will be available in the Quick Tables gallery for future use.

SEE ALSO For information about building blocks, see "Insert preformatted document parts" in Chapter 9, "Format document elements."

Key points

- To vary the layout of a document, you can divide text into columns. You can control the number of columns, the width of the columns, and the space between the columns.

- To clearly present a simple set of data, you can use tabs to create a tabbed list, with custom tab stops controlling the width and alignment of columns.

- You can create a table from scratch or convert existing text to a table. You can control the size of the table and its individual structural elements.

- By using the built-in table styles, you can quickly apply professional-looking cell and character formatting to a table and its contents.

- You can enhance a table and its contents by applying text attributes, borders, colors, and shading.

Practice tasks

Before you can complete these tasks, you must copy the book's practice files to your computer. The practice files for these tasks are in the **Word365SBS\Ch05** folder. You can save the results of the tasks in the same folder.

The Introduction includes a complete list of practice files and download instructions.

Present information in columns

Open the **AddColumns** document in Print Layout view, display formatting marks and rulers, and then perform the following tasks:

1. Select all the paragraphs except the heading and the first paragraph.

2. Lay out the selected text in three columns. Notice that a section break precedes the columns.

3. Justify all the text in the document except for the title.

4. With the cursor in the first column on the first page, use the commands in the **Columns** dialog to change the spacing to 0.2", applying the change to this section only.

5. Turn on automatic hyphenation for the document.

6. In the third column, change the hanging indent of the *NOTE* paragraph so that the text after the first line indents at the first mark (0.125").

7. At the bottom of page 1, insert a column break at the beginning of the *Take your Room Planner home* paragraph in the first column.

8. At the bottom of the third column on page 1, insert another column break at the beginning of the *If you're not sure* paragraph.

9. Save and close the document.

Create tabbed lists

Open the **CreateTabbedLists** document in Print Layout view, display formatting marks and rulers, and then perform the following tasks:

1. On the blank line at the end of the document, enter Location, press **Tab**, enter Discount Applies, press **Tab**, enter Hourly Rate, and then press **Enter**.

2. Add three more lines to the list by typing the following text, pressing the **Tab** key between each row entry and the **Enter** key at the end of each row.

In home	No	$50.00
Phone	Yes	$35.00
In store	Yes	$40.00

Apply bold formatting to the first line of the tabbed list.

3. Select all four lines of the tabbed list, including the headings.

4. Change the left indent of the list to **0.5"** and the spacing after each line to **0 pt**.

5. With the entire list still selected, set a centered tab at the **2.5**-inch mark and a right tab at the **4.5**-inch mark.

6. Save and close the document.

Present information in tables

Open the **CreateTables** document in Print Layout view, display formatting marks and rulers, and then perform the following tasks:

1. On the second blank line below *Please complete this form*, insert a table that contains five rows and five columns.

2. Merge the five cells in the first row into a single cell and center-align the cell content. Then enter Consultation Estimate in the cell as a table title.

3. Insert the following text in the cells of the second row, and then format the text as bold:

Type	Location	Consultant	Hourly Rate	Total

4. Insert the following text in the cells of the third row:

Window treatments	In home	Joan Lambert	$50.00	$50.00

5. Add two rows to the end of the table.

6. Merge the first four cells of the last row of the table into a single cell. Enter Subtotal in the cell, and then align the word with the center-right edge of the cell.

7. Create two new rows with the same formatting as the **Subtotal** row. Enter Add trip charge in the first cell of the first new row, and Total in the first cell of the second new row.

8. In each cell to the right of *Subtotal* and *Total*, enter the SUM formula and display the formula results.

9. In the cell to the right of *Add trip charge*, enter $10.00. Then update the results in the *Total* cell.

10. At the end of the document, under the *In-Home Trip Charge* heading, convert the tabbed list to a table.

11. Resize the columns to fit their longest entries.

12. In the last row of the table, replace the existing text in the first cell with 50+ miles, and replace the existing text in the second cell with Email for an estimate.

13. Add a third cell to the last row, and enter info@wideworldimporters.com in that cell.

14. Save and close the document.

Format tables

Open the **FormatTables** document in Print Layout view, and then perform the following tasks:

1. Select the table, and then display the **Table Styles** gallery.

2. Apply the **Grid Table 4 – Accent 1** table style to the table.

3. Select the table style checkboxes for the header row, total row, first column, and last column.

4. Apply banded formatting to the table rows.

5. Add an outside border to the last row in the table. The border should have the line style that features a thick line on top and a thin line below it, with a line weight of 3 points.

6. Apply orange shading to the last row of the table.

7. Save and close the document.

Add simple graphic elements

Many documents that you create in Word contain only text. Others might benefit from the addition of graphic elements to reinforce their concepts, to grab the reader's attention, or to make them more visually appealing.

The term *graphics* generally refers to several kinds of visual objects, including photos, clip-art images, diagrams, charts, and shapes. You can insert all these types of graphics as objects in a document and then size, move, and copy them.

This chapter guides you through procedures related to inserting, moving, and resizing pictures; editing and formatting pictures; attributing pictures and providing text alternatives; inserting screen clippings and icons; drawing and modifying shapes; adding WordArt text; and building equations in documents.

> 🔍 **SEE ALSO** For information about diagrams, see Chapter 7, "Insert and modify diagrams and 3D models." For information about charts, see Chapter 8, "Insert and modify charts."

In this chapter

- Insert, move, and resize pictures
- Edit and format pictures
- Provide additional information about pictures
- Insert screen clippings
- Insert and format icons
- Draw and modify shapes
- Build equations

Insert, move, and resize pictures

You can insert digital photographs and images created and saved in other programs into Word documents. Collectively, these types of images are referred to as *pictures*. You can use pictures to make documents more visually interesting or to convey information in a way that words cannot.

You can insert a picture into a document either from your computer or from an online source, such as the internet or your cloud storage drive.

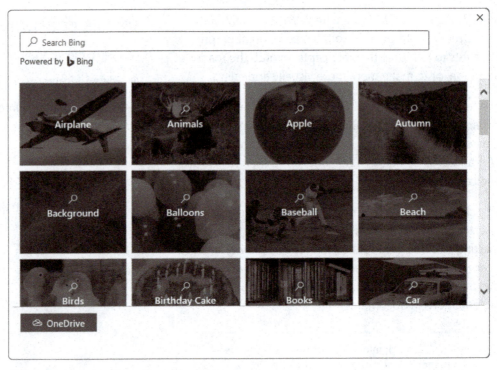

Choose an online storage location or search for an image

After you insert a picture, you can make it larger or smaller and position it anywhere you want on the page. A series of handles around a picture indicates that it's selected and can be moved or edited. A size handle appears at each corner and at the midpoint of each side. A rotate handle appears above the top midpoint of the picture. The Layout Options menu contains commands for formatting the appearance of a picture and controlling its position relative to text, images, and other page elements.

Rotate handle

Size handles

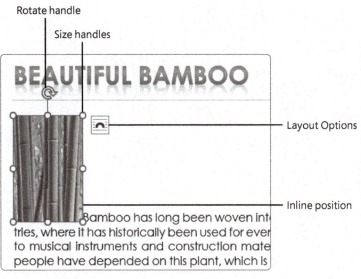

Layout Options

Inline position

An inline image at the beginning of a paragraph

By default, Word inserts pictures in line with the text, which means that it increases the line spacing to accommodate the picture. If you enter text adjacent to the picture, the bottom of the picture will align with the bottom of the text on the same line.

> **TIP** You can move or copy a picture just as you would anything else in Word: by selecting it and then either dragging it where you want it to go (to move it) or holding down the Ctrl key as you drag (to copy it).

To insert a picture from your computer

1. On the **Insert** tab, in the **Illustrations** group, select **Pictures**, and then select **This Device** to open the Insert Picture dialog.

2. In the **Insert Picture** dialog, browse to and select the picture (or pictures) you want to insert. Then select **Insert**.

> **TIP** If a picture might change, you can ensure that the document is always up to date by selecting the Insert arrow and then selecting Link To File to insert a link to the picture, or by selecting Insert and Link to both insert the picture and link it to its graphic file.

6

Graphic formats

Many common graphic formats store graphics as a series of dots, or *pixels*. Each pixel is made up of bits. The number of bits per pixel (bpp) determines the number of distinct colors that can be represented by a pixel.

The mapping of bits to colors isn't 1:1; it's 2^{bpp} In other words:

- 1 bpp = 2 colors

- 2 bpp = 4 colors

- 4 bpp = 16 colors

- 8 bpp = 256 colors

- 16 bpp = 65,536 colors

- 32 bpp = 4,294,967,296 colors

- 64 bpp = 18,446,744,073,709,551,616 colors

Image files that you'll use in a Word document are usually in one of the following file formats:

- **BMP (bitmap)** There are different qualities of BMPs.

- **GIF (Graphics Interchange Format)** This format is common for images that appear on webpages because the images can be compressed with no loss of information, and groups of them can be animated. GIFs store up to 8 bits per pixel, so they are limited to 256 colors.

To insert a picture from an online source

1. On the **Insert** tab, in the **Illustrations** group, select **Pictures**, and then select **Online Pictures**.

2. In the **Online Pictures** window, select an image category or enter a search term in the search box.

3. Browse to and select the picture you want to insert. Then select **Insert**.

- **JPEG (Joint Photographic Experts Group)** This compressed format works well for complex graphics such as scanned photographs. Some information is lost in the compression process, but often the loss is imperceptible to the human eye. Color JPEGs store 24 bits per pixel. Grayscale JPEGs store 8 bits per pixel.

- **PNG (Portable Network Graphic)** This format has the advantages of the GIF format but can store colors with 24, 32, 48, or 64 bits per pixel and grayscales with 1, 2, 4, 8, or 16 bits per pixel. A PNG file can also specify whether each pixel blends with its background color and can contain color correction information so that images look accurate on a broad range of display devices.

- **SVG (scalable vector graphics)** This format, a recent addition to those supported by Word, stores image data in XML format rather than in pixels. For more information about SVG images, see "Insert and format icons" later in this chapter.

Of the commonly available file formats, PNG is often the best choice for images other than photographs, because it allows for high-quality images with a small file size and supports transparency.

6

To move a picture

- Point to the image. When the cursor changes to a four-headed arrow, drag the picture to its new location.

To resize a picture

- Select the picture, and then do any of the following:

  - To change only the width of the picture, drag the left or right size handle.

  - To change only the height of the picture, drag the top or bottom size handle.

- To change both the height and the width of the picture without changing its aspect ratio, drag a corner size handle or set the **Height** or **Width** measurement in the **Size** group on the **Picture Format** tab. (Depending on the technique you use to set the measurements, the dimensions might not change until you press Enter or Tab or click or tap away from the measurement entry box.)

To position a picture on the page

1. Select the picture. Then, on the **Picture Format** tab, in the **Arrange** group, select the **Position** button to display the available text-wrapping options.

2. Point to a thumbnail to preview where that option will place the picture.

3. Select a thumbnail to move the picture to that location on the page.

To change how text wraps around a picture

1. Select the picture. Then, on the **Picture Format** tab, in the **Arrange** group, select the **Wrap Text** button to display the **Wrap Text** menu.

2. Do either of the following:

   - Point to an option to preview its effects, and then select an option.

   - Select **More Layout Options** to display the **Text Wrapping** page of the **Layout** dialog, select the option you want, and then select **OK**.

Edit and format pictures

After you insert any picture into a document, you can modify it by using the commands on the Picture Format tab. For example, you can do the following:

- Remove the background by designating the areas you want to keep or remove.

- Sharpen or soften the picture or change its brightness or contrast.

- Enhance the picture's color.

- Make one of the picture's colors transparent.

- Choose an effect, such as Pencil Sketch or Paint Strokes.

- Apply effects such as shadows, reflections, and borders; or apply combinations of these effects.

- Add a border consisting of one or more solid or dashed lines of whatever width and color you choose.

- Rotate the picture to any angle, either by dragging the rotating handle or by choosing a rotating or flipping option.

- Crop away the parts of the picture that you don't want to show on the page. (The picture itself is not altered—parts of it are simply covered up.)

All these changes are made to the representation of the picture on the page and do not affect the original picture.

The Picture Format tab contains the following groups:

- **Adjust**   This group contains commands that you can use to remove the picture's background, change the picture's brightness and contrast, recolor it, apply artistic effects to it, and compress it to reduce the size of the document containing it. From this group, you can also change a currently selected picture to a different one.

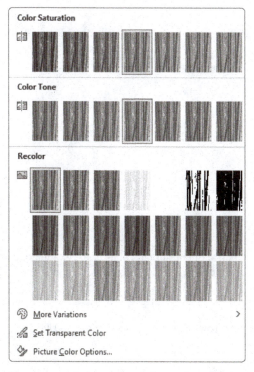

You can recolor pictures to match your document color theme

- **Picture Styles** This group offers a wide range of picture styles that you can apply to a picture to change its shape and orientation and to add borders and picture effects.

- **Accessibility** This group provides tools for adding a description to an image for someone who can't see or can't see well, or as an alternative description if the image content is unavailable or unclear. You can describe the image yourself or have Word generate the description for you. You can also indicate whether the image is unimportant to the content and can be skipped by screen-reading software.

- **Arrange** This group contains commands for specifying the position of the picture on the page with respect to other elements on the page.

You can control the position of the picture in relation to the surrounding text

> **SEE ALSO** For more information about positioning objects and wrapping text around them, see "Arrange objects on a page" in Chapter 10, "Organize and arrange content."

- **Size** You can use the commands in this group to crop and resize pictures.

If you like the changes you've made to a picture, you can copy its formatting and apply it to another picture. If you don't like the changes you've applied to a picture, you can undo them.

To select a picture for editing

- Click or tap the picture once.

To rotate a picture

- Select the picture, and then do any of the following:

  - Drag the circular rotate handle to the right or left.

  - On the **Picture Format** tab, in the **Arrange** group, select **Rotate**, and then select **Rotate Right 90°** or **Rotate Left 90°**.

  - On the **Picture Format** tab, in the **Arrange** group, select **Rotate**, and then select **More Rotation Options**. On the **Size** tab of the **Layout** dialog, in the **Rotate** section, enter or select a specific degree of rotation. Then select **OK**.

- Right-click or long-press (tap and hold) the picture, and then select **Size and Position**. On the **Size** tab of the **Layout** dialog, in the **Rotate** section, enter or select a specific degree of rotation. Then select **OK**.

To flip a picture

- Select the picture. On the **Picture Format** tab, in the **Arrange** group, select **Rotate**, and then select **Flip Vertical** or **Flip Horizontal**.

To crop a picture

1. Select the picture. On the **Picture Format** tab, in the **Size** group, select the **Crop** button (not the arrow) to display thick black handles on the sides and in the corners of the picture.

2. Drag the crop handles to define the area you want to crop to. The areas that will be excluded from the cropped picture are shaded.

6

Cropping a photo

3. When you finish defining the area, click or tap away from the picture, or select the **Crop** button again to apply the crop effect.

> **TIP** When cropping a picture, be careful not to drag a size handle instead of a crop handle; they're very close to each other. To redisplay the uncropped picture at any time, select the picture and then select the Crop button.

Or

- Select the picture. On the **Picture Format** tab, in the **Size** group, select the **Crop** arrow, and then do either of the following:

  - Select **Crop to Shape**, and then select a shape.

  - Select **Aspect Ratio**, and then select an aspect ratio.

You can crop photos to shapes

To frame or style a picture

1. Select the picture. On the **Picture Format** tab, in the **Picture Styles** group, select the **More** button to display the Picture Styles gallery.

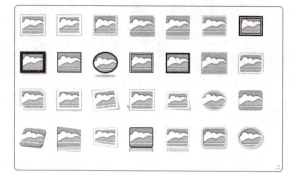

Apply frames, shadows, glows, and three-dimensional effects from the Picture Styles gallery

2. Point to any picture style to display a live preview of the style applied to the picture.

3. Select the picture style you want to apply.

To remove a background from a picture

1. Select the picture. On the **Picture Format** tab, in the **Adjust** group, select **Remove Background**. The Background Removal tool evaluates the picture and applies purple shading to the areas of the picture that it thinks you want to remove.

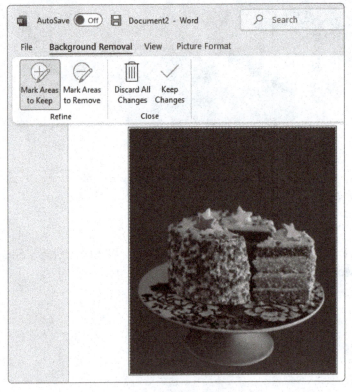

The accuracy of the estimate depends on the intricacy of the background

2. To adjust the area of the image that's marked for removal, do either or both of the following on the **Background Removal** tab:

   - Select **Mark Areas to Keep**, and then select any shaded areas of the photo that you'd like to keep.

   - Select **Mark Areas to Remove**, and then select any unshaded areas of the photo that you'd like to remove.

   Depending on the picture's complexity, you might need to make a lot of adjustments or only a few.

3. When you finish, select **Keep Changes** to display the results. You can return to the Background Removal tab at any time to make adjustments.

The background has been cleanly removed to leave only the cake

4. If you don't like the results and want to restore the background, select **Discard All Changes**.

To adjust the color of a picture

1. Select the picture. On the **Picture Format** tab, in the **Adjust** group, select **Color** to expand the gallery of color choices.

2. In the **Color** gallery, point to a thumbnail to preview its effect on the picture.

3. Select a thumbnail to apply the corresponding picture color to the picture.

6

To apply an artistic effect to a picture

1. Select the picture. On the **Picture Format** tab, in the **Adjust** group, select **Artistic Effects** to display the Artistic Effects gallery.

2. Point to any effect to display a live preview of the effect applied to the picture.

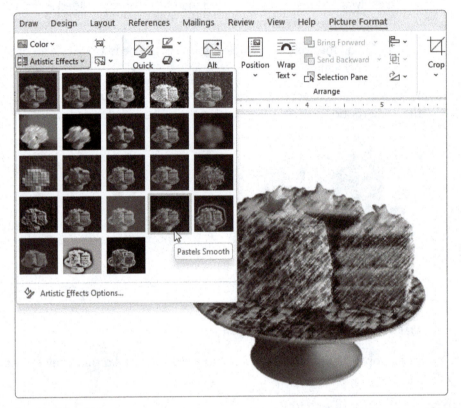

Try out all the effects

3. Select the effect that you want to apply.

To change the brightness, contrast, or sharpness of a picture

1. Select the picture you want to correct. On the **Picture Format** tab, in the **Adjust** group, select **Corrections** to display the picture correction options.

2. In the **Corrections** gallery, point to any thumbnail to display a live preview of its effect on the picture.

3. Select a thumbnail to apply the corresponding correction to the picture.

> **TIP** The following procedures apply to most images and objects, including pictures, shapes, and WordArt objects.

To copy the formatting of one picture to another picture

1. Select a picture that has color adjustments, color corrections, or a picture style applied to it.

2. On the **Home** tab, in the **Clipboard** group, select the **Format Painter** button.

3. Select another picture to apply to it the color adjustments, color corrections, or picture style from the first picture.

To discard changes made to a picture

1. Select the picture.

2. On the **Picture Format** tab, in the **Adjust** group, select the **Reset Picture** arrow, and then do either of the following:

   - Choose **Reset Picture** to discard formatting changes only.

   - Choose **Reset Picture & Size** to discard all formatting and size changes.

To compress a picture

1. Select the picture. On the **Picture Format** tab, in the **Adjust** group, select the **Compress Pictures** button.

2. In the **Compress Pictures** dialog, select the compression and resolution options you want to apply to the picture, and then select **OK**.

Use the compression option suitable for your content delivery format

Add video content to documents

Sometimes the best way to ensure that your audience understands your message is to show a video. Although it would be more common to embed a video in a Microsoft PowerPoint presentation than in a Word document, it's possible to do both. For example, you can embed a video recording directly onto a page, and then play the video when displaying the document electronically.

By using the Online Videos command on the Insert tab, you can insert a video onto a page from YouTube or from a website that provides an *embed code*—basically, an address that you can link to.

TIP If a publicly posted video clip has an embed code available, you can link to the online video rather than embedding it in the document. Word uses the embed code to locate and play the video. While the video remains available in its original location (and you have an active internet connection), you can access and play the video from the document at any time.

After you insert a video, you can format its representation on the page in all the ways that you can with a picture. You can move and resize it, display it in a frame of your choice, and even adjust the brightness or color contrast. The formatting you apply doesn't display when you play the video, however. Instead, the video plays against a gray screen in a frame on top of the Word document in its original format.

TIP You can add alt text for videos in the Alt Text pane. Word will not automatically generate alt text for videos. For more information about alt text, see the next section, "Provide additional information about pictures."

Provide additional information about pictures

Word has two features that make it easy to provide additional information about images that you insert in your documents. You can provide information about the image; the photographer, artist, or copyright holder; and the image licensing in the form of an *attribution*. Word automatically inserts image attributions when you insert an image by using the Online Pictures feature. You can manually insert attributions for pictures that you insert from your computer.

This Photo by Unknown Author is licensed under CC BY-NC-ND

An automatic attribution for an online image with Creative Commons licensing

The attribution provided for online pictures includes two important hyperlinks. The first is to the picture in its online location so that it can be seen in context. The second is to the applicable licensing information.

Attributions are provided as normal text within floating text boxes. You can modify the attribution text and move or rotate the text box. When you do, the attribution remains linked to, and part of, the picture object.

This Photo by Unknown Author is licensed under CC BY-NC-ND

A vertical attribution can save space and be less distracting

⚠️ **IMPORTANT** Pictures you acquire from the web are often copyrighted, meaning that you cannot use them without the permission of the image's owner. Sometimes owners will grant permission if you give them credit. Professional photographers usually charge a fee to use their work. Always assume that pictures are copyrighted unless the source clearly indicates that they are license free.

Alt text is an important accessibility feature that provides an alternative text description for images. This is useful for people who use screen readers, when the content of an image is unclear, or when the image doesn't render properly. Word automatically generates alt text when you insert a picture from your computer or generates it when you request it.

Auto-generated alt text is not always accurate, but it at least provides a starting point

You might use images in your documents that accompany and enhance text but don't provide additional information—for example, a decorative image in the document footer. You can mark these images as decorative to indicate to screen-reading software that it should skip over the image and its alt text.

To select an attribution for editing

- Select the picture. Point to the top of the attribution area (at the bottom of the picture). When the pointer changes to a four-headed arrow, click or tap to select the attribution text box.

To modify the attribution for an online picture

- Select the attribution text box, and then click or tap within the text and edit it.

To move an online picture attribution

- Select the attribution text box, and then drag it to the new location.

To rotate an online picture attribution

1. Select the attribution text box, and then drag the rotation handle.

2. Drag the text box size handle to match the text box width to the side of the picture you're aligning it with.

To add or edit alt text for a picture

1. Do either of the following:

   - Select the picture. On the **Format** tools tab, in the **Accessibility** group, select **Alt Text**.

   - Right-click the picture, and then select **Edit Alt Text**.

2. In the **Alt Text** pane, if Word doesn't generate alt text automatically or accurately, do either of the following:

   - In the text box, enter text that describes the image and gives it context.

   - Select **Generate a description for me**, and then edit the alt text in the text box if you want.

3. If the image is not important in context, select the **Mark as decorative** checkbox.

Insert screen clippings

Many people rely on the web as a source of information. At times, there might be information from the web or another window on your computer that you want to include in a Word document. For example, you might display an image of a page of a client's website in a sales proposal. Word includes a screen clipping tool that you can use to capture an image of anything visible on your computer screen and insert the image, called a *screen clipping* or *screenshot*, into your document. After you insert a screen clipping into your document, you can format it as you would any other picture.

There are two ways to insert content displayed on your computer into a Word document:

- You can insert a screenshot of the content of any open desktop app window.

- You can capture a screen clipping of any content.

To insert an image of an on-screen window

1. Display the window that you want to capture and size it to display its contents as you want to show them.

2. Switch to Word and position the cursor where you want to insert the screen content.

3. On the **Insert** tab, in the **Illustrations** group, select **Screenshot**. The Screenshot menu displays thumbnails of all the windows on your screen that are currently available to insert.

Some open windows aren't available from this menu and must be captured as clippings

4. On the **Screenshot** menu, select the window you want to insert an image of.

5. Resize the inserted image to suit your needs.

To capture a screen clipping from Word

1. Display the content that you want to capture.

2. Switch to Word and position the cursor where you want to insert the screen content.

3. On the **Insert** tab, in the **Illustrations** group, select **Screenshot**.

4. On the **Screenshot** menu, select **Screen Clipping**. The Word menu minimizes to the taskbar and a translucent white layer covers the entire display.

> **TIP** If you change your mind about capturing the screen clipping, press the Esc key to remove the white layer.

5. When the cursor changes to a plus sign, point to the upper-left corner of the area you want to capture, and then drag down and to the right to define the screen clipping borders.

The selected screen clipping area becomes clear

When you release the mouse button, Word captures the clipping, restores the window, and inserts the clipping.

Insert and format icons

A terrifically useful feature introduced in Office 365 (now Microsoft 365), and now available in Word, Excel, PowerPoint, and Outlook, is an extensive icon library, which is part of the Microsoft Stock Images library. At the time of this writing, over 3300 icons are available to insert from the Stock Images library into your Word documents.

Icons available from the Stock Images library

The Stock Images library is stored online. This is good, because Microsoft can easily add new icons to it, but not perfect, because it requires an internet connection to use it.

Provided that you're online, the icon library is easy to open and browse. The library is searchable and is divided into categories that make it a bit easier to find what you're looking for. If you want to enhance your document content with illustrations, it's worth perusing the icon library before looking elsewhere for these reasons:

- There are no rights or permission issues when using icons from the icon library.

- The icons provide clear and consistent representations of the image subjects.

- You can smoothly scale the icons to whatever size you need without worrying about them developing jagged edges.

- You can easily recolor the icons to fit the color scheme of your document.

- You can convert the icons to shapes, which allows you to ungroup the icon elements and recolor or otherwise modify them individually.

Work with scalable vector graphics

Word supports scalable vector graphics (SVG images), which sound fancy (and in fact, are) but can be used quite easily within Word and other Microsoft 365 apps by people who aren't professional graphic artists.

The icons provided with Word and other apps in the Microsoft 365 suite are scalable vector graphics. This file type might not be familiar to Word users (although it will quickly become more commonly known now that Word supports it). *Vector graphics* are composed of shapes, rather than pixels, which means that as you increase or decrease their size (scale them), their edges remain smooth rather than becoming pixelated, as the edges of the more commonly used GIF, JPG, and PNG image types do. In other words, they look just as good at 1,000 percent as they do at 100 percent.

Scalability is only one cool feature of SVG images. Another is that, rather than being simply a picture, the content of an SVG image is defined in XML format within the file and can be transformed, animated, and otherwise modified by using scripts and cascading style sheets (CSS files), or simply by selecting the image and recoloring it within Word or another Microsoft 365 app.

To insert an icon

1. Position the cursor where you want to insert the icon.

2. On the **Insert** tab, in the **Illustrations** group, select **Icons**.

3. Scroll through the icon library or select any category in the left pane to move to that section of the library.

4. Select each icon that you want to insert. You can select as many icons as you want. A check mark appears in the corner of each selected icon.

5. Select **Insert** to insert the selected icon or icons as individual pictures.

To convert an icon to one or more shapes

- Do either of the following:
  - Select the icon. On the **Graphics Format** tab, in the **Change** group, select **Convert to Shape**.
  - Right-click the icon, and then select **Convert to Shape**.

To resize, recolor, rotate, or otherwise modify an icon

- Select the icon, and then use the standard tools on the **Graphics Format** tab to modify it as you would any other picture object.

Draw and modify shapes

Word has an extensive library of shapes. Shapes can be simple, such as lines, circles, or squares; or more complex, such as stars, hearts, and arrows. Some shapes are three-dimensional (although most are two-dimensional). Some of these shapes have innate meanings or intentions, and others are simply shapes.

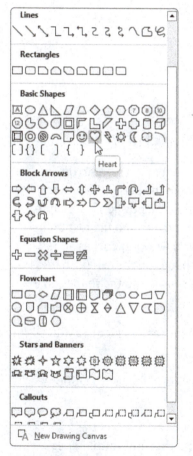

The shapes you can insert in a Word document

Shapes are available from the Shapes gallery. Pointing to any shape in the Shapes gallery displays a ScreenTip that contains the shape name.

Draw and add text to shapes

After you select a shape that you want to add to your document, you click or tap the page to insert it at its default size or drag to draw the shape at the size you want it on the page. Shapes are also text boxes, and you can enter text directly into them. You can format the text in shapes just as you would regular text.

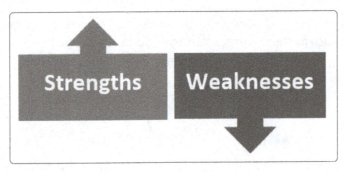

Shapes can help to visually reinforce a concept

Use the drawing canvas to draw shapes

If your picture consists of more than a few shapes, you might want to draw the shapes on a drawing canvas instead of directly on the page. The drawing canvas keeps the parts of the picture together, helps you position the picture, and provides a frame-like boundary between your picture and the text on the page. To open a drawing canvas, you select New Drawing Canvas at the bottom of the Shapes menu. You can then draw shapes on the canvas in the usual ways. You can resize and move the drawing canvas and the shapes on it as one unit.

If you prefer to always use the drawing canvas when creating pictures with shapes, do the following:

1. Display the Backstage view, select **Options**, and in the **Word Options** dialog, select **Advanced**.

2. On the **Advanced** page, in the **Editing Options** area, select the **Automatically create drawing canvas when inserting AutoShapes** checkbox, and select **OK**.

To create a shape on a page

1. On the **Insert** tab, in the **Illustrations** group, select the **Shapes** button.

2. On the **Shapes** menu, select the shape you want to insert.

> ✓ **TIP** If you select a shape button and then change your mind about drawing the shape, you can release the selection by pressing the Esc key.

3. When the cursor changes to a plus sign, do either of the following:

   - Click or tap on the page to create a shape of the default size.

   - Drag diagonally on the page to specify the upper-left and lower-right corners of the rectangle that surrounds the shape (the drawing canvas).

> ✓ **TIP** To draw a shape that has the same height and width (such as a circle or square), hold down the Shift key while you drag.

To add text to a shape

- Select the shape, and then enter the text you want to display on the shape. There is no cursor to indicate the location of the text; when you start typing, it appears on the shape.

Locate additional formatting commands

You control the area of the shape that is available for text by formatting the Text Box margins of the shape. This setting is gathered with many others in the Format Shape pane, which you can display by selecting the Shape Styles or WordArt Styles dialog launcher on the Picture Format or Shape Format tab. You can display different pages of settings by selecting the icons at the top of the pane.

In Word, the most frequently used formatting commands are located on the ribbon. If additional commands are available, the ribbon group includes a dialog launcher. Selecting the dialog launcher displays either a dialog or a control pane.

6

Move and modify shapes

You can change the size, angles, and effects applied to shapes. You can apply different colors to the outline and inside (fill) of a shape.

When you first draw a shape, and anytime you select it thereafter, a set of handles appears around the shape.

You can easily modify the shape, size, and angle of an image

You can use the handles to manipulate the shape in the following ways:

- Drag the side or corner handles (hollow circles) to change the size or aspect ratio of the shape.

- Drag the angle handles (yellow circles) to change the angles or curves of the shape. (Note that not all shapes have angle handles.)

- Drag the rotate handle (circling arrow) to rotate the shape.

With a little imagination, you can combine shapes to create more complex images.

To select a shape for editing

- Click or tap the shape once.

To select multiple shapes

- Select a shape, hold down the **Shift** or **Ctrl** key, and select each of the remaining shapes.

- Select one or more paragraphs to select all the shapes that are anchored to those paragraphs. (Note that this method doesn't activate the Format tab, but you can copy, cut, or delete the anchor paragraphs and associated shapes.)

To resize a shape

- Select the shape, and then do any of the following:

    - To change only the width of the shape, drag the left or right size handle.

    - To change only the height of the shape, drag the top or bottom size handle.

    - To change both the height and the width of the shape, drag a corner size handle.

    - To resize a shape without changing its aspect ratio, hold down the **Shift** key and drag a corner size handle or press an arrow key.

To rotate or flip a shape

1. Select the shape.

2. On the **Shape Format** tab, in the **Arrange** group, select the **Rotate Objects** button.

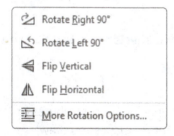

The menu illustrates the rotate and flip options

3. On the **Rotate Objects** menu, do either of the following:

    - Select the **Rotate** or **Flip** option you want.

    - Select **More Rotation Options**, enter or select a specific angle of rotation in the **Rotation** box on the **Size** tab of the **Layout** dialog, and then select **OK**.

> **TIP** You can rotate or flip any type of image. Rotating turns a shape 90 degrees to the right or left; flipping turns a shape 180 degrees horizontally or vertically.

Or

1. Select the shape.

2. Drag the **Rotate** handle in a clockwise or counterclockwise direction until the shape is at the angle of rotation you want.

To change a shape to another shape

1. Select the shape you want to change.

2. On the **Shape Format** tab, in the **Insert Shapes** group, select **Edit Shape**, select **Change Shape**, and then select the new shape.

Changing the shape doesn't affect the shape formatting or text.

Format shapes

When a shape is selected, the Format tab in the Drawing Tools tab group appears on the ribbon. You can use the commands on the Format tab to do the following:

- Replace the shape with another without changing the formatting.

- Change the fill and outline colors of the shape, and the effects applied to the shape.

- Separately, change the fill and outline colors and effects of any text that you add to the shape.

- Arrange, layer, and group multiple shapes.

Having made changes to one shape, you can easily apply the same attributes to another shape, or you can apply the attributes to all future shapes you draw.

When you have multiple shapes on a page, you can group them so that you can copy, move, and format them as a unit. You can change the attributes of an individual shape—for example, its color, size, or location—without ungrouping the shapes.

To format a shape

1. Select the shape that you want to format.

2. On the **Shape Format** tab, in the **Shape Styles** group, select the **More** button to display the Shape Styles gallery.

The Shape Styles gallery color options reflect the current color scheme

3. Point to any thumbnail to display a live preview of the formatting applied to the picture.

4. Select a thumbnail to apply the corresponding style.

Insert symbols

Some documents require characters not found on a standard keyboard. These characters might include the copyright (©) or registered trademark (®) symbols, currency symbols (such as € or £), Greek letters, or letters with accent marks. Or you might want to add arrows (such as ↗ or ↘) or graphic icons (such as ☎ or ✈).

Like graphics or shapes, symbols can add visual information or eye appeal to a document. However, they differ from graphics in that they are characters associated with a particular font.

Word gives you easy access to a huge array of symbols that you can easily insert into any document. To insert a recently used symbol:

1. On the **Insert** tab, in the **Symbols** group, select the **Symbol** button to display a list of recently used symbols.

2. Select a symbol in the list to insert it in your document.

3. If the symbol you need doesn't appear in the list, select **More Symbols** to open the **Symbol** dialog.

The Symbol dialog offers easy access to hundreds of symbols

4. Click or tap the symbol to select it, and then select the **Insert** button.

5. Select the **Close** button to close the Symbol dialog.

You can also insert some common symbols by typing key combinations. For example, if you enter two consecutive dashes followed by a word and a space, Word automatically changes the two dashes to a professional-looking em-dash (—). (This symbol gets its name from the fact that it was originally the width of the capital letter *M*.) These key combinations are controlled by the AutoCorrect feature. For information about displaying and modifying AutoCorrect options, see Chapter 16, "Customize options and the user interface."

You can review many of the available shortcuts for inserting frequently used symbols on the Special Characters page of the Symbol dialog.

To format text on a shape

1. Select the shape.

2. On the **Shape Format** tab, in the **WordArt Styles** group, modify the style, text fill, text outline, or text effects.

Or

- Select the text on the shape. Then do either of the following:

  - On the **Shape Format** tab, in the **WordArt Styles** group, modify the style, text fill, text outline, or text effects.

  - On the **Home** tab, in the **Font** and **Paragraph** groups, use the standard text-formatting commands.

To copy formatting from one shape to another

1. Select the shape from which you want to copy the formatting.

2. On the **Home** tab, in the **Clipboard** group, select the **Format Painter** button.

3. Select the shape you want to copy the formatting to.

To set formatting as the default for the active document

- Right-click the formatting source shape, and then select **Set as Default Shape**.

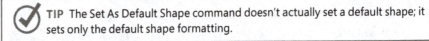

> **TIP** The Set As Default Shape command doesn't actually set a default shape; it sets only the default shape formatting.

To group shapes together as one object

1. Select all the shapes that you want grouped together.

2. On the **Shape Format** tab, in the **Arrange** group, select the **Group** button (when you point to this button, the ScreenTip that appears says *Group Objects*) and then, in the list, select **Group**.

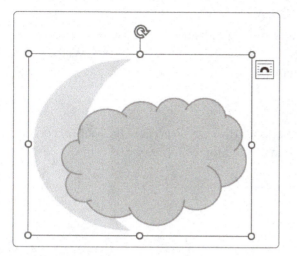

Grouped objects have a common set of handles

To move an entire group

1. Point to any shape in the group.

2. When the pointer changes to a four-headed arrow, drag the group to the new location.

To ungroup shapes

1. Select the group.

2. On the **Shape Format** tab, in the **Arrange** group, select the **Group** button, and then select **Ungroup**.

Build equations

You can insert mathematical symbols, such as π (pi) or ∑ (sigma, or summation), the same way you would insert any other symbol. But you can also create entire mathematical equations in a document. You can insert some predefined equations, including the quadratic formula, the binomial theorem, and the Pythagorean theorem, into a document with a few clicks or taps. If you need something other than these standard equations, you can build your own equations by using a library of mathematical symbols.

Equations are different from graphics in that they are accurately rendered mathematical formulas that appear in the document as fields. However, they are similar to graphics in that they can be displayed in line with the surrounding text or in their own space with text above and below them.

You can insert equations in two ways:

- **By inserting a predefined equation**   The Insert New Equation gallery contains several commonly used equations, including the following:

  - Area of circle

  - Binomial theorem

  - Expansion of a sum

  - Fourier series

  - Pythagorean theorem

  - Quadratic formula

  - Taylor expansion

  - Trig identity 1

  - Trig identity 2

  You can insert an equation from the gallery, or you can search the Office.com site for other predefined equations.

- **By building an equation from scratch**   Selecting the Equation button instead of its arrow inserts a field in which you can build an equation from scratch.

When you opt to build an equation from scratch, Word displays the Equation tab for equations. This tab provides access to mathematical symbols and structures such as fractions, scripts, radicals, integrals, and more.

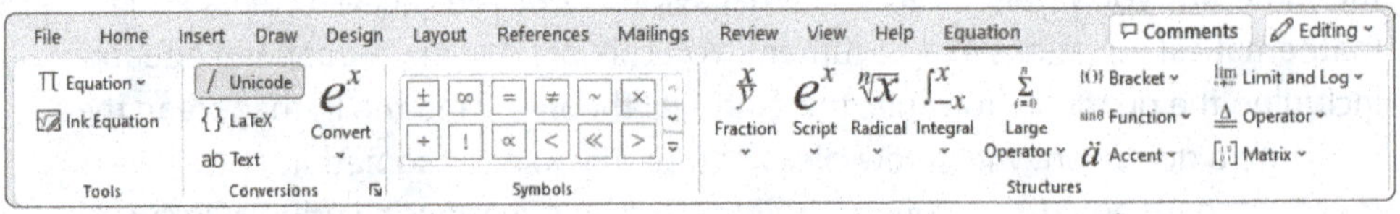

The Equation tab for equations offers easy access to mathematical symbols and structures

Selecting a button on the Equation tab—for example, the Fraction button—displays a gallery of related structures.

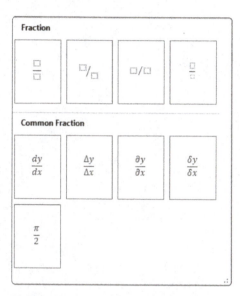

The Fraction gallery provides structures for forming fractions

By default, equations appear in professional, or two-dimensional, form. If you prefer linear form, which is easier to edit, you can change the equation accordingly. You can also specify how the equation should be aligned on the page—left, right, or center.

For even finer control over the equations you build, you can open the Equation Options dialog by selecting the Conversions dialog launcher on the Equation tab. Here, you can set many options that govern the appearance of equation expressions in a document, such as the following:

- The size of nested fractions
- The placement of integral limits
- The placement of *n*-ary limits
- The alignment of the equation
- The treatment of wrapped lines in the equation

Fine-tune the appearance of equation expressions in a document

If you build an equation that you know you'll want to reuse later, you can save it. When you save an equation, Word stores it as a building block. You can name the equation whatever you like. You can then access the equation from the Equation gallery, with other predefined equations.

> 🔍 **SEE ALSO** For information about building blocks, see "Insert preformatted document parts" in Chapter 9, "Format document elements."

Math AutoCorrect

Take advantage of Word's Math AutoCorrect feature to type mathematical symbols by hand. Math AutoCorrect defines dozens of text items that, when typed and followed by a space or punctuation mark, get automatically replaced by the corresponding symbol. All the Math AutoCorrect entries begin with a backslash (\\), followed by the name of the symbol. For example, to type a square root sign ($\sqrt{}$), type \\sqrt and then a space or punctuation mark. To see the complete list of Math AutoCorrect entries, either select Math AutoCorrect in the Equation Options dialog (see below) or select Options in Word's Backstage view, select Proofing, then AutoCorrect Options, and then Math AutoCorrect.

6

AutoCorrect		? ✕
AutoFormat		Actions
AutoCorrect	Math AutoCorrect	AutoFormat As You Type

☐ Use Math AutoCorrect rules outside of math regions

When Math AutoCorrect and AutoCorrect rules conflict, AutoCorrect rules will be used.

☑ Replace text as you type

Replace:	With:
‖	‖
...	...
::	∷
:=	≔
\\above	⊥
\\acute	ˊ
\\aleph	ℵ
\\alpha	α
\\Alpha	Α
\\amalg	⨿
\\angle	∠
\\aoint	∲
\\approx	≈
\\asmash	↓
\\ast	∗

[Recognized Functions...]   [Add]   [Delete]

[OK]   [Cancel]

Math AutoCorrect offers dozens of text replacements for math symbols

To insert a predefined equation

1. On the **Insert** tab, in the **Symbols** group, select the **Equation** arrow.

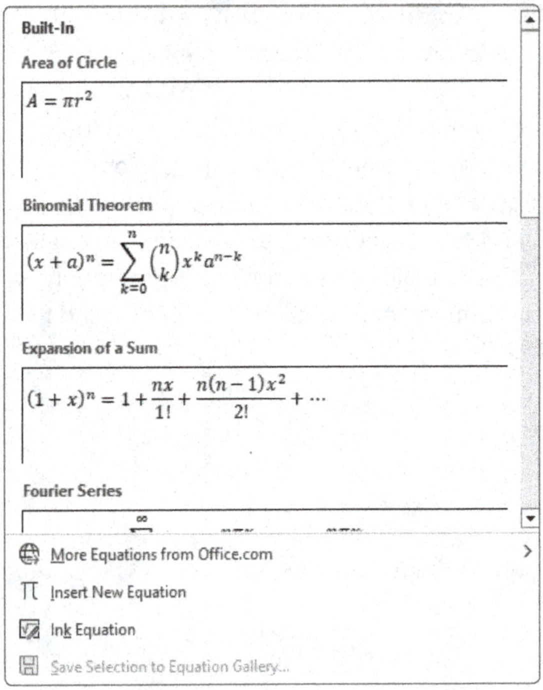

Built-In

Area of Circle

$$A = \pi r^2$$

Binomial Theorem

$$(x + a)^n = \sum_{k=0}^{n} \binom{n}{k} x^k a^{n-k}$$

Expansion of a Sum

$$(1 + x)^n = 1 + \frac{nx}{1!} + \frac{n(n-1)x^2}{2!} + \cdots$$

Fourier Series

🌐 More Equations from Office.com >

π Insert New Equation

Ink Equation

Save Selection to Equation Gallery...

Selecting a predefined equation inserts it into the document

2. On the **Insert an Equation** menu, in the **Built-In** gallery, select the equation you want to insert. (If necessary, scroll the gallery to display the available equations.)

To build an equation

1. On the **Insert** tab, in the **Symbols** group, select the **Equation** button (not the arrow) to insert an equation field into the document.

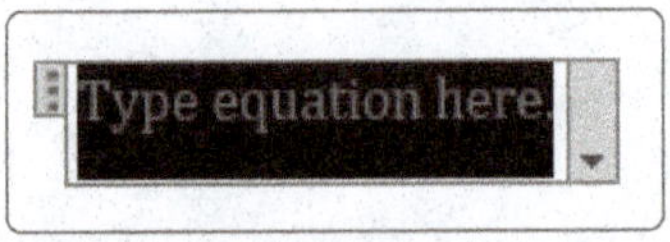

Type equation here

Word inserts a field in which you can build an equation

2. Enter an equation in the equation field.

To change the equation to linear form

1. Click or tap the equation to select it.

2. Do either of the following:

   - On the **Design** tab, in the **Conversions** group, select the **Convert** arrow, and then in the **Equation Options** list, select **Current-Linear**.

   - Select the arrow to the right of the equation, and then select **Linear** in the list that appears.

To change the relationship of the equation with the text

- To display the equation in line with the text rather than on its own line (the default), in the **Equation Options** list, select **Change to Inline**.

- If the equation is already displayed in line with the text and you want to set it apart on its own line, in the **Equation Options** list, select **Change to Display**.

To change the alignment of the equation

- In the **Equation Options** list, select **Justification**, and then select the alignment option you want (**Left**, **Right**, **Centered**, or **Centered as Group**).

> **TIP** You can change the font, size, and other attributes of the equation as you would any other type of text element. Simply select the equation, right-click the selection, and choose Font from the menu that appears. The Font dialog opens; change the settings as you want.

To save an equation

1. Select the equation.

2. In the **Equation Options** list, select **Save as New Equation** to open the Create New Building Block dialog.

3. In the **Name** box, replace the equation with a name you'll remember, and then select **OK**.

Key points

- You can use digital photographs and images created and saved in other programs to make documents more visually interesting or to convey information in a way that words cannot.

- You can include information from your computer screen in a document by capturing and inserting screenshots and screen clippings directly from within the document.

- You can add decorative elements or build complex illustrations within Word by using shapes and icons.

- Word has equation building tools that make it easy to build correctly formatted mathematical equations in a document.

Practice tasks

Before you can complete these tasks, you must copy the book's practice files to your computer. The practice files for these tasks are in the **Word365SBS\Ch06** folder. You can save the results of the tasks in the same folder.

The Introduction includes a complete list of practice files and download instructions.

Insert, move, and resize pictures

Open the **InsertPictures** document in Print Layout view, and then perform the following tasks:

1. Position the cursor in the first paragraph after the *Beautiful Bamboo* heading, before the word *Bamboo*.

2. Insert the **Bamboo1** picture from the practice file folder into the document, and move the text that follows to the next line.

3. Move the picture to the beginning of the second paragraph, before the word *There*, and move the text that follows to the next line.

4. Resize the picture to a height of **2"**.

5. Save and close the document.

Edit and format pictures

Open the **EditPictures** document in Print Layout view, and then perform the following tasks:

1. Do the following to the first picture in the document:

   - Crop the picture to a square shape.

   - Increase the contrast of the picture by 40 percent without changing the Brightness.

   - Change the picture's color setting to **Temperature: 8800K**.

   - Add a **Film Grain** artistic effect.

- Apply the **Rotated, White** picture style to the picture.

- Position the picture in the upper-right corner of the page.

- Change the text wrapping to **Tight**.

2. Do the following to the second picture in the document:

   - Remove the background from the picture.

   - Change the text wrapping to **Tight**.

3. Copy the formatting of the first picture to the second picture.

4. Reset the first picture to discard all formatting changes.

5. Save and close the document.

Provide additional information about pictures

Open the **AddInformation** document in Print Layout view, and then perform the following tasks:

1. Select the picture located below the first paragraph of text.

2. From the **Picture Format** tab, open the **Alt Text** pane.

3. Have Word generate a description of the photograph for you.

4. Edit the description to read Cozy bedroom with bed and desk.

5. On page 2, select the *[insert furniture picture here]* placeholder.

6. Display the **Online Pictures** window, and search for a photograph of furniture.

7. Select and insert a search result that you like.

8. Zoom in on the page if necessary to read the attribution inserted with the image.

9. Save and close the document.

Insert screen clippings

Open the **InsertClippings** document in Print Layout view, and then perform the following tasks:

1. Position the cursor on page **2** of the document, under the heading *Directions to the Bellevue Library*. Then minimize Word.

2. In your web browser, use the Bing Maps site (*www.bing.com/maps*) to display a map showing the location of the Bellevue Regional Library in Bellevue, Washington.

3. Insert a screen clipping of a portion of the map into the **InsertClippings** document.

4. Save and close the document.

Insert and format icons

Open the **InsertIcons** document in Print Layout view, and then perform the following tasks:

1. The document provides a template for an Idea of the Week award certificate or poster. Consider ways you could embellish this document to make it more interesting.

2. Position the cursor in the empty space below the text *[insert idea here]*.

3. From the **Insert** tab, open the **Insert Icons** window. Scroll through the window and look for icons that you could use to enhance this content.

4. In the **Communication** category, select the thought bubble and the email icon.

5. In the **Analytics** category, select the head that contains the light bulb.

6. In the **Celebration** category, select the clapping hands.

7. Insert the four selected icons and change their positioning to **Tight**.

8. Click or tap anywhere on the page away from the icons to release the selection, and then drag the icons to the following positions:

   - Position the head near *Idea of the Week* and the thought bubble above it.

   - Leave the clapping hands in the space below *[insert idea here]*.

   - Position the email envelope to the right of *ideas@blueyonderairlines.com*.

9. Resize the four icons as you like.

10. Select the thought bubble icon and, from the **Format** tab, fill the icon with the **Orange** color.

11. Ungroup the parts of the icon, converting it to a drawing object as you do so.

12. Select and fill each of the circles leading to the bubble with a different color.

13. Experiment with resizing and recoloring the other icons you inserted. Insert more icons if you want to!

14. Save and close the document.

Draw and modify shapes

Open a new blank document in Print Layout view, and then perform the following tasks:

1. In the upper-left corner of the page, from the **Block Arrows** section of the **Shapes** menu, insert an **Arrow: Curved Right** shape.

2. Change the shape's **Height** setting to **3"** and its **Width** setting to **2"**.

3. Create a copy of the shape and move the copy to the upper-right corner of the page.

4. Flip the copy of the shape horizontally so that it's a mirror image of the first shape.

5. From the **Rectangles** section of the **Shapes** menu, insert a **Rectangle** shape and move it so that its lower corners align with the points of each arrow. (You might have to adjust the size and position of the rectangle and the position of the arrows.)

6. In the rectangle, enter What goes around comes around.

7. Change the font of the text to **Century Gothic**, the size to **18** points, and the color to **Dark Blue**.

8. Group all the shapes as one object.

9. From the **Theme Styles** section of the **Shape Styles** gallery, apply the **Subtle Effect – Gold, Accent 4** style to the grouped object.

10. Ungroup the shapes.

11. Save the document in the practice file folder as MyShapes, and then close it.

Build equations

Create a new document in Word, and then perform the following tasks:

1. With the cursor in the first line of the document, insert the Pythagorean theorem predefined equation.

2. On the next line, insert a blank equation field.

3. In the equation field, enter (p-3)*.

4. Display the **Fraction** gallery and select the first thumbnail in the first row (**Stacked Fraction**) to insert structured placeholders for a simple fraction in the equation field.

5. Enter b in the top box of the fraction structure and enter 3 in the bottom box.

6. Change the equation to linear form.

7. Save the equation as a building block named Additional People Cost.

8. Display the **Insert an Equation** gallery. The equation you saved appears near the bottom of the gallery.

9. Save and close the document.

Part 3

Enhance document content

Insert and modify diagrams and 3D models

Diagrams are graphics that convey information. Business documents often include diagrams to clarify concepts, describe processes, and show hierarchical relationships. Word includes a powerful diagramming feature called SmartArt that you can use to create diagrams directly in your documents. By using these dynamic diagram templates, you can produce eye-catching and interesting visual representations of information.

SmartArt graphics can illustrate many different types of concepts. Although they consist of collections of shapes, SmartArt graphics are merely visual containers for information stored as bulleted lists. You can also incorporate pictures and other images to create truly spectacular, yet divinely professional, diagrams.

Microsoft 365 includes a library of three-dimensional models from which you can insert a variety of life-like content that you can modify to present from any angle. While three-dimensional graphics are more suited to online presentation in a program such as Microsoft PowerPoint, they can also add a sophisticated element to Word documents.

This chapter guides you through procedures related to creating and modifying SmartArt diagrams that include text and picture content, and inserting and modifying three-dimensional models.

In this chapter

- Create diagrams
- Modify diagrams
- Create picture diagrams
- Insert and modify 3D models

Create diagrams

Sometimes the concepts you want to convey to an audience are best presented in diagrams. You can easily create a dynamic, appealing diagram by using SmartArt graphics, which visually express information in predefined sets of shapes. SmartArt graphics can illustrate the following concepts:

- **List**   These diagrams visually represent lists of related or independent information—for example, a list of items needed to complete a task, including pictures of the items.

- **Process**   These diagrams visually describe the ordered set of steps required to complete a task—for example, the steps for getting a project approved.

- **Cycle**   These diagrams represent a circular sequence of steps, tasks, or events, or the relationship of a set of steps, tasks, or events to a central, core element—for example, the looping process for continually improving a product based on customer feedback.

- **Hierarchy**   These diagrams illustrate the structure of an organization or entity—for example, the top-level management structure of a company.

- **Relationship**   These diagrams show convergent, divergent, overlapping, merging, or containment elements—for example, how using similar methods to organize your email, calendar, and contacts can improve your productivity.

- **Matrix**   These diagrams show the relationship of components to a whole—for example, the product teams in a department.

- **Pyramid**   These diagrams illustrate proportional or interconnected relationships—for example, the amount of time that should ideally be spent on different phases of a project.

- **Picture**   These diagrams use pictures to illustrate the connections or relationships between multiple items—for example, a product and its accessories or components. See "Create picture diagrams" later in this chapter.

The layout of content in a SmartArt diagram is controlled by a behind-the-scenes bulleted list. When creating a SmartArt diagram in Word, you choose a layout first, and then populate the associated list in a window called the Text pane.

The dialog from which you choose the SmartArt graphic layout displays monochromatic representations of the layouts so that colors don't confuse the process of choosing a layout. The actual colors of the SmartArt diagram are based on the color scheme of the document, and you can choose from several different color patterns. The categories in the left pane of the dialog are not mutually exclusive, so some diagrams appear in more than one category.

Word includes about 140 SmartArt templates

> ✓ **TIP** After you create a SmartArt diagram, you can change its content, layout, and colors. For information about changing the diagram colors, see "Modify diagrams" later in this chapter.

Selecting a layout in the Choose A SmartArt Graphic dialog displays a color mockup of the diagram, a description of the layout, and information about any restrictions on the number of entries or list levels the layout supports.

After you choose a layout, Word inserts the basic diagram into the document and displays the Text pane containing placeholder information. You can enter more or less information than is required by the original diagram.

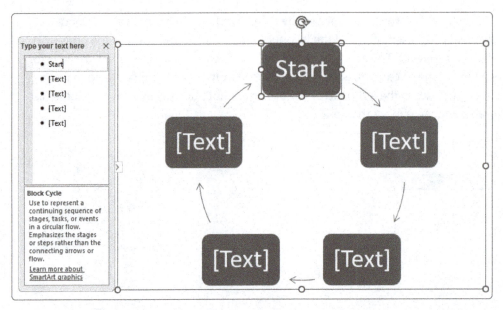

When you enter text in either the Text pane or the selected shape, that text also appears in the other location

You can insert and modify text either directly in the diagram shapes or in the associated Text pane. (You can hide the Text pane when you're not using it, and redisplay it if you need it.) The Text pane might display only a single-level bulleted list, or a multilevel list if the diagram layout supports multiple levels. You can expand the diagram either by adding more list items or by adding more shapes. Some diagram layouts support a specific number of entries, and others can be expanded significantly.

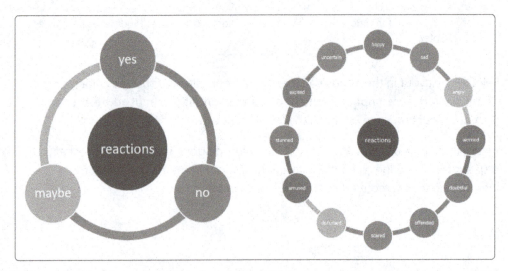

Increase or decrease the number of items displayed by a diagram to convey a more precise message

In layouts that support additional entries, Word adds shapes to the diagram to accommodate the content. Within a diagram, shapes of the same hierarchy level are the same size regardless of the amount of content each contains. The text within the shapes is also the same size. If a text entry is too long to fit a shape, the text size changes in all the shapes at that hierarchy level.

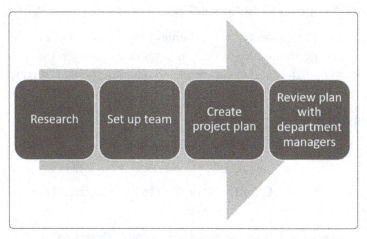

Word keeps your SmartArt diagrams looking professional by automatically adjusting text size as needed

> **✓ TIP** You can move, resize, and wrap text around SmartArt graphics just as you can other types of images. For information about configuring image layout options, see "Arrange objects on a page" in Chapter 10, "Organize and arrange content."

To create a diagram in a document

1. Position the cursor in the document where you want to insert the diagram.

2. Do either of the following to open the Choose A SmartArt Graphic dialog:

    -   On the **Insert** tab, in the **Illustrations** group, select **SmartArt**.

    -   Press **Alt+N+M**.

3. In the left pane, select a type of diagram. Then, in the center pane, select a diagram layout thumbnail to view an example, along with a description of what the diagram best conveys, in the right pane.

4. Select **OK** to insert the selected diagram at the cursor.

To enter text into diagram shapes

1. If the **Text** pane isn't open, select the diagram, and then do either of the following:

   - Select the chevron on the left side (in the middle) of the diagram frame to open the Text pane.

   - On the **SmartArt Design** tab, in the **Create Graphic** group, select **Text Pane**.

2. In the **Text** pane, select the first placeholder, and enter the text you want to display in the corresponding shape. Notice that the content you enter in the bulleted list appears immediately in the corresponding diagram shape. Then do any of the following:

   - Press the **Down Arrow** key to move to the next placeholder.

   - At the beginning of a list item, press **Tab** to increase the indent level of the current list item.

   - At the end of a list item, press **Enter** to add an item to the bulleted list and add a shape to the diagram.

   - Select an unused or unneeded placeholder and then press **Delete** to remove the item.

3. Repeat step 2 until you've entered all the diagram content.

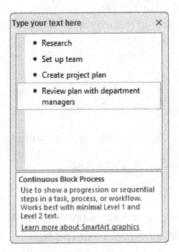

Use the Text pane both to enter text and to quickly review your text for errors

> **TIP** For a clean look, don't use ending punctuation for the text that appears in the SmartArt graphic shapes.

4. In the **Text** pane, select the **Close** button (the **X**).

Modify diagrams

After you create a diagram and add the text you want to display in it, you can move and size it to fit the space, and format it to achieve professional-looking results.

If the diagram layout you originally selected doesn't precisely meet your needs, choose a different layout. Some layouts preserve information that doesn't fit, and others don't; a message at the bottom of the Text pane provides information so you can make an informed decision.

7

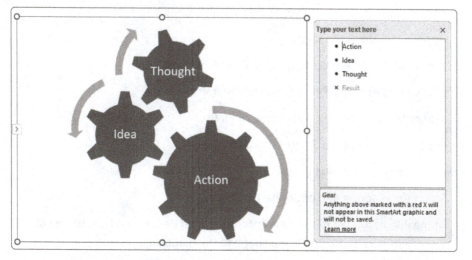

Some diagrams support only a limited number of text entries

When a SmartArt graphic is active, the ribbon includes two additional tabs: SmartArtDesign and Format.

Design tools for SmartArt graphics

You can make many changes directly on the diagram canvas, but if you prefer, you can also make changes from the ribbon.

From the SmartArt Design tab, you can make changes such as the following:

- Add, move, and change the hierarchy of shapes.
- Change to a different layout.
- Change the color scheme of the diagram.
- Change the effects applied to the diagram shapes.
- Reset the diagram to its default settings.

From the Format tab, you can make changes such as the following:

- Change the shape of an individual diagram shape—for example, change a square to a star to make it stand out.
- Change the size of an individual diagram shape.
- Apply a built-in shape style.
- Apply colors and effects to specific shapes.
- Apply WordArt text effects to the text in a shape.
- Add alternative text (alt text) to the diagram.
- Position and resize the SmartArt graphic.

To add a shape to a SmartArt graphic

1. Select the diagram and open the **Text** pane.
2. At the end of any list item, press **Enter** to add an item to the bulleted list at the same level and a corresponding shape to the diagram.
3. If you want to make the new item a subitem of the original item, press **Tab** to demote the bulleted list item and change the corresponding shape.

Or

1. Select the diagram shape next to which you want to add a new shape.
2. To add a shape at the same level, on the **SmartArt Design** tab, in the **Create Graphic** group, select the **Add Shape** button to add a shape to the diagram and corresponding item to the bulleted list.

Or

1. Select the diagram shape next to which you want to add a new shape.

2. To add a shape at another level, on the **SmartArt Design** tab, in the **Create Graphic** group, select the **Add Shape** arrow, and then select one of the following (only valid shape options are active):

   - Add Shape After

   - Add Shape Before

   - Add Shape Above

   - Add Shape Below

   - Add Assistant

> ⚠️ **IMPORTANT** Some SmartArt graphics support only a limited number of shapes. If you want to add a shape to a diagram to accommodate more text, change to a diagram that supports more shapes.

To remove a shape from a SmartArt graphic

1. Do either of the following to select the shape you want to remove:

   - In the diagram, select the shape.

   - In the **Text** pane, select the list item.

2. Press the **Delete** key.

To move a shape in a SmartArt graphic

- In the diagram, point to the shape. When the cursor changes to a four-headed arrow, drag the shape by its border to a different position.

- In the **Text** pane, drag the list item to a different position.

7

To change the hierarchy of shapes in a SmartArt graphic

> ⚠ **IMPORTANT** You can promote and demote shapes only in SmartArt layouts that support multiple levels of content.

1. In the diagram, select a shape.

2. On the **SmartArt Design** tab, in the **Create Graphic** group, do either of the following:

   - Select the **Promote** button to increase the level of the selected shape or list item.

   - Select the **Demote** button to decrease the level of the selected shape or list item.

Or

- In the **Text** pane, click or tap at the beginning of a list item. Then do either of the following:

  - Press **Tab** to demote the list item (and the shape).

  - Press **Shift+Tab** to promote the list item (and the shape).

To change a SmartArt graphic to a different layout

1. Select the diagram.

2. On the **SmartArt Design** tab, in the **Layouts** group, select the **More** button to expand the **Layouts** gallery. (Or, if the gallery is collapsed into a group button, select the **Change Layout** group button.)

   This view of the gallery displays only the available diagram layouts for the currently selected diagram layout category.

3. In the **Layouts** gallery, do either of the following:

   - Select a thumbnail to change the diagram to the new layout in the same category.

   - At the bottom of the gallery, select **More Layouts** to display the Choose A SmartArt Graphic dialog. Locate and select the layout you want to apply, and then select **OK**.

To change the color scheme of a SmartArt graphic

1. On the **SmartArt Design** tab, in the **SmartArt Styles** group, select **Change Colors** to display the SmartArt coloring options in the current color scheme.

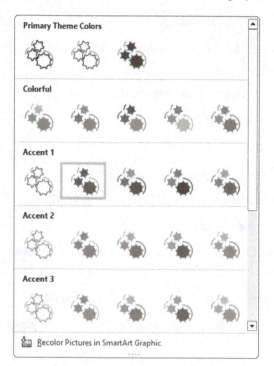

The Change Colors gallery options are based on the document color scheme

2. Point to any color set to display a live preview of that option. Select the color set you like to apply it to the diagram.

To change the effects applied to the shapes in a SmartArt graphic

1. Select the diagram. On the **Format** tab, in the **Shape Styles** group, select the **Shape Effects** button.

2. On the **Shape Effects** menu, select an effect category. Then, in the **Variations** section of the effect menu, point to any thumbnail to display a live preview of the effect.

3. Select a thumbnail to apply that effect to the diagram.

To reset a SmartArt graphic to its default formatting

- Select the diagram, and on the **SmartArt Design** tab, in the **Reset** group, select **Reset Graphic**.

To change the shape of an individual diagram shape

1. Right-click or long-press (tap and hold) the diagram shape you want to change, and then select **Change Shape**.

2. In the **Shape** gallery, select any shape to change the diagram shape.

To change the size of an individual diagram shape

- Select the shape, and then do either of the following:
  - Drag the sizing handle until the shape is the size you want.
  - On the **Format** tab, in the **Size** group, set the **Height** and **Width**.

To apply colors and effects to specific shapes

- Select a shape. On the **Format** tab, in the **Shape Styles** group, do either of the following:
  - From the **Shape Styles** gallery, apply a preformatted set of styles.
  - From the **Shape Fill**, **Shape Outline**, or **Shape Effects** menu, apply individual style formats.

To apply WordArt text effects to the text in a shape

1. Do either of the following:
   - Select the diagram to apply WordArt text effects to all the text in a diagram.
   - Select a shape to apply WordArt text effects to only the selected shape.

2. On the **Format** tab, in the **WordArt Styles** group, select the **More** button to display the Quick Styles gallery.

3. In the **Quick Styles** gallery, point to any thumbnail to display a live preview of the effect.

4. Select a thumbnail to apply the effect to the selected shape or shapes.

> **TIP** For a custom WordArt effect, select the text fill color, the text outline color, and the text effect individually from the corresponding menus in the WordArt Styles group.

Create picture diagrams

Most SmartArt graphics present text information in shapes, but some can display pictures instead of, or in addition to, text. Most SmartArt graphic categories include some
picture options, but picture diagrams are also available in their own category to help
you locate them if you specifically want to create a diagram that includes pictures.

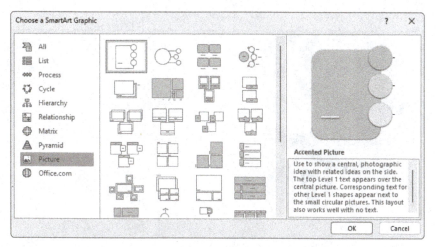

Diagrams that include spaces for pictures have "Picture" in the layout name

You can insert pictures into a SmartArt graphic from the same sources you can insert
them into a document: your computer or a connected storage location, a SharePoint
library, a OneDrive or OneDrive for Business storage folder, or the internet. As always,
take care when reusing pictures you find on the internet to ensure that you don't
violate someone's copyright.

When you insert or select a picture in a SmartArt graphic, the SmartArt Design,
Format, and Picture Format tabs are active. You can edit pictures you insert in diagrams the same way you edit those you insert directly into documents.

To insert a picture diagram in a document

1. Position the cursor in the document where you want to insert a picture diagram.

2. On the **Insert** tab, in the **Illustrations** group, select **SmartArt** to open the
   Choose A SmartArt Graphic dialog.

3. In the left pane, select **Picture** to display the picture diagram options. Then in
   the middle pane, select any thumbnail to display information about the diagram and the number of pictures you can use in it.

4. In the **Choose a SmartArt Graphic** dialog, select **OK** to insert the selected picture diagram template.

To replace a picture placeholder in a diagram

1. In the **Text** pane or in a diagram shape, select the **Insert Picture** icon to open the Insert Pictures window.

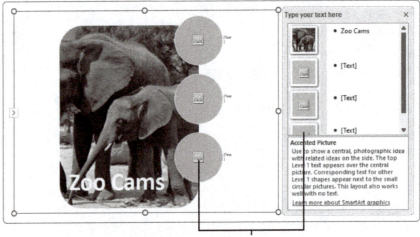

Insert Picture icons

Word makes it easy to insert pictures in a picture diagram

2. In the **Insert Pictures** window, which displays the locations from which you can insert pictures into the diagram, select the source you want to use.

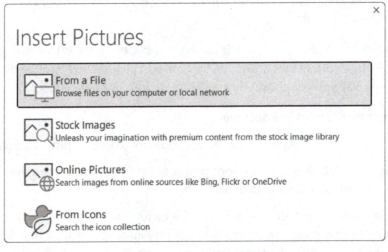

The Insert Pictures window provides access to local and online resources

3. Browse to and select the picture you want to use. Then select **Insert** to replace the picture placeholder.

Insert and modify 3D models

Word includes features that enable you to insert, manipulate, and format three-dimensional models in your documents.

3D models depict a chicken selecting a treat from a cornucopia

Insert 3D models

You can select models from the 3D Models online library or another source, or create your own in Microsoft Paint 3D, 3D Builder, or another 3D-modeling program. Supported 3D model file types include:

- 3D Manufacturing Format (*.3mf)
- Binary GL Transmission Format (*.glb)
- Filmbox Format (*.fbx)
- Object Format (*.obj)
- Polygon Format (*.ply)
- SketchUp Format (*.skp)
- StereoLithography Format (*.stl)

Access to the 3D Models library is free. The library includes a wide variety of objects in categories as diverse as Clothing, Dinosaurs, and Space—and if you don't find what you need, you can create your own by using Microsoft Paint 3D.

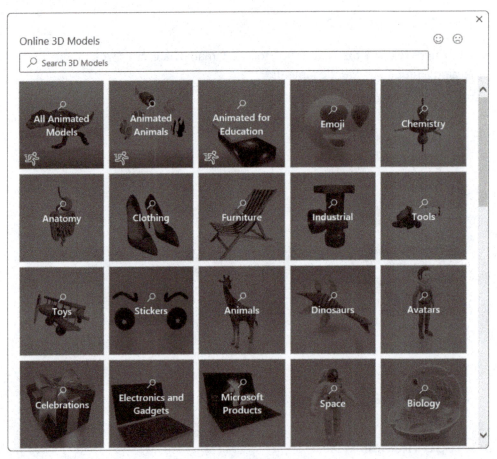

The 3D Models online library is available from Microsoft 365 and Paint 3D

Some of the 3D models available from the 3D Models library are animated. Animated models are obviously effective only when you display them on-screen—in a PowerPoint slideshow or electronically distributed document—rather than in a printed Word document.

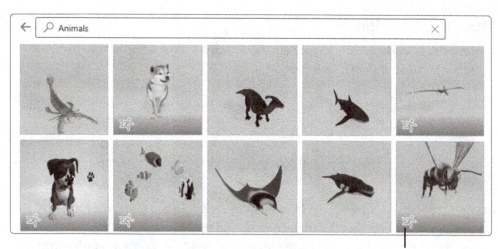

This icon indicates an animated 3D model

Animated models are indicated by a running-person icon

To insert a 3D model from the online library

1. On the **Insert** tab, in the **Illustrations** group, select **3D Models** (or select the **3D Models** arrow, and then select **Stock 3D Models**).

2. In the **Online 3D Models** window, do either of the following:

   - Enter a search term in the search box, and then press **Enter** to display related models.

   - Select a category tile to display models in that category.

3. Locate the model you want to insert, select the tile, and then select **Insert**.

To insert a 3D model from a local file

1. On the **Insert** tab, in the **Illustrations** group, select the **3D Models** arrow (not the button), and then select **This Device**.

   The Insert 3D Model dialog opens to your 3D Objects folder. This is the default folder for saving three-dimensional models from Paint 3D.

2. In the **Insert 3D Model** dialog, browse to the file you want to insert, and then select **Insert**.

Modify 3D models

Commands for working with 3D models are available from the Format tab that appears when a 3D model is selected.

The The 3D Model tab for an animated 3D model

The primary actions you take with 3D models are rotating and tilting the model to change the viewer's perspective of the model, and then panning and zooming to change the display of the model on the drawing board. Selecting a three-dimensional model displays additional handles you can use for these actions.

Animated 3D models have one or more associated motion patterns. The available motion patterns are called *scenes*. Some animated models have only one scene (for example, the animated toaster shows toast popping out of the toaster). Others have multiple scenes. The available motion patterns for each model are labeled Scene 1, Scene 2, and so on. The motion associated with each scene is specific to the model. If a 3D model has multiple motion pattern scenes, you can easily switch among them.

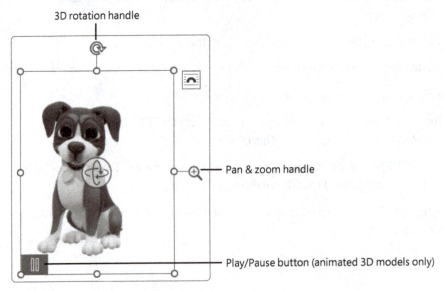

Handles that are specific to 3D model actions

You can choose from a preset view or rotate the model freely. Preset views include Front, Back, Left, Right, Top, Bottom, and combinations such as Above Back Left.

Preset options for displaying a three-dimensional dog

When working with an animated 3D model, you can also choose the scene or action pattern you want to display.

> **SEE ALSO** For any 3D model, you can add alt text to the image and change its position, text wrapping, alignment, and size by using standard techniques. For information about these techniques, see Chapter 6, "Add simple graphic elements."

To rotate a 3D model to a preselected perspective

1. Select the model.

2. On the **3D Model** tab, in the **3D Model Views** gallery, select one of the available perspectives.

To rotate a 3D model freehand

1. Select the model. A rotation handle appears in the center of the drawing object.

2. Drag the rotation handle in the direction you want to rotate the model.

To magnify a 3D model in the existing drawing space

1. Select the model.

2. On the **3D Model** tab, in the **Size** gallery, select **Pan & Zoom**. A magnifying glass handle appears to the right of the model.

3. Point to the magnifying glass. When the pointer changes to a double-headed vertical arrow (the Pan & Zoom handle), drag up or down to increase or decrease, respectively, the size of the model.

After you release the handle, only the portion of the model within the original drawing space is visible.

4. Drag the model within the drawing space to reveal the portion you want to display.

To change the motion pattern of an animated 3D model

1. Select the model.

2. On the **3D Model** tab, in the **Play 3D** group, select **Scenes**, and then select the model animation you want to apply (such as Scene 1 or Scene 2).

Key points

- You can use the SmartArt feature to easily create a sophisticated diagram that conveys a process or the relationship between hierarchical elements.

- Diagrams are dynamic illustrations you can customize to produce precisely the effect you want.

- You can use a picture diagram to neatly lay out pictures on a page.

- You can insert sophisticated three-dimensional models into documents and position them at the angle you want. You can format 3D models as you can other graphic elements.

Practice tasks

Before you can complete these tasks, you must copy the book's practice files to your computer. The practice files for these tasks are in the **Word365SBS\Ch07** folder. You can save the results of the tasks in the same folder.

The Introduction includes a complete list of practice files and download instructions.

Create diagrams

Open the **CreateDiagrams** document, and then perform the following tasks:

1. Position the cursor below the existing page title.

2. Open the **Choose a SmartArt Graphic** dialog and review the available layouts. Select any layout that interests you to display information about it in the right pane.

3. Display the **Cycle** category of layouts. Select the **Hexagon Radial** layout, and then select **OK** to create the diagram in the document.

4. If the **Text** pane for the SmartArt graphic isn't already open, open it. Notice that the Text pane displays two levels of bullets. The first-level bullet populates the center hexagon, and the second-level bullets populate the six surrounding hexagons.

5. In the **Text** pane, select the first bullet and then enter My Health. The words appear in the center hexagon.

6. In the **Text** pane, select the second bullet, enter Physical, and then press the **Down Arrow** key to move to the third bullet. The word appears in one of the outer hexagons.

7. Repeat step 6 to enter Mental and Emotional in the next two hexagons.

8. In the diagram, select one of the empty outer hexagon shapes, and then select it again to activate the text insertion point. In the hexagon, enter Financial.

9. Repeat step 8 to enter Social and Spiritual in the final two outer hexagons.

10. Save and close the document.

Modify diagrams

Open the **ModifyDiagrams** document, and then perform the following tasks:

1. The Balance diagram on the page displays balance scales that can have up to four shapes stacked on each side. Select the **Balance** diagram. If the **Text** pane doesn't automatically open, open it.

2. In the **Text** pane, click or tap at the end of the word *Family*, and then press **Enter** to create a new second-level bullet and add a corresponding shape to the diagram. Notice that with three shapes on each side, the scale moves to show that the two sides are balanced.

3. In the new shape, enter Sports.

4. From the **SmartArt Design** tab, add a shape to the **Work** side of the diagram. Notice that the scale tips to show that there are more shapes on the **Work** side. In the new shape, enter Household management. Notice that the text resizes to fit the default size of the shape.

5. In the diagram, select the word *Life*. From the **Format** tab, apply a WordArt style of your choice. Then apply a WordArt style to the word *Work*.

6. Select the entire diagram. On the **SmartArt Design** tab, display the **Change Colors** gallery, and select the thumbnail of the color and pattern you want to use.

7. Display the **SmartArt Styles** gallery. Point to each of the thumbnails to display a live preview of the style. Then apply the style you like best.

8. Move the **Troop leader** and **Coach** shapes from the **Work** side of the diagram to the **Life** side. Notice that when there is more content than the shape supports, the unused content is dimmed and preceded by an X.

9. Select the diagram and expand the **Layouts** gallery. Point to each of the other layouts to find one you can use to illustrate this same information. Select the layout you like best.

10. Experiment with any other modifications you'd like to make to the diagram.

11. Save and close the document.

Create picture diagrams

Open the **CreatePictograms** document, and then perform the following tasks:

1. Position the cursor below the existing page title.

2. Open the **Choose a SmartArt Graphic** dialog and select the **Picture** category.

3. Select any picture diagram layout that interests you to display information about it in the right pane.

4. Select the **Bending Picture Blocks** layout, and then select **OK** to insert the diagram in the document.

5. Populate the diagram by inserting the **Chickens**, **Penguins**, and **Tiger** pictures from the practice file folder into the picture placeholders.

6. Enter the corresponding animal names next to the pictures.

7. Add a shape to the diagram. Insert the **Fish** picture and corresponding name in the new shape.

8. Select the four shapes that contain animal names. From the **Format** tab for SmartArt, apply a different shape style.

9. Close the **Text** pane, and then select the **Tiger** picture. From the **Format** tab for pictures, crop the picture so the animal fills the width of the picture shape.

10. Make any other improvements you want to the graphics.

11. From the **SmartArt Design** tab, apply a color set and effects of your choice.

12. Save and close the document.

Insert and modify 3D models

Open the **Create3DModels** document, and then perform the following tasks:

1. From the practice file folder, insert the **Astronaut** and **Globe** 3D models.

2. Experiment with rotating the globe model freely. Notice that you can turn the globe in all directions on its axis.

3. Apply the **Above Front Left** view to the astronaut model.

4. Use the **Pan & Zoom** tools to display only the astronaut's head and shoulders within the drawing object.

5. Delete the astronaut model from the document.

6. From the 3D Model library, insert the animated astronaut 3D model.

7. Apply the different scenes to the animated astronaut.

8. Experiment with ways in which you can work with the animated astronaut and planet within the document.

9. Save and close the document.

Insert and modify charts

You'll often find it helpful to reinforce the argument you make in a document by providing facts and figures. When it's more important for your audience to understand trends than identify precise values, use a chart to present numerical information in visual ways.

You can create a chart directly in a document or import a completed chart from another app. The chart takes on the design elements of the document template and blends in with the rest of the document content. You can modify the chart layout and the included elements to provide the visual imagery that you want.

This chapter guides you through procedures related to creating, modifying, and formatting charts.

In this chapter

- Create charts
- Modify charts
- Format charts

Create charts

Easily add a chart to a document to help identify trends that might not be obvious from looking at numbers. Word 365 has 17 chart categories. Some categories include two-dimensional and three-dimensional variations.

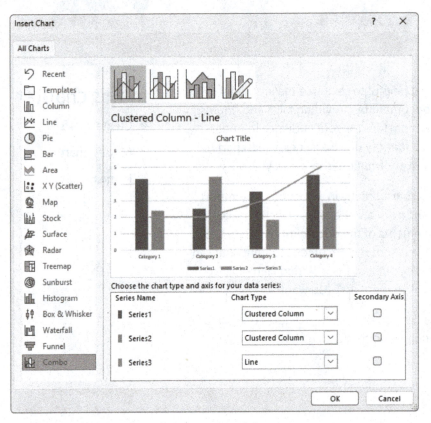

In the Insert Chart dialog, choose from many types of charts

The most frequently used chart categories include:

- **Column**   These charts show how values change over time.

- **Line**   These charts show erratic changes in values over time.

- **Pie**   These charts show how parts relate to the whole.

> 🔍 **SEE ALSO** For information about creating pie charts, see the sidebar "Pie charts" later in this chapter.

- **Bar**   These charts show the values of several items at one point in time.

You can display multiple types of data by creating a combo (combination) chart. Combo charts display multiple data series independently on a common axis.

A combo chart that combines a line chart and a column chart

When you create a chart in Word, you specify the chart type and then Word opens a linked Microsoft Excel worksheet that contains sample data appropriate to the selected chart type. You replace the sample data in the worksheet with your own data, and the chart in the adjacent document window adapts to display your data.

8

> ⚠ **IMPORTANT** The procedures in this chapter assume that you have Excel installed on your computer. If you don't have Excel, the procedures might not work as described.

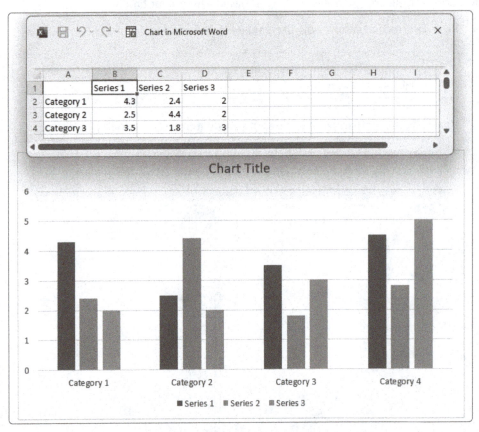

A new chart inserted in a Word document and the chart's associated Excel worksheet

Enter the data directly into the linked worksheet or copy and paste it from an existing Microsoft Access table, Word table, or Excel worksheet.

After you plot the data in the chart, you can move and size the chart to fit the space available on the page, change the flow of text around the chart, and add and remove chart elements to most clearly define the chart content for the audience. You can edit the data in the worksheet at any time—both the values and the column and row headings. Word replots the chart to reflect your changes.

When a chart is active, you work with the chart and its components by using commands from the Chart Design and Format tabs on the ribbon, and the Chart Elements, Chart Styles, and Chart Filters panes that open when you select the corresponding buttons to the right of the chart. The Layout Options button is also available.

> **TIP** The Chart Filters button appears only if it is appropriate for the active chart.

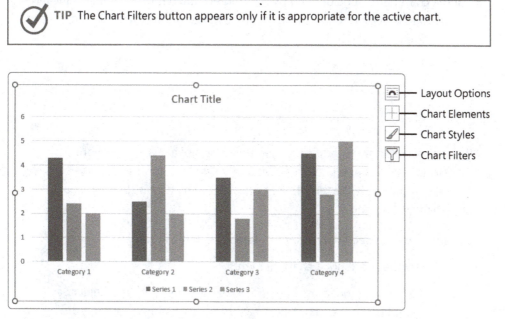

Manage a chart from the ribbon or from option panes

If you decide that the type of chart you initially selected doesn't adequately depict your data, you can change the type at any time.

To create a chart on a page

1. On the **Insert** tab, in the **Illustrations** group, select the **Chart** button.

2. In the left pane of the **Insert Chart** dialog, select a chart category to display the chart variations in the right pane.

3. In the right pane, select the chart type that you want to create, and then select **OK** to insert a sample chart and open its associated Excel worksheet containing the plotted data.

4. In the linked Excel worksheet, enter the values to be plotted, following the pattern of the sample data.

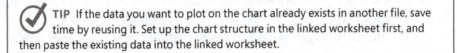

> **TIP** If the data you want to plot on the chart already exists in another file, save time by reusing it. Set up the chart structure in the linked worksheet first, and then paste the existing data into the linked worksheet.

5. If the chart data range defined by the colored outlines doesn't automatically expand to include new data, drag the blue handle in the lower-right corner of the range to expand it.

6. Close the Excel window.

Custom chart templates

If you make extensive modifications to the design of a chart, you might want to save it as a template. Then, when you want to plot similar data in the future, you can apply the template as a custom chart type instead of manually making the changes.

To save a customized chart as a template, follow these steps:

1. Select the chart (not a chart element).

2. Right-click or long-press (tap and hold) the chart, and then select **Save as Template** to open the Save Chart Template dialog displaying the contents of your Charts folder.

TIP The default Charts folder is the *AppData\Roaming\Microsoft\Templates\Charts* subfolder of your user profile folder.

3. Enter a name for the chart template in the **File name** box, and then select **Save**.

You can work with custom chart templates in the following ways:

- To locate a custom chart type, open the **Chart Type** or **Change Chart Type** dialog, and then select **Templates**.

- To delete a custom chart type, display the **Templates** folder in the **Chart Type** or **Change Chart Type** dialog. In the lower-left corner, select **Manage Templates**. Then, in the File Explorer window that opens, right-click the template and select **Delete**.

To insert a chart from Excel onto a page

1. In the source workbook, select the chart border.

2. Copy the chart to the Clipboard.

3. Switch to Word, display the page, and then paste the chart from the Clipboard.

To change the type of a selected chart

1. On the **Chart Design** tab, in the **Type** group, select **Change Chart Type**.

2. In the **Change Chart Type** dialog, select a category on the left and a chart type at the top, and then select **OK**.

> ✓ **TIP** When you select a chart type in the top row, the dialog displays a preview of that chart type as applied to the current data. Point to the preview to display a larger version.

Modify charts

You can modify a chart by changing the data or elements that it displays.

Manage chart data

The Excel worksheet is composed of rows and columns of cells that contain values, which in charting terminology are called *data points*. Collectively, a set of data points is called a *data series*. Each worksheet cell is identified by an address consisting of its column letter and row number—for example, A2. A range of cells is identified by the address of the cell in the upper-left corner and the address of the cell in the lower-right corner, separated by a colon—for example, A2:D5.

By default, a chart is plotted based on the series of data points in the columns of the attached worksheet, and these series are identified in the legend. You can easily switch the chart to base it on the series in the rows instead, or you can select specific cells of the worksheet data to include in the chart.

You can edit the chart data at any time, either in the linked worksheet window or in Excel. The ribbon is available only when you open the worksheet in Excel.

To select a chart for editing

1. Point to a blank area of the chart, outside of the plot area (the rectangular area bordered by the chart axes).

2. When the *Chart Area* ScreenTip appears, click or tap once.

To open the linked chart data worksheet in Word

- Right-click the chart, and then select **Edit Data**.

- Select the chart. Then, on the **Chart Design** tab, in the **Data** group, select the **Edit Data** button (not the arrow).

>  **TIP** The chart must be active (surrounded by a frame) when you make changes to the data in the worksheet; otherwise, the chart won't automatically update.

To open the linked chart data worksheet in Excel

1. In Word, select the chart.

2. On the **Chart Design** tab, in the **Data** group, select the **Edit Data** arrow, and then select **Edit Data in Excel**.

> **TIP** If you open the worksheet in the linked window and then need access to commands on the ribbon, open the worksheet in Excel by selecting the Edit Data In Microsoft Excel button on the Quick Access Toolbar of the linked window.

To switch the data across the category and series axes

1. Open the linked chart data worksheet.

2. In Word, on the **Chart Design** tab, in the **Data** group, select the **Switch Row/Column** button.

> **TIP** The Switch Row/Column button is active only when the linked worksheet is open.

To select worksheet data for editing

- To select a cell, click or tap it.

- To select a column, click or tap the column header (the letter at the top of the column).

- To select a row, click or tap the row header (the number at the left end of the row).

- To select multiple cells, columns, or rows, do either of the following:

  - Select the first element, and then hold down the **Shift** key as you select subsequent elements.

  - Drag through adjacent cells, columns, or rows.

- To select an entire worksheet, select the **Select All** button (the triangle in the upper-left corner of the worksheet, at the intersection of the row and column headers).

To change the area of a worksheet included in the chart

- Drag the blue sizing handle in the lower-right corner of the range to expand or contract it.

Different colors identify the series, categories, and values

To filter the chart to display only specific data

1. Select the chart, and then select the **Chart Filters** button to display the Chart Filters pane. The Chart Filters pane lists all the series and categories in the data set.

   > **TIP** The Chart Filters button appears only if it is appropriate for the active chart.

2. Point to any series or category to emphasize it.

3. Clear the checkboxes of the series or categories you do not want to plot on the chart.

   > **TIP** To select or clear all the checkboxes in a group at once, use the Select All checkbox.

4. At the bottom of the **Chart Filters** pane, select **Apply** to replot the data.

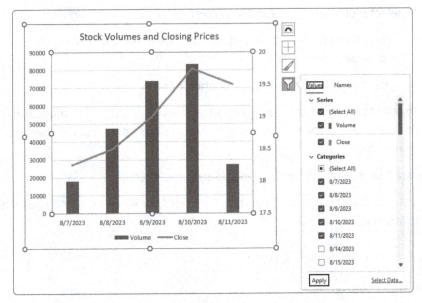

Filtering a chart to display only specific series and categories

5. Select the **Chart Filters** button to close the **Chart Filters** pane.

> **SEE ALSO** For information about working with the Chart Elements button, see "Modify the display of chart elements," next; for information about working with the Chart Styles button, see "Format charts" later in this chapter.

Modify the display of chart elements

Each data point in a data series is represented graphically in the chart by a data marker. The data is plotted against an x-axis (referred to as the *horizontal axis* or *category axis*) and a y-axis (referred to as the *vertical axis* or *value axis*). (Three-dimensional charts also have a z-axis, which is referred to as the *depth axis* or *series axis*.)

The primary components of a chart on a page include the following:

- **Chart area**   The entire area within the chart frame.

- **Plot area**   The rectangular area bordered by the axes.

- **Data markers**   Graphical representations of the values, or data points, of each data series in the linked worksheet.

You can add chart elements to the chart components to help explain the data.

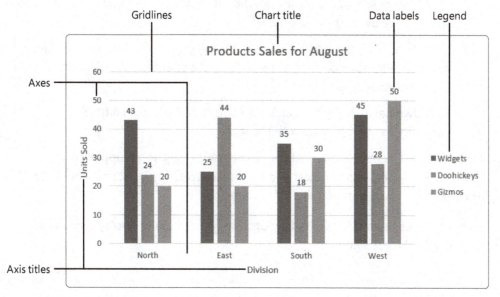

Some default and optional chart elements

The available chart elements include the following:

- **Axes**   These elements control the display of the category and value axis labels, not the display of the data.

- **Axis titles**   These identify the categories, values, or series along each axis.

- **Chart title**   The name by which you identify the chart. The chart title can appear above the chart or overlaid across the center of the chart.

- **Data labels**   These identify the exact values represented by the data markers on the chart. They can be displayed inside or outside of the data markers.

- **Data table**   This table provides details of the plotted data points in table format, essentially mimicking the worksheet. A data table can incorporate a legend.

- **Error bars**   These indicators mark a fixed amount or percentage of deviation from the plotted value for one or more series.

- **Gridlines**   Major and minor horizontal and vertical gridlines identify measurement points along each axis and help to visually quantify the data points.

- **Legend**   This listing correlates the data marker color and name of each data series. The legend can be displayed on any side of the plot area.

- **Lines**   On charts that plot data that doesn't touch the category axis (such as an area chart or line chart), these lines drop from the plotted points to the corresponding value on the category axis.

- **Trendline**   This line marks a value that is calculated on all the series values in a category. It most commonly marks the average of the values but can also be based on other equations.

- **Up/down bars**   These bars indicate the difference between the high and low values for a category of data in a series.

All the chart elements are optional, and some chart types don't support all the elements. For example, a pie chart doesn't display axes or gridlines because they wouldn't be a logical part of that type of data display.

Each chart type has a set of Quick Layouts that you can use to display or position specific sets of chart elements.

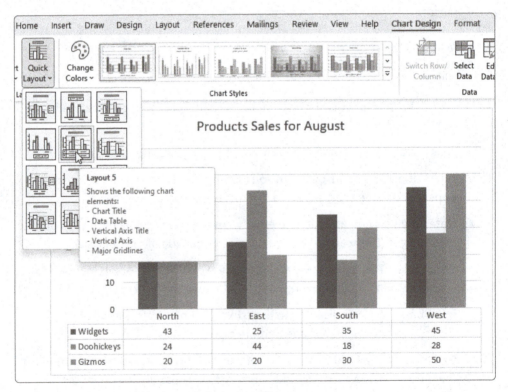

Apply a Quick Layout to quickly change multiple chart elements

The Quick Layouts are preset combinations of the available chart elements. When the preset layouts don't produce the chart you want, you can create a custom layout by mixing and matching different chart elements. You control the display of chart elements from the Add Chart Element menu on the Chart Design tab, and from the Chart Elements pane that opens when you select the Chart Elements button to the right of the chart.

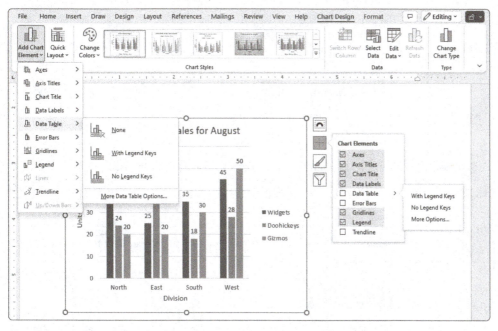

The menu and pane include only chart elements that apply to the current chart type

You can apply the same chart elements from both locations. The Add Chart Element menu provides a bit more visual guidance than the Chart Elements pane but is farther from the chart.

You can adjust a chart layout by adding, deleting, moving, and sizing chart elements. To perform any of those tasks, you must first select the element. The following table describes some of the options available for common chart elements.

Chart element	Options
Axes	Primary Horizontal, Primary Vertical, or both
Axis Titles	Primary Horizontal, Primary Vertical, or both
Chart Title	Above Chart or Centered Overlay
Data Labels	Center, Inside End, Inside Base, Outside End, or Data Callout
Data Table	With Legend Keys or No Legend Keys
Error Bars	Standard Error, Percentage, or Standard Deviation
Gridlines	Primary Major Horizontal, Primary Major Vertical, Primary Minor Horizontal, Primary Minor Vertical, or any combination of the four options
Legend	Right, Top, Left, or Bottom
Lines	Drop Lines or High-Low Lines
Trendline	Linear, Exponential, Linear Forecast, or Moving Average
Up/Down Bars	(On or Off)

TIP Use standard techniques to add pictures, shapes, and independent text boxes to pages to enhance charts.

To apply a preset layout to a chart

- Select the chart. On the **Chart Design** tab, in the **Chart Layouts** gallery, select the **Quick Layout** button, and then select the layout you want.

To display the Add Chart Element menu

- Select the chart. On the **Chart Design** tab, in the **Chart Layouts** group, select the **Add Chart Element** button.

To display the Chart Elements pane

- Select the chart, and then select the **Chart Elements** button that appears to the right of the chart.

To specify which chart elements to display on the chart

1. Select the chart, and then open the **Add Chart Element** menu.

2. On the **Add Chart Element** menu, select the chart element, and then select one or more options to select or clear them.

Or

1. Select the chart, and then open the **Chart Elements** pane.

2. In the **Chart Elements** pane, do either of the following:

   - Clear the checkbox for the chart elements you want to remove from the chart.

   - Select the checkbox for the chart elements you want to open on the chart. Select the arrow that appears to the right of the element to display the options menu for that element, and then select the option you want.

Pie charts

Unlike column, bar, and line charts, which plot at least two series of data points, pie charts plot only one series, with each data point, or *slice*, reflecting a fraction of the whole series. If you plot a multi-series chart and then change the chart type to a pie chart, Word hides all but the first series, retaining the hidden information in case you change back to a chart type capable of showing more than one series. Switch to a different series by selecting the Chart Filters button to the right of the chart, selecting the series you want in the Series area of the Chart Filters pane, and selecting Apply.

When you plot a pie chart, you can use an effective formatting option that isn't available with multi-series chart types. To draw attention to individual data points, you can "explode" the pie by dragging individual slices away from the center. Or double-click a slice to select it and open the Format Data Point pane, where you can set a precise Angle Of First Slice and Point Explosion percentage.

To change the size of a selected chart or chart element

- Point to any sizing handle (the hollow dots around the chart frame), and when the pointer changes to a double-headed arrow, drag in the direction you want the chart to grow or shrink.

> **TIP** If an element cannot be resized, it doesn't have sizing handles when selected.

To change the position of a selected chart element

- Point to the border around the element, away from any handles, and when the four-headed arrow appears, drag the chart to the new location.

To rotate a three-dimensional chart layout

1. Right-click the chart, and then select **3-D Rotation**.

2. In the **3-D Rotation** area of the **Effects** page of the **Format Chart Area** pane, set the angle of rotation for each axis.

Format charts

Quickly format a chart and its individual parts by applying fills, outlines, and effects to the following components:

- **Chart area**   Specify the background fill, the border color and style, effects such as shadows and edges, the three-dimensional format and rotation, and the size and position. You can also attach text to be displayed when someone points to the chart.

- **Plot area**   Specify the background fill, the border color and style, effects such as shadows and edges, and the three-dimensional format and rotation.

- **Data markers**   Specify the background fill, the border color and style, effects such as shadows and edges, and the three-dimensional format. You can also precisely determine the gap between data points.

- **Legend**   Specify the background fill, the border color and style, and effects such as shadows and edges. You can also specify the legend's position and whether it can overlap the chart.

- **Axes**   Specify the background fill, the line color and style, effects such as shadows and edges, and the three-dimensional format and rotation. For the category axis, you can also specify the scale, add or remove tick marks, adjust the label position, and determine the starting and maximum values. You can set the number format (such as currency or percentage), and set the axis label alignment.

- **Gridlines**   Specify the line color, line style, and effects such as shadows and edges.

- **Data table**   Specify the background fill, the border color and style, effects such as shadows and edges, and the three-dimensional format. You can also set table borders.

- **Titles**   Specify the background fill, the border color and style, effects such as shadows and edges, and the three-dimensional format. You can also set the title's alignment, direction, and angle of rotation.

If you don't want to spend a lot of time formatting individual chart elements, you can apply a predefined chart style to create a sophisticated appearance with a minimum of effort. Chart styles affect only the formatting of the chart components and elements; they don't change the presence of the chart elements.

The Chart Styles pane has two pages: Style and Color. From the Style page, you can preview and apply the chart styles. From the Color page, you can change the colors that are used in the chart without affecting other document elements.

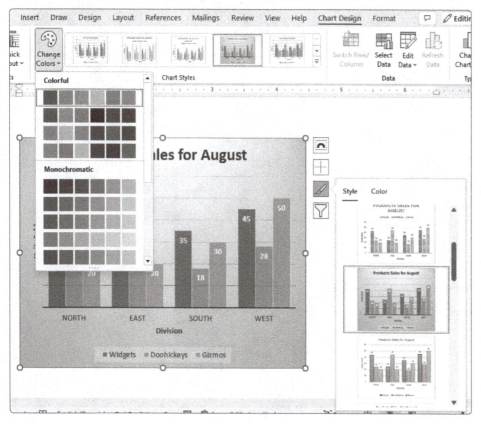

Change the chart colors or style without changing the template

You can apply these same styles and colors from the Chart Styles group on the Chart Design tab. From the Format tab, you can apply shape styles and WordArt styles to chart elements.

You can fine-tune the formatting of a selected chart element in its Format pane. Each type of element has a specific Format pane. Most Format panes have settings that are divided into multiple pages, such as Fill & Line, Effects, Size & Position, and an Options page that is specific to the selected chart element. You can display different options by selecting the elements in the pane header.

Format Axis	Format Axis
Axis Options ∨ Text Options	Axis Options ∨ **Text Options**
◇ ◯ ▦ ▥	**A** A A≡
∨ Axis Options	**∨ Text Fill**
Bounds	○ No fill
Minimum `0.0` Auto	● Solid fill
Maximum `60.0` Auto	○ Gradient fill
Units	○ Picture or texture fill
Major `10.0` Auto	○ Pattern fill
Minor `2.0` Auto	
Horizontal axis crosses	Color ⬦ ▾
● Automatic	Transparency ⊢——— `0%` ↕
○ Axis value `0.0`	**∨ Text Outline**
○ Maximum axis value	● No line
Display units `None` ▾	○ Solid line
☐ Show display units label on chart	○ Gradient line
☐ Logarithmic scale Base `10`	
☐ Values in reverse order	
> Tick Marks	
> Labels	
> Number	

Commands for formatting different elements are on separate pages of the pane

To apply a chart style to a chart

- Select the chart, and then do either of the following:

  - On the **Chart Design** tab, in the **Chart Styles** gallery, select the style you want.

  - Select the **Chart Styles** button, and then on the **Style** page of the **Chart Styles** pane, select the style you want.

To change the colors of chart elements without changing the theme colors

- Select the chart, and then do either of the following:

  - On the **Chart Design** tab, in the **Chart Styles** gallery, select **Change Colors**, and then select the color set you want.

  - To the right of the chart, select the **Chart Styles** button, and then on the **Color** page of the **Chart Styles** pane, select the style you want.

To select a chart component for formatting

- On the chart, click or tap the element once.

- If the element is difficult to identify or select, on the **Format** tab, in the **Current Selection** group, display the **Chart Elements** list, and then select the component you want.

> **TIP** If you want to activate the chart (that is, select the chart area), be sure to click or tap a blank area inside the chart frame. Clicking any of the chart's elements will activate that element, not the chart as a whole.

To apply a preset style to a selected chart component

- On the **Format** tab, in the **Shape Styles** gallery, select the style you want.

To apply a fill color, outline color, or effect to a selected chart component

- On the **Format** tab, in the **Shape Styles** group, select the **Shape Fill**, **Shape Outline**, or **Shape Effects** button, and then select the option you want.

To apply a WordArt style to the text in a selected chart

- On the **Format** tab, in the **WordArt Styles** group, expand the **Quick Styles** gallery if necessary and then select the style you want.

8

To apply WordArt style components to a selected chart component

- In the **WordArt Styles** group, select the **Text Fill**, **Text Outline**, or **Text Effects** button, and then select the option you want.

To open the Format pane for a chart element

- Do any of the following:

  - Double-click the chart element.

  - Right-click the element, and then select **Format Element**.

  - At the top of an open **Format** pane, select the downward-pointing triangle to the right of the **Options** label, and then select an element to open that Format pane.

- If you have trouble double-clicking a smaller chart element, on the **Format** tab, in the **Current Selection** group, display the **Chart Elements** list, and then select the element you want.

> **TIP** To open the Format Major Gridlines pane, right-click any gridline, and then select Format Gridlines. To open the Format Data Table pane, right-click the selected data table, and then select Format Data Table.

Key points

- A chart is often the most efficient way to present numeric data with at-a-glance clarity.

- You can select the type of chart and change the appearance of its elements until it clearly conveys key information.

- Existing data in a Word table, Excel workbook, Access database, or other structured source can easily be copied and pasted into the associated chart worksheet, eliminating time-consuming typing.

Practice tasks

Before you can complete these tasks, you must copy the book's practice files to your computer. The practice files for these tasks are in the **Word365SBS\Ch08** folder. You can save the results of the tasks in the same folder.

The Introduction includes a complete list of practice files and download instructions.

Create charts

Open the **CreateCharts** document, and then perform the following tasks:

1. Position the cursor in the blank paragraph below the *Regional Averages* heading.

2. Insert a chart, using the **3-D Clustered Column** chart type (the fourth chart from the left in the **Column** category).

3. In the linked chart data worksheet, select and delete all the sample data, leaving only the colors that identify the series, categories, and values.

4. In cell **B1**, enter March. Then press the **Tab** key to enter the heading on the chart and move to the next cell of the worksheet.

> **TIP** To move within the plotted data, press Tab to move to the right in the same row, Shift+Tab to move to the left, Enter to move down in the column (or to the beginning of a data entry series), or Shift+Enter to move up.

5. In cells **C1** through **E1**, enter June, September, and December.

> **TIP** If you were entering a sequential list of months, you could enter *January* and then drag the fill handle in the lower-right corner of the cell to the right to fill subsequent cells in the same row with the names of the months.

When you enter *December*, notice that it's outside of the table data area and doesn't appear on the chart in the document. You'll fix this in the next practice task.

6. In cells **A2** through **A4**, enter Minimum, Average, and Maximum, pressing the **Enter** key between entries.

7. In cell **B2**, enter 37, and press **Tab**. Notice that a corresponding column appears in the chart.

8. In cells **C2** through **E2**, enter 54, 53, and 29, pressing **Tab** to move from cell to cell. After you enter the last number, press **Enter** to move to cell **B3**.

9. Enter the following data into the chart worksheet, noticing as you enter data that the chart columns and scale change to reflect the data.

	B	C	D	E
3	47	67	66	35
4	56	80	70	41

10. Close the **Chart in Microsoft Word** window.

    Notice that the temperatures on the chart are grouped by category rather than by month, and the December temperatures are missing. You'll fix these issues in the next practice task.

11. Open the **Temperatures** workbook from the practice file folder in Excel. Select the chart on the worksheet and copy it to the Clipboard.

12. Return to the **CreateCharts** document. Position the cursor in the blank paragraph after the *Local Averages* heading, and then paste the chart from the Clipboard into the document. Notice that the chart takes on the color scheme of the document.

13. The chart type used for this data, Stacked Column, sums the minimum, average, and maximum temperatures for each month.

14. Change the chart type of the *Local Averages* chart to **Line with Markers** (the fourth chart from the left in the **Line** category) to display the three temperature series individually.

15. Save and close the document. Then close the workbook.

Modify charts

Open the **ModifyCharts** document, and then perform the following tasks:

1. Select the chart and open the linked chart data worksheet in Word.

2. In the worksheet, drag the blue handle so that the colored cells include only those that contain content (A1:E4). Notice that the December data appears in the chart.

3. In the document, select the chart. Then switch the data across the category and series axes to display the temperatures in groups by month.

4. In the worksheet, change the text in cells **B1:E1** to Spring, Summer, Fall, and Winter. Then close the linked chart data worksheet.

5. Open the **Chart Filters** pane, and then do the following:

   a. Point to each item in the **Series** and **Category** areas of the pane to high-light those values on the chart.

   b. Clear all the checkboxes in the **Series** area, and then select only the **Average** checkbox.

   c. Select **Apply** to modify the chart.

6. Repeat step 5 to display only the **Minimum** and **Maximum** series values.

7. From the **Quick Layout** gallery on the **Chart Design** tab, apply **Layout 9** to the chart. Notice that this adds a chart title, axis titles, and a legend to the chart area.

8. Add the following elements to the chart:

   • Primary Minor Horizontal gridlines

   • Data labels

   > **TIP** You can add data labels to the chart only from the Chart Elements pane, not from the Add Chart Elements menu.

9. Remove the horizontal **Axis Title** placeholder from the chart.

10. Replace the vertical **Axis Title** placeholder with Degrees Fahrenheit.

11. Replace the **Chart Title** placeholder with Regional Averages.

12. Select the legend. Drag its top border to align with the top horizontal gridline, and its bottom border to align with the bottom horizontal gridline. Notice that the legend entries move to fill the space.

13. Drag the chart title to the right so that it right-aligns with the legend. Then click or tap outside the chart to view the results.

14. Experiment with any other chart modification procedures that interest you. Then save and close the document.

Format charts

Open the **FormatCharts** document, and then perform the following tasks:

1. Select the chart. From the **Chart Styles** gallery on the **Chart Design** tab, apply **Style 8** to the chart. Notice that the legend changes location.

2. Change the colors of the chart elements to the **Monochromatic Palette 9** color set without affecting the document theme.

3. Select the legend. From the **Shape Styles** gallery on the **Format** tab, apply a **Moderate Effect** (5th line) of your choice.

4. Select the chart title. From the **WordArt Styles** gallery, apply a WordArt style of your choice. Then change the fill and outline colors and add a shadow effect if the WordArt style doesn't already have one.

5. Select the vertical axis title, and change the font size to **12** points.

6. Select the plot area (not the chart area) and double-click it to open its Format pane. In the **Format Plot Area** pane, explore the various options that are available for formatting this component.

7. At the top of the pane, select the downward-pointing arrow next to **Plot Area Options**, and select another chart component or element to display its Format pane.

8. Experiment with any other chart formatting procedures that interest you. Then save and close the document.

Format document elements

You've already explored some of the more common graphic elements that you can add to a document, such as pictures, diagrams, and charts. These elements reinforce concepts or help make a document more visually appealing. You can also add other types of visual elements, such as document page backgrounds, which can be colors, textures, patterns, or pictures; and watermarks, which display text or an image behind the text on each page.

You can draw attention to specific information and add graphic appeal by incorporating preformatted document parts, also called *building blocks* or *Quick Parts*, into a document. These are combinations of drawing objects (and sometimes pictures) in a variety of formatting styles that you can select to insert elements such as cover pages, quotations pulled from the text (called *pull quotes*), and sidebars. Many of the built-in building blocks have graphic elements that coordinate with Office themes to add an extra visual impact to your document. You can use themed header, footer, and page number building blocks to provide useful information to readers, or you can create these page elements from scratch.

This chapter guides you through procedures related to formatting the page background; inserting a background watermark; inserting headers, footers, and page numbers; and inserting preformatted document parts.

In this chapter

- Format the page background
- Insert a background watermark
- Insert headers, footers, and page numbers
- Insert preformatted document parts

Format the page background

Whether you're creating a document that will be printed, viewed on a computer, or published on the internet and viewed in a web browser, you can make the document pages stand out by changing the page background. You can configure a solid color background or apply any of the following effects:

- **Gradient** Select a premade gradient or choose two colors and the direction you want the gradient to flow—for example, horizontal, diagonal down, or from the center—to have Word blend them for you.

Configure fill effects with multiple colors and in a variety of directions

- **Texture** Word offers 24 predefined textures, including textures designed to resemble papyrus, denim, woven mat, water droplets, granite, cork, and wood. In addition to these, you can apply textures saved as image files on your own computer, and even locate additional textures online.

A page with the Water Droplets texture applied to the background

- **Pattern**   Word offers a variety of predefined patterns, such as polka dots, stripes, and checkerboards—and even plaid. In addition to choosing a pattern, you select a foreground and background color.

Word provides a preview of the selected effect in the Sample box

9

TIP When you use a texture or pattern background, Word configures it to repeat seamlessly across the page.

- **Picture**   Use a picture from your computer or any connected online storage locations as the document background.

Use any photo as the page background

Insert a background picture from the Texture tab or Picture tab of the Fill Effects dialog, though with slightly different results. Inserting an image from the Texture tab adds it to the Texture gallery.

Another way to change the background of your document is to apply a border. This is a good way to provide some definition to your document. Word offers several border styles from which to choose, including Box, Shadow, 3-D, and more. You can also change the style, color, and thickness of the border. For a bit more pizzazz, apply an Art border. Options include borders made of stars, suns, flowers, and more.

A blank page with an art border applied

When it comes to backgrounds, the trick is to not overdo it. The effects should be subtle enough that they do not interfere with the text or other elements on the page or make the document difficult to read.

> ✅ **TIP** To make it easier to see the effect of your background changes on your document, display the whole page in the app window by selecting the One Page button in the Zoom group on the View tab.

To apply a solid background color

1. On the **Design** tab, in the **Page Background** group, select the **Page Color** button.

2. On the **Page Color** menu, do either of the following:

   - In the **Theme Colors** or **Standard Colors** palette, select a color swatch.

   - Select **More Colors**, use the commands in the **Colors** dialog to select a custom color, and then select **OK**.

To configure a preset gradient page background

1. On the **Page Color** menu, select **Fill Effects** to display the Gradient tab of the Fill Effects dialog.

2. In the **Colors** area, select **Preset**.

3. Under **Preset colors**, select a background. The Variants and Sample areas change to show variations of the background.

4. In the **Shading styles** area, select the options to observe their effects in the Variants and Sample areas, and then select the shading style you want.

5. Select **OK**.

To configure a gradient color page background

1. Display the **Gradient** tab of the **Fill Effects** dialog.

2. In the **Colors** area, select **One color** or **Two colors**.

3. In the color palette or palettes, select the colors you want to use. The Variants and Sample areas change to show variations of the background.

4. If you selected a one-color gradient, drag the **Darkness** slider until the colors in the Sample area look the way you want.

5. In the **Shading styles** area, select the options to observe their effects in the Variants and Sample areas, and then select a shading style.

6. Select **OK**.

To configure a textured page background

1. Display the **Texture** tab of the **Fill Effects** dialog.

2. In the texture gallery, select the options to observe their effects in the Sample area, and then select a texture swatch.

3. Select **OK**.

To configure a patterned page background

1. Display the **Pattern** tab of the **Fill Effects** dialog.

2. In the **Foreground** and **Background** color charts, select the colors you want to use for the pattern.

3. In the pattern gallery, select the options to observe their effects in the Sample area, and then select a pattern tile.

4. Select **OK**.

To configure a picture page background

1. Display the **Picture** tab of the **Fill Effects** dialog.

2. Select the **Select Picture** button to open the Insert Pictures dialog. Then do one of the following:

   - In the **From a file** area, select **Browse**. Then locate and select the picture you want to use and select **Insert**.

   - In the **Bing Image Search** area, enter a search word or phrase in the search box and press **Enter**. A dialog containing pictures that match the word or phrase you entered appears; select the picture you want to use and select **Insert**.

   - In the **OneDrive** area, select **Browse**. Then locate and select the picture you want to use and select **Insert**.

3. Select **OK**.

> ⚠️ **IMPORTANT** Word fills the page with as much of the picture as will fit. If one copy of the picture doesn't completely fill the page, Word inserts another copy, effectively "tiling" the image. If the picture is particularly large, only a portion of it will be visible. If you want to display the entire picture, resize it in a graphics app and then reselect it as the page background.

To remove the page background

1. On the **Design** tab, in the **Page Background** group, select the **Page Color** button.

2. On the **Page Color** menu, select **No Color**.

To apply a simple border

1. In the **Page Background** group, select the **Page Borders** button to display the Page Border page of the Borders And Shading dialog.

2. In the **Setting** area of the **Borders and Shading** dialog, select the type of border you want.

3. In the **Style**, **Color**, **Width**, and **Art** boxes, select the options you want.

4. When the border in the **Preview** box looks the way you want, select **OK**.

9

Insert a background watermark

A *watermark* is a faint text or graphic image that appears on the page behind the main content of a document. A common use of a text watermark is to indicate a status such as *DRAFT* or *CONFIDENTIAL*.

Simple Room Design

With the Room Planner, you'll never make a design mistake again. Created by acclaimed interior designers to simplify the redecorating process, this planning tool incorporates elements of color, dimension, and style to guide your project. It includes a furniture location guide; room grid; drawing tools; and miniature furniture, rugs, accessories, and color swatches that match our large in-store selection. Here's how to use the planner to create the room of your dreams!

Look at how your home is decorated and note the things you like and dislike. Pay special attention to the color scheme and to how each room "feels" to you. Is it inviting? Does it feel comfortable? Does it relax you or does it invigorate you?

Focus on the room(s) you would most like to change. Brainstorm all the things you would change in that room if you could. Don't give a thought to any financial considerations; just let your imagination go wild! It might be helpful to write down all the negatives and positives. You don't need to come up with solutions all at once. Just be clear on what you like and what you hate about that room.

Visit our showroom and purchase a Room Planner. While you're there, look around and see what really appeals to you. Sometimes entire rooms are designed around just one or two special pieces, so don't be afraid to fall in love with something that doesn't seem to fit into your overall scheme. Go with what you love, and the rest will fall into place.

Take your Room Planner home and get to work! Adjust the planner so that it models the room dimensions. Don't forget to place the windows and doors. Arrange the furniture placeholders to mirror how your room is currently set up. Add the current colors, too.

This is where the fun begins! Start changing things around a bit. Move the furniture, add different colors, and watch the room come together! Here's where you can tell if that rich red rug you saw in the showroom enhances or overwhelms your room. What about that overstuffed chair that caught your eye? Place a furniture or accessory shape, and then color it. Does it look great or is it too jarring? Change the color... does that help? Don't forget about the walls. Try different colors to see the effect on the room overall.

When you're sure you have the right look and feel, take a break. Put the planner away and sleep on your design for a day or two. Then review it again. Does it still look perfect, or is something not quite right? You might need to "live" with the new plan for a few days, especially if you've made big changes. When everything feels just right to you, you're ready for the next big step!

Come back to the store. Look again at the pieces you liked during your last visit and see if you still love them. If you're not quite sure, go back to your planner for a little more tweaking. If you are sure, take a look around the store one more time to see if anything else catches your eye. Then make your

Text watermarks can be any color

Word offers various predefined text watermarks, including CONFIDENTIAL, DO NOT COPY, and URGENT watermarks. These watermarks can be positioned diagonally or horizontally on the page. Additional predefined text watermarks are available from Office.com.

In addition, you can create a custom text watermark that features whatever text you like. For example, you might create a text watermark that includes the name of your organization. When you create a custom text watermark, you can select the font, size, and color of the text, whether it appears diagonally or horizontally, and whether it is solid or semitransparent.

If you want to dress up the pages of your document without taking attention from the main text, you might consider displaying a graphic watermark, such as a company logo or an image that subtly reinforces your message. Watermarks are visible in printed and online documents, but because they are faint, they don't interfere with the display of the document's main text.

Use a picture, such as a company or team logo, as a watermark

By default, the Watermark feature adds a watermark to all pages of your document except the title page (if the document includes a title page). If you want to add the watermark to only specific pages, you can do so by adding it in the header or footer defined for those pages.

To add a predefined watermark to a document

1. Open the document to which you want to add a watermark.

2. On the **Design** tab, in the **Page Background** group, select the **Watermark** button to display the Watermark gallery and menu.

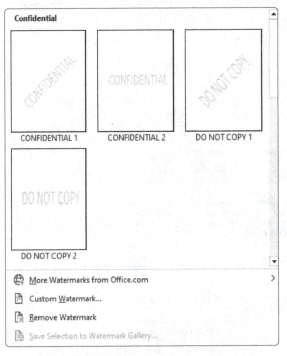

The predefined watermark categories are Confidential, Disclaimers, and Urgent

3. In the gallery, select a watermark to insert it in light gray on every page of the document.

> **TIP** Since the beginning of this book series, the More Watermarks From Office.com menu item has provided access to no additional online content.

To add a custom text watermark

1. On the **Watermark** menu, select **Custom Watermark** to open the Printed Watermark dialog.

2. Select **Text watermark**.

3. If necessary, in the **Language** list, select the language you want.

4. In the **Text** box, enter the text you want to appear in your watermark.

5. In the **Font**, **Size**, and **Color** boxes, choose the options you want.

6. If you want to reduce the opacity of the watermark color, select the **Semitransparent** checkbox.

7. In the **Layout** area, select either **Diagonal** or **Horizontal**.

Configure a custom picture or text watermark

8. Do either of the following:

    *   Select **Apply** to apply the watermark to the document but leave the dialog open so that you can review the effect and make adjustments if you want.

    *   Select **OK** to apply the watermark and close the dialog.

To add a picture watermark to a document

1. Open the **Printed Watermark** dialog and select **Picture watermark**.

2. Select the **Select Picture** button to open the Insert Pictures window. Then do one of the following:

   - To use a picture from your computer or a connected storage drive, in the **From a file** area, select **Browse** to open the Insert Picture dialog.

   - To use a picture from your connected OneDrive cloud storage, in the **OneDrive** area, select **Browse**.

   - To use a picture that appears in an online search, in the **Bing Image Search** area, enter a word or phrase in the search box and press **Enter** to display pictures that match the search term.

3. Locate and select the picture you want to use, and then select **Insert**.

4. In the **Printed Watermark** dialog, in the **Scale** list, select the scale you want to use.

> ✓ **TIP** If you're not sure what scale to choose, select Auto. Word will scale the picture automatically.

5. If you want the picture to appear washed out, select the **Washout** checkbox.

6. Do either of the following:

   - Select **Apply** to apply the watermark to the document but leave the dialog open, so that you can review the effect and make adjustments if you want.

   - Select **OK** to apply the watermark and close the dialog.

To add a watermark to every other page of a document

1. Open the document header or footer.

2. On the **Header & Footer** tab, in the **Options** group, select the **Different Odd & Even Pages** checkbox.

3. Move to any odd or even page header or footer.

4. Follow the procedure to insert a predefined, custom text, or picture watermark.

5. On the **Header & Footer** tab, in the **Close** group, select **Close Header & Footer**.

> **SEE ALSO** For information about working with document headers and footers, see the next topic, "Insert headers, footers, and page numbers." For information about working with document sections, see "Control what appears on each page" in Chapter 12, "Finalize and distribute documents."

To add a watermark to specific pages of a document

1. Insert section breaks at the beginning and end of the document content for which you want to display the watermark. Use a continuous section break or a section break that creates a page break.

2. Open the header or footer within the section you want to watermark.

3. On the **Header & Footer** tab, in the **Navigation** group, ensure that **Link to Previous** is not selected for the current section or the one that follows it.

4. Position the cursor in the header or footer of the section you want to watermark.

5. Follow the procedure to insert a predefined, custom text, or picture watermark.

6. Scroll through the document to ensure that the watermark appears in only the intended section.

7. On the **Header & Footer** tab, in the **Close** group, select **Close Header & Footer**.

To remove a watermark

- Display the **Watermark** menu and select **Remove Watermark**.

Insert headers, footers, and page numbers

You can display information on every page of a document in regions at the top and bottom of a page by selecting a style from the Header or Footer gallery. Word displays dotted borders to indicate the header and footer areas, and displays a Design tab on the ribbon. You can enter and format information in the header and footer by using the same techniques you do in the document body and by using commands on the Design tab.

Headers and footers are highly customizable. You can have a different header and footer on the first page of a document and different headers and footers on odd and even pages. You can manually insert text or graphic elements in a header or footer, select common elements (such as page number, date and time, or a document property) from a menu, or insert a preformatted building block. (For more information about building blocks, see the next topic, "Insert preformatted document parts.") You can also mix different headers, footers, and document themes to create a document that has the look and feel you want.

Headers and footers can include any information you want to display

> **TIP** If your document contains section breaks, each successive section inherits the headers and footers of the preceding section unless you break the link between the two sections. You can then create a different header and footer for the current section. For information about sections, see "Control what appears on each page" in Chapter 12.

It's common to insert page numbers in a document that will be printed. You can manually insert a page number element in a header or footer or use one of the many predefined header, footer, or page number objects Word provides on the Design tab for headers and footers. These predefined page number options insert the number in the header, footer, left margin, or right margin. They may also include the word "Page," document properties such as the title or total number of pages, and themed graphic elements.

To insert custom header or footer content

1. Activate the header or footer by using either of these methods:

   - Position the cursor anywhere in the document. On the **Insert** tab, in the **Header & Footer** group, select the **Header** button or the **Footer** button, and then select the corresponding **Edit** command on the menu.

   - In Print Layout view, double-click in the top margin of a page to activate the header or in the bottom margin to activate the footer.

2. In the header or footer area, do any of the following:

   - Insert and format content by using the standard commands.

   - From the **Insert** group on the **Design** tab, insert the date, time, an image, or document information you want to include.

   - Use the preset tabs to align content at the left margin, in the center, and at the right margin, or modify the tabs to meet your needs.

3. In the **Close** group, select the **Close Header and Footer** button.

> ⚠ **IMPORTANT** If your document includes a cover page, the header or footer should first appear on the second page of the file and display page number 1. Cover pages are counted separately from document pages.

To insert a preformatted header or footer

1. On the **Insert** tab, in the **Header & Footer** group, select the **Header** button or the **Footer** button.

2. In the **Header** gallery or the **Footer** gallery, select the design you want.

9

3. Replace any text placeholders and enter any other information you want to appear.

4. In the **Close** group, select **Close Header and Footer**.

To insert the current date or time in a header or footer

1. In the header or footer, position the cursor where you want the date or time to appear.

2. On the **Header & Footer** tab, in the **Insert** group, select the **Date & Time** button (the ScreenTip shows Insert Date and Time).

3. In the **Date and Time** dialog, do the following, and then select **OK**:

   - Select the format in which you want the date or time to appear in the header or footer.

   - If you want Word to update the date or time in the header each time you save the document, select the **Update automatically** checkbox.

To navigate among headers and footers

- Click or tap in the header or footer area, and then on the **Header & Footer** tab, in the **Navigation** group, do any of the following:

   - Select the **Go to Header** button to move the cursor to the header area at the top of the page.

   - Select the **Go to Footer** button to move the cursor to the footer area at the bottom of the page.

   - Select the **Next** button to move to the header or footer area of the next section.

   - Select the **Previous** button to move to the header or footer area of the previous section.

To modify standard header or footer settings

1. On the **Header & Footer** tab, in the **Options** group, do any of the following:

   - Select the **Different First Page** checkbox if you want to use a different header or footer on the first page of the document. You might want to do this if, for example, the first page of the document is a cover page.

- Select the **Different Odd & Even Pages** checkbox if you want to use different headers or footers for odd pages and for even pages. Select this option if the content of the header or footer is not centered and the document content will be viewed on facing pages.

- Clear the **Show Document Text** checkbox if you find that you're distracted by the main document text when working in the header or footer.

2. In the **Position** group, set the **Header from Top** or **Footer from Bottom** distance.

3. In the **Close** group, select the **Close Header and Footer** button.

To change the format of page numbers

1. On the **Insert** tab or **Header & Footer** tab (when the header or footer is active), in the **Header & Footer** group, select the **Page Number** button, and then select **Format Page Numbers**.

2. In the **Page Number Format** dialog, in the **Number format** list, select the format you want.

3. Select any other options you want, and then select **OK**.

To insert a page number building block independently of a header or footer

1. On the **Insert** tab, in the **Header & Footer** group, select the **Page Number** button.

2. On the **Page Number** menu, select one of the following to display building blocks with page numbers in those locations:

   - Top of Page

   - Bottom of Page

   - Page Margins

   - Current Position

3. Scroll through the submenu to review the available page number building blocks, and then select the one you want to insert.

To delete a header or footer

■ Activate the header or footer. Press **Ctrl+A** to select all the content of the header or footer, and then press the **Delete** key.

■ On the **Insert** tab, in the **Header & Footer** group, select **Header** or **Footer**, and then select the corresponding **Remove** command.

9

Insert preformatted document parts

To simplify the creation of professional-looking text elements, Word 365 comes with ready-made visual representations of text, known as *building blocks*, which are available from various groups on the Insert tab. Headers and footers, which were covered in the previous topic, are one type of building block.

In addition to inserting headers and footers, you can insert the following types of building blocks:

- **Cover page** Quickly add a formatted cover page to a document such as a report by selecting a style from the Cover Page gallery. The cover page includes text placeholders for elements such as a title so that you can customize the page to reflect the content of the document.

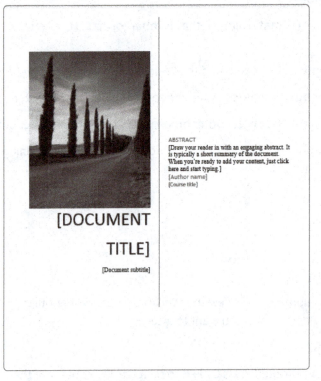

Add document-specific information to the basic cover page

- **Text box**   To reinforce key concepts and also alleviate the monotony of page after page of plain text, insert text boxes such as sidebars and quote boxes by selecting a style from the Text Box gallery. The formatted text box includes placeholder text that you replace with your own.

> With the Room Planner, you'll never make a design mistake again. Created by acclaimed interior designers to simplify the redecorating process, this planning tool incorporates elements of color, dimension, and style to guide your project. It includes a furniture location guide; room grid; drawing tools; and miniature furniture, rugs, accessories, and color swatches that match our large in-store selection. Here's how to use the planner to create the room of your dreams!
>
> Look at how your home is decorated and note the things you like and dislike. Pay special attention to the color scheme and to how each room "feels" to you. Is it inviting? Does it feel comfortable? Does it relax you or does it invigorate you?
>
> [GRAB YOUR READER'S ATTENTION WITH A GREAT QUOTE FROM THE DOCUMENT OR USE THIS SPACE TO EMPHASIZE A KEY POINT. TO PLACE THIS TEXT BOX ANYWHERE ON THE PAGE, JUST DRAG IT.]
> [Cite your source here.]
>
> Focus on the room(s) you would most like to change. Brainstorm all the things you would change in that room if you could. Don't give a thought to any financial considerations; just let your imagination go wild! It might be helpful to write down all the negatives and positives. You don't need to come up with solutions all at once. Just be clear on what you like and what you hate about that room.
>
> Visit our showroom and purchase a Room Planner. While you're there, look around and see what really appeals to you. Sometimes entire rooms are designed around just one or two special pieces, so don't be afraid to fall in love with something that doesn't seem to fit into your overall scheme. Go with what you love, and the rest will fall into place.

Placeholder text provides instructions

Most building blocks include text fields that contain placeholders for information. For example, a cover page building block might contain placeholders for the date, title, subtitle, author name, company name, or company address. You can replace this text by selecting it and then typing over it with text of your own. For example, you can replace the Document Title placeholder text on a cover page with the actual title of your document.

> **TIP** If any of the required information—such as Author—is already saved with the properties of the document into which you're inserting the cover page, Word inserts the saved information instead of the placeholders. For information about document properties, see "Prepare documents for electronic distribution" in Chapter 12.

Of course, you're not restricted to the default contents of the building block. You can change the building block in any way that you want to—altering the text and various visual elements. For example, if you insert a text box building block, you can change the box's size and other characteristics by using the Format tab that appears when the box is selected. Think of the building box as a convenient starting point.

You can display all available building blocks in the Building Blocks Organizer dialog. The left pane of this dialog displays a complete list of all the building blocks available on your computer. Selecting a building block in the left pane displays a preview in the right pane, along with its description and behavior.

The Building Blocks Organizer includes all available building blocks

Initially, the building blocks are organized by type, as reflected in the Gallery column. If you want to insert building blocks of the same design in a document—for example, a cover page, footer, header, quote box, and sidebar all in the Whisp design—you might want to select the Name column heading to sort the list alphabetically by design name. Some elements, such as bibliographies, equations, tables of contents, tables, and watermarks, are not part of a design family and have their own unique names.

You can display a dialog containing all the information about a selected building block in a more readable format. To do so, select the building block you want to learn more about, and then select the Edit Properties button in the lower-left corner of the Building Blocks Organizer dialog. Although you can use this dialog to change the properties associated with any building block, be cautious when doing so. If you change the properties assigned to a building block that came with Word, you might accidentally render it unusable.

The Modify Building Block dialog

If you frequently use a specific element in your documents, such as a formatted title-subtitle-author arrangement at the beginning of reports, you can define it as a custom building block. It will then become available from the Quick Parts gallery.

> **SEE ALSO** For information about saving frequently used text as a building block, see "Create custom building blocks" in Chapter 15, "Create custom document elements."

To display all available building blocks

- On the **Insert** tab, in the **Text** group, select the **Quick Parts** button, and then select **Building Blocks Organizer** to open the Building Blocks Organizer dialog.

To insert and modify a cover page

1. On the **Insert** tab, in the **Pages** group, select the **Cover Page** button to display the gallery of available cover pages.

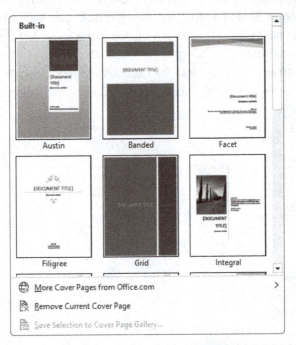

Thumbnails display cover page designs and standard text layout

2. Scroll through the **Cover Page** gallery to display the available options, and then select a thumbnail to insert the cover page at the beginning of the document.

3. Select a placeholder, select the arrow that appears, and then do either of the following:

   - Enter the text you want to use for the selected placeholder. As you enter the text, its appearance on the page reflects the character formatting applied to the placeholder.

   - If a control appears, such as for the date, use the control to enter the information required.

To insert a text box building block

1. On the **Insert** tab, in the **Text** group, select the **Text Box** button to display the available text box building blocks.

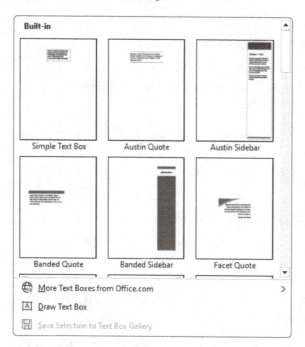

Predefined text boxes share graphic elements with themes

2. Scroll through the gallery to review the available text boxes, and then select the one you want to insert.

Insert and link custom text boxes

If you prefer to start from scratch rather than using one of the preformatted text box building blocks, you can draw and format your own text box. Here's how:

1. On the **Insert** tab, select **Text Box**, and then select **Draw Text Box**.

2. Drag to draw a box of the approximate size you want anywhere on the page.

3. Enter the text and format it the way you would any other text.

4. Optionally, select the text box frame and format the text box shape, outline, fill, and other properties by using the commands on the **Format** tab.

When a text box has a solid border, you can reposition it by dragging it to another location or by pressing the arrow keys. You can rotate it by dragging the rotate handle and change its size by dragging the size handles around its frame.

You can link text boxes so that text flows from one to the next. To do so:

1. Ensure that the second text box is empty.

2. Select the first text box.

3. On the **Format** tab, in the **Text** group, select **Create Link**. The pointer shape changes to a pitcher.

4. Point to the second text box. When the pointer changes to a pouring pitcher, click or tap once.

Text boxes are not accessible to adaptive technologies, so if you want to ensure that a text-reading program can access the content of your document, do not use a text box.

Key points

- A background color, texture, pattern, or picture can really give a document pizzazz, but be careful that it doesn't overwhelm the text.

- By using a watermark, you can flag every page of a document with a faint word, such as "Confidential," or a faint picture. Watermarks appear behind the text of the document, so the text can still be read.

- Word comes with predefined building blocks that you can use to quickly add graphic elements to a document.

9

Practice tasks

Before you can complete these tasks, you must copy the book's practice files to your computer. The practice files for these tasks are in the **Word365SBS\Ch09** folder. You can save the results of the tasks in the same folder.

The Introduction includes a complete list of practice files and download instructions.

Format the page background

Create a new document in Word, and then perform the following tasks.

1. Apply a solid page background color of your choice.

2. Configure the page background to display a gradient, using any two colors of your choice and the **From Center** shading.

3. Configure the page background to display the **Woven Mat** texture.

4. Configure the page background to display the **Light Horizontal** pattern, using any two colors of your choice.

5. Configure the page background to display the **Clouds** picture from the practice file folder.

6. Remove the page background.

7. Apply a dark blue, double-line **Shadow** page border that is ½ **pt** wide.

8. Save and close the document.

Insert a background watermark

Open the **AddWatermarks** document in Print Layout view, and then perform the following tasks:

1. Apply the **ASAP 2** watermark, and then remove it.

2. Create a text watermark with the text First Draft.

3. Style the watermark with the **Century Gothic** font and make it red, semitransparent, and horizontal.

4. Remove the watermark.

5. Begin creating a picture watermark.

6. Use the commands in the **Insert Pictures** dialog to locate and insert the **Logo.jpeg** picture from the practice file folder.

7. Select a scale of **500%**, select the **Washout** checkbox, and select **OK**.

8. Save and close the document.

Insert headers, footers, and page numbers

Open the **InsertHeadersFooters** document in Print Layout view, and then perform the following tasks:

1. Move the cursor to the top of the first page after the cover page.

2. Insert a **Banded** header from the built-in headers menu. Notice that the document title appears in the header automatically.

3. Add a built-in **Banded** footer. Notice that page numbers appear in the footer automatically, and that page numbering begins on the first page after the cover page.

4. Remove the footer, leaving the header in place.

5. Re-create the footer and, at the left end of the footer, insert a date that will update automatically. Use the date format of your choice.

6. Press the **Tab** key twice to move the cursor to the right end of the footer, and then add page numbers in the current position in the **Large Color** style. Notice that the color matches the theme color of the document.

7. In the **Close** group, select the **Close Header and Footer** button.

8. Save and close the document.

Insert preformatted document parts

Open the **InsertBuildingBlocks** document in Print Layout view, and then perform the following tasks:

1. Move the cursor to the top of the document.

2. Add a **Banded** cover page, select the **Document Title** placeholder, and enter Office Procedures.

3. If your name has not been entered automatically in the author placeholder, select the placeholder and enter your name.

4. Select the **Company Name** placeholder and enter Consolidated Messenger.

5. Select the **Company Address** placeholder and enter 1234 Main Street, New York, NY, 90012.

6. On page **2** of the document, to the left of the *Warehouse* heading, insert a **Banded Quote** text box.

7. Select the placeholder text and type Consolidated Messenger believes in opportunity for all! We are an equal-opportunity employer. Then click or tap anywhere outside the text box building block.

8. Save and close the document.

Organize and arrange content

Word provides many tools for organizing and arranging the content of a document. For example, you can use outlining tools to display the hierarchy of content within a document, and you can rearrange content in the Navigation pane and in Outline view. Word also has positioning and alignment tools that you can use to precisely position objects and control their alignment and stacking order.

You can also use the table functionality in Word to control the positions of blocks of information on the page in nested tables. For example, a table with two columns and two rows can hold a set of four paragraphs, four bulleted lists, or four tables in a format in which you can easily compare their data.

This chapter guides you through procedures related to reorganizing document outlines, arranging objects on a page, and using tables to control page layout.

In this chapter

- Reorganize document outlines
- Arrange objects on a page
- Use tables to control page layout

Reorganize document outlines

When you create a document, you can divide the document into logical sections by using headings. Heading styles define not only formatting but also outline levels. These outline levels are visible in the Navigation pane and also in Outline view.

> **SEE ALSO** For information about formatting headings by using styles, see "Apply built-in styles to text" in Chapter 4, "Modify the structure and appearance of text." For general information about styles, see "Create and modify styles" in Chapter 15, "Create custom document elements."

Manage content in the Navigation pane

When working in Print Layout view, you can display a hierarchical structure of the document headings in the Navigation pane. By default, the Navigation pane displays document content styled as Heading 1, Heading 2, or Heading 3. You can display up to nine heading levels in the Navigation pane. (The display is controlled by the outline level rather than by the heading name.) If you use custom styles, you can set the outline levels of the styles to control the Navigation pane content.

You can reorganize document content by dragging headings in the Navigation pane. You can also promote, demote, or remove sections by using commands on the Navigation pane shortcut menu.

Navigation ▼ ✕

Search document 🔍▾

Headings   Pages   Results

10

Organize and arrange content

▲ Reorganize document outlines

   ▲ Manage content in the Navigation pane

      To display the Navigation pane

      To change the outline levels displayed in the Navigation pane

      To move a document section in the Navigation pane

   ▲ Manage content in Outline view

      To display a document in Outline view

      To change the outline levels displayed in Outline view

      To collapse or expand a single document section in Ou...

      To expand the entire document in Outline view

      To promote or demote a heading in Outline view

      To move a document section in Outline view

      To close Outline view

   ▲ Arrange objects on a page

      To display the Selection pane

      To select an object

      To position an object on a page

      To change the way text wraps around an object

      To anchor an object to a paragraph or page

      To align an object on the page

Context menu:
← Promote
→ Demote
New Heading Before
New Heading After
New Subheading
✕ Delete
Select Heading and Content
Print Heading and Content
Expand All
Collapse All
Show Heading Levels ›

10

You work with a document in the Navigation pane in much the same way you do in Outline view

To display the Navigation pane

- On the **View** tab, in the **Show** group, select the **Navigation Pane** checkbox.

To change the outline levels displayed in the Navigation pane

- Right-click or long-press (tap and hold) anywhere in the **Navigation** pane, select **Show Heading Levels**, and then select the lowest outline level that you want to display.

To move a document section in the Navigation pane

- In the **Navigation** pane, drag the heading of the section you want to move to the new location. (A bold horizontal line indicates the drop location.)

Manage content in Outline view

When you format headings by using Word's built-in heading styles, it's easy to view and organize the document in Outline view. In this view, you can hide all the body text and display only the headings at and above a particular level. You can also rearrange the sections of a document by moving their headings. When you display a document in Outline view, Word displays the document with a hierarchical structure, and the Outlining tab appears on the ribbon between the File and Home tabs.

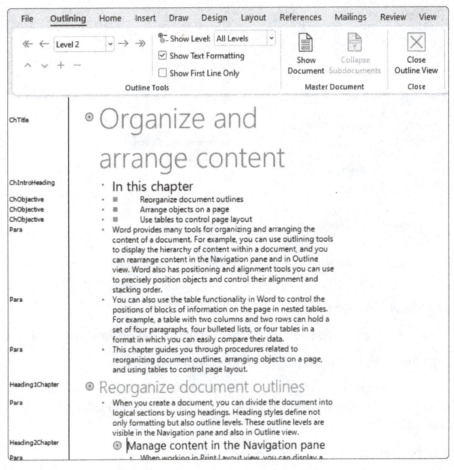

A document in Outline view

The indentations and symbols used in Outline view to indicate the level of a heading or paragraph in the document's structure don't appear in the document in other views or when you print it.

To easily reference paragraph styles while working in Outline view, you can display the style area pane to the left of the document. For information about displaying and resizing the style area pane, see "Display different views of documents" in Chapter 2, "Create and manage documents."

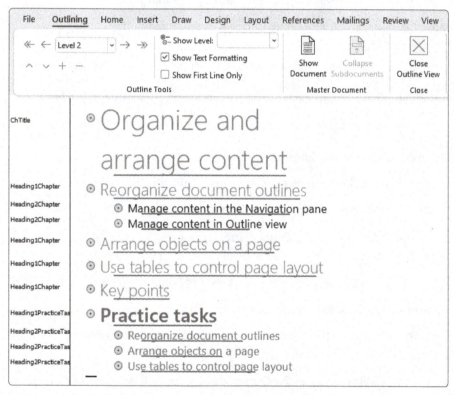

Wavy lines indicate collapsed content

You can use commands in the Outline Tools group of the Outlining tab to do the following:

- Display only the headings at a specific level and above. Word displays a double dotted line under the heading if the document contains text below it.

- Collapse or expand a specific heading.

- Expand the entire outline to display the document in its entirety.

- Promote or demote headings or body text by changing their level.

- Move headings and their text up or down in the document.

> ✓ **TIP** Select the buttons in the Master Document group to create a master document with subdocuments that you can then display or hide. The topic of master documents and subdocuments is beyond the scope of this book. For information, use the Search box at the top of the Word window.

To display a document in Outline view

- On the **View** tab, in the **Views** group, select **Outline**.

To change the outline levels displayed in Outline view

- On the **Outlining** tab, in the **Outline Tools** group, in the **Outline Level** list, select **Level *n***, where *n* is the lowest level of heading you want to display.

- Press **Alt+Shift+*n***, where *n* is the lowest level of heading you want to display.

To collapse or expand a single document section in Outline view

- Position the cursor in the heading of the section you want to collapse or expand. Then do either of the following:

  - On the **Outlining** tab, in the **Outline Tools** group, select the **Collapse** or **Expand** button.

  - Press **Alt+Shift+Minus Sign** to collapse the section or **Alt+Shift+Plus Sign** to expand the section.

To expand the entire document in Outline view

- On the **Outlining** tab, in the **Outline Tools** group, in the **Show Levels** list, select **All Levels**.

- Press **Alt+Shift+A**.

To promote or demote a heading in Outline view

- Position the cursor in the heading you want to promote or demote. Then do either of the following:

  - In the **Outline Tools** group, select the **Promote** or **Demote** button.

  - Press **Alt+Shift+Left Arrow** to promote the heading or **Alt+Shift+Right Arrow** to demote the heading.

> **TIP** Promoting or demoting a heading also promotes or demotes subheadings within that section to maintain the content hierarchy.

To move a document section in Outline view

- Select the plus sign to the left of the heading to select the section. Then do either of the following:

  - In the **Outline Tools** group, select the **Move Up** button or **Move Down** button as many times as necessary to move the section to the target location.

  - Press **Alt+Shift+Up Arrow** or **Alt+Shift+Down Arrow** as many times as necessary to move the section to the target location.

To close Outline view

- On the **Outlining** tab, in the **Close** group, select **Close Outline View** to display the document in Print Layout view.

10

Arrange objects on a page

In previous chapters, you learned basic ways to position an object, such as a picture or shape, on a page. When you position an object on a page, text wraps around that object by default. You're not limited to the basic settings you've explored thus far, however. In fact, you can position objects and change text-wrap settings in several ways. The Position gallery of layout options is available for most objects from the object's contextual tab (such as the Picture Format tab for a picture or the Shape Format tab for a shape). These options position the object in a specific location relative to the page margins.

The Position gallery offers several preconfigured position options

The Layout Options menu, which appears when you insert or select an object, provides text-wrapping options.

From the Layout Options menu, quickly set a text-wrapping option

The standard text-wrapping options include the following:

- **In Line with Text**   As its name suggests, when you choose this option, the object is placed in line with the text. The text doesn't wrap around the object.

- **Square**   When you choose Square, text wraps around the object in a square shape.

- **Tight**   Choose this option if you want text to wrap more tightly around the object.

- **Through**   The effects of this setting are most obvious when you insert an irregularly shaped object. When this option is selected, text appears to go through the object, filling in any blank spaces within it.

- **Top and Bottom**   This option places the object on its own line, with no text on either side of it.

- **Behind Text**   When you choose this option, the object is placed behind, or underneath, any existing text.

- **In Front of Text**   This setting lays the object on top of existing text, thereby obscuring it.

10

You can display the Layout dialog from either the Position menu or the Layout Options menu. The Text Wrapping tab of the Layout dialog offers the same text-wrapping styles as the Layout Options menu. In addition, you can fine-tune text-wrapping settings—for example, indicating whether text should wrap on both sides of the object and how far the object should be from the text.

For more exact text wrapping, configure the settings on the Text Wrapping tab

For more position settings, including settings for specifying whether the position is absolute or relative (more on that in a moment), you can use the commands on the Position tab of the Layout dialog. The available positions vary based on the selected text-wrapping option.

Layout   ?   ✕

| Position | Text Wrapping | Size |

Horizontal

○ A̲lignment   `Left`   ⌄   relative to   `Column`   ⌄

● Book layout   `Inside`   ⌄   of   `Margin`   ⌄

○ Absolute p̲osition   `0.02"`   ⇅   to the right of `Column`   ⌄

○ R̲elative position   `        ` ⇅   relative to   `Page`   ⌄

Vertical

○ Alig̲nment   `Top`   ⌄   relative to   `Page`   ⌄

● Absolute po̲sition   `2.7"`   ⇅   belo̲w   `Paragraph` ⌄

○ Relat̲ive position   `        ` ⇅   relative to   `Page`   ⌄

Options

☑ Move object with text   ☑ Allow o̲verlap

☐ L̲ock anchor   ☑ Layout in table cell

OK   Cancel

You can fine-tune position settings on the Position tab

When you choose a text-wrapping option other than In Line With Text, you can specify that an object be positioned in a specific location on the page or relative to a page element, or you can anchor it to a paragraph so it moves with the content.

You can also use alignment commands to align objects with the margins and with each other. You access these commands from the Align menu on the Format tab.

10

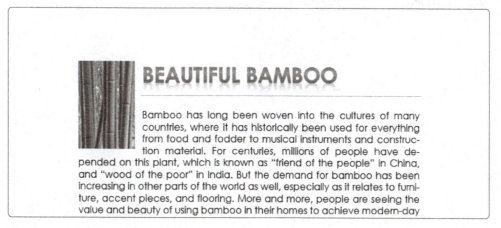

The picture is aligned with the top and left page margins

You can move an object manually by dragging it to another position on the page. To make it easier to align objects, you can display a grid that divides the page content area into squares of specific dimensions.

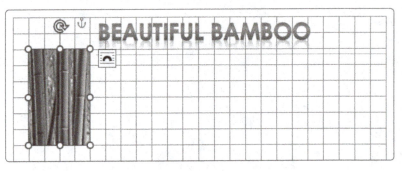

You can display a grid to help with aligning objects

You can change the grid settings in the Grid And Guides dialog. You can choose whether to display alignment guides, such as margins, and whether items should be *snapped*, or automatically aligned, to the grid or to other objects. You can also change the size of the grid.

If you insert several objects and then position them so that they overlap, they are said to be *stacked*. The stacking order (which object appears on top of which) is initially determined by the order in which you inserted the objects, but it can also be determined by other factors, such as the type of text wrapping assigned to each object. If all the objects have the same kind of text wrapping, you can change their order. You do so by using buttons in the Arrange group on the Format tab, or from the Selection pane, which displays a list of all the objects on the page.

Manage objects from the Selection pane

To display the Selection pane

- On the **Home** tab, in the **Editing** group, select **Select**, and then in the list, select **Selection Pane**.

- Select the object. Then on the object's **Format** tab, in the **Arrange** group, select the **Selection Pane** button.

To select an object

- On the page, select the object.

- In the **Selection** pane, select the object's name.

To position an object on a page

1. Select the object.

2. On the object's **Format** tab, in the **Arrange** group, select the **Position** button to display the Position gallery and menu.

3. Do either of the following:

   - In the **Position** gallery, point to a thumbnail to display a live preview of that option's effect on the position of the object. When you find the position you like, select the corresponding thumbnail.

   - On the **Position** menu, select **More Layout Options** to display the **Position** tab of the **Layout** dialog. In the **Horizontal** and **Vertical** areas, specify the absolute or relative position you want. Then select **OK**.

10

To change the way text wraps around an object

1. Select the object, and then select the **Layout Options** button that appears next to the selected object.

2. In the **Layout Options** gallery, select the text-wrapping option you want to apply.

Or

1. Select the object.

2. On the object's **Format** tab, in the **Arrange** group, select the **Wrap Text** button and then select **More Layout Options** to open the Layout dialog with the Text Wrapping tab displayed.

3. In the **Wrapping style** area, choose the text wrapping you want to apply.

4. In the **Wrap text** area, indicate whether the text should wrap on both sides, on the left side only, on the right side only, or on the largest side only.

5. In the **Distance from text** area, specify the minimum distance between each side of the object and the text.

6. Select **OK**.

To anchor an object to a paragraph or page

1. Position the object next to or within the paragraph you want to anchor it to, or in the position where you want to anchor it.

2. Select the object.

3. On the object's **Format** tab, in the **Arrange** group, select the **Wrap Text** button, and then do either of the following:

   - To anchor the object to the paragraph, select **Move with Text**.

   - To anchor the object to the page location, select **Fix Position on Page**.

To align an object on the page

1. Select the object.

2. On the object's **Format** tab, in the **Arrange** group, select **Align**, and then select one of the six alignment options at the top of the menu.

⊫	Align <u>L</u>eft
⊕	Align <u>C</u>enter
⊧	Align <u>R</u>ight
⫿	Align <u>T</u>op
⊡	Align <u>M</u>iddle
⊔	Align <u>B</u>ottom
⊪	Distribute <u>H</u>orizontally
⊟	Distribute <u>V</u>ertically
	Align to <u>P</u>age
✓	<u>A</u>lign to Margin
	Align Selected <u>O</u>bjects
	Use Alignment G<u>u</u>ides
	View Gridli<u>n</u>es
#	<u>G</u>rid Settings...

The Align menu provides easy access to all the alignment options

> ✓ **TIP** When objects have a text-wrapping setting other than In Line With Text, use the options on the Align menu to align multiple objects horizontally or vertically. You can also distribute selected objects equally between the first and last objects in the selection.

To display or hide gridlines in the content area

- On the object's **Format** tab, in the **Arrange** group, select the **Align** button, and then select **View Gridlines**.

10

To change grid settings

1. On the object's **Format** tab, in the **Arrange** group, select the **Align** button, and then select **Grid Settings** to open the Grid And Guides dialog.

Specify the location and functionality of the on-screen alignment guides and grid

2. Make any changes you want, and then select **OK**.

To manually move an object

1. Select the object.

2. Drag the selected object to the target location.

> ✓ **TIP** If the grid is displayed and has been configured to allow snapping, the object will snap to the nearest gridline when it is dropped. To move an object without snapping it to the grid, hold down the Ctrl key while pressing an arrow key. The object will move in tiny increments.

To change the stacking order of objects

1. Select the object that you want to move.

2. On the object's **Format** tab, in the **Arrange** group, do one of the following:

   - Select the **Bring Forward** button to move the selected object one position closer to the top of the stack.

   - In the **Bring Forward** list, select **Bring to Front** to move the object to the top of the stack.

   - Select the **Send Backward** button to move the selected object one position closer to the bottom of the stack.

   - In the **Send Backward** list, select **Send to Back** to move the object to the bottom of the stack.

To hide objects on the page

1. Open the **Selection** pane. The eye icon to the right of each object indicates that it is currently visible on the page.

2. In the **Selection** pane, do either of the following:

   - To hide one object, select the eye icon to the right of the object name.

   - To hide all objects in the document, select the **Hide All** button.

   The eye icon changes to a small horizontal bar, indicating that an object is hidden.

To display hidden objects

- In the **Selection** pane, do either of the following:

   - To display one object, select the bar icon to the right of the object's name.

   - To display all the objects in the document, select the **Show All** button.

10

Use tables to control page layout

Most people are accustomed to thinking of a table as a means of displaying data in a quick, easy-to-grasp format. But tables can also serve to organize content in creative ways. For example, suppose you want to display two tables next to each other. The simplest way to do this is to first create a page-width table that has only one row and two columns, and then insert one of the tables you want to display in the first cell and the other table in the second cell. When the outer table borders are hidden, these nested tables appear side by side.

Consultation Fee			Trip Charges	
Location	**Hourly Rate**		**Distance**	**Fee**
In home	$50.00		0-10 miles	No charge
Phone	$35.00		11-20 miles	$10.00
In store	$40.00		Over 20 miles	$20.00

These tables are nested within the cells of a one-row, two-column table

As with regular tables, you can create a nested table in one of three ways:

- From scratch
- By formatting existing information
- By inserting Microsoft Excel data

And just like with other tables, you can format a nested table either manually or by using one of the ready-made table styles.

> **TIP** Use tables to organize a mixture of elements such as text, tables, charts, and diagrams. For more information about creating tables, see Chapter 5, "Organize information in columns and tables."

Structure content for accessibility

If you're designing your document with accessibility in mind, be aware that screen readers and other assistive devices access content linearly—from left to right, row by row—whereas you might expect a person looking at the table to read its content from top to bottom, column by column. Some screen readers have a table reading mode that can help to ameliorate this problem, so if you're arranging content by using a simple table layout, this won't present as much of an issue (although the content meaning might still be less clear than when presented in normal text or in a list). If you create a fancy table layout that includes cells of varying heights and widths, with some merged cells and some split cells, it's likely that the screen reader will access and deliver the content out of order. Keep this in mind if you intend to deliver your content in an electronic format, and certainly if your organization is required to adhere to accessibility standards.

To create a nested table

1. In a document, position the cursor where you want to insert the nested table.

2. On the **Insert** tab, in the **Tables** group, select the **Table** button.

3. In the **Insert Table** gallery, select the box corresponding to the size of table you want for the container table.

> ⚠ **IMPORTANT** It's inadvisable to create a container table of more than two columns. The procedures in this topic assume a two-column container table.

4. Create or locate the first table you want to nest within the container table, and click or tap anywhere within it.

5. On the **Layout** tab, in the **Table** group, select **Select**, and then select **Select Table**.

10

6. On the **Home** tab, in the **Clipboard** group, select **Cut** or **Copy** to move or copy the selected table to the Clipboard.

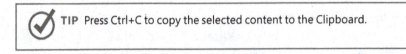

> **TIP** Press Ctrl+C to copy the selected content to the Clipboard.

7. In the container table, right-click the left table cell, and then under **Paste Options**, select the **Nest Table** button to insert the table you copied into the cell and adjust the height of the container table to fit the nested table.

8. Create or locate the second table you want to nest within the container table, and then cut or copy the table to the Clipboard.

9. In the container table, select the right table cell, and then on the **Home** tab, in the **Clipboard** group, select **Paste** to insert the second table as a nested table.

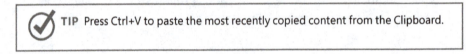

> **TIP** Press Ctrl+V to paste the most recently copied content from the Clipboard.

To format a nested table

1. Point to the container table, and then click or tap the table selector that appears just outside of its upper-left corner to select the table. (Be sure you select the container table and not the nested table.)

2. On the **Table Design** tab, in the **Borders** group, in the **Borders** list, select **No Border** to remove the borders from the container cells.

Key points

- If you take the time to apply heading styles to a document, you can use the document's outline to rearrange its sections, either in Outline view or in the Navigation pane.

- You can position an object in relation to the text that surrounds it and in relation to other objects on the page.

- By using tables in creative ways, you can place information in nonlinear arrangements for easy comparison or analysis.

10

Practice tasks

Before you can complete these tasks, you must copy the book's practice files to your computer. The practice files for these tasks are in the **Word365SBS\Ch10** folder. You can save the results of the tasks in the same folder.

The Introduction includes a complete list of practice files and download instructions.

Reorganize document outlines

Open the **ReorganizeOutlines** document in Print Layout view, and then perform the following tasks:

1. Display the document in Outline view.

2. In the **Word Options** dialog, set the style area pane width to 1", and then return to the document.

3. Use the commands on the **Outlining** tab to display only level 1 headings.

4. Expand the **General Administration** section, and then collapse it again.

5. Show all levels of the outline.

6. Promote the **Contact Information** heading to level 1, and then demote it back to level 2.

7. Move the **Warehouse** section up so that the heading and the text within it appear above the Office heading.

8. Close the outline to display the document in Print Layout view.

9. Open the **Navigation** pane.

10. In the **Navigation** pane, drag the *Warehouse* heading back to its original location, below the Office section.

11. Close the document, saving your changes if you want.

Arrange objects on a page

Open the **ArrangeObjects** document in Print Layout view, display formatting marks, and then perform the following tasks:

1. With the cursor next to the first word in the second paragraph, *There*, insert the **Bamboo1** picture from the practice file folder.

2. Use the buttons in the **Position** gallery to position the picture in the top center of the page, with square text wrapping.

3. Use the picture's **Layout Options** menu to set the text wrapping to **Tight**.

4. Use the commands on the **Text Wrapping** tab of the **Layout** dialog to set the text wrapping to **Right only**, with a 0.5" gap between the picture and text on all sides.

5. Use the commands on the **Position** tab of the **Layout** dialog to set the picture at a horizontal absolute position 2 inches to the right of the left margin, and a vertical absolute position 2 inches below the top margin.

6. With the cursor again next to the first word in the second paragraph, insert the **Bamboo2** picture from the practice file folder.

7. Use the buttons in the **Position** gallery to position the picture in the middle of the page, with square text wrapping.

8. Anchor the picture so that it moves with the text.

9. Select the paragraph containing the **Bamboo2** picture and move it to the end of the document. Notice that the picture moves with the paragraph.

10. Undo the move.

11. Anchor the picture so that it's in a fixed position on the page.

12. Select the paragraph containing the **Bamboo2** picture and move it to the end of the document. Notice that this time, the picture stays where it was on the page.

13. Undo the move.

14. Use the commands on the **Align Objects** menu to align the **Bamboo2** picture on the left side of the page.

15. Display the gridlines.

16. Drag the **Bamboo2** picture to the upper-left corner of the document, on top of the **Bamboo1** picture, using gridlines to align it.

17. Hide the gridlines.

18. Bring the **Bamboo1** picture to the front of the stack.

19. Open the **Selection** pane and use it to hide either picture. Notice that the eye icon changes to a small horizontal bar to indicate that the object is hidden.

20. Redisplay the object.

21. Close the document, saving your changes if you want.

Use tables to control page layout

Open the **ControlLayout** document in Print Layout view, display formatting marks, and then perform the following tasks:

1. With the cursor on the line above the *Consultation Fee* table, insert a table that contains two columns and one row.

2. Cut the *Consultation Fee* table, and right-click in the left cell of the table you just created.

3. Use the options on the shortcut menu to nest the table into the container table.

4. Cut the *Trip Charges* table, and then click (don't right-click) or tap in the right table cell of the container table.

5. Use any method described in this chapter to nest the *Trip Charges* table into the container table.

6. Remove the borders from the container table.

7. Close the document, saving your changes if you want.

Part 4

Review and finalize documents

Collaborate on documents

It's not unusual for several people to collaborate on the development of a document. Collaboration is simplest when contributors review electronic documents on a computer screen rather than paper printouts. On-screen review is very efficient; you can provide legible feedback, implement specific changes, and save trees at the same time.

If you save a file in a shared location, multiple people can review and edit the document at the same time. This highly efficient method of collaboration is called *coauthoring*. Another method of gathering feedback from multiple reviewers is to send a file to each reviewer and then merge the reviewed versions into one file that displays all the changes. This is less efficient but has its benefits.

Word provides many tools that simplify document-collaboration processes. You can make changes without deleting the original content, provide feedback in comments, and respond to comments and queries from other reviewers. To protect a document from unwanted changes, you can restrict the editing options so that Word tracks all changes, allows only certain types of changes, or doesn't allow changes at all.

This chapter guides you through procedures related to marking up and reviewing documents, comparing and merging document versions, restricting the changes that people can make to documents that you share with them, and coauthoring documents.

In this chapter

- Mark up documents
- Display and review document markup
- Compare and combine documents
- Control content changes
- Coauthor documents

Mark up documents

Comments and tracked changes are collectively referred to as *markup*. Markup is used during the content-development and review processes and is particularly useful for bringing changes, suggestions, and comments to the attention of multiple members of a collaborative authoring group.

Insert comments

A *comment* is a note attached to an anchor within the text. The anchor can be text or any type of object, or simply a location; wherever it is, Word displays the comment in the right margin of the document.

Word automatically adds your name and a time stamp to the comment

Each comment is inside a container that is fully visible when the comment is active (when you point to or select it). Comment containers are referred to as *balloons*. Balloons can be used for the display of various types of markup.

You can insert comments for many reasons, such as to ask questions, make suggestions, provide reference information, or explain edits. You insert and work with comments by using the commands in the Comments group on the Review tab and on the Comments menu at the right end of the ribbon.

> ✅ **TIP** You can customize the colors that Word uses to mark text edits, content moves, and structural changes in tables. The custom colors don't travel with the document, though, so they'll be visible only to you.

Comments group Comments pane Comments button

The commands in the Comments group make it easy to navigate and remove comments

> **TIP** Display documents in Print Layout view so that all the collaboration commands are available.

To display the Comments pane

- To the right of the ribbon tabs, select the **Comments** button.

- On the **Review** tab, in the **Comments** group, select the **Show Comments** arrow (not the button), and then in the list, select **List**.

To insert a comment

1. Select the text or object to which you want to anchor the comment.

2. Do one of the following:

   - On the **Review** tab, in the **Comments** group, select **New Comment**.

   - In the **Comments** pane, select **New**.

   - Press **Alt+I+M**.

3. In the comment balloon that appears in the right margin or in the **Comments** pane, enter the comment.

> **TIP** Comments are usually simple text but can include other elements and formatting such as images and active hyperlinks.

11

4. Post the comment by doing either of the following:

- Select the **Post comment** button (labeled with a paper airplane) below the comment text box.

- Press **Ctrl+Enter**.

> ⚠️ **IMPORTANT** Until you post the comment, Word does not allow you to create, reply to, or edit other comments. In the Comments pane, "Another comment is in progress" displays in the Reply area of the other comment balloons, and "Please post your comment" displays in red below the in-progress comment. You must scroll the Comments pane to locate and post (or cancel) the comment. This feature of Word 365 comments is the subject of a significant amount of internet commentary and one that can easily cost an editor a significant amount of time and frustration.

Track changes

When two or more people collaborate on a document, one person usually creates and "owns" the document, and the others review it—adding or revising content to make it more accurate, logical, or readable. When reviewing a document in Word, you can track your changes so they are available for review and retain the original text for comparison or reversion. You manage change tracking from the Tracking group on the Review tab.

Tracking dialog launcher

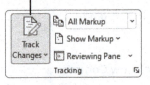

A shaded button indicates that change tracking is active

> ✅ **TIP** Turning on the change-tracking feature tracks changes only in the active document, not in any other open documents.

When change tracking is on, Word tracks insertions and deletions and the movement and formatting of content. When you display a document in All Markup view, tracked changes are indicated by different font colors and formatting. The default formatting is as follows:

- Insertions are in the reviewer-specific color and underlined.

- Deletions are in the reviewer-specific color and crossed out (struck through).

- Formatting changes are indicated in balloons in the markup area.

- Moves are green and double-underlined.

- All changes are indicated in the left margin by a vertical line.

> As with comments, mMultiple people can track changes in a document. Word tracks insertions and deletions and the movement and formatting of content. When you display a document in All Markup view, tracked changes are indicated by different font colors and formatting. The default formatting is as follows:
>
> - Insertions are in the reviewer-specific color and underlined.
> - Deletions are in the reviewer-specific color and crossed out.
> - Formatting changes are indicated in balloons in the markup area.
> - Moves are green and double-underlined.
> - All changes are indicated in the left margin by a vertical line.
>
> Multiple people can track changes in a document. Word assigns a color to each person's changes and uses that color to format inserted and deleted text. If you prefer to select a color for your own changes, you can do so. You can also modify the formatting that indicates each type of change. For example, you could have Word indicate inserted text by formatting it as bold, italic, or with a double underline. Note, however, that this change would be valid only for your profile on the computer you make the change on and would not affect change formatting on other computers.

Moved text is green, and a double underline indicates its new location

11

Multiple people can track changes in a document. Word assigns a color to each person's changes and uses that color to format inserted and deleted text. If you prefer to select a color for your own changes, you can do so. You can also modify the formatting that indicates each type of change. For example, you could have Word indicate inserted text by formatting it as bold, italic, or with a double underline. Note, however, that this change would be valid only for your profile on the computer you make the change on and would not affect change formatting on other computers.

Modify the types of changes that are tracked and the markup colors

If you want to ensure that other reviewers track their changes to a document, you can turn on and lock the change-tracking feature and (optionally) require that reviewers enter a password to turn it off.

A new feature in this version of Word allows you to turn on change tracking only for yourself or for everyone who edits the document.

> **SEE ALSO** For information about forcing change tracking by restricting editing, see "Control content changes" later in this chapter.

To turn on change tracking for everyone

- On the **Review** tab, in the **Tracking** group, select the **Track Changes** button (not its arrow).

- On the **Review** tab, in the **Tracking** group, select the **Track Changes** arrow, and then select **For Everyone**.

- Press **Ctrl+Shift+E**.

To turn on change tracking for only yourself

- On the **Review** tab, in the **Tracking** group, select the **Track Changes** arrow, and then select **Just Mine**.

To turn off change tracking

- On the **Review** tab, in the **Tracking** group, select the **Track Changes** button (not its arrow).

> **SEE ALSO** For information about keyboard shortcuts, see the appendix, "Keyboard shortcuts."

To track changes without displaying them on the screen

1. On the **Review** tab, in the **Tracking** group, select the **Display for Review** arrow.

2. In the **Display for Review** list, select **Simple Markup** or **No Markup**.

> **SEE ALSO** For more information about the markup views, see "Display and review document markup" later in this chapter.

To specify the color of the changes you track in any document

1. On the **Review** tab, select the **Tracking** dialog launcher to open the **Track Changes Options** dialog.

2. Select **Advanced Options** to open the **Advanced Track Changes Options** dialog.

3. In the **Color** lists adjacent to **Insertions**, **Deletions**, and **Formatting**, select the color you want to use for that type of change in Word documents on the current computer.

4. Select **OK** in each open dialog to close them and save your changes.

To prevent reviewers from turning off change tracking

1. On the **Review** tab, in the **Tracking** group, select the **Track Changes** arrow, and then select **Lock Tracking**.

2. In the **Lock Tracking** dialog, enter and reenter a password to prevent other people from turning off change tracking.

Use a password that you'll remember, or make a note of it in a secure location so you can find it later

3. In the **Lock Tracking** dialog, select **OK**. The Track Changes button becomes unavailable.

To unlock change tracking

1. On the **Review** tab, in the **Tracking** group, select the **Track Changes** arrow, and then select **Lock Tracking**.

2. In the **Unlock Tracking** dialog, enter the password you assigned when you enabled this feature, and then select **OK**.

Unlocking tracking doesn't turn off change tracking; you must do that separately

Display and review document markup

After reviewers provide feedback by making changes and entering comments, you can review the tracked changes and comments and choose how you'd like to process them.

Display markup

Usually you would display and review all types of markup at one time—insertions, deletions, moves, formatting changes, and comments. However, if you prefer, you can choose to display only certain types of markup or only markup from specific reviewers.

Word has four basic Display For Review options that govern the display of tracked changes in a document. The options are:

- **Simple Markup**   This default markup view displays a red vertical line in the left margin adjacent to each tracked change. Markup is hidden.

- **All Markup**   This view displays a gray vertical line in the left margin adjacent to each tracked change, and formats inserted, deleted, and moved content to reflect the settings in the Advanced Track Changes Options dialog.

> **SEE ALSO** For information about controlling markup formatting, see "Mark up documents" earlier in this chapter.

- **No Markup**   This view hides comments and displays the current document content as though all changes have been accepted. Changes that you make in this view are tracked (if change tracking is turned on) and visible when markup is shown.

- **Original**   This view displays the original document content without any markup.

Depending on your view settings, comments are shown in one of the following ways:

- In balloons in the Comments pane

- In balloons in the right margin

- Hidden and indicated by highlighting in the text

You can select the comment icon or point to the highlight to display the comment text.

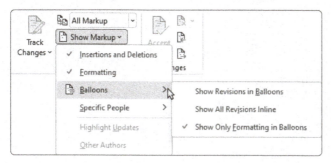

The individual markup display options

After you select a Display For Review option, you can additionally filter the display of markup in these ways:

- Individually control the display of comments, insertions and deletions, and formatting.

- Show all markup inline or in balloons, or keep comments in balloons and insertions, deletions, and moves inline.

- Display or hide markup by reviewer.

You can display and manage all the comments in the document in the new Comments pane, which opens to the right of the document text. From within the Comments pane, you can create, edit, reply to, resolve, and delete comment threads.

Manage comment threads in the Comments pane

If you prefer to display all comments and tracked changes in a document at one time, you can do so in the Revisions pane. By default, this pane opens to the left of the document text (and to the right of the Navigation pane, if that is open) at the same height as the document content area. If you want to, you can dock it on the right side of the window instead.

Revision details — [pointing to a pane showing:]

Revisions

∨ **288 revisions**
   Insertions: 121
   Deletions: 115
   Moves: 18
   Formatting: 17
   Comments: 17

Joan Lambert Inserted
***insert G04xx07 no crop callouts*

Type a new message

Type your message in the composition box, and click the Send button

G04xx07 callouts: Callout around the Send button

G04xx07: The composition box to send a message.

Joan Lambert Deleted

Group Chats

Joan Lambert Moved up [1]

Group chats allow you to include multiple people in a conversation. Group chats take place outside of a channel, so only members of the chat can communicate.

Joan Lambert Formatted
Left: 1", Right: 1", Bottom: 1", Width: 8.5", Height: 11"

Joan Lambert Commented
AU: Do you want to include something about embedding and attaching pictures?

Information about the number and type of revisions is available at the top of the Revisions pane

11

From the ribbon, you can also display the Revisions pane horizontally. By default, the horizontal pane stretches across the bottom of the Word app window. If you prefer, you can drag it to the top of the window.

When the Comments pane or Revisions pane is docked, the content pane becomes narrower (or shorter, if you display the horizontal Revisions pane) to make space for the pane. You can undock the pane so that it floats independently of the app window and doesn't take space away from the content pane. The floating pane has a vertical format, but you can change its height and width to fit wherever it's convenient. The best display location depends on the amount of space you have available on your device screen or screens.

To change the display of markup in a document

- To switch between Simple Markup view and All Markup view, select the red or gray vertical line in the margin to the left of any tracked change.

Or

1. On the **Review** tab, in the **Tracking** group, select the **Display for Review** arrow (to the right of the current markup view).

2. In the **Display for Review** list, select **Simple Markup**, **All Markup**, **No Markup**, or **Original**.

To display specific types of markup in balloons

1. In the **Display for Review** list, select **All Markup**.

2. In the **Show Markup** list, select **Balloons**, and then select **Show Revisions in Balloons**, **Show All Revisions Inline**, or **Show Only Formatting in Balloons**.

To hide or display all markup of a specific type

- On the **Review** tab, in the **Tracking** group, select **Show Markup**, and then select **Comments**, **Insertions and Deletions**, or **Formatting**.

 TIP A check mark to the left of a markup type indicates that elements of that type are visible in views of the document that display those elements.

To display only markup by a specific person

1. On the **Review** tab, in the **Tracking** group, select **Show Markup**.

2. In the **Show Markup** list, select **Specific People**, and then select the name of any reviewer whose comments you don't want to display.

To display individual comments in Simple Markup view

- Select a comment icon to display the comments on that line in comment balloons.

- Point to a comment icon to highlight the comments on that line in the colors associated with the comments' authors.

> **TIP** The reviewer name is taken from the user information stored with the user account. If you're signed in to Word with a Microsoft account, Word tracks revisions by the name associated with your Microsoft account. If the instance of Word you're working in is not linked to a Microsoft account, you can change the stored user information on the General page of the Word Options dialog. Changing your user information affects revision tracking only when you aren't signed in with a Microsoft account.

To display comments in the margin

- On the **Review** tab, in the **Comments** group, select the **Show Comments** button.

- On the **Review** tab, in the **Comments** group, select the **Show Comments** arrow (not the button), and then select **Contextual**.

To display the Comments pane

- To the right of the ribbon tabs, select the **Comments** button.

- On the **Review** tab, in the **Comments** group, select the **Show Comments** arrow (not the button), and then in the list, select **List**.

To display the Revisions pane

- On the **Review** tab, in the **Tracking** group, select the **Reviewing Pane** button (not the arrow).

> **TIP** Selecting the button opens the Revisions pane in its most recent location. The default location in each new Word session is to the left of the page.

11

Or

1. In the **Tracking** group, select the **Reviewing Pane** arrow.

2. In the **Reviewing Pane** list, do either of the following:

   - Select **Reviewing Pane Vertical** to display the pane to the left or right of the document.

   - Select **Reviewing Pane Horizontal** to display the pane below the ribbon or above the status bar.

To display a breakdown of revision types

- In the **Revisions** pane, to the left of the revision summary, select the **Expand** button (the v).

To change the location of the Comments pane or Revisions pane

- Drag the pane by its header to any of the following locations:

  - Dock the pane vertically to the left or right side of the app window or against any other vertical pane.

  - Dock the pane horizontally below the ribbon or above the status bar.

  - Drag the pane inside or outside the app window to float it independently.

To change the width or height of the floating Comments pane or Revisions pane

1. Point to the right or top border of the pane.

2. When the pointer changes to a double-headed arrow, drag the border.

To close the Comments pane or Revisions pane

- In the upper-right corner of the pane, select the **Close** button.

- On the **Review** tab, in the **Tracking** group, select **Reviewing Pane**.

Review and respond to comments

All the comments in a document are available for review, regardless of who created them. You can scroll through a document and review the comments as you come to them, or you can jump from comment to comment by selecting comments in the Comments pane or buttons on the ribbon, or by using the commands on the Comments menu.

> **TIP** If a document contains both comments and tracked changes, selecting the Next or Previous button in the Changes group on the Review tab moves sequentially among these elements, whereas selecting the Next or Previous button in the Comments group or Comments menu moves only among comments.

When reviewing comments, you can take the following actions:

- Respond to individual comments to provide further information or request clarification.

- Mark individual comments or comment threads as Resolved to indicate that you've processed them and retain them for later reference.

- Delete individual comments that you no longer require.

- Filter the comments by author.

- Delete all visible comments at the same time.

- Delete all comments in the document at the same time.

The ability to mark comments as Resolved is a useful feature. Marking a comment as Resolved leaves the comment intact but minimizes and recolors the comment elements so that it doesn't distract from the document content in the way that an active comment does.

An example of a tracked comment before and after being marked as Resolved

11

To move among only comments

- In the **Comments** pane or **Revisions** pane, select any comment to move to that comment in the document.

- On the **Review** tab, in the **Comments** group, select the **Next** or **Previous** button to jump from balloon to balloon.

- Scroll through the document to visually locate comment balloons.

To activate a comment for editing

- In the comment balloon, select the **Edit comment** icon (the pencil).

To respond to a comment

- In the comment balloon, enter your comment in the **Reply** box and then select the **Post reply** button or press **Ctrl+Enter** to post your reply.

To mark a comment as Resolved or reactivate a Resolved comment

- Right-click or long-press (tap and hold) the comment highlight (in the text), and then select **Resolve Comment**.

- In the comment balloon, select the **More thread actions** button (...) and then select **Resolve thread**.

> ✓ **TIP** It isn't possible to resolve individual comments in a multi-comment thread. The first comment in a thread is treated as a thread.

To delete a comment

- In the comment balloon, select the **More thread actions** button (...) for a comment without replies, and then select **Delete thread**.

- In the comment balloon, select the **More comment actions** button (...) for any reply within a thread, and then select **Delete comment**.

- Right-click the comment highlight (in the text), and then select **Delete Comment**.

To delete a comment thread

- Activate the comment balloon, and then on the **Review** tab, in the **Comments** group, select the **Delete** button.

- In the comment balloon, select the **More thread actions** button (...) for the first comment in a thread, and then select **Delete thread**.

Review and process tracked changes

As with comments, you can scroll through a document and review insertions, deletions, content moves, and formatting changes as you come to them, or you can jump from change to change by selecting buttons on the ribbon or by using the Revisions pane. You also have the option of accepting or rejecting multiple changes at the same time.

Here are some typical scenarios for reviewing and processing changes that you might consider:

- Display a document in Simple Markup view or No Markup view so you're viewing the final content. If you're happy with the document content in that view, accept all the changes at the same time.

- Display a document in All Markup view. Scan the individual changes visually. Individually reject any change that doesn't meet your requirements. As you complete the review of a section that meets your requirements, select the content of that section and approve all the changes within your selection.

- Display a document in All Markup view. Move to the first change. Accept or reject the change to move to the next. (You can perform both actions with one click.)

When reviewing tracked changes, you can take the following actions:

- Accept or reject individual changes.

- Select a section of content and accept or reject all changes therein at the same time.

- Filter the changes and then accept or reject all visible changes at the same time.

- Accept or reject all changes in the document at the same time.

To move among tracked changes and comments

- On the **Review** tab, in the **Changes** group, select the **Next** or **Previous** button.

- In the **Revisions** pane, select any change or comment to move to it in the document.

To display the time and author of a tracked change

- Point to any revision in the text to display a ScreenTip identifying the name of the reviewer who made the change and when the change was made.

To accept a selected tracked change and move to the next tracked change

- On the **Review** tab, in the **Changes** group, select the **Accept** button.

11

Or

1. On the **Review** tab, in the **Changes** group, select the **Accept** arrow.

2. In the **Accept** list, select **Accept and Move to Next**.

To accept a selected tracked change and remain in the same location

- Right-click the change, and then select **Accept Deletion**, **Accept Insertion**, or **Accept Format Change**.

- On the **Review** tab, in the **Accept** list, select **Accept This Change**.

To reject a selected tracked change and move to the next tracked change

- On the **Review** tab, in the **Changes** group, select the **Reject** button.

- On the **Review** tab, in the **Reject** list, select **Reject and Move to Next**.

To reject a selected tracked change and remain in the same location

- Right-click the change, and then select **Reject Deletion**, **Reject Insertion**, or **Reject Format Change**.

- On the **Review** tab, in the **Reject** list, select **Reject This Change**.

To accept or reject all the changes in a section of text

- Select the text. Then do either of the following:

  - On the **Review** tab, in the **Changes** group, select the **Accept** button or the **Reject** button.

  - Right-click the selected text, and then select **Accept Change** or **Reject Change**.

To accept or reject all the changes in a document

- On the **Review** tab, in the **Accept** list, select **Accept All Changes**.

- On the **Review** tab, in the **Reject** list, select **Reject All Changes**.

To accept or reject all the changes of a certain type or from a certain reviewer

- On the **Show Markup** menu, configure the settings to display only the changes you want to accept or reject. Then do either of the following:

  - On the **Review** tab, in the **Accept** list, select **Accept All Changes Shown**.

  - On the **Review** tab, in the **Reject** list, select **Reject All Changes Shown**.

Remember to check for errors

It's a good idea to check for spelling issues in a document after you finish processing changes because, for example, it's easy to accidentally end up with a missing or extra space in the document. If the Check Spelling As You Type option is on (as it is by default), you can scroll through the document and visually scan for wavy red underlines that indicate suspected spelling errors or double blue underlines that indicate suspected grammar errors. To be entirely thorough, you can run the Check Document tool and respond to each issue it identifies.

SEE ALSO For more information about checking spelling and grammar, see "Locate and correct text errors" in Chapter 12, "Finalize and distribute documents."

Compare and combine documents

Sometimes you might want to compare several versions of the same document. Word supports two types of document-version comparison:

- Comparing a document to a separate copy of the document. For example, if you sent individual document copies out for review by several colleagues and want to compare their edited versions with the original document.

- Comparing a document to a previous version of the same document. For example, if you've been working in a document without tracking changes and you want to identify all the changes made since a version saved a month ago.

Compare and combine separate copies of a document

Instead of comparing multiple open documents visually, you can tell Word to compare the documents and either move the changes from one document into the other or create a new document that contains the changes from both documents.

11

By default, when you compare documents, Word generates a composite document that shows all the differences between the two documents as tracked changes. If you want to review the specific changes and the before-and-after versions independently, you can display the source documents in the same window.

Scrolling any version of the documents you're comparing or combining scrolls all three

If you're working on a document that is stored in a Microsoft SharePoint document library, the Compare menu also includes options for comparing the open document to other versions of itself.

> **TIP** Word can't compare or combine documents that have Protection turned on to restrict changes.

You can compare any two documents. To compare multiple edited documents to one original, combine all the edited documents into one, and then compare them with the original.

To compare or combine two documents and annotate changes

1. Start from a blank document or any existing document.

2. On the **Review** tab, in the **Compare** group, select **Compare** to track changes from only one document or **Combine** to track changes from both documents.

3. In the **Compare Documents** or **Combine Documents** dialog, under **Original document**, select the arrow to expand the alphabetical list of documents you've recently worked with.

4. If the document you want to designate as the first document appears in the list, select it. If not, select **Browse** (the first item in the list) to display the **Open** dialog. In the dialog, navigate to the document you want, select it, and then select **Open**.

5. Use the same technique in the **Revised document** area to select the document you want to designate as the second document.

6. In the **Label changes with** box or boxes, enter the name or names you want Word to assign as the reviewer when marking differences between the documents.

> **TIP** When comparing documents, you specify the reviewer for only the revised document; when combining documents, you specify reviewers for both documents.

11

Indicate the differences to identify and how to label them

7. If the dialog doesn't include the **Comparison settings** and **Show changes** areas, select the **More** button to display them.

8. In the **Comparison settings** area of the dialog, select the checkboxes of the content differences you want to annotate.

> ⊘ **TIP** By default, Word marks changes at the word level in a new document. You have the option to show changes at the character level and to show them in one of the two documents rather than in a third document. Until you're comfortable with the compare and combine operations, it's safest to retain the default settings in the Show Changes area.

9. In the **Compare Documents** or **Combine Documents** dialog, select **OK** to create the combined document.

> ⊘ **TIP** If you compare documents that contain conflicting formatting, a message box will ask you to confirm which document's formatting should be used.

To hide or display comparison source documents

■ In the **Compare Result** document window, on the **Review** tab, in the **Compare** group, select **Show Source Documents**, and then select **Hide Source Documents** or the option to show one or both source documents.

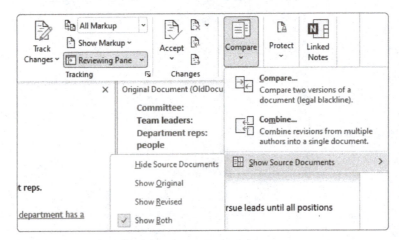

Word shows both source documents by default

Compare separate versions of a document

By default, Word automatically saves a temporary copy of your open documents every 10 minutes. Automatically saved versions of the document are displayed in the Manage Document area of the Info page of the Backstage view.

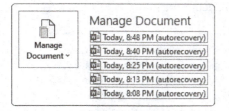

Easily review or recover an earlier version of a document

To display a previous version of a document

■ On the **Info** page of the Backstage view, in the **Manage Document** list, select the version you want to display.

To compare a document to a previous version

1. Display the previous version of the document.

2. On the information bar at the top of the previous version, select **Compare**.

To roll back to a previous version of a document

1. Display the previous version of the document.

2. On the information bar at the top of the previous version, select the **Restore** button.

To change how often Word automatically saves document recovery versions

1. Display the **Save** page of the **Word Options** dialog.

2. In the **Save AutoRecover information every** box, enter the number of minutes Word should allow to pass before saving a recovery version of the document.

3. Select **OK** to close the dialog.

11

Control content changes

Sometimes you'll want to allow people to display the contents of a document but not make changes to it. Other times you'll want to allow changes, but only of certain types, or only if they're tracked for your review. This section includes information about ways that you can protect the content of a document.

> **TIP** When considering content protection options, keep in mind that storing documents within a document-management system that has version control can save you a lot of trouble. Word includes a built-in version-tracking system that you can use to compare and restore previous versions of a document that are stored on your computer. SharePoint document libraries provide access to previous versions of documents checked in by any team member.

Restrict actions

To prevent people from introducing inconsistent formatting or unwanted changes into a document, you can restrict the types of changes that an individual document permits, in the following ways:

- **Restrict formatting** Limit formatting changes to a specific list of styles that you select, or to the recommended minimum style set, which consists of all the styles needed by Word for features such as tables of contents. (The recommended minimum set doesn't necessarily include all the styles used in the document.) Restricting formatting prevents anyone from adding or applying styles that you don't want in your document.

> **SEE ALSO** For more information about styles, see "Apply character formatting" and "Apply built-in styles to text" in Chapter 4, "Modify the structure and appearance of text."

- **Restrict editing** Limit changes to comments, tracked changes, or form field content, or permit no changes at all.

You can implement these types of restrictions from the Restrict Editing pane. When restrictions are turned on, the Restrict Editing pane provides information about the actions you can perform in the document. Ribbon buttons that apply restricted formats are unavailable (grayed out).

Restrict formatting so that other people don't make unapproved content or formatting changes

> **SEE ALSO** For information about locking the change-tracking feature without restricting editing, see "Track changes" earlier in this chapter.

To display the Restrict Editing pane

- On the **Info** page of the Backstage view, select **Protect Document**, and then select **Restrict Editing**.

- On the **Review** tab or **Developer** tab, in the **Protect** group, select the **Restrict Editing** button.

> **SEE ALSO** The Developer tab is hidden by default. For information about displaying and hiding tabs, see "Customize the ribbon" in Chapter 16, "Customize options and the user interface."

To restrict the styles permitted in a document

1. Display the **Restrict Editing** pane.

2. In the **Formatting restrictions** area of the **Restrict Editing** pane, select the **Limit formatting to a selection of styles** checkbox, and then select **Settings** to display the **Formatting Restrictions** dialog.

The Allow AutoFormat option permits Word to apply automatic formatting, such as list formatting

3. Select the permitted styles by doing one of the following:

   - To allow only the recommended minimum style set, select **Recommended Minimum.**

   - To allow only specific styles, select **None** and then, in the **Checked styles are currently allowed** list box, select the checkboxes of the styles you want to allow.

   - To allow all styles and restrict only formatting, select **All.**

4. Select the permitted formatting by doing any of the following:

   - To permit Word to automatically format elements such as hyperlinks, bulleted lists, and numbered lists that aren't specified by a style, select the **Allow AutoFormat to override formatting restrictions** checkbox.

   - To permit only the current document theme, theme colors, and theme fonts, select the **Block Theme or Scheme switching** checkbox.

   - To permit only the current style set, select the **Block Quick Style Set switching** checkbox.

5. Select **OK** to implement the restricted set of styles. Word displays a message warning you that restricted styles will be removed.

Microsoft Word   ✕

❓ This document may contain formatting or styles that aren't allowed. Do you want to remove them?

                         [Yes]   [No]

Word displays this warning regardless of whether the document contains restricted styles

6. In the message box, select **Yes** to remove any restricted formatting and revert restricted styles to Normal.

7. In the **Start enforcement** area of the **Restrict Editing** pane, select **Yes, Start Enforcing Protection** to open the **Start Enforcing Protection** dialog.

People who don't know the password can't turn off the restrictions

8. If you want to require a password to turn off the restrictions, enter the password in the **Enter new password** and **Reenter password to confirm** boxes. Otherwise, leave the boxes blank.

9. In the **Start Enforcing Protection** dialog, select **OK** to turn on the restrictions.

To restrict the editing permitted in a document

1. Display the **Restrict Editing** pane.

2. In the **Editing restrictions** area of the pane, select the **Allow only this type of editing in the document** checkbox.

3. In the **Allow only this type of editing in the document** list, select one of the following:

   - **Tracked changes**

   - **Comments**

   - **Filling in forms**

   - **No changes (Read only)**

4. In the **Start enforcement** area of the **Restrict Editing** pane, select **Yes, Start Enforcing Protection** to open the Start Enforcing Protection dialog.

5. If you want to require a password to turn off the restrictions, enter the password in the **Enter new password** and **Reenter password to confirm** boxes. Otherwise, leave the boxes blank.

6. In the **Start Enforcing Protection** dialog, select **OK** to turn on the restrictions.

To remove restrictions for specific people

1. Display the **Restrict Editing** pane.

2. In the **Editing restrictions** area of the pane, select the **Allow only this type of editing in the document** checkbox, and then select either **Comments** or **No changes (Read only)** as the type of editing you want to permit for all users. An Exceptions section appears in the pane.

3. In the document, select the content that you want to permit a specific person or specific people to freely edit.

4. In the **Exceptions** area, if the **Groups** or **Individuals** box does NOT list the people or person you want to permit to edit the selection, do the following:

   a. Select **More users** to open the **Add Users** dialog.

b. Enter the user credentials of the person or people you want to allow to freely edit the selection.

When granting restriction exceptions to multiple people, separate the entries by using semicolons

c. In the **Add Users** dialog, select **OK**.

5. In the **Exceptions** area, select the checkbox that precedes each group or person you want to permit to edit the selection.

6. If you want to permit the editing of additional sections of content, repeat steps 3 through 5.

7. In the **Start enforcement** area of the **Restrict Editing** pane, select **Yes, Start Enforcing Protection** to open the **Start Enforcing Protection** dialog shown in the earlier procedure to restrict the styles permitted in a document.

8. In the **Start Enforcing Protection** dialog, select **User authentication**, and then select **OK** to turn on the restrictions.

To remove editing and formatting restrictions

1. Display the **Restrict Editing** pane.

2. At the bottom of the pane, select **Stop Protection**.

3. The **Unprotect Document** dialog opens regardless of whether a password is required.

When protecting a document, always use a password you can remember, because it can't be reset

4. In the **Unprotect Document** dialog, enter a password in the **Password** box if one is required. Otherwise, leave the **Password** box blank. Then select **OK** to remove the restrictions.

Restrict access by using a password

Sometimes, you might want to allow only certain people to open and change a document. The simplest way to do this for an individual document is to assign a password to protect the file. Then, anyone who wants to modify the document must enter a password when opening it.

You can assign a password to a document while working in the document or when saving the document. Word offers two levels of password protection:

- **Encrypted** The document is saved in such a way that people who do not know the password cannot open it at all.

- **Unencrypted** The document is saved in such a way that only people who know the password can open it, make changes, and save the file. People who don't know the password can open a read-only version. If they make changes and want to save them, they must save the document with a different name or in a different location, preserving the original.

Assigning a password to open a document encrypts the document; assigning a password to modify the document does not encrypt it

> ⚠ **IMPORTANT** Don't use common words or phrases as passwords, and don't use the same password for multiple documents. After assigning a password, make a note of it in a safe place. If you forget it, you won't be able to open the password-protected document.

To recommend against changes to a document

1. Display the **Save As** page of the Backstage view.

2. Using locations in the **Places** list, the current folder, or recent folders as a starting point, navigate to the folder you want to save the document in. If necessary, select **Browse** to display the Save As dialog.

3. If you want to protect a copy of the document instead of the original, enter a name for the copy in the **File name** box.

4. Near the lower-right corner of the **Save As** dialog, select **Tools**. Then in the **Tools** list, select **General Options**.

5. In the **General Options** dialog, select the **Read-only recommended** checkbox, and then select **OK**.

To prevent unauthorized changes by setting a password

1. On the **Save As** page of the Backstage view, navigate to the folder you want to save the password-protected document in. If necessary, select **Browse** to display the Save As dialog.

2. If you want to protect a copy of the document instead of the original, enter a name for the copy in the **File name** box.

3. Near the lower-right corner of the **Save As** dialog, select **Tools**. Then in the **Tools** list, select **General Options**.

4. In the **General Options** dialog, enter the password you want to assign to the document in the **Password to modify** box. Then select **OK** to display the Confirm Password dialog.

> **TIP** As you enter the password, Word obscures it for security.

5. In the **Confirm Password** dialog, enter the same password in the **Reenter password to modify** box, and then select **OK** to set the password.

6. In the **Save As** dialog, select **Save**. If Word prompts you to overwrite the original document, select **Yes**.

11

To test the security of a password-protected document

1. Open the document and verify that Word displays the **Password** dialog.

2. Enter an incorrect password, select **OK**, and verify that Word denies you access to the document.

To open a password-protected document for reading

1. Open the document.

2. In the **Password** dialog, select the **Read Only** button to open a read-only version of the document.

> **TIP** When using the default settings, Word opens the document in Read Mode.

To open a password-protected document for editing

1. Open the document.

2. In the **Password** dialog, enter the password that you assigned to the document, and then select **OK** to open a read/write version of the document.

To remove password protection from an unencrypted document

1. On the **Save As** page of the Backstage view, in the **Current Folder** area, select the current folder.

2. At the bottom of the **Save As** dialog, in the **Tools** list, select **General Options**.

3. In the **General Options** dialog, select the contents of the **Password to modify** box, press **Delete**, and then select **OK**.

4. In the **Save As** dialog, select **Save**.

To prevent document access by setting a password

1. Display the **Info** page of the Backstage view.

2. Select **Protect Document**, and then select **Encrypt with Password**.

After you assign the password, you'll no longer be able to open the document without it

3. In the **Encrypt Document** dialog, enter the password you want to assign in the **Password** box, and then select **OK**.

4. In the **Confirm Password** dialog, enter the same password in the **Password** box, and then select **OK**.

The Info page of the Backstage view displays the protected status of the document

5. Close the document and save your changes.

Or

1. On the **Save As** page of the Backstage view, navigate to the folder you want to save the password-protected document in. If necessary, select **Browse** to display the **Save As** dialog.

2. If you want to make a password-protected copy of the document, enter a name for the copy in the **File name** box.

3. Near the lower-right corner of the **Save As** dialog, select **Tools**. Then in the **Tools** list, select **General Options**.

4. In the **General Options** dialog, enter the password you want to assign to the document in the **Password to open** box. Then select **OK** to display the **Confirm Password** dialog.

5. Enter the same password in the **Reenter password to modify** box, and then select **OK** to set the password.

6. In the **Save As** dialog, select **Save**. If Word prompts you to overwrite the original document, select **Yes**.

To remove password encryption from a document

1. Open the document and enter the correct password.

2. On the **Info** page of the Backstage view, in the **Protect Document** list, select **Encrypt with Password**.

3. In the **Encrypt Document** dialog, delete the password from the **Password** box, and then select **OK**.

Coauthor documents

Whether you work for a large company or a small organization, you might need to collaborate with other people on the development of a document. Regardless of the circumstances, it can be difficult to keep track of different versions of a document produced by different people. If you store a document in a shared location such as a SharePoint document library or Microsoft OneDrive folder, multiple people can edit the document simultaneously.

After you save a document to a shared location, you can open and edit the document just as you would if it were stored on your computer. Other people can also open and edit the document either by browsing to it or from an invitation that you send. This facilitates efficient collaboration between people regardless of location, schedule, or time zone.

The process of inviting people to edit a shared file depends on the storage location. The file is automatically shared with other people who have access to the SharePoint document library or OneDrive folder. You can create links that allow other people to edit or view the file from the Share pane.

Provide read or write access to an online document

The sharing links you create can have unique audience and access settings. For example, you can create a link that allows anyone to edit the document, a different link that allows read-only access, and another that allows a specific person to edit the document for a limited period of time.

Sharing settings
Legal Contract.docx

Share the link with

🌐 Anyone ⓘ

👥 **Specific people**
Share with specific people you choose using their name, group, family, or email

More settings

✎ Can edit

📅 Expires Saturday, Jan 6, 2024

Apply   Cancel

Limit access to specific people and time periods

After you configure the link, you can have it sent through Outlook with a brief message that you compose in the Send Link pane, or you can copy the link and paste it into an email message, instant message, or other communication form, and send it to the people you want to invite to edit the file.

When other people open a shared file for editing, Word alerts you to their presence by displaying their user badge (a round badge displaying a photo or initials) on the ribbon.

Selecting an editor's user badge displays options for tracking the work that person is doing in the document and communicating with him or her. If the file is stored on SharePoint, you have the option of chatting with other editors directly in the document. Otherwise, you have an email option.

An alert appears as each editor opens the document

Word keeps track of the content that people are editing so you can see where other people are working in a document. If change tracking is turned on, you can see the changes they're making.

Active editing point

You can use Outlook ~~2019~~ to manage multiple email accounts, including ~~multiple~~ Microsoft Exchange <u>accounts</u> ~~Server or~~ Office 365 accounts, <u>internet mail</u> <u>accounts (such as Gmail),</u> and their associated contacts, calendars, and other elements. Even if you use Outlook only for sending and receiving email messages, it can be challenging to keep track of them and to locate specific information that you're looking for. Fortunately, Outlook provides many simple yet useful features that you can use to organize messages and other Outlook items and to quickly find information you need.

Word indicates the areas of the document that are being edited

When you turn on change tracking in a Word document, you can turn it on for all editors or only for yourself. If each person working in the document tracks his or her changes, the tracked changes remain available so that the document owner can accept or reject them when the team has finished working on the document.

To make a document available for coauthoring

- Save the document to a SharePoint document library or OneDrive folder.

To begin coauthoring a document

1. If the document is stored in a SharePoint document library, do NOT check it out.

2. Open the document directly from the document library or OneDrive folder.

3. Edit the document as you would normally. Other editors can join the document from the same location.

11

To create and copy a link that allows anyone to edit a file stored in OneDrive

■ To the right of the ribbon tabs, select the **Share** button, and then select **Copy Link**. Word creates the link and copies it to the Office Clipboard.

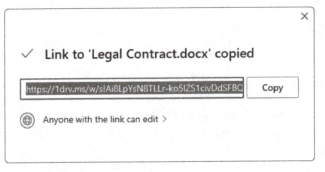

Quickly create and copy a link

Or

1. To the right of the ribbon tabs, select the **Share** button, and then select **Share**.

2. In the **Copy link** section of the pane, to the right of **Anyone with the link can edit**, select **Copy**.

To invite other people to edit or view a file stored in OneDrive

1. Do either of the following to display the **Share** pane:

   • To the right of the ribbon tabs, select the **Share** button, and then select **Share**.

   • In the left pane of the Backstage view, select **Share**.

2. In the **Send link** section of the pane, at the blinking insertion point below **Anyone with the link can edit**, enter the email addresses of the people you want to invite to edit the document, pressing **Tab** or **Enter** after each address.

3. If you want to place restrictions on the link, select the **Anyone with the link can edit** link above the recipient list to open the Sharing Settings pane, and then do any of the following:

   • To make the link work for only specific people, select **Specific people**.

   • To prevent link recipients from changing the document, select **Can edit**, and then select **Can view**.

- To expire the link on a specific date, select (click or tap) **MM/DD/YYYY** and then select the expiration date from the calendar, or drag to select **MM/DD/YYYY** and then enter the expiration date.

- To require a password in addition to the link, select **Set password**, and then enter the password.

- Select **Apply** after changing the sharing settings to return to the Share Link pane.

4. In the message area below the recipient list, enter any message you want to include in the sharing invitation.

5. Select **Send** to create and send an email message that contains your message and a link to the document on OneDrive.

To move to the location in a document where another editor is working

1. On the ribbon, select the user badge of the editor you want to locate.

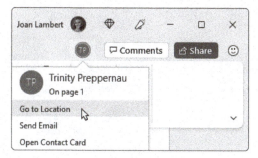

Easily locate edits other people are making

2. On the menu, select **Go to Location**.

To begin a chat in a document stored on SharePoint

- On the ribbon, select the user badge of the editor you want to chat with, and then select **Chat**.

Key points

- You can insert comments in a document to ask questions or explain suggested edits.

- You can track the revisions you make to a document without losing the original text. Word assigns different revision-tracking colors to multiple reviewers so you can easily identify change sources.

- You can merge multiple versions of a document so that the changes in all versions are tracked in one document.

- If only specific people should work on a document, you can protect it with a password. You can also restrict the types of changes people can make or force all changes to be tracked.

- Multiple people can simultaneously edit a document stored in a SharePoint document library or on OneDrive.

Practice tasks

Before you can complete these tasks, you must copy the book's practice files to your computer. The practice files for these tasks are in the **Word365SBS\Ch11** folder. You can save the results of the tasks in the same folder.

The book's Introduction includes a complete list of practice files and download instructions.

Mark up documents

Open the **TrackChanges** document in Word, display the document in Print Layout view, and then perform the following tasks:

1. Turn on change tracking.

2. Display the Comments pane.

3. In the last column of the table, select the words *some good*, and then attach the comment They carry the new Ultra line.

4. Configure the review settings to display the **All Markup** view of changes and to display only formatting in balloons.

5. If necessary, scroll through the document to display the table. Perform these tasks in the *Fabrikam* row of the table:

   - In the *Prices* column, delete the word *much* from the phrase *Some much lower*.

   - In the *Service* column, insert but slow after the word *Adequate*.

6. Perform these tasks in the *Northwind Traders* row of the table:

   - In the *Quality* column, replace the word *Poor* with Substandard.

   - Point to the deleted word and then to the inserted word to display information about the changes in ScreenTips.

7. Configure the review settings to display revisions in balloons instead of inline.

8. Restore the inline revision indicators and remove the balloons.

9. Move the last sentence of the paragraph (*Traveling for business...*) to the beginning of the paragraph. If necessary, insert a space after the sentence.

10. Turn off change tracking.

11. Configure the review settings to display the Simple Markup view.

12. Save and close the document.

Display and review document markup

Open the **ReviewComments** document in Word, display the document in Print Layout view, and then perform the following tasks:

1. Configure the review settings to display the **Simple Markup** view of changes.

2. Display only revisions made by Elizabeth Jones.

3. Move to the first comment shown in the document, which is attached to the word *competitors*. Delete the comment.

4. Move to the second comment, which is attached to the word *Adequate* in the *Service* column of the table. Point to the word in the table to display a ScreenTip that contains the name of the person who inserted the comment and the date and time the comment was inserted. Notice that the ScreenTip displays more information than the comment bubble.

5. Select the **Reply to Comment** button in the second comment bubble. In the reply box, enter If you had been a real customer, would you have left?

6. Display the **Revisions** pane on the left side of the app window. Then drag the pane away from the side of the window so that it floats independently.

7. In the **Revisions** pane, expand the detailed summary of revisions and note the types of revisions in the document.

8. Configure the review settings to display revisions made by all reviewers.

9. Scroll through the revisions in the pane, and then close it.

10. Configure the review settings to display the **All Markup** view of changes.

11. Hide all comments in the document.

12. Move between the tracked changes in the document.

    - Accept all the changes in the text paragraph.

    - Process the changes in the table as follows:

        - Reject the table formatting change.

        - Accept the deletion of the word *much*.

- Reject the changes associated with the addition of the words *but slow*.

- Accept both changes associated with the replacement of *Poor* with *Substandard*.

13. Configure the review settings to display the **No Markup** view of changes. Then change the balloon setting to the one you like best.

14. Save and close the document.

Compare and combine documents

Open a new, blank document in Word, and then perform the following tasks:

1. Compare the **MergeDocs1** and **MergeDocs2** documents by using the following settings:

   - Label unmarked changes from **MergeDocs2** with your name.

   - Select all available comparison settings.

   - Mark the differences in a separate document.

2. When Word completes the comparison, ensure that the **Revisions** pane is open on the left, the merged document in the center, and the two original documents on the right.

> **TIP** If the Revisions pane is not open, select Reviewing Pane in the Tracking group on the Review tab. If the source documents are not displayed, select the Compare button, select Show Source Documents, and then select Show Both.

3. In the center pane, scroll through the document to review all the revisions, and then in the **Revisions** pane, scroll through the individual revisions. Before changes can be accepted in the document, conflicting changes must be resolved.

4. In the **Revisions** pane, locate the deleted instance of *March* and then accept the deletion.

5. Select each change that remains in the **Revisions** pane to display that location in the three document panes.

6. Select the merged document in the center pane to activate it. Then accept all the changes in the document at the same time.

7. Close the **Revisions** pane, and then close the two windows on the right side of the screen.

8. Save the merged document as MyMergedDocument, and then close it.

Control content changes

Open the **ControlChanges** document, and then perform the following tasks:

1. Save a copy of the document, naming the copy MyControlChanges, and require the password P@ssw0rd1 to modify the document but no password to read the document.

2. Configure the document options to recommend that people open a read-only copy of the document.

3. Close the document, and then open a read-only version of it.

4. Attempt to make a change and verify that you can't save the changed document.

5. Close the document, and then use the password to open an editable version of it.

6. Remove the password protection from the document.

7. Encrypt the document and require the password P@ssw0rd2 to open it.

8. Restrict the formatting in the document to only the recommended minimum styles.

9. Block users from switching schemes or style sets.

10. Turn on the restrictions and remove any formatting and styles that don't meet the requirements you selected. Notice the changes to the document.

11. Configure the editing restrictions so that you can edit only the first paragraph of the document and other people aren't permitted to make any changes.

12. Save and close the document.

Coauthor documents

There is no practice task for this topic because it requires that documents be stored in a shared location.

Finalize and distribute documents

When you finish developing a document, you'll often want to distribute either a printed version or an electronic version. Before committing the document to paper, you should check that the pages are efficiently laid out and that there are no glaring problems, such as spelling errors or headings that print on separate pages from their text. Word provides several tools that you can use to ensure the accuracy of your content and control page layout. When you're ready to print, you can control precisely how many copies and what parts of your document appear on paper.

If you intend to distribute your document electronically, Word provides tools for ensuring that the document doesn't contain unresolved revisions, hidden text, or identifying information that you might not want to provide to other people. It also provides tools for indicating that a document is final and ready to distribute, and makes it easy to send the document by using email.

This chapter guides you through procedures related to locating and correcting text errors, previewing and adjusting page layout, controlling what appears on each page, preparing documents for electronic distribution, and printing and sending documents.

In this chapter

- Locate and correct text errors

- Preview and adjust page layout

- Control what appears on each page

- Prepare documents for electronic distribution

- Print and send documents

Locate and correct text errors

In the days of handwritten and typewritten documents, people might have tolerated a typographical or grammatical error or two because correcting such errors without creating a mess was difficult. Word-processing apps such as Word have built-in spelling and grammar checkers, so documents that contain these types of errors are likely to reflect badly on their creators.

> **TIP** Although Word can help you eliminate misspellings and grammatical errors, its tools are not infallible. You should always read through your document to catch any problems that the Word tools don't detect—for example, homonyms such as *their, there,* and *they're.*

Word provides three tools to help you avoid editorial errors:

- **AutoCorrect**   This feature corrects common spelling and grammatical errors, replaces text codes with mathematical symbols, and automatically applies formatting based on text cues. AutoCorrect has a built-in list of frequently misspelled words and their correct spellings. If you frequently misspell a word that AutoCorrect doesn't change, you can add it to the list in the AutoCorrect dialog. If you deliberately enter a word that is on the AutoCorrect list and don't want to accept the AutoCorrect change, you can undo the correction.

> **SEE ALSO** For information about modifying the AutoCorrect settings, see the "Manage proofing options" section of "Change default Word options" in Chapter 16, "Customize options and the user interface."

- **Error indicators**   Word indicates possible spelling errors with red wavy underlines, possible grammatical errors with blue double underlines, and refinements such as clarity, conciseness, and vocabulary choices with gold dotted underlines.

> **TIP** Word's grammar checker helps identify phrases and clauses that don't follow traditional grammatical rules, but it's not always accurate. It's easy to get in the habit of ignoring blue double underlines. However, it's wise to scrutinize them all to be sure that your documents don't contain any embarrassing mistakes.

- **Editor pane**   This pane identifies the number of spelling, grammar, and wording issues it finds in the document. When you select a spelling or grammar error in the document, the Editor pane displays possible alternative spellings or word choices. You can also display information about the grammar rule that applies to the flagged text.

  When you select flagged text in the Clarity or Conciseness area of the Editor pane, the pane displays suggestions for better word choices.

  At the top of the Editor pane is the Editor Score, which is a percentage value that reflects the number of suggestions that Word is making to improve the document, relative to the length of the document. The greater the number of spelling and grammar errors, and the more suggestions Word makes in the Refinements section of the Editor pane, the lower the Editor Score. Increase your document's score by fixing (or ignoring) errors and by implementing (or ignoring) suggested refinements.

Editorial issues are underlined in the text and managed from the Editor pane

> ✓ **TIP** Word saves your responses to suggested spelling and grammar changes with the document. If you choose to ignore a flagged error, the error will not be reflagged when you check again in the same document.

From the Grammar Settings dialog, you can specify the grammatical issues and refinements you want the Editor to check for. This dialog contains several categories of options for grammar and refinement.

The Grammar category contains more than 100 issues that Word can check for, including the following:

- Academic Degrees
- Adjective Used instead of Adverb
- Adjective Used instead of Noun
- Adjective Used instead of Verb
- Adverb instead of Adjective
- Agreement within Noun Phrases
- "An" "And" Confusion
- Capitalization
- Capitalization of "March" and "May"
- Capitalization of Personal Titles
- Comma after Conjunction
- Comma after Greetings
- Comma before Contrast
- Comma before Prepositional Phrase
- Comma before Quotations
- Comma Missing after Introductory Phrase
- Comma Splice
- Comma Used instead of Conjunction
- Comma with Conjunction
- Comma with Conjunctive Adverbs
- Commas around Descriptive Clause
- Commas with Nonrestrictive Relative

- Commas with Parenthetical
- Commas with Restrictive Relative
- Commonly Confused Phrases
- Commonly Confused Words
- Comparative Use
- Correlative Conjunction Mismatch
- Date Formatting
- Divide Word
- Embarrassing Words
- Fused Sentence
- Hyphenation
- Incomplete Correlative Conjunction Pair
- Incorrect Auxiliary
- Incorrect Comma
- Incorrect Determiner
- Incorrect Intensifier
- Incorrect Negation
- Incorrect Number Ending
- Incorrect Preposition
- Incorrect Pronoun Case
- Incorrect Quantifier
- Incorrect Reflexive Pronoun Use

- Incorrect Tag Question
- Incorrect Use of "That"
- Incorrect Verb Form
- Incorrect Verb Form after Auxiliary
- Indefinite Article
- Indirect Questions
- Misheard Phrases
- Missing Auxiliary
- Missing Coordinating Conjunction
- Missing Comma
- Missing Comma between Adjectives
- Missing Determiner
- Missing End Punctuation
- Missing Object
- Missing Preposition
- Missing Quantifier
- Missing Quotation Marks
- Missing Relativizer or Interrogative
- Missing Semicolon or Period
- Missing Subject
- Missing Subordinating Conjunction
- Missing Verb
- Modal Confusion
- Multiple Modals
- Noun Number
- Participle or Adjective Form
- Possessive and Plural Forms

- Pronoun Number
- Punctuation
- Question Mark Missing
- Redundant Colon
- Redundant Comma before Complement Clause
- Redundant Comma before Object
- Redundant Comma following Subject
- Redundant Noun Phrase
- Redundant Question Mark
- Repeated Auxiliary
- Semicolon Use
- Sentence Fragment
- Spacing
- Subject-Verb Agreement
- Too Many Determiners
- Too Many Verbs
- Unnecessary Adverb
- Unnecessary Conjunction
- Unnecessary Determiner
- Unnecessary Hyphen
- Unnecessary Preposition
- Unnecessary Prepositional Phrase
- Unnecessary Pronoun
- Unnecessary Quantifier
- Use of Plain Verb Form
- Use of the Word "Lack"
- Use of "Will" and "Would"

12

- Verb Use
- Verb Used instead of Noun
- "Which" "Who" Confusion
- "Who" "Whom" Confusion
- Wrong Noun
- Word Order

- Word Split
- Wrong Conjunction
- Wrong Suffix
- Wrong Verb
- Wrong Verb Tense

In the Clarity category, you can choose to check for these types of clarity issues:

- Adjective Order
- Adverb Placement
- Double Negation
- Jargon
- Number Words
- Passive Voice
- Passive Voice with Unknown Actor

- Sentence Structure
- Simpler Wording
- Split Infinitives
- Use of Euphemisms
- Verb Number with Collective Noun
- Whether vs If

In the Conciseness category, you can choose to check for these types of issues:

- Conjunction Overuse
- Nominalizations
- Progressive Use

- Wordiness
- Words Expressing Uncertainty

The following table lists other refinements you can check for.

Category	Issue
Formality	Colloquial Verb Phrase
	Contractions
	Informal Language
	Missing Auxiliary in Question
	Number Formatting
	Opinion Markers
	Preposition at End of Clause
	Slang
	Subjunctive Mood

Inclusiveness	Age Bias
	Cultural Bias
	Ethnic Slurs
	Gender Bias
	Gendered Pronouns
	Gender-Specific Language
	Racial Bias
	Sexual Orientation Bias
	Socio-economic Bias
Punctuation Conventions	Comma with Adverbials
	Oxford Comma
	Unnecessary Commas
	Punctuation Required with Quotes
	Space between Sentences
Resume	Avoid First-Person References
	Superfluous Expressions
	Unsuitable Expressions
	Vague Quantifiers
	Vague Verbs
Sensitive Geopolitical References	Geopolitical References
Vocabulary	Clichés
	Collective Nouns
	Conventional Phrasing
	Locale-Specific Words
	Profanity
	Region-Specific Words
	Vague Adjectives
	Vague or Superfluous Adverbs
	Weak Verbs

12

> **TIP** Specify the behavior of the spelling and grammar checker from the Proofing page of the Word Options dialog. For information, see the "Manage proofing options" section of "Change default Word options" in Chapter 16.

To undo an AutoCorrect correction

- Before entering any new text, do any of the following:
  - On the Quick Access Toolbar, select the **Undo** button.
  - Press **Ctrl+Z**.
  - Point to the bar that appears below the word, and then select **Undo**.

To display the Editor pane

- On the **Home** tab, in the **Editor** group, select **Editor**.
- On the **Review** tab, in the **Proofing** group, select **Editor**.
- Press **F7**.

To fine-tune the level of detail the Editor pane checks for

1. Display the Editor pane.

2. Select any category in the Corrections or Refinements section.

3. At the bottom of the pane that appears, select **Settings** to display the Proofing page of the Word Options dialog.

4. Under **When correcting spelling and grammar in Word**, select **Settings** to open the Grammar Settings dialog.

> ✓ **TIP** The default selected checkboxes in the Grammar Settings dialog change depending on whether you have Grammar & Refinements or Grammar selected as the Writing Style in the Proofing page of the Word Options dialog.

5. In the **Grammar Settings** dialog, below each section, select or clear the checkboxes. The **Punctuation Conventions** section contains two dropdown lists:
   - **Punctuation Required with Quotes**   Select **don't check, inside,** or **outside** from the list.
   - **Space Between Sentences**   Select **don't check, one space,** or **two spaces** from the list.

6. Select **OK** in both the Grammar Settings and Word Options dialog to close them.

To review flagged text from within the body of the document

1. Right-click or long-press (tap and hold) any word or phrase marked with an underscore. Word displays suggestions to correct or improve the current spelling or wording at the top of the shortcut menu.

As you know, operateing an import business that sells a new item such as Quirggels in the global arena requires careful consideration of current economic and environmental conditions, as well as of political issues that could affect our ability to maintain a viable business. When we select our product sorces, we strive to not only to improve the local economy but to to ensu̱...

but we are commited to...

			sources		Read Aloud
abc Spelling	>		bases, informants, upwellings		Change All
X Cut			Add to Dictionary		Add to AutoCorrect
Copy			Ignore All		AutoCorrect Options...
Paste Options:			See More		

This is a exciting and ch...
corporate office to disc...
that you are unable to v...
(925) 555-0167, through...
our corporate address.

...mail at

Search "sorces"

In the meantime, here i̱...
and suppliers, a travel ṉ...
statement, which outlin...
Contoso.

A⁾ Read Aloud

Translate

...ional material that includes a list of products
...rchasing agents in the field, and our mission
...o supporting grass-root businesses such as

Sincerely,

Link >

New Comment

The shortcut menu lists spelling options from the dictionary and related actions

> **SEE ALSO** For information about the Link option on the shortcut menu, see the sidebar "Hyperlink to additional resources" in Chapter 13, "Reference content and content sources."

2. Select any of the suggestions to replace the word or phrase.

To review and correct the spelling, grammar, and clarity or conciseness in a document

1. Display the **Editor** pane.

2. If spelling changes are recommended, select **Spelling** to display the Spelling page of the Editor pane, and then do any of the following:

   - To continue the review without changing the highlighted word, select **Ignore Once** or **Ignore All**.

   - Select **Add to Dictionary** to add the word to the dictionary on your computer.

   - Select the correct spelling of the word in the **Suggestions** list or select the downward-pointing arrow at the end of the word and select **Change All** to change all instances of this word in the document.

12

- If the selection is identified as a repeated word, select **Ignore Once** to continue the review without making a change, or select **Delete Repeated Word** to delete the highlighted instance of the duplicated word.

The Editor pane highlights misspelled or duplicated words and suggests corrections

3. If grammatical changes are recommended, select **Grammar** to display the Grammar page of the Editor pane, review the guidance, and then do one of the following:

   - Select the correct usage in the **Suggestions** list to change the selection to the new usage.

   - Select **Ignore Once** to continue the review without making a change.

   - Select **Don't check for this issue** (if available) to ignore this instance and avoid having it flagged anywhere else in the document.

4. If recommendations appear in any of the categories in the Refinements section, select a category to display that page in the Editor pane. To address each issue, do one of the following:

   - Select the suggestion in the **Suggestions** list to implement the change.

   - Select **Ignore Once** to continue the review without making a change.

   - Select **Don't check for this issue** to ignore this instance and avoid having the same issue flagged anywhere else in the document.

5. When you select a button to fix or ignore the issue, the Editor pane moves to the next word in that category for which Word has a suggestion. After the last Editor pane recommendation has been addressed within a category, the main page of the Editor pane is displayed, and a checkmark appears next to the category you've finished reviewing. Select the next category that contains an editorial recommendation and repeat the preceding steps that apply to that category.

6. Select the **Close** button to close the Editor pane. When a message indicating that it has finished checking the document appears, select **OK**.

To turn off the automatic spelling checking function

1. Display the **Proofing** page of the **Word Options** dialog.

2. In the **When correcting spelling and grammar in Word** section, clear the **Check spelling as you type** checkbox.

To specify the grammar and style issues Word checks for

1. Display the **Proofing** page of the **Word Options** dialog.

2. In the **When correcting spelling and grammar in Word** section, select the **Settings** button to open the Grammar Settings dialog. By default, most grammar and refinement options are selected.

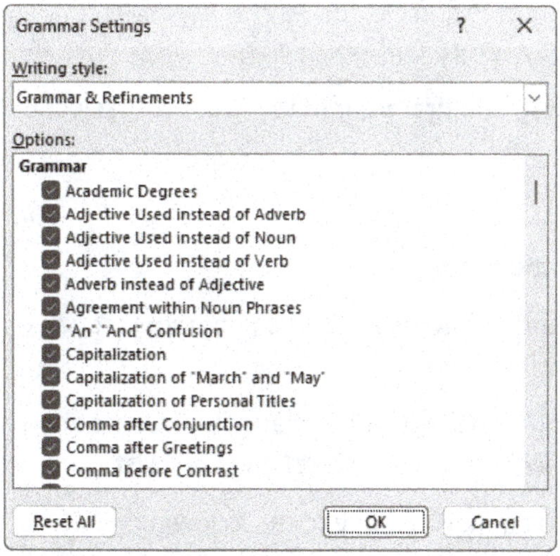

Specify the types of grammar and style issues Word checks for

3. In the **Grammar Settings** dialog, use the Writing Style list to select either Grammar & Refinements or Grammar.

12

4. Clear the checkboxes of any grammar or refinement issues you don't want Word to check for. Then select **OK**.

> ✅ **TIP** Typically, the issues you might want to ignore are those for which you consistently select Ignore when running a spelling and grammar check from the Review tab.

To hide underlines that indicate spelling or grammar errors or clarity issues

1. Display the **Proofing** page of the **Word Options** dialog.

2. In the **Exceptions for** list, do either of the following:

   - Select **All New Documents** to hide error indicators until you change this selection.

   - Select a specific document file name to hide error indicators in that document.

3. In the **Exceptions for** section, select one or both of the following checkboxes:

   - Hide spelling errors in this document only

   - Hide grammar errors in this document only

To clear hidden errors and check spelling and grammar against the current criteria

1. Display the **Proofing** page of the **Word Options** dialog.

2. In the **When correcting spelling and grammar in Word** section, select the **Recheck Document** button.

To manage a custom dictionary

1. Display the **Proofing** page of the **Word Options** dialog.

2. In the **When correcting spelling in Microsoft Office programs** section of the page, select **Custom Dictionaries**.

3. The Custom Dictionaries dialog displays the dictionaries that Office apps consult. Select one of the dictionaries, and then select **Edit Word List**.

4. In the dialog for the selected dictionary, do any of the following:

   - To review the content of the dictionary, scroll through the **Dictionary** pane.

   - To remove a word from the dictionary, select it in the **Dictionary** pane, and then select **Delete**.

- To clear the entire dictionary, select **Delete All**.

- To add a word to the dictionary, enter it in the **Word(s)** box and then select **OK**.

The dictionary includes words that you've added from the Editor pane, from the shortcut menu, or manually

Preview and adjust page layout

12

Working on your document in the default Print Layout view means that you always know how the document content will appear on the printed page. While you're working in the document, you can use the commands in the Page Setup group on the Layout tab to adjust the page settings (such as the margins and page orientation) to best suit your content and delivery method. If you're planning to deliver the document at a page size other than the default, you can format the document to display and print correctly by changing the paper size.

Although the layout of each page is visible in Print Layout view, it's also a good idea to preview the whole document before you print it. This gives you more of a high-level overview of the document than when you're working directly in the content. Previewing is essential for multipage documents but is helpful even for one-page documents. You can preview a document as it will appear when printed, on the Print page of the Backstage view. The preview area shows exactly how each page of the document will look when printed on the selected printer.

The Print page displays a preview of the document as it will appear when printed

> **TIP** Press Ctrl+P to display the Print page of the Backstage view. For more information about keyboard shortcuts, see the appendix, "Keyboard shortcuts," at the end of this book.

If you don't like what appears in the preview pane of the Print page, you don't have to leave the Backstage view to make adjustments. The left pane of the Print page provides access to many of the commands available in the Page Setup group on the Page Layout tab, allowing you to change the following document settings while previewing their effect on the printed page:

- **Orientation** You can switch the direction in which a page is laid out on the paper. The default orientation is Portrait, in which the page is taller than it is wide. You can set the orientation to Landscape, in which the page is wider than it is tall.

- **Paper size** You can switch to one of the paper sizes available for the selected printer.

- **Margins** Changing the margins of a document changes where information can appear on each page. You can select one of Word's predefined sets of top, bottom, left, and right margins, or set custom margins.

All the pages of a document have the same orientation and margins unless you divide the document into sections. Then each section can have independent orientation and margin settings.

> SEE ALSO For more information about sections, see "Control what appears on each page" later in this chapter.

By default, hidden text does not print with the document. If your document contains hidden text that you want to print, you can configure that option in the Print settings.

If you want to configure multiple print layout settings in one place, or configure settings for only specific sections of the document, use the Page Setup dialog. This dialog provides the most comprehensive set of tools for page layout.

> ⚠ IMPORTANT You must have a printer installed to perform the following procedures. On a default installation of Microsoft 365, the Microsoft Print to PDF and Microsoft XPS Document Writer options appear in your Printers list. You can perform the procedures by using one of those options or an actual local or network printer connection.

To adjust page layout settings from the Page Setup dialog

1. Do either of the following:

   - On the **Print** page of the Backstage view, at the bottom of the left pane, select **Page Setup**.

   - On the **Layout** tab, select the **Page Setup** dialog launcher.

2. In the **Page Setup** dialog, do any of the following:

   - On the **Margins** tab, make the margin adjustments you want.

     > SEE ALSO For information about working with margins, see the procedure "To modify document margins" later in this topic.

   - On the **Paper** tab, make any necessary changes to the paper settings.

   - On the **Layout** tab, make the layout adjustments you want.

3. When you're satisfied with your settings, select **OK**.

12

To preview a document as it will appear when printed

- Display the **Print** page of the Backstage view. The page navigator below the preview pane indicates the number of pages the document will print on. Then do any of the following:

  - To move between pages, select the **Next Page** or **Previous Page** button, or enter the number of the page you want to display in the page navigator box.

  - To preview multiple pages, reduce the magnification until two or more pages fit in the preview pane.

Move between pages, zoom in or out, or fit a page to the available space

> ✓ **TIP** If you want to preview a multipage document as it will look when printed on both sides of the page and bound, add a blank page or a cover page to the beginning of the document before previewing it.

- To display a single page at the largest size that fits in the preview pane, select the **Zoom to Page** button in the lower-right corner.

To modify document margins

1. From the **Print** page of the Backstage view, do either of the following to display the margin settings:

   - In the **Settings** area, select the current margin setting to display the **Margins** menu.

*Select from predefined margin settings
or set your own*

> **TIP** While editing a document, you can display the same Margins menu by selecting the Margins button in the Page Setup group on the Layout tab.

12

- At the bottom of the left pane, select the **Page Setup** link to display the Margins tab of the Page Setup dialog.

Mirror Margins is a good choice for double-sided documents

2. From the menu or in the dialog, configure the margin settings as you want them. The preview area reflects the change.

Or

1. On the **Layout** tab, in the **Page Setup** group, select **Margins**.

2. On the **Margins** menu, select the predefined margin settings you want, or select **Custom Margins** and set your margins how you want them from the **Page Setup** dialog.

To change the page orientation

1. On the **Print** page of the Backstage view, in the **Settings** area, select the current orientation to display the **Orientation** menu.

2. Select either **Landscape Orientation** or **Portrait Orientation**. The preview area reflects the change.

To include hidden text when printing documents

1. Open the **Word Options** dialog, and then select **Display**.

2. In the **Printing options** area of the **Display** page, select the **Print hidden text** checkbox. Then select **OK**.

> ⚠ IMPORTANT Changing the Print Hidden Text option in the Word Options dialog changes this setting for all documents.

Control what appears on each page

When a document includes more content than will fit between its top and bottom margins, Word creates a new page by inserting a *soft page break* (a page break that moves if the preceding content changes). If you want to break a page in a place other than where Word would normally break it, you can insert a manual page break (also called a *hard page break*). As you edit the content of a document, Word changes the location of the soft page breaks but not of any manual page breaks.

> ⚠ IMPORTANT It's important to set manual page breaks and layout options from the beginning of a document to the end because each change you make affects the content from that point forward.

12

If a paragraph breaks so that most of it appears on one page but its last line appears at the top of the next page, the line is called a *widow*. If a paragraph breaks so that its first line appears at the bottom of one page and the rest of the paragraph appears on the next page, the line is called an *orphan*. These single lines of text can make a document hard to read, so by default Word specifies that a minimum of two lines should appear at the top and bottom of each page. As with so many other aspects of Word, however, you have control over this setting.

You can also control the following options for keeping content together on a page:

- **Keep with next**   Prevents Word from breaking a page between the selected paragraph and the following paragraph.

- **Keep lines together**   Prevents Word from breaking a page within the paragraph.

- **Page break before**   Inserts an invisible page break before the paragraph.

A small black square in the left margin indicates that one of the Keep options is on for that paragraph

> ✅ **TIP** By selecting Keep With Next instead of inserting a page break, you allow the content to move from page to page as long as it stays with the following paragraph. You can apply these options to individual paragraphs, or you can incorporate them into the styles you define for document elements such as headings. For information about styles, see "Create and modify styles" in Chapter 15, "Create custom document elements."

When you want to format part of a document differently from the rest—for example, with page layout settings different from those of the surrounding text—you do so by inserting section breaks above and below it. A common example of this is when you need to print a wide table on a page with a Landscape orientation within a report with a Portrait page orientation. Word uses four types of section breaks:

- **Next Page**   Starts the following section on the next page

- **Continuous**   Starts a new section without affecting page breaks

- **Even Page**   Starts the following section on the next even-numbered page

- **Odd Page**   Starts the following section on the next odd-numbered page

When you display hidden formatting marks, a section break appears in Print Layout view as a double-dotted line from the preceding paragraph mark to the margin, with the words *Section Break* and the type of section break in the middle of the line.

> ✓ **TIP** Formatting selected text in columns automatically inserts section breaks. For more information, see "Present information in columns" in Chapter 5, "Organize information in columns and tables."

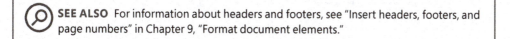

Processing a Personal Check Invoice¶
If the customer is going to mail a check to us rather than paying via credit card, follow these steps:¶

1. → Create the customer invoice.¶
2. → Send the invoice to the customer.¶
3. → Enter Tentative in the customer's Access account until you receive the check and the check has cleared the bank.··Section Break (Next Page)···································

¶

¶

4. → ¶

Shipping Quick Reference¶

Package for shipment¤	
Customer information, existing account?¤	¤
PO for payment with existing account?¤	¤
Shipping company/method of shipment?¤	¤
Delivery when?¤	¤
Invoice and tracking slip¤	¤
Process order¤	¤
Paperwork to customer¤	¤

The heading and table move to the next page, after the section break indicator

You can configure individual page layout, page setup, and headers and footers for each section.

> 🔍 **SEE ALSO** For information about headers and footers, see "Insert headers, footers, and page numbers" in Chapter 9, "Format document elements."

12

To insert a manual page break

■ Position the cursor where you want to insert the page break in the document, and then do any of the following:

- On the **Insert** tab, in the **Pages** group, select **Page Break**.

- On the **Layout** tab, in the **Page Setup** group, select **Breaks**, and then select **Page**.

- Press **Ctrl+Enter**.

To control paragraph page break settings

1. Select the paragraph or paragraphs that you want to modify.

2. On the **Layout** tab, select the **Paragraph** dialog launcher to open the Paragraph dialog. Then select the **Line and Page Breaks** tab.

Filled checkboxes indicate that the setting is not the same for all selected content

3. On the **Line and Page Breaks** tab, do any of the following:

   - Select the **Widow/Orphan control** checkbox to have Word control widows and orphans.

   - Select the **Keep with next** checkbox to prevent Word from breaking a page between the selected paragraph and the following paragraph.

   - Select the **Keep lines together** checkbox to prevent Word from breaking a page within the paragraph.

   - Select the **Page break before** checkbox to have Word break a page before the paragraph.

To insert a section break

1. Position the cursor where you want to insert the section break in the document.

2. On the **Layout** tab, in the **Page Setup** group, select **Breaks**, and then do any of the following:

   - Select **Next Page** to start the new section at the top of the next page.

   - Select **Continuous** to start a new section without affecting page breaks.

   - Select **Even Page** to start the following section on the next even-numbered page.

   - Select **Odd Page** to start the following section on the next odd-numbered page.

To remove a page break or section break

- Click or tap at the left end of the break, or select the break, and then press the **Delete** key.

12

Prepare documents for electronic distribution

When a document is complete, you can distribute it in two ways: printed on paper or electronically. When you distribute a printed document, only the printed information is visible to the reader. When you distribute a document electronically, you should ensure that no confidential information is attached to the file and that it can be viewed by the people you're sending it to. Some of the information attached to the document is available with the document properties on the Info page of the Backstage view. You can change or remove some types of information from this page and more types of information from either the Document Panel or the Properties dialog.

> **SEE ALSO** For information about properties, see "Display and edit file properties" in Chapter 2, "Create and manage documents."

Many documents go through several revisions, and some are scrutinized by multiple reviewers. During this development process, documents can accumulate information that you might not want in the final version, such as the names of people who worked on the document, the time spent working on the document, and comments that reviewers have added to the file. There might also be hidden tracked changes. This information is not a concern if the final version is to be delivered as a printout. However, it has become very common to deliver documents electronically, making this information available to anyone who wants to read it.

Word includes these three tools that you can use to check for hidden and personal information, accessibility issues, and version compatibility issues:

- **Document Inspector**   Automates the process of finding and removing all extraneous and potentially confidential information.

Inspect Document

Check for Issues ˅

Before publishing this file, be aware that it contains:

- Document properties, document server properties and content type information
- Headers
- Characters formatted as hidden text
- Custom XML data
- Content that people with disabilities are unable to read

The Inspect Document area displays information about the document content

- **Accessibility Checker**   Identifies document elements and formatting that might be difficult for people with certain kinds of disabilities to read or for assistive devices such as screen readers to access.

  This tool checks for many common accessibility issues and provides explanations and recommendations for fixing them. You can leave the Accessibility Checker open while you work; its contents will automatically update to indicate the current issues. After you run the Accessibility Checker, information about document content issues is also shown in the Inspect Document area of the Info page of the Backstage view.

> **TIP** For more information about designing documents for accessibility, run the Accessibility Checker and then select the Read More About Making Documents Accessible link at the bottom of the Accessibility pane.

- **Compatibility Checker** Identifies formatting and features not supported in earlier versions of Word.

After you determine that a document is ready to distribute, you can mark the document as final so that other people know that they should not make changes to the released document.

To inspect a document for common issues

1. Display the **Info** page of the Backstage view.

2. In the **Inspect Document** area on the left side of the **Info** page, select the **Check for Issues** button, and then select **Inspect Document** to open the Document Inspector dialog, which lists the items that will be checked.

3. If Word prompts you to save changes to the file, select **Yes**.

4. Clear the checkboxes for any of the properties you don't want to check for, and then select **Inspect** to view the **Document Inspector** report on the presence of the properties you selected. In addition to the basic properties displayed in the Properties section of the Info page, the Document Inspector might return information on headers and footers and custom XML data.

12

Document Inspector ? ✕

Review the inspection results.

⊘ **Comments, Revisions, and Versions**
No items were found.

! **Document Properties and Personal Information** [Remove All]
The following document information was found:
* Document properties
* Author
* Document server properties

⊘ **Task Pane Add-ins**
We did not find any Task Pane add-ins.

⊘ **Embedded Documents**
No embedded documents were found.

⊘ **Macros, Forms, and ActiveX Controls**
No macros, forms, or ActiveX controls were found.

⊘ **Ink**
Inspects the document for Ink.

⊘ **Collapsed Headings**
Inspects the documen

! **Custom XML Data** [Remove All]
Custom XML data was found.

! **Headers, Footers, and Watermarks** [Remove All]
The following items were found:
* Headers
* Footers
Headers and footers may include shapes such as watermarks.

⊘ **Invisible Content**
No invisible objects found.

⊘ **Hidden Text**
No hidden text was found.

⚠ Note: Some changes cannot be undone.

[Inspect] [Close]

The Document Inspector evaluates up to 11 categories of information

5. Review the results, and then select the **Remove All** button for any category of information that you want to remove.

 TIP You can choose to retain content identified by the Document Inspector if you know that it is appropriate for distribution.

6. In the **Document Inspector** dialog, select **Reinspect**, and then select **Inspect** to verify the removal of the properties and other data you selected.

7. When you're satisfied with the results, close the **Document Inspector** dialog.

To inspect a document for accessibility issues

1. Do either of the following:

   - On the **Info** page of the Backstage view, select **Check For Issues**, and then select **Check Accessibility** to display the Accessibility pane.

   - On the **Review** tab, in the **Accessibility** group, select **Check Accessibility**.

2. In the **Accessibility** pane, review the inspection results and make any changes you want to the document.

3. When you're done, do either of the following:

   - Select the **X** in the upper-right corner of the **Accessibility** pane to close the pane.

   - Leave the pane open to continue checking for accessibility issues as you work with the document.

To check a document for compatibility with earlier versions of Word

1. On the **Info** page of the Backstage view, select the **Check Compatibility** button to run the Compatibility Checker.

2. In the **Microsoft Word Compatibility Checker** dialog, review the results, make any changes you want, and then select **OK**.

> **TIP** By default, Word always checks for compatibility whenever you save a document. If you don't want Word to do this, clear the Check Compatibility When Saving Documents checkbox in the Microsoft Word Compatibility Checker dialog.

12

Accessibility issues

Whenever you create a document that will be distributed electronically, particularly if it will be displayed as a webpage, think about whether its content will be accessible to all the people you want to reach. For example, consider the following:

- Not all people will display the document in the same version of Word or in the same web browser in which you preview it.

- Some people might set their default web browser font sizes larger than usual or display their web browser content at an increased zoom level.

- Some people can't differentiate changes in color. Others might have their computers configured to display a high-contrast color scheme that changes the default colors of text so they can read it better.

- People with visual impairments might use an assistive device such as a screen reader to "read" content to them from the document or webpage.

- Web browsers might be configured to hide certain page elements.

- A slow connection might prevent the display of large images.

If you intend to publish the document on a public webpage, consider also whether the terms that your prospective viewers might search for are accessible to search engines.

You can do some things to make a document display more uniformly on-screen (or on paper) and be more accessible to assistive devices and internet search engines:

- Use styles to format content, rather than applying manual formatting. This allows readers to move directly to specific headings from the document Navigation pane, and to apply style sets that use legible fonts and high-contrast colors to make content easier to read on the screen.

- Similarly, when specifying colors, use the theme colors so that they change appropriately when viewers choose high-contrast themes.

- If your content includes graphics, add a caption to each image and add a written description of the image to the image properties as alternative text (frequently referred to as *alt text*). The alt text is displayed in place of the image when the image can't be displayed on-screen. It can also be read aloud by screen readers.

- Also to assist screen readers, wrap text around images by using the In Line With Text setting so that images do not interrupt text.

- Do not use watermarks or background colors, patterns, or images that might interfere with the readability of the document content.

- Present information in the standard content of the document rather than in text boxes. Content in text boxes might not be accessible to screen readers.

- To ensure that screen readers can access content in the intended reading order, present it in text paragraphs rather than in tabbed lists or tables. If you must present information in a table, follow these guidelines:

  - Use the standard table formats—don't "draw" the table manually, merge or split cells, or nest tables. Variances in the table might cause assistive devices to incorrectly interpret the content.

  - If your table will span multiple pages, select the option to repeat the header row so that the headers are both visible and accessible to assistive devices.

  - Add alt text and captions to tables in case they are incorrectly displayed or interpreted.

- When formatting hyperlinks, provide ScreenTip text.

SEE ALSO For information about creating ScreenTips for hyperlinks, see the sidebar "Hyperlink to additional resources" in Chapter 13.

12

To mark a document as final

1. On the **Info** page of the Backstage view, in the **Protect Document** area, select **Protect Document**, and then select **Mark As Final**. A message tells you that the document will be marked as final and then saved.

2. In the message box, select **OK**. A message tells you that the document has been marked as final, the status property has been set to Final, and typing, editing commands, and proofing marks are turned off.

3. In the message box, select **OK**. The document title bar indicates that the document is read-only (no changes can be saved), and the Protect Document area indicates that the file has been marked as final.

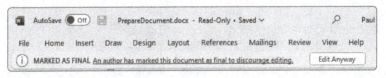

The Info page reminds people that the file is final

4. Select the **Return** button (the arrow) above the Backstage view page tabs to return to the document. Notice that only the ribbon tabs are visible; the commands are hidden. Word displays an information bar, notifying you that the document has been marked as final.

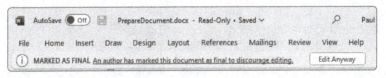

The information bar discourages people from making casual changes

To remove the Final designation and read-only protection from a file that has been marked as final

- On the information bar, select **Edit Anyway**.

- On the **Info** page of the Backstage view, select **Protect Document** and then **Mark as Final**.

Print and send documents

When you're ready to distribute your document to other people, you can do so either by printing it on paper or by sending or posting the file for people to access electronically.

The available printing options change, depending on the selected printer. This is either the default or the most recently used printer. You can display a list of installed printers on the Print page of the Backstage view.

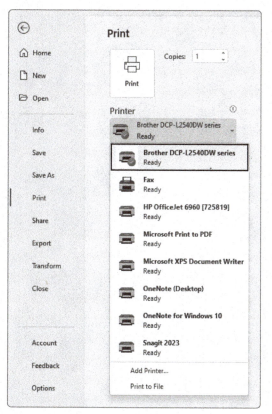

Apps you can print to, such as Microsoft OneNote, are available with local and network printers

> **TIP** You can display a ScreenTip that contains information about a printer, such as the printer status, manufacturer, model, and connection method, by selecting it in the Printer list and then pointing to it. You can manage the apps and printers shown on the Printer menu from the Devices And Printers Control Panel window.

From the Settings area of the Print page, you can specify what part of the document is printed and whether markup (tracked changes) is indicated in the printed document. In addition, you have the option of printing the following information instead of the document content:

- Document properties

- Tracked changes

- Styles

- AutoText entries

- Custom shortcut keys

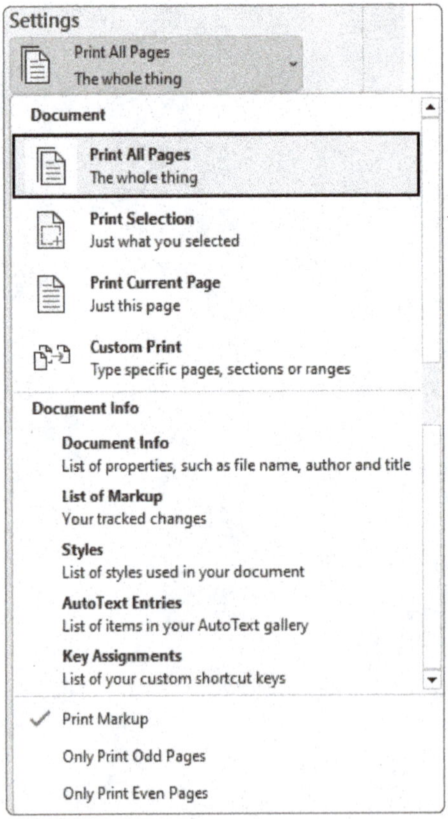

You can choose to print all or part of a document, or to print information stored with the document

You can choose to print a multipage document on one or both sides of the paper. If your printer supports double-sided printing, you have the option of flipping the double-sided page on the long edge or the short edge (depending on how you plan to bind and turn the document pages).

> **IMPORTANT** Some of the settings on the Print page of the Backstage view depend on the functionality supported by your printer. These settings might vary when you select a different device in the Printer list.

You can choose to print multiple copies of a document and whether to print collated pages (all pages of each copy together) or uncollated pages (all copies of each page together).

Finally, you have the option of specifying the number of pages to print per sheet of paper, up to 16. You can use this option to print a booklet with two pages per sheet that will be folded in the middle. You might also use this option to save paper when you're printing a long document, but bear in mind that as the number of pages per sheet increases, the size of the content printed on the page decreases.

> **TIP** If your printer has multiple paper trays or a manual paper feeder, you can select the paper source you want to use, on the Paper page of the Page Setup dialog.

When Outlook is set as your default email app, you can send a document from Word while you're working in the file. You have the option of sending a copy of the file as a message attachment or, if the file is stored in a shared location, you can send a link to the file.

> **IMPORTANT** To use the Email sharing option, you must have Outlook installed and configured on your computer. If you're running another email app, the Email option will be available on the Share page of the Backstage view but might not generate an email message.

12

Share a Word document as a link or as an attachment to an Outlook email message

When using the Share function, an interesting option is to send a document as a PDF file. When you choose this option, Word creates the selected version of the document and attaches it to an email message for you to send. The PDF file is not saved to your computer.

> **✓ TIP** If you have an account with a fax service provider that permits the transmission of fax messages by email, you can select the Send As Internet Fax option and provide the fax number to address the message in the format required by the fax service. For example, if your fax service provider is Contoso and the fax number is (425) 555-0199, the email might be addressed to 14255550199@contoso.com. The fax service relays the message electronically to the recipient's fax number.

To print one copy of a document with the default settings

- Display the **Print** page of the Backstage view, and then select the **Print** button.

- If you have the Quick Access Toolbar visible, on the Quick Access Toolbar, select the **Quick Print** button.

> **TIP** You can add the Quick Print button to the Quick Access Toolbar from the Customize Quick Access Toolbar menu.

To print multiple copies of a document

1. Display the **Print** page of the Backstage view.

2. In the **Copies** box at the top of the page, enter the number of copies you want to print.

3. Select **Print** to print the specified number of copies of the document on the selected printer and return to the document.

To print only specific pages of a document

1. On the **Print** page of the Backstage view, select the first box in the **Settings** area to open a list of page options.

2. In the list, do any of the following:

   - Select **Print All Pages** to print the entire document. This is the default setting if there's currently no content selected in the document.

     > **TIP** If you first select text in the document and then display the Print page of the Backstage view, the Print Selection option will be active. Then when you select the Print button, Word will print only the selected text.

   - Select **Print Current Page** to print the page currently shown in the preview pane.

   - Select **Custom Print**, and then in the **Pages** box, enter the specific pages (in the format 1,3 or 1-3), sections (in the format s1 or s1-s3), or ranges (in the format p1s1-p3s2) you want to print.

3. Select the **Print** button to print the specified pages of the document on the selected printer and return to the document.

To select a printer

1. Display the **Print** page of the Backstage view.

2. In the **Printer** area, select the active printer to display the list of installed printers and print apps.

3. In the list, select the printer you want to use.

12

To display printer status information

- On the **Print** page of the Backstage view, point to the **Information** icon in the upper-right corner of the **Printer** area, or to the selected printer name, to display a ScreenTip that contains printer status information.

To send a document by email from within Word

1. Open the **Share** window:

   - Select the **Share** button near the upper-right corner of the Word window.

   - Select **File** to open Backstage view, and then select **Share**.

2. Select **Send a Copy**, and then do one of the following:

   - Select **Word Document** to attach a copy of the document to an email message.

   - Select **PDF** to create a PDF version of the document and attach it to an email message.

3. If Outlook isn't already running, Word starts it before generating the email message. Enter your password if you're prompted to do so.

4. Enter the message recipient(s), add a subject line, type some explanatory text, and then send the email.

To send a link to a document from within Word

1. Open the **Share** window:

   - Select the **Share** button near the upper-right corner of the Word window.

   - Select **File** to open Backstage view, and then select **Share**.

2. To configure the link settings, select **Anyone With a Link Can Edit**. In the Link Settings dialog, choose whether recipients can edit or only view the document, set an optional expiration date and password, and then select **Apply**.

3. In the **To** box, start entering the name or email address of the person with whom you want to share the link, and then select that person when they appear in the search results. Repeat as needed for each person with whom you want to share the link.

4. In the **Message** area, enter an explanatory message.

5. Select **Send**.

Key points

- Rely on AutoCorrect to correct common misspellings. Correct other spelling, grammatical, and style errors as you enter text, or check the entire document in one pass.

- You should always preview a document before printing it. You can efficiently preview a document and adjust most page layout settings from the Print page of the Backstage view.

- You can insert line breaks, page breaks, and section breaks to control the way content breaks on and across pages.

- Before distributing a document electronically, you can use the Document Inspector to remove information that you don't want other people to see. You can use the Accessibility Checker and Compatibility Checker to ensure that your document content is available to all readers.

- You can print a document to a local or network printer, and configure the printer settings, from the Print page of the Backstage view.

- From the Share window, you can send a link to a document or send a document as an attachment to an email message. You can send the original document or, if you want to ensure that the document appears to recipients exactly as you have laid it out, you can have Word create and send a PDF file.

12

Practice tasks

Before you can complete these tasks, you must copy the book's practice files to your computer. The practice files for these tasks are in the **Word365SBS\Ch12** folder. You can save the results of the tasks in the same folder.

The Introduction includes a complete list of practice files and download instructions.

> ⚠ **IMPORTANT** You must have a printer installed to perform some of the following procedures. On a default installation of Microsoft 365, the Microsoft Print To PDF and Microsoft XPS Document Writer options appear in your Printers list. You can perform the procedures by using one of those options or an actual local or network printer connection.

Locate and correct text errors

Open the **CorrectErrors** document, and then perform the following tasks:

1. In the first paragraph, display a list of suggested spellings for the word *operateing* (the first word with a red wavy underline). In the list, select **operating** to replace the misspelled word.

2. Position the cursor at the beginning of the document, and then do the following:

   - Review each error that the Editor pane identifies and correct it as appropriate.

   - When the spelling checker flags the business's item name, *Quirggels*, add the name to the custom dictionary so that Word doesn't flag it as an error in the future.

3. Save and close the document.

Preview and adjust page layout

Open the **PreviewPages** document, and then perform the following tasks:

1. Display the print preview of the document and zoom out to show both pages side by side in the preview pane.

2. Change the margins to **Wide**. Notice that the change is immediately reflected in the preview pane, and the page navigator indicates that the document now has three pages.

3. Scroll through the preview pane to display the new third page.

4. From the **Print** page, open the **Page Setup** dialog. Turn on **Mirror margins** to set margins for facing pages. Then set the **Inside** margin to 2.5".

5. Review the other page settings and then return to the preview pane.

6. If you have a printer installed, print the document and compare it to what was shown on the screen. Then save and close the document.

Control what appears on each page

Open the **ControlLayout** document, display formatting marks, and then perform the following tasks:

1. Scroll through the document, noticing any awkward page breaks, such as a topic or list that starts close to the bottom of a page.

2. Near the bottom of page 1 and continuing on to page 2, select the paragraph that begins with *The front office space*. Turn on the **Keep lines together** setting for the selection to move the entire paragraph to the beginning of the next page so that it's not split over two pages.

3. At the bottom of page 2 and top of page 3, select the *Office Supplies* heading and the two lines that follow the heading. Turn on the **Keep with next** setting for the selected text.

4. Insert a **Next Page** section break immediately before the *Shipping Quick Reference* heading.

5. In the new section, set the **Margins** to **Wide** so the table better fits the page.

6. Return to the document and review your changes. Then save and close the document.

Prepare documents for electronic distribution

Open the **PrepareDocument** document, and then perform the following tasks:

1. On the **Info** page, notice the document properties that are shown.

2. Run the **Document Inspector** to check the document for all the default issues, and then do the following:

   - Examine the results of the report.

   - Remove all document properties and personal information from the document.

- If custom XML data was found, remove that.

- Leave the headers and footers in the document.

- Reinspect the document and verify the removal of the properties and XML data.

3. Close the **Document Inspector** dialog and notice the changes in the properties shown in the **Properties** area of the **Info** page.

4. Mark the document as **Final**. Notice the results on the **Info** page of the Backstage view. Then return to the document content and notice the results there.

5. Select the **Insert** tab to temporarily expand it, and notice that all the buttons are inactive (dimmed). Then click or tap away from the tab to hide it. Word displays an information bar, notifying you that the document has been marked as final.

6. Save and close the document.

Print and send documents

Open the **PrintDocument** document, and then perform the following tasks:

> ⚠️ **IMPORTANT** You must have an active printer connection to complete this exercise. You must also have configured Outlook to connect to your email account.

1. Display the **Print** page of the Backstage view. Notice that this is a two-page document. The colored document background is not displayed in the preview pane, because it will not be printed.

2. In the **Printer** area, display the list of installed printers, and then select the printer you want to use. Notice whether any of the available print options change.

3. Display the **Printer Status** ScreenTip for the selected printer.

4. Configure the print settings to print only page 2, and to print two copies of that page. Then print the document and confirm that it printed correctly as configured.

5. From the **Share** window, send the document to yourself as an email message attachment. Then send the document to yourself as a PDF file attachment.

6. Review the received messages and their attachments to confirm the expected behavior.

7. Close the open documents.

Part 5

Use advanced Word functions

Reference content and content sources

Word includes many types of reference tools that you can use to help readers locate information in or about a document. Many of these reference tools pull information directly from the document content based on its formatting. For example, you can format paragraphs as headings and then insert a table of contents built from those headings. Similarly, you can insert index tags and then generate an index that references or links to them, or insert citations and then generate a bibliography from them.

In addition, you can insert named bookmarks as anchors you can hyperlink to for cross-referencing purposes. You can also provide supporting information without interrupting the flow of the primary content by inserting information in footnotes or endnotes.

Another way to reference information that exists within a document or as a document property is by inserting a field that references the property. Changes to the property are automatically reflected in the fields that reference it. By using fields in this way, you can easily generate custom documents by updating the document properties.

This chapter guides you through procedures related to inserting bookmarks and cross-references, displaying document information in fields, inserting and modifying footnotes and endnotes, creating and modifying tables of contents, creating and modifying indexes, and citing sources and compiling bibliographies.

In this chapter

- Insert bookmarks and cross-references

- Display document information in fields

- Insert and modify footnotes and endnotes

- Create and modify tables of contents

- Create and modify indexes

- Cite sources and compile bibliographies

Insert bookmarks and cross-references

Although you'll most often use the Navigation pane and the Find And Replace dialog to move around a document, Word provides two other tools you can use to jump easily to designated places within the same document: bookmarks and cross-references.

Whether the document you're reading was created by you or by someone else, you can insert bookmarks to flag information to which you might want to return later. Like a physical bookmark, a Word bookmark marks a specific named place in a document. Each bookmark is identified by a unique name. (Bookmark names can contain only letters, numbers, and underscore characters.)

You can quickly go directly to any bookmark from the Bookmark dialog, from the Go To tab of the Find And Replace dialog, or from a hyperlink. Bookmarks are hidden by default, but you can configure Word options to display their markers. The markers indicate only the bookmark locations. Bookmarks that mark individual locations are indicated by large, gray I-beams. Bookmarks that mark spans of text are indicated by gray square brackets at the beginning and end.

I-beams and brackets indicate bookmarks

You can create cross-references to bookmarks, headings, figures, tables, numbered items, footnotes, endnotes, and equations. Word automatically creates anchors for all these items other than bookmarks. Cross-references can include hyperlinks so that selecting a cross-reference in the electronic document takes the reader directly to the specified location.

---

4. Storage

4.1 No bicycles, tricycles, scooters, roller skates, skateboards, wagons, toys, or other personal belongings shall be stored or left in any Common Area.

4.2 No trailers, boats, vans, campers, house trailers, buses, or trucks shall be stored in any parking space in any Common Area. (See 6. Parking for more information.)

4.3 No Owner shall use his or her garage to store personal belongings in such a way that there is not enough space for his or her vehicles.

Cross-references become shaded when the cursor is in them

To insert a bookmark

1. Do either of the following:

   - Position the cursor in the location where you want to insert the bookmark. This is usually at the beginning of the content you want to reference.

   - Select the text you want to include in the bookmark.

2. On the **Insert** tab, in the **Links** group, select the **Bookmark** button to open the Bookmark dialog.

The most recent bookmark is selected so you can quickly reinsert it

3. In the **Bookmark name** box, enter a name for the bookmark you want to create (or replace the name that is currently in the Bookmark Name box).

4. Select **Add** or press **Enter**.

> ✓ **TIP** Bookmark names cannot contain characters other than letters, numbers, and underscores. If you enter a prohibited character (such as a space or hyphen), the Add button becomes inactive. To name bookmarks with multiple words and maintain readability, either run the words together and capitalize each word (known as *camel case*) or replace the spaces with underscores.

To display bookmarks in text

1. From the Backstage view, open the **Word Options** dialog, and then select the **Advanced** page.

2. In the **Show document content** area of the **Advanced** page, select the **Show bookmarks** checkbox.

Word Options

	Show document content
General	
Display	☑ Show background colors and images in Print Layout view
Proofing	☐ Show text wrapped within the document window
Save	☐ Show picture placeholders ⓘ
Language	☑ Show drawings and text boxes on screen
Accessibility	☑ Show bookmarks
	☐ Show text boundaries
Advanced	☐ Show crop marks
Customize Ribbon	☐ Show field codes instead of their values

Display bookmark indicators in a document

3. Select **OK**.

To go to any bookmark

- Open the **Bookmark** dialog, and then do either of the following:

  - In the **Bookmark name** list, double-click the bookmark you want to go to.

  - Select the bookmark you want to go to, and then select **Go To**.

Or

1. Do either of the following to display the Go To tab of the Find And Replace dialog:

   - On the **Home** tab, in the **Editing** group, in the **Find** list, select **Go To**.

   - Press **Ctrl+G**.

2. In the **Go to what** list, select **Bookmark**. Then do either of the following in the **Enter bookmark name** list:

   - Select the bookmark you want.

   - Enter the name of the bookmark you want.

3. Select **Go To**.

To insert a cross-reference to a bookmark or document element

> ✓ **TIP** Word doesn't add text to introduce the cross-reference, so it's a good idea to enter text such as *See also* before the cross-reference.

1. On the **Insert** tab, in the **Links** group, select the **Cross-reference** button to open the Cross-reference dialog.

Cross-reference many types of content

2. In the **Reference type** list, select the type of item you want to reference (for example, Heading).

Hyperlink to additional resources

Many documents include URLs of websites that the reader can visit to obtain additional information related to the document topic. When a document will be viewed electronically, the URLs can be formatted as hyperlinks so readers can access the websites directly from the document. Hyperlinks can also provide direct access to bookmarks or headings in the document, or to a separate file; or you can use a hyperlink to create a new document or to open a pre-addressed email message window.

Hyperlinks are most frequently in text format, but you can attach a hyperlink to any object—for example, an image such as a shape, logo, or picture. Selecting the hyperlinked object then takes you directly to the linked location. Editing the object doesn't disrupt the hyperlink; however, deleting the object also deletes the hyperlink.

Word automatically adds hyperlink functionality and applies the Hyperlink format when you enter a standard website address and then press the Spacebar or Enter key.

To attach a hyperlink to text or an object, follow these steps:

1. Select the text or object that you want to hyperlink from.

2. On the **Insert** tab, in the **Links** group, select the **Link** button (not the arrow) to open the Insert Hyperlink dialog (or press **Ctrl+K**).

3. In the **Insert reference to** list, select the text you want the cross-reference to display. For example, when cross-referencing to a bookmark, you can display the bookmark text (when the bookmark includes a span of text), the page or paragraph number of the bookmark, or the word *above* or *below* depending on the location of the bookmark in relation to the location of the cross-reference.

4. If you want the cross-reference to include a hyperlink, select the **Insert as hyperlink** checkbox. If you plan to distribute the document only on paper, it isn't necessary to hyperlink the cross-reference.

5. In the **For which** *item* pane, select the specific item you want to reference.

6. Select **Insert**, and then select **Close**.

7. Review the cross-reference and add any words or punctuation necessary to assist the reader.

8. In the **Link to** list, select the type of target you're linking to. Often this is a webpage or another place in the file.

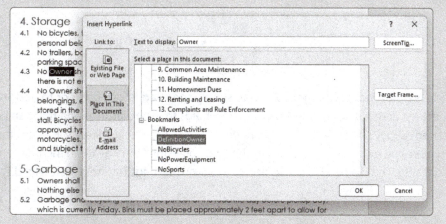

Link to internal and external locations

9. Do either of the following, and then select **OK**:

   - If you're linking to a webpage, select **Existing File or Web Page** in the Link To box and then enter the URL in the **Address** box.

   - If you're linking to a heading or bookmark in the current file, select **Place in This Document** in the Link To box and then select the target in the **Select a place in this document** pane.

13

To go to a cross-referenced location

- In the document, hold down the **Ctrl** key, and then select the cross-reference.

> ✓ **TIP** Pointing to the inserted cross-reference displays a ScreenTip containing information about the cross-reference target.

> ⚠ **IMPORTANT** If you delete the target of a cross-reference, you must manually delete the cross-reference text by selecting and deleting it as you would any other text. If you modify an item you have designated as the target of a cross-reference, delete the existing cross-reference and create a new one.

Display document information in fields

A *field* is a placeholder that tells Word to supply specified information or to perform a specified action in a specified way. You use fields to insert information that can be updated quickly if the information changes. You can't enter fields directly in a document by typing; you must tell Word to insert the field you want. One way to do this is from the Field dialog. This dialog also allows access to various settings for the selected field type.

The Field dialog provides a comprehensive list of all the available fields

More often, however, you will insert preconfigured fields, which you can do by selecting various options on the Insert tab. For example, selecting the Date & Time button in the Text group on the Insert tab opens the Date And Time dialog, which you can use to insert a date and time field. When you insert a date and time field, Word retrieves the date and time from your computer's internal calendar or clock. You can set a date and time field to be updated every time you open a document or whenever you save the document, or you can lock the field so it doesn't update at all.

Specify the date and time format you want

Another type of preconfigured field you might want to insert in a document—for example, in its header or footer—is one that contains a document property, such as the author, title, or last modification date. You can easily insert this type of information from the Document Property submenu of the Quick Parts menu. (If you edit the contents of the field in the document, the change is carried over to the list of properties displayed on the Info page in Backstage view.)

For more information, see *Microsoft Word Step by Step (Office 2021 and Microsoft 365)* by Joan Lambert.

The Author document property automatically provides the document author's name

> **SEE ALSO** For information about document properties, see "Prepare documents for electronic distribution" in Chapter 12, "Finalize and distribute documents."

13

To insert a date and time field

1. Position the cursor in the document where you want to insert the field.

2. ·On the **Insert** tab, in the **Text** group, select the **Date & Time** button to open the Date And Time dialog.

> ✓ **TIP** If you want to insert a date and time field in a header or footer, you can also open the Date And Time dialog from the Design tab. For more information about headers and footers, see "Insert headers, footers, and page numbers" in Chapter 9, "Format document elements."

3. In the **Available formats** list, select the date and time format you want.

4. Select the **Update automatically** checkbox. The field will update each time you open the document. If you don't select this checkbox, Word inserts the date and time as static text rather than as a field.

5. Select **OK**.

To edit a date and time field so it's updated when the file is saved

1. Right-click or long-press (tap and hold) the date and time field, and then select **Edit Field** to open the Field dialog and display the properties and options for the current field.

2. In the **Categories** list, select **Date and Time** to filter the **Field names** list to display only the fields that relate to dates and times.

3. In the **Field names** list, select **SaveDate**.

4. In the **Date formats** list, select the format you want.

5. Select the **Preserve formatting during updates** checkbox.

6. Select **OK**.

To manually update a date and time field

- Select the field, and then select the **Update** button that appears above it.

- Right-click the field and select **Update Field**.

The field will update to the current date and time, to the date and time it was last saved, or to the date and time it was last printed, depending on the setting of the field.

To lock a selected date and time field

- Press **Ctrl+F11**.

> 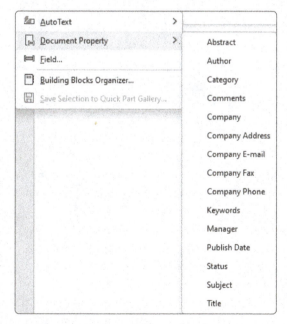 **TIP** To unlock the field, select it, and then press Ctrl+Shift+F11.

To insert a document property field

- On the **Insert** tab, in the **Text** group, select the **Quick Parts** button, select **Document Property**, and then select the document property you want to insert.

🔠 AutoText >	
📄 Document Property >	Abstract
🔳 Field...	Author
📄 Building Blocks Organizer...	Category
🔲 Save Selection to Quick Part Gallery...	Comments
	Company
	Company Address
	Company E-mail
	Company Fax
	Company Phone
	Keywords
	Manager
	Publish Date
	Status
	Subject
	Title

Insert document property fields into your document

13

Insert and modify footnotes and endnotes

When you want to make a comment about a statement in a document—for example, to explain an assumption or cite the source for a different opinion—you can enter the comment as a footnote or an endnote. Doing so inserts a number or symbol called a *reference mark* in the body of your document. The associated comment appears with the same number or symbol, either as a footnote at the bottom of the page or as an endnote at the end of the document or document section. In most views, footnotes or endnotes are divided from the main text by a horizontal note separator line.

You can insert and manage footnotes and endnotes by using the commands in the Footnotes group on the References tab.

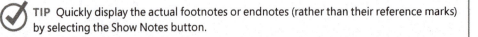

*Footnotes appear on the same page as
their reference marks, and endnotes
appear at the end of the document*

> ✓ **TIP** Quickly display the actual footnotes or endnotes (rather than their reference marks) by selecting the Show Notes button.

You can use commands in the Footnote And Endnote dialog to change various settings, such as where the footnote or endnote should appear, how it should be laid out, and what number format to use. By default, footnote reference marks use the *1, 2, 3* number format, and endnote reference marks use the *i, ii, iii* number format.

To insert a footnote

1. Click or tap in the document where you want the footnote reference mark to appear.

2. On the **References** tab, in the **Footnotes** group, select **Insert Footnote**.

3. Word creates a blank footnote at the bottom of the page and displays a blinking cursor. Enter the footnote text, and then click or tap anywhere outside of the footnote area to return to the document.

To insert an endnote

1. Click or tap in the document where you want the endnote reference mark to appear.

2. On the **References** tab, in the **Footnotes** group, select **Insert Endnote**.

3. Word creates a blank endnote at the end of the document and displays a blinking cursor. Enter the endnote text, and then click or tap anywhere outside of the endnote area to return to the document.

To convert a footnote to an endnote

- Right-click the footnote, and then select **Convert to Endnote**.

To convert an endnote to a footnote

- Right-click the endnote, and then select **Convert to Footnote**.

To move among footnote or endnote references

- On the **References** tab, in the **Footnotes** group, select the **Next Footnote** button.

- In the **Footnotes** group, in the **Next Footnote** list, select **Next Footnote**, **Previous Footnote**, **Next Endnote**, or **Previous Endnote**.

13

To display footnotes or endnotes

- Double-click a reference mark in the body of the document to display its corresponding footnote or endnote.

- On the **References** tab, in the **Footnotes** group, select the **Show Notes** button to display the list of footnotes or endnotes.

To change the number format of footnotes or endnotes

1. On the **References** tab, select the **Footnotes** dialog launcher to open the Footnote And Endnote dialog.

2. In the **Location** area of the **Footnote and Endnote** dialog, select **Footnotes** or **Endnotes** to indicate the element you want to modify.

3. In the **Format** area, in the **Number format** list, select the number format you want to use.

4. Select **Apply**.

To delete a footnote or endnote

- In the document text, select the footnote or endnote marker, and then press **Delete**.

Create and modify tables of contents

When you create a long document that includes headings, such as an annual report or a catalog with several sections, you might want to add a table of contents to the beginning of the document to give your readers an overview of the document content and help them navigate to specific sections. In a document that will be printed, you can indicate with a page number the page where each heading is located. If the document will be distributed electronically, you can link each entry in the table of contents to the corresponding heading in the document so readers can jump directly to the heading with a click or tap.

Office Procedures

▤ ▾ ▤ Update Table...

Contents

The table of contents is a field that can be updated

By default, Word creates a table of contents based on the document headings (as indicated by the styles Heading 1, Heading 2, and so on). Word can also create a table of contents based on outline levels or on fields you insert in the document. When you tell Word to create a table of contents, Word identifies the entries and inserts the table at the cursor as a single field.

> ⊘ **SEE ALSO** For information about applying styles, see "Apply built-in styles to text" in Chapter 4, "Modify the structure and appearance of text."

13

The Table Of Contents controls are available from the References tab. In the Table Of Contents gallery, you can select from three standard options:

- **Automatic Table 1**   This option inserts the heading *Contents* and a table of contents that references all Heading 1, Heading 2, and Heading 3 paragraphs.

- **Automatic Table 2**   This option inserts the heading *Table of Contents* and a table of contents that references all Heading 1, Heading 2, and Heading 3 paragraphs.

- **Manual Table**   This option inserts the heading *Table of Contents* and a table of contents that contains placeholders that don't reference any specific document content.

Choose from three main options in the Table Of Contents gallery

Entries in a table of contents are formatted by using nine levels of built-in TOC styles (TOC 1, TOC 2, and so on). By default, Word uses the styles assigned in the template attached to the document. If you want to use a different style, you can create a custom table from the Table Of Contents dialog. Here, you can choose from several formats, including Classic, Distinctive, Fancy, Modern, Formal, and Simple. (The Print Preview and Web Preview panes display a preview of the selected format.) You can also apply a different tab leader—that is, the set of characters used between the text and the corresponding page number in the table of contents. After you create a table of contents, you can format it manually by selecting text and then applying character or paragraph formatting or styles. (However, if you regenerate the table, the manual formatting will be replaced, so do this only after the table is final.)

Choose a different set of formatting styles for your table of contents

13

> **TIP** The TOC styles are based on the Body font of the document theme. Each style has specific indent and spacing settings. If you create a table of contents based on the document template, you can customize the TOC styles during the creation process. To do so, select From Template in the Formats list. Then select the Modify button. The Style dialog opens, displaying the nine TOC styles. You can modify the font, paragraph, tabs, border, and other formatting of these styles the same way you would modify any other style. For information about creating styles, see "Create and modify styles" in Chapter 15, "Create custom document elements."

You can modify the elements on which Word bases the table at any time, and update the table quickly to reflect your changes. If you change a heading in the document or if edits to the text change the page breaks, you can update the table of contents to reflect those changes. You have the option of updating only the page numbers, or—if you have changed, added, or deleted headings—you can update (re-create) the entire table.

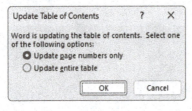

If headings or page breaks change, you can easily update the table of contents

You can use the table of contents to navigate within your document. For example, you can hold down the Ctrl key and click a heading in a table of contents to access the corresponding section in the text.

Contents
General Administration ....
Contact Information ....
Facilities ....
Office ....

Current Document
Ctrl+Click to follow link

Hyperlink navigation functionality is built in to the table of contents

Other reference tables

Tables of figures

If a document includes figures, tables, or equations, you can easily create a table of figures so readers can locate and quickly navigate to them. A table of figures is built from the tools in the Captions group on the References tab of the ribbon. You must insert a caption for each figure, table, or equation you want to include, and then generate the table.

Tables of authorities

If a legal document contains items such as regulations, cases, and statutes identified as legal citations, you can tell Word to create a table of authorities. In the table, citations are categorized as cases, statutes, rules, treatises, regulations, constitutional provisions, or other authorities.

Word uses the citations to create this type of table the same way it uses headings to create a table of contents and captions to create a table of figures. You must insert a citation for each legal reference you want to include, and then generate the table.

To insert a table of contents for a document with headings

1. Position the cursor in the document where you want to insert the table of contents.

2. On the **References** tab, in the **Table of Contents** group, select the **Table of Contents** button to display the **Table of Contents** menu.

3. In the **Table of Contents** gallery, select the table of contents style you want.

To create a custom table of contents

1. Position the cursor in the document where you want to add a custom table of contents.

2. On the **References** tab, in the **Table of Contents** group, select the **Table of Contents** button, and then select **Custom Table of Contents** to open the Table Of Contents dialog.

13

3. In the **General** area of the **Table of Contents** tab, do the following:

    - In the **Formats** list, select the style set you want to apply to the TOC elements.

    - If you want to change the formatting, select **Modify**, redefine the formatting of each TOC level you want to change, and then select **OK**.

    - In the **Show levels** list, select the number of outline levels you want the TOC to include.

    - If you want to include only specific styles in the TOC, select **Options**, select the styles you want and clear the selection of the styles you don't want, and then select **OK**.

    The Print Preview and Web Preview panes reflect your changes.

4. In the Print Preview area of the tab, do the following:

    - If you want to exclude page numbers from the TOC, clear the **Show page numbers** checkbox.

    - If you want to display the page numbers immediately after the TOC entries, clear the **Right align page numbers** checkbox.

    - In the **Tab leader** list, select the leader option you want.

5. Select **OK**.

To update a table of contents

1. Do either of the following to display the Update Table Of Contents dialog:

    - Click anywhere in the table of contents to select it, and then select the **Update** button that appears above the table.

    > **TIP** The table of contents is contained in one large field. When you select it, you select the entire field. If you accidentally delete the table of contents, select the Undo button or press Ctrl+Z to bring it back. For information about fields, see "Display document information in fields" earlier in this chapter.

    - On the **References** tab, in the **Table of Contents** group, select the **Update Table** button.

2. In the dialog, do either of the following:

   - Select **Update page numbers only** to update the page numbers but not the headings.

   - Select **Update entire table** to update the headings and page numbers.

3. Select **OK**.

To jump to a location in the document from the table of contents

1. Point to any entry in the table of contents.

2. Press and hold the **Ctrl** key. The pointer changes to a hand.

3. Select the entry to move directly to that heading.

> **SEE ALSO** For more information about linking to other parts of a document, see "Insert bookmarks and cross-references" earlier in this chapter.

To delete a table of contents

1. On the **References** tab, in the **Table of Contents** group, select the **Table of Contents** button.

2. Select **Remove Table of Contents**.

Create and modify indexes

To help readers find specific concepts and terms they might not be able to readily locate by looking at a table of contents, you can include an index at the end of a document. Word creates an index by compiling an alphabetical listing with page numbers based on index entry fields you mark in the document. As with a table of contents, an index is inserted as a single field.

> **TIP** You don't need to create indexes for documents that will be distributed electronically, because readers can use the Navigation pane to find the information they need. For more information, see "Find and replace text" in Chapter 3, "Enter and edit text."

13

Generate an index for your document to help readers find important topics

In the index, an entry might apply to a word or phrase that appears on one page or that is discussed on several pages. The entry might have related subentries. For example, in the index to this book, the main index entry *text effects* might have below it the subentries *applying* and *live preview of*. An index might also include cross-reference entries that direct readers to related entries. For example, the main index entry *text wrapping breaks* might be cross-referenced to *line breaks*. You can use cross-references to direct readers to index terms they might not think of when looking for specific information.

> ✓ **TIP** When building an index, bear in mind the terms readers are likely to look up. For example, one reader might expect to find information about cell phones by looking under *cell*, whereas another might look under *mobile*, another under *phones*, and another under *telephones*. A good index will include all four entries.

Before you can generate an index for your document, you must insert index entry fields throughout the document. Word then compiles the entries in these fields into the index. To insert an index entry field into the document, you use the Mark Index Entry dialog. In this dialog, you can do the following:

- Modify the selected text to alter how it appears in the index.

- Add a subentry.

- Designate the entry as a cross-reference, one-page entry, or, if the selected text spans multiple pages, a page-range entry. In the case of page-range entries, Word creates a bookmark for the selected text and prompts you to enter a name for it in the Mark Index Entry dialog.

- Format the page number associated with the entry—for example, to make it appear bold or italic in the index.

Edit, add a subentry to, and otherwise adjust the index entry in this dialog

After you set the options in the dialog, you can insert an index entry field adjacent to the selected text by selecting Mark, or adjacent to every occurrence of the selected text in the document by selecting Mark All.

> **TIP** The Mark Index Entry dialog remains open to simplify the process of inserting multiple index entry fields, so you don't have to select the Mark Entry button for each new entry. You can move the dialog off to the side so it doesn't block the text you're working with.

Index entry fields are formatted as hidden. They are not visible unless you display formatting marks and hidden characters. When the index entry field is visible, the entry appears in the document enclosed in quotation marks within a set of braces, with the designator *XE* and a dotted underline.

To compile an index based on the index entries in a document, you work in the Index dialog.

You use the Index dialog to set up the index

In this dialog, you can specify the following:

- Whether the index formatting should use styles from the current template or be based on one of four predefined formats, which you can preview in the Print Preview box

- Whether page numbers should be right-aligned, and if so, whether they should have dotted, dashed, or solid tab leaders

- Whether the index should be indented, with each subentry on a separate line below its main entry, or run-in, with subentries on the same line as the main entries

- The number of columns you want

When you select OK in the Index dialog, Word calculates the page numbers of all the entries and subentries, consolidates them, and inserts the index as one field in the specified format at the specified location in the document.

You can edit the text of the index generated from the entries, but the changes you make are not permanent. If you regenerate the index, the original entries will be restored. It's more efficient to edit the text within the quotation marks in the index entry fields. You can move and copy index entries by using the same techniques you would for regular text. If you make changes to a document that affect index entries or page numbering, you can update the index.

To mark a word or short phrase as an index entry

1. Select the word or phrase you want to mark. Then do any of the following to open or activate the Mark Index Entry dialog:

   - On the **References** tab, in the **Index** group, select the **Mark Entry** button.

   - Press **Alt+Shift+X**.

   - If the **Mark Index Entry** dialog is already open, select its title bar.

   Notice that the selected word or phrase has already been entered in the Main Entry box.

2. If you want, select the text and enter text—for example, making a word plural or lowercase.

> **TIP** Index entries appear in the index exactly as they appear in the Mark Index Entry dialog. For consistency, make all nouns (except proper nouns) plural and lowercase, and all verbs gerund (ending in "ing").

3. Do either of the following:

   - Select **Mark** to insert an index entry field next to just this occurrence of the selected word or phrase.

   - Select **Mark All** to insert index entry fields adjacent to every occurrence of the selected word or phrase in the document.

> **TIP** Index entries are case sensitive. If you mark an entry that is lowercase, any uppercase instances of the word or phrase will not be indexed, because their capitalization does not match the selected word. The Mark Index Entry dialog remains open even after you insert the index entry, so you can quickly add more index entries. When you're finished marking index entries, simply close the dialog.

13

To mark text that is longer than one page as an index entry

1. Select the text segment you want to mark.

2. Open the **Mark Index Entry** dialog or, if it's already open, select its title bar to activate it.

3. The selected text appears in the Main Entry box. Replace the text segment with an appropriate index entry.

4. Select **Page range**.

5. In the **Bookmark** field, enter a bookmark name for the selected text.

> ✅ **TIP** Bookmark names can contain only numbers, letters, and underscore characters. To name bookmarks with multiple words, either run the words together and capitalize each word or replace the spaces with underscores for readability.

6. Select the **Mark** button.

To add a cross-reference to an index entry

1. After marking a word, phrase, or longer text as an index entry, without leaving the **Mark Index Entry** dialog, in the **Options** area, select the **Cross-reference** option. Notice that the cursor moves to the space after the word *See* in the adjacent box.

2. Without moving the cursor, enter the text you want to use for a cross-reference. This text should exactly match another index entry in the document.

3. Select **Mark** to insert a cross-reference to the new index entry adjacent to the current index entry.

To enter a subentry for an index entry

1. Select the word or phrase you want to mark.

2. Open the **Mark Index Entry** dialog or, if it's already open, select its title bar to activate it.

3. In the **Subentry** box, enter the subentry.

4. Select **Mark** to insert an index entry with the entry and subentry separated by a colon.

To edit an index entry

- Click within the index entry in the document (not in the Mark Index Entry dialog) and then make the changes you want.

To insert an index in a document

1. In a document with previously marked index entries, position the cursor where you want to insert the index—usually at the end of the document.

2. On the **Home** tab, in the **Paragraph** group, select the **Show/Hide ¶** button to hide formatting marks, fields, and content formatted as hidden.

> ⚠ **IMPORTANT** When hidden content is visible, the document might not be paginated correctly. Always turn off the display of formatting marks and hidden characters before creating an index.

3. On the **References** tab, in the **Index** group, select the **Insert Index** button to open the Index dialog.

4. Optionally, change the number of columns and the format.

5. Select **OK** to compile an index based on the index entries you previously marked.

To delete an index entry

1. On the **Home** tab, in the **Paragraph** group, select the **Show/Hide ¶** button to show formatting marks, fields, and content formatted as hidden.

2. Scroll to the index entry you want to delete.

3. Select the entire entry and press the **Delete** key.

> ✓ **TIP** Dragging through any part of an index entry field that includes one of the enclosing braces selects the entire field. If you find it hard to select only the entry, try pointing to the right of the closing brace (}) and dragging slightly to the left.

13

To update an index

- Click anywhere in the index, and then, on the **References** tab, in the **Index** group, select the **Update Index** button.

- Right-click the index and then select **Update Field**.

Cite sources and compile bibliographies

Many types of documents you create might require bibliographies that list the sources of the information in or referenced in the documents. Whether your sources are books, periodicals, websites, or interviews, you can record details about them. You can also select a common style guide, such as *The Chicago Manual of Style*, to have Word automatically list your sources in that style guide's standard format.

Bibliography

American Bamboo Society. (2023, March 15). Retrieved from https://www.bamboo.org
Bourdain, A. (1997). *Gone Bamboo*. Villard Publishers.
Lewis, D., & Miles, C. (2007). *Farming Bamboo*. Lulu Press.

A bibliography formatted to meet the specifications of The Chicago Manual of Style

Word offers a tool called the Source Manager to help you keep track of sources and to ensure that you reference them in the proper format. When you enter source information, Word stores the information in a separate file on your computer's hard drive so you can cite the sources in any document you create. The Source Manager offers easy access to this master list of sources, in addition to access to the list of sources cited in your current document.

The Source Manager accumulates sources from all documents, so if other documents already contain citations, their source information might appear here

> **TIP** To add a source in the master list to the current document, select it in the Master List box in the Source Manager dialog and then select Copy to copy it to the Current List box.

To create sources, you use the Create Source dialog. In this dialog, you can select the type of source—for example, whether it's a book, a journal article, or other type of source. You can then enter the author of the source, the title of the source, and other key information. If the source has multiple authors, you can open the Edit Name dialog to enter them all.

Record information about content sources for your bibliography

Within your document, you can cite the sources you create by using the Source Manager dialog or by using the Insert Citation menu available from the Citations & Bibliography group of the References tab. You can also use the Insert Citation menu to create new citations as you work and to set placeholders for citations, which you can fill in later. When you add a citation to the document, it appears alongside the associated text in the format you specified—for example, *The Chicago Manual of Style*.

13

> flooring. More and more, people are seeing the value and beauty of using bamboo in their homes to achieve modern-day fashion with an ethnic flavor. Entire books have been written on the subject (American Bamboo Society, 2023), including *Big Bad Bamboo* and *Bamboo, Family Style*.

This document includes a citation

If you know you need to insert a citation, but you don't have all the information about your source handy, you can insert a placeholder. Then, when you gather the information you need, you can update the placeholder.

After you enter citations in a document, you can compile their sources into a list with one of three headings: *Bibliography*, *References*, or *Works Cited*. (The heading you choose is usually specified by the organization or person for whom you are preparing the document, such as your company, your instructor, or the publication in which you intend to publish the document.) You can also insert a source list without a heading.

Built-In

Bibliography

Bibliography
Chen, Jacky. 2003. *Citations and References*. New York: Contoso Press.
Haas, Jonathan. 2005. *Creating a Formal Publication*. Boston: Proseware, Inc.
Kramer, James David. 2006. *How to Write Bibliographies*. Chicago: Adventure Works Press.

References

References
Chen, Jacky. 2003. *Citations and References*. New York: Contoso Press.
Haas, Jonathan. 2005. *Creating a Formal Publication*. Boston: Proseware, Inc.
Kramer, James David. 2006. *How to Write Bibliographies*. Chicago: Adventure Works Press.

Works Cited

Works Cited
Chen, Jacky. 2003. *Citations and References*. New York: Contoso Press.
Haas, Jonathan. 2005. *Creating a Formal Publication*. Boston: Proseware, Inc.
Kramer, James David. 2006. *How to Write Bibliographies*. Chicago: Adventure Works Press.

🔖 Insert Bibliography

Save Selection to Bibliography Gallery...

Choose from three built-in styles or insert a bibliography with no heading

When you compile a bibliography, Word inserts it at the cursor as one field. You can edit the text of a bibliography, but if the source information changes, it's more efficient to edit the source in the Source Manager and then update the bibliography the same way you would update a table of contents or index.

To set the style rules for citations

1. On the **References** tab, in the **Citations & Bibliography** group, display the **Style** list.

The available styles change from time to time

2. In the style list, select the style guide you want Word to use when creating the bibliography.

To create a bibliography source

1. In the **Citations & Bibliography** group, select the **Manage Sources** button to open the Source Manager dialog.

2. In the **Source Manager** dialog, select **New** to open the Create Source dialog.

3. In the **Type of Source** list, select the type of source (book or magazine, for example) you want to add.

> ⚠ **IMPORTANT** The fields in the Bibliography Fields For section and the required data vary depending on the type of source and style guide you select.

4. In the **Bibliography Fields for** *Style* area, enter the required bibliographic data.

5. Select **OK** to add the source to both the **Master List** and the **Current List**.

To create a source with multiple authors

1. In the **Create Source** dialog, select **Edit** to open the Edit Name dialog.

2. In the **Add name** area, enter an author's name in the **Last**, **First**, and/or **Middle** boxes, and then select **Add** to add the name to the Names box.

3. Repeat step 2 to add other authors, selecting **Add** after each author.

If a source has more than one author, create a multiple-name entity

4. Reorder the names as needed by selecting a name in the **Names** box and then selecting the **Up** or **Down** button to change its place in the order.

5. When you're finished adding authors, select **OK**.

6. In the **Create Source** dialog, enter the bibliographic data, and then select **OK**.

7. In the **Source Manager** dialog, select **Close**.

To insert a citation to an existing source in a document

1. Position the cursor in the document at the location where you want to insert a citation.

2. On the **References** tab, in the **Citations & Bibliography** group, select the **Insert Citation** button to display the list of available sources.

	Ame23
	American Bamboo Society, (2023)
	Bourdain, Anthony
	Gone Bamboo, (1997)
	Lewis, Daphne, Miles, Carol
	Farming Bamboo, (2007)
	Add New Source...
	Add New Placeholder...

Cite sources from the Insert Citation menu

3. On the **Insert Citation** menu, select a source to insert it in the document.

To create a source while inserting a citation

1. On the **Insert Citation** menu, select **Add New Source** to open the Create Source dialog.

2. Enter source information as described in the procedure "To create a bibliography source" earlier in this topic.

3. Select **OK** to add the citation to the document and add the source information to both the Master List and the Current List in the Source Manager.

To insert a citation placeholder

1. On the **References** tab, in the **Citations & Bibliography** group, select **Insert Citation**, and then select **Add New Placeholder**.

2. In the **Placeholder Name** dialog, enter a descriptive name for the placeholder (without spaces), and then select **OK**.

To update a placeholder

1. Do either of the following:

   - Select the placeholder in the document, select the arrow that appears, and then select **Edit Source**.

   - In the **Source Manager** dialog, in the **Current List** box, select the placeholder, and then select **Edit**.

2. In the **Edit Source** dialog, enter the necessary source information, and then select **OK**.

13

To generate and insert a bibliography

1. In the **Citations & Bibliography** group, select the **Bibliography** button to display the Bibliography gallery.

2. Select a bibliography format from the gallery to insert a bibliography containing all the citations in the document in alphabetical order.

To update a bibliography

- Select anywhere in the bibliography to activate it. Then, above the bibliography, select the **Update Citations and Bibliography** button.

- Right-click the bibliography, and then select **Update Field**.

Key points

- Bookmarking information makes it easy to locate or reference the information later.

- You can display document information such as the title and author in fields that automatically update within the document.

- You can provide peripheral or supporting information in footnotes at the bottom of each page or endnotes at the end of the document.

- A table of contents provides an overview of the topics covered in a document and helps readers navigate quickly to a topic heading.

- After marking index entries for key concepts, words, and phrases, you can compile an index to the document's content.

- Word can keep track of information sources and compile a bibliography of cited sources that meets the requirements of a specific writing style guide.

Practice tasks

Before you can complete these tasks, you must copy the book's practice files to your computer. The practice files for these tasks are in the **Word365SBS\Ch13** folder. You can save the results of the tasks in the same folder.

The Introduction includes a complete list of practice files and download instructions.

Insert bookmarks and cross-references

Open the **InsertBookmarks** document in Print Layout view, and then perform the following tasks:

1. Position the cursor at the beginning of the *10. Building Maintenance* heading (don't select any text).

2. Insert a bookmark named BuildingMaintenance.

3. In section 10.3, select the bulleted list, and then add a bookmark named LimitedCommonAreas.

4. Use the commands on the **Advanced** page of the **Word Options** dialog to display bookmarks in the document.

5. Use any of the methods described in this chapter to go to each bookmark in turn.

6. At the end of section 4.2, enter See also followed by a space and a period.

7. Position the cursor before the period, and then insert a hyperlinked cross-reference to the section 6 heading.

8. Use the cross-reference to go directly to section 6.

9. Save and close the document.

Display document information in fields

Open the **DisplayFields** document in Print Layout view, and then perform the following tasks:

1. Display the document's headers and footers.

2. Activate the document footer, and then position the cursor at the left end of the footer.

3. Use the commands in the **Date and Time** dialog to insert a field that displays both the date and time and that updates automatically.

4. Edit the field to change it to a **SaveDate** field that displays both the date and time and preserves formatting during updates.

5. Save the document.

6. Update the footer to display the time you saved the document.

7. Lock the **SaveDate** field, and then save the document again.

8. Right-click the field. Notice that the **Update Field** command is not available.

9. Unlock the **SaveDate** field.

10. In the middle of the footer, insert the **Author** document property field.

11. If your name doesn't appear in the field, display the **Info** page of the Backstage view, expand the **Properties** list to include the **Author** property, and enter yourself as the author. Then return to the document to verify that the field displays your name.

12. Save and close the document.

Insert and modify footnotes and endnotes

Open the **InsertFootnotes** document in Print Layout view, and then perform the following tasks:

1. In the first paragraph after the heading *Moving to a New Home*, locate the word *mulch*. Insert a footnote immediately after the word.

2. In the footnote area at the bottom of the page, enter Grass makes a good mulch, because it's high in nitrogen and silica.

3. In the second paragraph under the heading *Moving to a New Home*, insert an endnote immediately after the word *trench*.

4. In the endnote area at the end of the document, enter Examine the trench each fall to determine whether any rhizomes have tried to cross it. If so, cut them off.

5. Convert the endnote to a footnote.

6. Move the cursor to the beginning of the document, and then go to the first footnote reference.

7. Double-click the footnote reference mark to display the corresponding footnote.

8. Display the list of footnotes in the document.

9. Change the format of the footnote markers from numbers to symbols. Notice the effect of the change.

10. Save and close the document.

Create and modify tables of contents

Open the **CreateTOC** document in Print Layout view, and then perform the following tasks:

1. With the cursor positioned at the beginning of the document, insert an **Automatic Style 2** table of contents. Review the table of contents, and then delete it.

2. Position the cursor at the beginning of the document, and then open the **Table of Contents** dialog.

3. Use the commands in the dialog to insert a **Formal** table of contents with no tab leader.

4. From the table of contents, go directly to the *Phone System* heading in the document.

5. In the heading, replace the word *Phone* with Telecommunications.

6. Update the entire table of contents, and verify that it reflects the change in the heading.

7. Save and close the document.

Create and modify indexes

Open the **CreateIndexes** document in Print Layout view, display formatting marks, and then perform the following tasks:

1. At the beginning of the document, in the first bulleted list item, select the word *Declaration*. Then mark all instances of that word in the document as index entries.

2. In section 2.3, select the word *sports*. Mark only this instance of the word as an index entry.

3. In section 3.2, select the word *animal*. Mark all instances of the word as index entries, but change the main entry to animals.

4. In section 3.3, in the first bulleted list item, select the word *dog*. Mark all instances of the word as index entries. Then add a *See* cross-reference from *dog* to *animals*.

5. In section 5.1, mark the first instance of the word *garbage* as an index entry. Then add the subentry recycling.

6. In section 11.4, select the entire bulleted list.

7. In the **Mark Index Entry** dialog, replace the text in the **Main entry** box with delinquency.

8. In the **Options** area of the dialog, select **Page Range**.

9. In the **Bookmark** field, enter delinquency. Then select **Mark**.

10. If you want to create a more extensive index, add other index entries.

11. Position the cursor at the end of the document, after the *Index* heading.

12. Hide formatting marks so they don't affect the page numbers of the index entries.

13. Insert an index in the **Simple** format, with page numbers right-aligned and with dots as tab leaders. Review the index. Notice that the *delinquency* entry points to an invalid bookmark.

14. Show formatting marks, fields, and content formatted as hidden.

15. In section 11.4, delete the *delinquency* index entry.

16. Hide formatting marks, and then update the index.

17. Save and close the document.

Cite sources and compile bibliographies

Open the **CompileBibliography** document in Print Layout view, and then perform the following tasks:

1. Set the bibliography style to **Chicago Sixteenth Edition**.

2. Create a new source in the **Source Manager** by using the following information:

   Type of Source: **Book**

   Author: Jeremy Nelson

   Title: Big Bad Bamboo

   Year: 2015

   Publisher: Litware, Inc.

3. Create a second source in the **Source Manager**, this time using the commands in the **Edit Name** dialog to accommodate multiple authors. Use the following information:

   Type of Source: **Book**

   Authors: Lisa Miller and Harry Miller

   Title: Bamboo, Family Style

   Year: 2014

   Publisher: Lucerne Publishing

4. Close the **Source Manager** dialog.

5. In the first paragraph of the document, position the cursor immediately after *Big Bad Bamboo*, and then insert the Nelson citation.

6. Position the cursor immediately after *Bamboo, Family Style*, and then insert the Miller citation.

7. Move the cursor to the end of the document, and then insert the bibliography. Use the **Bibliography** option.

8. In the first paragraph of the document, position the cursor after *Entire books have been written on the subject*, and insert a new citation with the following information:

   Type of Source: **Web site**

   Corporate Author: American Bamboo Society

   Name of Web Page: Bamboo Resources

   Year: 2010

   URL: www.americanbamboo.org/bamboo-resources.php

9. Update the bibliography and verify that it includes the new citation.

10. Save and close the document.

Merge data with documents and labels

Many organizations communicate with customers or members by means of letters, newsletters, and promotional pieces that are sent to everyone on a mailing list. You can use a reasonably simple process called *mail merge* to easily insert specific information from a data source into a Word document to create personalized individual items such as form letters, labels, envelopes, or email messages. You can also use this process to create a directory, catalog, or other listing that incorporates information from the data source.

The primary requirement for a mail merge operation is a well-structured data source. You can pull information from a variety of data sources—even your Microsoft Outlook address book—and merge it with a starting document or a content template to create the output you want. Word provides a wizard that can guide you through the processes, but this chapter provides information about each of the individual processes so you can quickly get started with your merging projects.

This chapter guides you through procedures related to starting the mail merge process, choosing and refining data sources, choosing the output type and starting documents, previewing the results and completing the merge, and creating individual envelopes and labels.

In this chapter

- Understand the mail merge process
- Start the mail merge process
- Choose and refine the data source
- Insert merge fields
- Preview and complete the merge
- Create individual envelopes and labels

Understand the mail merge process

The process for creating a mail merge document is straightforward and logical. All the tools for performing mail merge operations are available from the Mailings tab. From this tab, you can run the wizard or perform individual steps of the mail merge process on your own.

Mail merge tools are located on the Mailings tab

Three important terms used when discussing mail merge processes include:

- **Data source**   The file or storage entity that contains the variable information you want to pull into the merge output.

- **Field**   A specific category of information, such as a first name, last name, birth-date, customer number, item number, or price.

- **Record**   A set of the information that goes in the fields—for example, informa-tion about a specific person or transaction. A record doesn't have to contain information for every field, but it must have a placeholder for any missing information.

The mail merge process varies slightly depending on whether you're creating one document per record or one document containing all the records. However, the basic process is this:

1. Identify a data source that contains the records you want to use.

2. Create a document into which you want to merge the records.

3. In the document, identify the fields from the data source that you want to merge into the document.

4. Preview the results and make any necessary adjustments.

5. Merge the data into the document to either create one or more new docu-ments or to print the merge results directly to the printer.

You can perform the mail merge process by using the commands on the Mailings tab of the ribbon, or you can get step-by-step guidance from the Mail Merge wizard. The wizard displays options in a series of panes, and you choose the options you want. If you're new to mail merge, the wizard can provide a helpful framework. If you're comfortable with the mail merge process and know what you want to create, it can be faster to perform the steps manually.

To use the Mail Merge wizard

1. Start Word and display the **Mailings** tab.

2. In the **Start Mail Merge** group, select **Start Mail Merge**, and then select **Step-by-Step Mail Merge Wizard**.

3. In each of the six panes of the wizard, select an option or provide the requested information.

4. In the last pane, specify whether to send the merge output directly to the printer or to create one or more documents that you can review and save.

Start the mail merge process

For most mail merge projects, you need a starting document that provides structure and common content, and that identifies the locations where you want to insert data. You specify the data to merge into each location by inserting *merge fields*. The merge fields pull data from the data source fields into the starting document. To identify the data fields available for the mail merge operation, you must select the data source and import its records into the Mail Merge Recipients list.

The best starting point varies based on the type of output that you want to create. The output categories include letters, email messages, envelopes, labels, and directories.

In this topic, we discuss ways of getting started with a mail merge process based on the output type.

14

> **TIP** If you find that you need help, start the wizard from any point in the process and move back to make changes or forward to keep the work you've done.

Get started with letters

If you're creating a form letter or similar document, you can write the document, connect to the data source, and then insert the merge fields; or you can start with a blank document, connect to the data source, and then insert the merge fields as you write the document. Either way, you can't insert merge fields in a document until you connect to the data source.

If you're creating a document that must go through a review process, it's easier to do that before you connect to the data source; otherwise, the document tries to connect to the data source each time a reviewer opens it. When that's the case, you can insert placeholders in the document where you plan to insert merge fields later. You can set off the placeholders from the real text by using brackets or highlighting to indicate to reviewers that the placeholders aren't final content, and to make them easy to locate later.

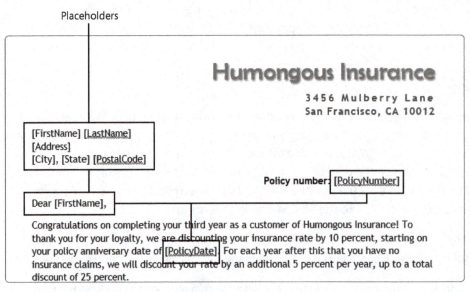

It's easiest to write and edit your document before starting the mail merge process

If you need help creating a document for your intended purpose, you can use any of the Word content templates. A wide variety of templates is available from the New page of the Backstage view.

To start a letter mail merge

1. Open a blank document or a document that contains the static content you want to pull data into.

2. On the **Mailings** tab, in the **Start Mail Merge** group, select **Start Mail Merge**.

3. On the **Start Mail Merge** menu, select **Letters**. There is no visible change to the document.

4. To continue and complete the process:

    a. Use the procedures described in "Choose and refine the data source" later in this chapter to identify the data source and available fields.

    b. Create or edit the document content, and use the procedures described in "Insert merge fields" later in this chapter to insert the merge fields.

    c. Use the procedures described in "Preview and complete the merge" later in this chapter to finish creating the letter.

Get started with labels

The mail merge processes for labels are designed not only for stickers but also for name tags, badge inserts, business cards, tab inserts for page dividers, CD labels, postcards, notecards, printable magnets, and anything else that you print onto paper or other sheet-fed media that is divided into fixed areas. Many of these products are available from office supply and craft supply retailers. Well-known manufacturers of label materials include Avery and 3M, but there are many others.

> **SEE ALSO** For more information about creating mailing labels, see "Create individual envelopes and labels" later in this chapter.

14

When generating labels from a data source, you're usually printing data from multiple records onto each sheet, but you can also print a full sheet of each record.

When creating labels, you select the manufacturer and product number of the specific printing media, and then Word creates a table that defines the printable area of the label sheet. You insert merge fields into the first cell as a template for all the other cells, format the content as you want it, and then copy the cell content to the other fields. If you're making sheets of labels that pull data from multiple records, each additional field starts with a «Next Record» tag that signals Word to move to the next record.

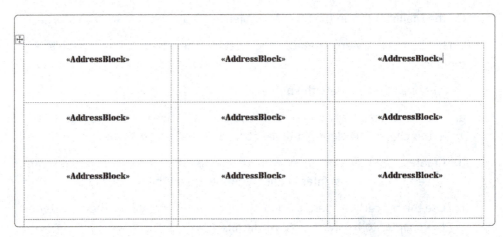

The starting document for an address label mail merge

It's important that you select the correct manufacturer and product because the document page setup is very precisely controlled to match the media.

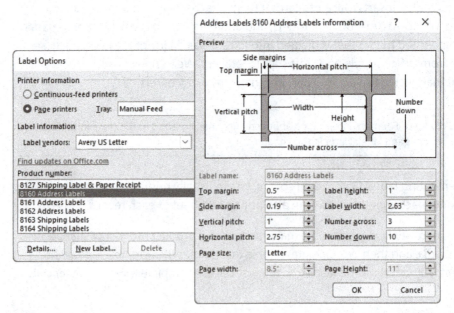

The definition for each label product includes the dimensions of the printable and nonprintable areas of the sheet

To start a label mail merge

1. Open a blank document and display paragraph marks and formatting symbols.

2. On the **Mailings** tab, in the **Start Mail Merge** group, select **Start Mail Merge**.

3. On the **Start Mail Merge** menu, select **Labels**. The Label Options dialog opens.

Thousands of label products are available from this dialog

4. In the **Printer information** area, choose the correct printer type for the label forms and, for standard printers, choose the input tray (or manual feed) for the label sheets.

5. On the label package, identify the manufacturer and product number of the labels you will use. In the **Label information** area, do the following:

   • In the **Label vendors** list, select the label manufacturer.

   • In the **Product number** list, select the product number.

> **TIP** To save time, click or tap in the Product Number box and press the keyboard key corresponding to the first character of the product number to jump to that section of the list. Then scroll to locate the specific product number. If the label product you're using isn't in the list, select Find Updates On Office.com to refresh the list.

14

6. In the **Label Options** dialog, select **OK** to return to the document. Word creates the label form in which you will enter the merge fields and any static content.

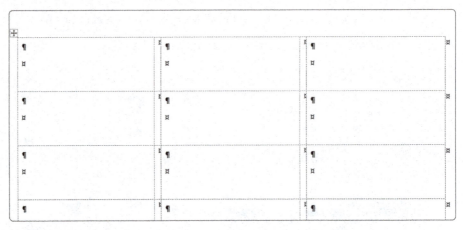

Ensure that paragraph symbols and formatting marks are shown before continuing

7. To continue and complete the process:

   a. Use the procedures described in "Choose and refine the data source" later in this chapter to identify the data source and available fields.

   b. Create or edit the static label content, and use the procedures described in "Insert merge fields" later in this chapter to insert the merge fields.

   c. Use the procedures described in "Preview and complete the merge" later in this chapter to finish creating the labels.

Get started with email messages

When you want to send the same information to all the people on a list—for example, all your customers, or all the members of a club or your family—you don't have to print letters and physically mail them. Instead, you can use mail merge to create a personalized email message for each person in a data source. As with a form letter that will be printed, you can either use the Mail Merge wizard or use the buttons on the Mailings tab to insert merge fields into a document. These merge fields will be replaced with information from the specified data source, and the starting document will be converted to individual email messages.

Many email messages need no merge fields other than a greeting line.

«GreetingLine»

Thank you for your recent visit to our store. It was a pleasure to discuss your decorating plans and offer suggestions.

As you requested, we have added your name to our online mailing list. You will receive our monthly newsletter, as well as advance notice of upcoming sales and special in-store events. You can also visit our website at www.wideworldimporters.com for a schedule of events, links to online decorating resources, articles on furniture care, and more.

Questions? Contact us by email at customerservice@wideworldimporters.com, or call (925) 555-0167 during business hours.

If you want to edit the custom greeting, right-click the merge field and then select Edit Greeting Line

Because email messages tend to be less formal than printed letters, you might want to start the messages with a custom greeting rather than one of the predefined greeting options (*Dear* and *To*).

Word connects to Outlook to send the email messages. You can find the sent messages in your Outlook Sent Mail folder.

Attaching files to email merge messages

The native mail merge features of Word don't provide a method for attaching a file or files to the email messages that you generate from Word. If this is something that you want to do, however, there is a workaround.

If you're looking for a simpler method of attaching files to outgoing email merge messages, there are many third-party add-ins that enable you to do this, either for free or for a fee, depending on the number of messages you send. Search online for "mail merge with attachments" to return a current list of solution providers.

14

To start an email mail merge

1. Open a blank document or a document that contains the static content you want to pull data into.

2. On the **Mailings** tab, in the **Start Mail Merge** group, select **Start Mail Merge**.

3. On the **Start Mail Merge** menu, select **E-mail Messages**. Word displays the current content in Web view.

> (🔍) **SEE ALSO** For information about the available views, see "Display different views of documents" in Chapter 2, "Create and manage documents."

4. To continue and complete the process:

   a. Use the procedures described in the next section ("Choose and refine the data source") to identify the data source and available fields.

   b. Create or edit the document content, and use the procedures described in "Insert merge fields" later in this chapter to insert the merge fields.

   c. Use the procedures described in "Preview and complete the merge" later in this chapter to finish creating the messages.

Choose and refine the data source

The mail merge process combines variable information from a data source with static information in a starting document. The basic data source requirement is the same regardless of the output format: it must be a container that stores information in a consistent structure.

	A	B	C	D	E	F
1	FirstName	LastName	Address	City	State	PostalCode
2	Patrick	Wedge	151 Fir Drive	Bangor	AK	10136
3	Pia	Westermann	221 Mahogany Dr	San Antonio	ND	10218
4	Greg	Yvkoff	791 Beech			
5	Lee	Chia	79 Beech R			
6	Joseph	Matthews	895 Gum B			
7	James	Van Eaton	742 Madro			
8	Humberto	Acevedo	421 Hawth			
9	Anette	Grohsmüller	956 Cypres			
10	David	Hodgson	292 Maple			
11	Jim	Wickham	547 Gum A			
12	Paulo	Lisboa	855 Beech			
13	Ty	Carlson	760 Willow			
14	Amy	Recker	566 Yucca			

```
FirstName,LastName,Address,City,State,PostalCode
Patrick,Wedge,151 Fir Drive,Bangor,AK,10136
Pia,Westermann,221 Mahogany Dr,San Antonio,ND,10218
Greg,Yvkoff,791 Beech Terrace,Toledo,MT,10367
Lee,Chia,79 Beech Rd,Houston,ND,10537
Joseph,Matthews,895 Gum Bay,Evansville,OK,10826
James,Van Eaton,742 Madrone St,Rockford,IN,11374
Humberto,Acevedo,421 Hawthorn Ct,Tucson,MA,11491
Anette,Grohsmüller,956 Cypress Ln,Denver,AL,12097
David,Hodgson,292 Maple Terrace,Youngstown,WY,12642
Jim,Wickham,547 Gum Ave,St. Louis,VT,12864
Paulo,Lisboa,855 Beech Bay,Gainesville,NM,12999
Ty,Carlson,760 Willow Ave,Chattanooga,SC,13291
Amy,Recker,566 Yucca Ct,Montgomery,LA,13322
```

Data sources store information in a consistent structure

Most data source structures store data in a tabular format, with fields identified at the top and records following. The most straightforward example of this, and the one we work with throughout this chapter, is a Microsoft Excel workbook.

Each field in a data source must be identified by a unique name so you can pull data from the field into the starting document. In Excel, the field names are the table column headers.

The Mail Merge Recipients dialog displays all the records from the data source

Select an existing data source

The full list of acceptable data source file types is lengthy. Typical data sources include Excel worksheets and delimited text files, but you can also pull data from tables in Microsoft Word, Access, or SQL Server; from a Microsoft Outlook contacts list; or from a variety of other, less common sources.

14

```
All Files (*.*)
All Data Sources (*.odc;*.mdb;*.mde;*.accdb;*.accde;*.ols;*.udl;*.dsn;*.xlsx;*.xlsm;...
Office Database Connections (*.odc)
Access Databases (*.mdb;*.mde)
Access 2007 Database (*.accdb;*.accde)
Microsoft Office Address Lists (*.mdb)
Microsoft Office List Shortcuts (*.ols)
Microsoft Data links (*.udl)
ODBC File DSNs (*.dsn)
Excel Files (*.xlsx;*.xlsm;*.xlsb;*.xls)
Web Pages (*.htm;*.html;*.asp;*.mht;*.mhtml)
Rich Text Format (*.rtf)
Word Documents (*.docx;*.doc;*.docm)
All Word Documents (*.docx;*.doc;*.docm;*.dotx;*.dot;*.dotm;*.rtf;*.htm;*.html)
Text Files (*.txt;*.prn;*.csv;*.tab;*.asc)
Database Queries (*.dqy;*.rqy)
OpenDocument Text Files (*.odt)
```

All the file types that are accepted as data sources

> **TIP** If your company or organization uses another contact-management system, you can probably export information to one of these formats. Delimited text files are the most basic format of structured information storage and should be an export option from any other information storage system.

The data source doesn't have to be stored on your computer; the wizard can link to remotely stored data. If the data source is stored on a server that requires you to sign in, you can provide your credentials and, optionally, store your password.

> **TIP** It isn't necessary for the data source file to be closed during the import operation; you can import records from an open file, edit and save the file, and refresh the list with the changes.

If you use Outlook to manage your Microsoft Exchange or Exchange Online email, contacts, and calendar information, you can import data from an Exchange account contacts folder to use as a mail merge data source. The Mail Merge wizard polls your Outlook data folders and provides a list of contacts folders that you can use. When you choose a contacts folder, the wizard imports the contacts list.

It's likely that your contacts list contains a variety of contacts—clients, employees, friends, relatives, and other people you have corresponded with. Many of these contacts might not be current, and many of them might not be people to whom you want to direct the specific form letter or email message that you're creating. But that's okay; you can import the entire contacts list and then use the filtering function in the Mail Merge Recipients dialog to identify only those people you want to include in your current mail merge project.

Mail Merge Recipients

This is the list of recipients that will be used in your merge. Use the options below to add to or change your list. Use the checkboxes to add or remove recipients from the merge. When your list is ready, click OK.

Data Source	☑	LastName	FirstName	Address	City	Sta
CustomerList.xlsx	☑	Wedge	Patrick	151 Fir Drive	Bangor	AK
CustomerList.xlsx	☑	Westermann	Pia	221 Mahogany Dr	San Antonio	ND
CustomerList.xlsx	☑	Yvkoff	Greg	791 Beech Terrace	Toledo	MT
CustomerList.xlsx	☑	Chia	Lee	79 Beech Rd	Houston	ND
CustomerList.xlsx	☑	Matthews	Joseph	895 Gum Bay	Evansville	OK
CustomerList.xlsx	☑	Van Eaton	James	742 Madrone St	Rockford	IN
CustomerList.xlsx	☑	Acevedo	Humberto	421 Hawthorn Ct	Tucson	MA
CustomerList.xlsx	☑	Grohsmüller	Anette	956 Cypress Ln	Denver	AL
CustomerList.xlsx	☑	Hodgson	David	292 Maple Terrace	Youngstown	WV

Data Source

CustomerList.xlsx

Refine recipient list

- ↓ Sort...
- Filter...
- Find duplicates...
- Find recipient...
- Validate addresses...

Edit...   Refresh

OK

A selected checkbox indicates that a record will be included in the mail merge

> **SEE ALSO** For information about filtering records for a mail merge, see "Refine the data source records" later in this topic.

To select an existing data source

1. On the **Mailings** tab, in the **Start Mail Merge** group, select **Select Recipients** to display the data source options.

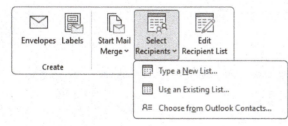

- Type a New List...
- Use an Existing List...
- R≡ Choose from Outlook Contacts...

Choose or create a data source file

14

2.   On the **Select Recipients** menu, do either of the following:

-   Select **Use an Existing List**. In the **Select Data Source** dialog, browse to and select the data source file, and then select **Open**.

-   Select **Choose from Outlook Contacts**. If the **Select Contacts** dialog opens, select the contacts folder that you want to import, and then select **OK**.

Create a new data source

If the information that you want to include in your data source isn't already stored in a file or address list, you can create a Microsoft Office Address List while working in the Mail Merge wizard. The wizard saves your list as a table in an Access database (.mdb) file in the My Data Sources subfolder of your Documents folder.

The process of entering information through the Address List interface is somewhat tedious, because you must manually populate each field—so if you have a lot of records, it's easier to enter your data into an Excel worksheet. However, it's fine for an impromptu mail merge process, such as creating a set of name tags for a meeting.

Creating a simple list in the wizard

You're not limited to collecting contact information; you can add, remove, and reorder the fields to store the type of data that's pertinent to your mail merge process.

To create a data source from the Mailings tab

1. On the **Mailings** tab, in the **Start Mail Merge** group, select **Select Recipients**, and then select **Type a New List**.

2. In the **New Address List** dialog, do the following:

   a. Select **Customize Columns**. Add any fields to the column list that you plan to include in the mail merge operation. To keep things tidy, remove any fields that you don't plan to use.

   b. Enter the information for each record, selecting **New Entry** to create another.

3. When you finish, select **OK**.

4. In the **Save Address List** dialog, provide a name for the database file, and then select **Save**.

Refine the data source records

The data source you choose doesn't have to be specific to the item you're creating. For example, you could create postcards announcing an in-store sale only for customers who live in the area or create gift certificates only for people who have birthdays in the next month.

If you don't want to include all the data source records in your mail merge operation, you can now whittle down the list to those you want. Use the following processes to remove a record from the recipient list:

- **Filter the list on one or more fields** Filter the list to display only the records that you want to include, or to locate (and then remove) the records that you want to exclude.

- **Remove duplicates** The wizard can help to identify entries that might be duplicates. Either clear the checkboxes for the duplicate versions that you don't want to use, or remove the entries from the data source file, save the file, and refresh the recipients list.

- **Manually exclude records** Each record has a checkbox. Clearing the checkbox removes the record from the mail merge operation.

Excluding records from the mail merge operation doesn't remove them from the Mail Merge Recipients list or from the original data source file. They will still be available for you to use in this or another mail merge operation.

14

In addition to limiting the set of information used in a mail merge, you can also sort the records to specify the order in which they appear in the mail merge document— for example, in postal code order for a bulk mailing.

> ⚠ **IMPORTANT** The Refine Recipient List area of the Mail Merge Recipients dialog includes a Validate Addresses link. A third-party address-validation tool is required to validate addresses. If you don't already have one of these tools, selecting the link displays a message that an address validation add-in is required and provides a link to a list of validation tools that work with Word. You can use these tools to validate mailing addresses against US postal regulation standards to filter out recipients whose mailing addresses don't appear to be valid.

To display the Mail Merge Recipients list

- On the **Mailings** tab, in the **Start Mail Merge** group, select **Edit Recipient List**.

To filter the recipients list to display only records you want to include

1. Display the **Mail Merge Recipients** list.

2. In the **Refine recipient list** area, select **Filter** to display the Filter Records tab of the Filter And Sort dialog.

3. In the **Field** list, select the field you want to filter by.

4. In the **Comparison** list, select one of the following:

   - Equal to

   - Not equal to

   - Less than

   - Greater than

   - Less than or equal

   - Greater than or equal

   - Is blank

   - Is not blank

   - Contains

   - Does not contain

5. In the **Compare to** list, enter the criterion for the field filter.

6. To apply multiple criteria, select **And** or **Or** in the leftmost list and then enter the additional criteria.

A multi-filter operation that returns only specific insurance policy subscribers

7. In the **Filter and Sort** dialog, select **OK**. Records not displayed in the filtered list are not included in the mail merge operation.

To filter records out of the recipients list

1. Following the instructions in the previous procedure, filter the **Mail Merge Recipients** list to display the records you want to exclude.

2. Select the checkbox in the column heading area (twice if necessary) to clear the checkboxes of all the records returned by the filter operation.

Clearing a checkbox removes a record from the recipient list but not from the data source

3. In the **Refine recipient list** area, select **Filter** to redisplay the Filter Records tab of the Filter And Sort dialog.

4. On the **Filter Records** tab, select the **Clear All** button, and then select **OK** to remove the filter. The records that you excluded while the filter was applied are still excluded.

To remove duplicate records from the recipients list

1. Display the **Mail Merge Recipients** list.

2. In the **Refine recipient list** area, select **Find duplicates** to display records that have similar field entries.

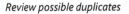

| Find Duplicates | | | | | | ? ✕ |

The following entries appear to be duplicates. Use the checkboxes to select the entries you want to include in your merge.

Data Source		LastName	FirstName	Address	City	State
Policyholders.xl...	☑	Charles	Mathew	14 Lilac Court	Zanesville	LA
Policyholders.xl...	☑	Charles	Matthew	14 Lilac Court	Zanesville	LA
Policyholders.xl...	☑	Clayton	Jane	290 Willow Drive	Newark	TX
Policyholders.xl...	☑	Clayton	Jane			
Policyholders.xl...	☑	Untch	Hans-Walter	483 Conifer Drive	Las Vegas	LA
Policyholders.xl...	☑	Untch	Hans-Walter	483 Conifer Drive	Las Vegas	LA

| | | | | | OK | Cancel |

Review possible duplicates

3. In the **Find Duplicates** dialog, clear the checkboxes of any records that you want to exclude from the mail merge operation. Then select **OK**.

To sort records in a data source

1. Display the **Mail Merge Recipients** list.

2. To sort the records by one field, select the field name (the column header) of the field you want to sort by. (Select the field name again to sort in the opposite order.)

   Or

To sort the records by multiple fields, do the following:

a. In the **Refine recipient list** area, select **Sort** to display the Sort Records tab of the Filter And Sort dialog.

Sort by up to three fields

b. In the **Sort by** list, select the first field you want to sort by. Then select the adjacent **Ascending** or **Descending** option to specify the sort order.

c. In the first **Then by** list, select the second field you want to sort by, and the adjacent **Ascending** or **Descending** option.

d. In the second **Then by** list, specify the third sort field and order, or select **(None)**.

e. In the **Filter and Sort** dialog, select **OK**.

To manually exclude records from the recipients list

1. Display the **Mail Merge Recipients** list.

2. If necessary, sort or filter the list to locate records.

3. Clear the checkboxes of any records that you want to exclude from the mail merge operation.

14

Refresh data

You can save and close the document at any point in the mail merge process. When you reopen the document, if you've already connected to the data source and inserted merge fields, Word prompts you to refresh the data connection.

The recipient list reflects changes to the source data when you reopen the document

You can also refresh the data manually at any time from within the document by selecting the Refresh button in the Data Source area of the Mail Merge Recipients dialog.

Insert merge fields

In the document, merge fields are enclosed in chevrons (« and »). However, you can't simply type the chevrons and the field name; you must insert the merge field by using the commands on the Mailings tab. This creates a link from the merge field to the data source field.

The commands that you use to insert merge fields in a starting document are in the Write & Insert Fields group on the Mailings tab.

The tools for inserting fields in mail merge documents

Every field in the data source is available to insert as an individual merge field. Two additional merge fields that pull information from the data source are available to save you time:

- **Address Block**   This merge field inserts elements of a standard address block (the recipient's name, company name, and postal address) that you select so you can insert all the information with one merge field.

Customize the Address Block merge field

- **Greeting Line**   This merge field inserts a personalized salutation or substitutes a generic salutation for records that are missing the necessary information.

Select from multiple greetings and name forms

14

After you insert the first merge field in a document, the Highlight Merge Fields button in the Write & Insert Fields group on the Mailings tab becomes active. Select this button to highlight (in gray) all the merge fields in the document so they're easier to locate.

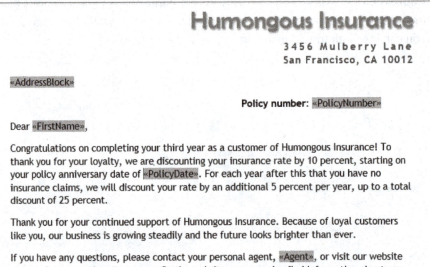

Highumongous Insurance

3456 Mulberry Lane
San Francisco, CA 10012

«AddressBlock»

Policy number: «PolicyNumber»

Dear «FirstName»,

Congratulations on completing your third year as a customer of Humongous Insurance! To thank you for your loyalty, we are discounting your insurance rate by 10 percent, starting on your policy anniversary date of «PolicyDate». For each year after this that you have no insurance claims, we will discount your rate by an additional 5 percent per year, up to a total discount of 25 percent.

Thank you for your continued support of Humongous Insurance. Because of loyal customers like you, our business is growing steadily and the future looks brighter than ever.

If you have any questions, please contact your personal agent, «Agent», or visit our website at www.humongousinsurance.com. On the website, you can also find information about our referral program, through which you can earn additional discounts and other rewards.

Highlight the merge fields to more easily locate them and verify that they aren't placeholders

> **IMPORTANT** Before you can perform the procedures in this topic, you must select a data source. For more information, see "Choose and refine the data source" earlier in this chapter.

To insert a single merge field

1. Position the cursor in the location where you want to insert the merge field.

2. On the **Mailings** tab, in the **Write & Insert Fields** group, select **Insert Merge Field**, and then select the field you want to insert.

To insert a customized address block

1. Position the cursor in the location where you want to insert the address block.

2. On the **Mailings** tab, in the **Write & Insert Fields** group, select **Address Block**.

3. In the **Insert Address Block** dialog, select the address block elements you want to include and select the format for the recipient's name.

4. In the **Preview** box displaying your first data record, check that the address block looks correct. You can move through additional records to check further.

5. When you finish, select **OK**.

To insert a customized greeting line

1. Position the cursor in the location where you want to insert the Greeting Line merge field.

2. On the **Mailings** tab, in the **Write & Insert Fields** group, select **Greeting Line**.

3. In the **Insert Greeting Line** dialog, select the greeting line elements you want to include and the generic format for records that don't have the elements you specify.

4. In the **Preview** box displaying your first data record, check that the greeting looks correct. You can move through additional records to check further.

5. When you finish, select **OK**.

To modify a customized merge field

- Right-click or long-press (tap and hold) the merge field and then select **Edit Address Block** or **Edit Greeting Line**.

Preview and complete the merge

After you specify the data source you want to use and enter merge fields in the main document, you can preview the effect of merging the records into the documents, and then perform the actual merge. You can further filter the source data during the preview process. When you're ready, you can either send the merged documents directly to the printer or merge them into a new document. If you merge to a new document, you have another chance to review and, if necessary, edit the merged documents before sending them to the printer.

14

> ⚠ **IMPORTANT** Before you can perform the procedures in this topic, you must select a data source and insert merge fields. For more information, see "Choose and refine the data source" and "Insert merge fields" earlier in this chapter.

To preview merged documents

1. Display the starting document with merge fields in place and the data source attached.

2. On the **Mailings** tab, in the **Preview Results** group, select **Preview Results** to display the data source information in place of the merge fields.

3. In the **Preview Results** group, do any of the following:

   - Select the **Next Record** or **Previous Record** button to move through the data source one record at a time.

   - Select the **First Record** or **Last Record** button to move to the first or last record in the data source.

   - Select **Preview Results** again to redisplay the merge fields.

To merge data to a new document

1. On the **Mailings** tab, in the **Finish** group, select **Finish & Merge**, and then **Edit Individual Documents**. The Merge To New Document dialog opens.

Limit the merge to one record or a range of records

2. In the **Merge to New Document** dialog, indicate the record or records that you want to merge, and then select **OK**.

To merge data and print the resulting file

1. On the **Mailings** tab, in the **Finish** group, select **Finish & Merge**, and then **Print Documents**.

2. In the **Merge to Printer** dialog, indicate the record or records that you want to merge, and then select **OK**.

3. In the **Print** dialog, select your printer, configure any additional printer settings that are necessary, and then select **OK**.

To merge data and email the resulting messages

1. On the **Mailings** tab, in the **Finish** group, select **Finish & Merge**, and then **Send Email Messages**. The Merge To E-mail dialog opens.

Merge to E-mail	? X
Message options	
To:	EmailAddress ⌄
Subject line:	Thank you for your business!
Mail format:	HTML ⌄
Send records	
● All	
○ Current record	
○ From: ___ To: ___	
	OK Cancel

You specify the address field and subject line before sending the messages

2. In the **Message options** area, do the following:

    a. In the **To** list, select the field that contains the recipients' email addresses.

    b. In the **Subject line** box, enter the message subject you want the email message to display.

    c. In the **Mail format** list, select **Attachment**, **Plain text**, or **HTML**.

3. In the **Send records** area, indicate the record or records that you want to merge. Then select **OK**.

Create individual envelopes and labels

14

If you want to print a lot of envelopes or mailing labels based on data source fields, you can use the mail merge function to create documents, and then print the documents onto envelopes or sheet-fed labels rather than regular paper.

However, you can also use the Envelopes and Labels commands to create one or more individually addressed envelopes or address labels. Because these functions are related to "mailing" envelopes or packages, they are located on the Mailing tab of the ribbon with the mail merge functionality.

Generate individual envelopes

The Envelope function prints a delivery address and can also print a return address and electronic postage, if you have the necessary software installed. You can manually enter the delivery address, or you can pick it up from a document (usually a letter) that contains an address.

Edit the address information before creating or printing the envelope

> ✓ **TIP** Save time by storing the return address with your user information. The address then appears by default as the return address in the Envelopes And Labels dialog.

When creating envelopes, you can specify the envelope size, the address locations, and the fonts for the addresses. You can also specify the paper source, the envelope feed method (horizontally or vertically and face up or face down), and the alignment of the envelope. Then Word configures the page layout options and print options as required for your selections.

Position the addresses on the envelope exactly where you want them

When you create an envelope based on an address in a letter, you can print the envelope immediately, or add the envelope page to the document and then print the envelope and letter later.

Adding the envelope to the document inserts it as a separate document section with unique page layout settings

14

> ⚠️ **IMPORTANT** The electronic postage options on the Envelopes tab of the Envelopes And Labels dialog require the installation of an electronic postage add-in. Selecting an electronic postage option displays a message box that directs you to a list of electronic postage providers. However, at the time of this writing, the only available add-in works only with Word 2013. Additional add-ins might be available by the time you read this book; when they are, you can print electronic postage directly onto envelopes.

To save your mailing address for use in Word documents

1. Open the **Word Options** dialog, and then select the **Advanced** tab.

2. On the **Advanced** page, in the **General** section, enter your name and address in the **Mailing Address** box. Then select **OK**.

To set up an envelope with a manually entered address

1. Open any document.

2. On the **Mailings** tab, in the **Create** group, select **Envelopes** to open the Envelopes And Labels dialog.

   The Return Address box contains your user name or your mailing address if you saved that in the Word Options dialog. (If you saved and then deleted your mailing address, the Return Address box might be blank.)

3. In the **Return address** area, do either of the following:

   - Review the return address information and modify it as necessary.

   - If you plan to print to envelopes that have a preprinted return address, select the **Omit** checkbox.

4. In the **Delivery address** box, enter the name and address that you want Word to print on the envelope.

To set up an envelope from an address in a document

1. Open the document and select the address.

2. On the **Mailings** tab, in the **Create** group, select **Envelopes** to open the Envelopes And Labels dialog with the selected address in the Delivery Address box. The Return Address box contains your user name, and your return address if you've saved that in Word.

3. Review the addresses and make any changes you want. If you plan to print on an envelope that has a preprinted return address, select the **Omit** checkbox in the **Return address** area.

To configure or confirm the envelope printing options

1. At the bottom of the **Envelopes** tab of the **Envelopes and Labels** dialog, select **Options** to open the Envelope Options dialog.

2. On the **Envelope Options** tab, set the envelope size, delivery address font and position, and return address font and position.

3. On the **Printing Options** tab, set the feed method, rotation, and paper source.

> ⚠ **IMPORTANT** If the printer shown at the top of the Printing Options tab is not the correct printer, select OK in each of the open dialogs to save your settings and return to the source document. Then select the correct printer in the source document and return to the Envelopes And Labels dialog to finish creating the envelope.

4. Select **OK** to return to the Envelopes And Labels dialog.

To print or save an envelope

- After you set up the envelope and configure the envelope printing options, do either of the following:

  - Load an envelope into the printer in the orientation configured in the Envelope Options dialog. Then at the bottom of the **Envelopes and Labels** dialog, select **Print** to print the envelope.

  - At the bottom of the **Envelopes and Labels** dialog, select **Add to Document** to insert the envelope content as a separately formatted section at the beginning of the current document. Then save the document.

14

Generate individual mailing labels

The Labels function is designed to print one address (a delivery address or a return address) onto a sheet of labels, to create either a single label or a full sheet of the same label. Instead of selecting an envelope size, you select a label form by first selecting the label manufacturer and then selecting the specific product number. Word sets up a document to precisely match the content layout areas of the selected form.

Elizabeth Jones 123 Plumeria Court Hibiscus Hill, UT 98765	Elizabeth Jones 123 Plumeria Court Hibiscus Hill, UT 98765	Elizabeth Jones 123 Plumeria Court Hibiscus Hill, UT 98765
Elizabeth Jones 123 Plumeria Court Hibiscus Hill, UT 98765	Elizabeth Jones 123 Plumeria Court Hibiscus Hill, UT 98765	Elizabeth Jones 123 Plumeria Court Hibiscus Hill, UT 98765
Elizabeth Jones 123 Plumeria Court Hibiscus Hill, UT 98765	Elizabeth Jones 123 Plumeria Court Hibiscus Hill, UT 98765	Elizabeth Jones 123 Plumeria Court Hibiscus Hill, UT 98765
Elizabeth Jones 123 Plumeria Court	Elizabeth Jones 123 Plumeria Court	Elizabeth Jones 123 Plumeria Court

The content cells defined by the table match the printing areas of the label sheets

As discussed in "Get started with labels" earlier in this chapter, the term "labels" refers not only to rectangular stickers, but also to many other things that you print onto sheet-fed media that is divided into fixed areas. You can use the Labels function to print on any of these. It's important that you select the correct form because the print areas are very specifically defined.

To set up individual mailing labels

1. Open any document.

2. On the **Mailings** tab, in the **Create** group, select **Labels** to open the Envelopes And Labels dialog.

3. In the **Address** area, do either of the following:

    -   If you've saved your return address information in Word and want to create a return address label, select the **Use return address** checkbox to insert the saved address into the Address box. Then review the return address information and modify it as necessary.

- Enter the name and address that you want Word to print on the label.

Envelopes and Labels	?	×

Envelopes　__Labels__

Address:　　　　　　　　　　　　　　▦ ▾ ☐ Use return address

Elizabeth Jones
123 Plumeria court
Hibiscus Hill, UT 98765|

Print
- ⦿ Full page of the same label
- ☐ Single label

　　Row: 1 ⇕　Column: 1 ⇕

Label
Avery US Letter, 8160 Address La...
Address Labels

Before printing, insert labels in your printer's manual feeder.

[Print]　[New Document]　[Options...]　[E-postage Properties...]

[Cancel]

Although the field specifies an address, you can print any text on the labels

4. In the **Print** area, do either of the following to correctly configure the label output:

   - If you want to print one full sheet of labels, select **Full page of the same label**.

   - If you want to print only one label, select **Single label** and then enter the row and column of the position on the sheet of the label you want to print on.

   > **TIP** This feature permits you to easily reuse a partial sheet of blank labels.

14

5. In the **Label** area, confirm that the label type is the correct one for the printed label forms you're using. If it isn't, configure the label settings in the **Label Options** dialog.

> **SEE ALSO** For information about configuring label settings, see "Get started with labels" earlier in this chapter.

To print or save a mailing label

■ After you set up the label and configure the label printing options, do either of the following:

- Load a label form into the printer in the manner configured in the Label Options dialog. Then at the bottom of the **Envelopes and Labels** dialog, select **Print** to print the label.

- At the bottom of the **Envelopes and Labels** dialog, select **New Document** to generate a new document that contains the merged labels. Then save the document.

Key points

■ The mail merge process is that of merging variable information from a data source into the static content of a main document such as a letter, envelope, sheet of labels, or email message.

■ Mail merge data sources are organized into sets of information, called records, with each record containing the same items of information, called fields.

■ You insert merge field placeholders into the main document to tell Word where to merge fields from the data source.

■ You don't have to use all the records from a data source for a mail merge; you can filter the data and exclude specific records.

■ The mail merge process can create a new document that you can edit or save, or you can send the results directly to your printer or to email recipients.

Practice tasks

Before you can complete these tasks, you must copy the book's practice files to your computer. The practice files for these tasks are in the **Word365SBS\Ch14** folder. You can save the results of the tasks in the same folder.

The Introduction includes a complete list of practice files and download instructions.

Understand the mail merge process

Start Word, open a new blank document, and then perform the following tasks:

1. Start the Mail Merge wizard and investigate the options provided therein.

2. Using the wizard, create any mail merge item you want. Use the **CustomerList** workbook from the practice file folder as your data source.

3. If you create a mail merge document, save it as MyMerge, and then close it.

Start the mail merge process

Open the **StartMerge** document from the practice file folder, and then perform the following tasks:

1. Start a letter mail merge. Notice that the document doesn't change.

2. Start an email mail merge. Notice that the document view changes to Web Layout.

3. Start a label mail merge and investigate the options in the Label Options dialog. Choose a label vendor and product number, and display the label details.

4. Create the label sheet and allow Word to replace the contents of the **StartMerge** document when prompted to do so.

5. Close the document without saving it.

Choose and refine the data source

Open the **RefineData** document, and then perform the following tasks:

1. Start a letter mail merge. Select the **CustomerList** workbook from the practice file folder as the data source, and select the **Customers$** table of the workbook when prompted to do so.

2. Sort the recipient list alphabetically, in ascending order, by the customers' last names.

3. Remove duplicate records from the recipient list.

4. Filter the list to display only those records for customers who live in either the state of Texas (TX) or the state of Louisiana (LA).

5. Manually exclude all the Louisiana (LA) records from the recipient list, and then return to the letter.

6. From the **Select Recipients** menu, create a new data source. Add your name and the names of two other people. Add any other information you want, and then save the new list as **PracticeList.mdb**.

7. Save and close the document.

Insert merge fields

Open the **InsertFields** document, and then perform the following tasks:

1. Start a letter mail merge. Select the **PolicyholdersList** workbook from the practice file folder as the data source, and select the **PolicyHolders$** table of the workbook when prompted to do so.

2. Replace each placeholder in the document with its corresponding merge field.

3. Save the **InsertFields** document, but don't close it.

4. Create a new blank document and start a new letter mail merge. Use the same data source as in step 1.

5. Open the **Insert Address Block** dialog. Review the settings and make any changes you want, and then insert the merge field.

6. In the document, two lines below the address block, insert a **Greeting Line** merge field.

7. Save the document as MyFields, and then close it. Leave the **InsertFields** document open for the next set of practice tasks.

Preview and complete the merge

Complete the previous set of practice tasks to modify the **InsertFields** document. Then perform the following tasks:

1. Use the tools in the **Preview Results** group on the **Mailings** tab to preview the results of completing the mail merge. Then redisplay the merge fields.

2. Merge the data source into the document to create a new document. Save the document as MyLetter, and then close it.

3. Redisplay the **InsertFields** document and follow the procedure to merge the output directly to the printer. (If you don't want to print the file, select **Cancel** in the final dialog.)

4. Follow the procedure to merge the output to email messages. Explore the settings, and then select **Cancel**.

5. Save and close the document.

Create individual envelopes and labels

Open the **CreateEnvelopes** document, and then perform the following tasks:

1. Open the **Word Options** dialog and display the **Advanced** page. In the **General** section, check whether you have saved your mailing address. If you haven't, do so now.

2. In the document, select the letter recipient's name and address, and then open the **Envelopes and Labels** dialog. Verify that the **Return Address** box contains your mailing address, and the **Delivery Address** box contains the letter recipient's name and address.

3. In the **Envelope Options** dialog, configure the envelope printing options and then, if you want, load an envelope into your printer, and print the addresses onto the envelope.

4. Save and close the **CreateEnvelopes** document.

5. Create a new blank document.

6. Display the **Labels** tab of the **Envelopes and Labels** dialog. If your saved mailing address isn't already shown in the Address box, select the **Use return address** checkbox to add your saved information to the **Address** box.

7. Configure the merge output to print one full sheet of labels.

8. Do either of the following:

   - If you have a sheet of labels to print to, configure the label settings. Then load a sheet of labels into the printer and print the addresses onto the labels.

   - If you don't have a sheet of labels, generate a new document that contains the merged labels. Then save the document as MyLabels, and close it.

Create custom document elements

When it comes to maximizing your efficiency while creating documents in Word, styles and templates are among the most powerful tools available to you.

You can greatly enhance your efficiency when developing a series of related custom documents by creating themes that specify the colors and fonts to use, styles that specify the formatting appropriate to the document, and templates that store and apply those styles. You can also create building blocks that save preformatted content segments to insert into any document.

This chapter guides you through procedures related to creating and modifying styles, creating and managing custom themes, creating and attaching templates, and creating custom building blocks.

In this chapter

- Create and modify styles
- Create and manage custom themes
- Create and attach templates
- Create custom building blocks

Create and modify styles

Even if you don't want to create your own templates, it's very useful to know how to create and modify styles. When you apply direct character formatting or paragraph formatting, you affect only the selected characters or paragraphs. If you change your mind about how you want to format a particular element, you'll have to change the formatting manually everywhere it is applied. When you format characters or para-graphs by applying a style, you can change the way all those characters or paragraphs look simply by changing the style definition. Making one change can completely change the look of the document.

You can modify existing styles or create new styles. When you modify a style, docu-ment content with that style applied reflects your changes immediately. When you create or modify styles, you can choose to apply the changes in the current document only or in all documents based on the template you're working in.

Modify the content of the Style gallery for the current template by adding and removing styles so the styles you want are available from the gallery and so the styles you rarely use don't distract you.

A customized Style gallery

Adding and removing styles in the gallery doesn't affect the styles in the Styles pane. If you create or modify styles and don't want to save them as part of a template, you can save the style definitions as a custom style set.

To open the Modify Style dialog

- In the **Style** gallery, right-click or long-press (tap and hold) the style you want to modify, and then select **Modify**.

- In the **Styles** pane, point to the style you want to modify, select the arrow that appears to the right of the style name, and then select **Modify**.

- In the **Apply Styles** dialog, select the style you want to modify, and then select **Modify**.

To modify an existing style

1. Apply the style you want to modify to a paragraph or selected text.

2. Adjust the formatting so that the paragraph or selection looks the way you want it.

3. Do either of the following to update the style definition with the new formatting:

   - In the **Style** gallery, right-click the style, and then select **Update** *<style>* **to Match Selection**.

   - In the **Styles** pane, point to the style, select the arrow that appears to the right of the style name, and then select **Update** *<style>* **to Match Selection**.

Or

15

1. Open the **Modify Style** dialog for the style.

2. In the **Formatting** area or from the **Format** menu, change the settings to achieve the look you want.

Modify any aspect of a paragraph style

3. To save the style modification in the template, select **New documents based on this template** (otherwise, the style will be modified in this document only).

4. Select **OK**.

> **SEE ALSO** For information about configuring a custom personal templates location, see "Change default Word options" in Chapter 16, "Customize options and the user interface."

To create a simple style

1. Apply the formatting that you want to include in the style to a paragraph or selection of text.

2. On the **Home** tab, in the **Styles** group, select the **More** button (below the scroll arrows) and then, on the menu, select **Create a Style**.

   A minimized version of the Create New Style From Formatting dialog opens.

Create New Style from Formatting	?	×

   Name:

   Style1

   Paragraph style preview:

   ∝ Style1

OK	Modify...	Cancel

   The Paragraph Style Preview area displays the style formatting

3. In the **Create New Style from Formatting** dialog, enter a name for the style in the **Name** box.

4. Do either of the following:

   - Select **OK** to create the style as shown in the preview pane.

   - Select **Modify** to open the full version of the Create New Style From Formatting dialog (identical to the Modify Style dialog shown in the previous procedure), make any changes to the style that you want, and then select **OK** to create the style.

15

To create a style that is linked to other styles

> ✓ **TIP** To save steps later, insert the cursor within an existing style that you want to base the new style on, and then apply the formatting that you want to that style.

1. Do either of the following to open the full version of the Create New Style From Formatting dialog:

   - In the lower-left corner of the **Styles** pane, select the **New Style** button.

   - Open the minimal version of the dialog, and then select **Modify**.

Basing a style on another simplifies global updates

2. In the **Name** box, enter a name for the style.

3. In the **Style based on** list, verify or select the style on which you want to build the new style. Updating the base style updates all styles based on it.

4. Do either of the following:

   - In the **Formatting** section, select the font, font size, font effects, font color, alignment, line spacing, space before and after, and indent.

   - Select **Format**, and then from the Format list, format the font, paragraph, tabs, border, language, frame, numbering, shortcut key, or text effects.

5. If you're creating a paragraph style, in the **Style for following paragraph** list, select the style that you want to create when the user presses **Enter** in a paragraph of this style.

6. If you want to include this style in the Style gallery, select the **Add to the Styles gallery** checkbox.

7. If you want to automatically update the style definition whenever formatting is applied to this style in a document, select the **Automatically update** checkbox. (You probably don't want to select this, because it can modify the style when you don't want it to.)

8. If you want to save the style as part of the currently attached document template, select **New documents based on this template**.

9. Select **OK**.

To add a style to the Style gallery

- In the **Styles** pane, do either of the following:

  - Right-click the style, and then select **Add to Style Gallery**.

  - Point to the style, select the arrow that appears, and then select **Add to Style Gallery**.

Managing the application of a style from the Styles pane

Or

1. Open the **Modify Style** dialog for the style.

2. Select the **Add to the Styles gallery** checkbox, and then select **OK**.

To remove a style from the Style gallery

- In the **Styles** pane, point to the style, select the arrow that appears, and then select **Remove from Style Gallery**.

- In the **Styles** pane or **Style** gallery, right-click the style, and then select **Remove from Style Gallery**.

Managing a style from the Style gallery

Or

1. Open the **Modify Style** dialog for the style.

2. Clear the **Add to the Styles gallery** checkbox, and then select **OK**.

To save the current style definitions as a style set

1. On the **Design** tab, in the **Document Formatting** group, select the **More** button (in the lower-right corner of the gallery pane) to expand the Style Set gallery and menu.

2. On the menu, select **Save as a New Style Set**.

3. In the **Save as a New Style Set** dialog, enter a name for the style set in the **File name** box.

4. Select **Save** to save the style set in the QuickStyles folder and add it to the Style Set gallery.

> **SEE ALSO** For information about switching style sets, see "Apply built-in styles to text" in Chapter 4, "Modify the structure and appearance of text."

To delete a custom style

- In the **Styles** pane, select the arrow to the right of the style, select **Delete** or **Revert To** *<style>*, and then select **Yes** to confirm the deletion.

> **TIP** The Delete command appears on the menu for styles that aren't based on other styles. The Revert To command appears for styles that *are* based on other styles. You can't delete a built-in style, but if you've modified it, you can revert it back to its original formatting.

Create and manage custom themes

Chapter 4 contains information about applying themes, changing the default theme, and changing the colors, fonts, or effect styles of a theme within an individual document.

If you create a combination of theme elements that you would like to use with other documents, save the combination as a new theme. By saving the theme in the default Document Themes folder, you make the theme available in the Themes gallery. However, you don't have to store custom themes in the Document Themes folder; you can store them anywhere on your hard disk, on removable media, or on a network location.

> **TIP** The default Document Themes folder is stored inside a subfolder of your user profile folder. To find it, navigate in File Explorer to C:\Users*<user name>*\AppData\Roaming\Microsoft\Templates\Document Themes. (In a corporate environment with managed computer configurations, the user profile folder might be in a custom location.) AppData is a hidden folder, so you can either show hidden items in File Explorer (from the View menu) and navigate from This PC to the Document Themes folder or enter the path in the File Explorer address bar and then press Enter or select the Go button.

15

If multiple people create corporate documents for your company, you can ensure that everyone's documents have a common look and feel by assembling a custom theme and making it available to everyone. Use theme elements that reflect your corporate colors, fonts, and visual style, and then save the theme to a central location or send the theme file by email and instruct your colleagues to save it to the default Document Themes folder.

Themes and theme components are stored in this folder

To save a custom theme

1. Within a document, apply a base theme, and then modify the theme colors, fonts, and effects the way you want them.

2. On the **Design** tab, in the **Document Formatting** group, select **Themes**.

3. At the bottom of the **Themes** menu, select **Save Current Theme** to display the contents of the Document Themes folder in the Save Current Theme dialog.

4. In the **File name** box, replace the suggested name, and then select **Save**.

To apply a custom theme

1. Display the **Themes** menu. If the Document Themes folder contains custom themes, they're available in a Custom section at the top of the Themes menu. (If the Document Themes folder is empty, the Themes menu doesn't display the Custom section.)

2. In the **Custom** section of the **Themes** menu, select the theme.

To apply a theme from a nonstandard location

1. On the **Design** tab, in the **Document Formatting** group, select **Themes**.

2. At the bottom of the **Themes** menu, select **Browse for Themes**.

3. In the **Choose Theme or Themed Document** dialog, browse to the theme you want to apply, and then select **Open**.

To find the location of your Document Themes folder

1. On the **Design** tab, in the **Document Formatting** group, select **Themes**.

2. At the bottom of the **Themes** menu, select **Save Current Theme**.

3. In the **Save Current Theme** dialog, select the folder icon at the left end of the address bar to display the full path to the Document Themes folder.

To delete a custom theme

- Open File Explorer, browse to the **Document Themes** folder, and delete the theme file.

- In Word, display the **Themes** menu, right-click the custom theme, and then select **Delete**.

Note that the second method removes the theme choice from the gallery but doesn't remove the theme file from your Themes folder.

15

Create and attach templates

Although most Word users rarely need to concern themselves with this fact, all Word documents are based on templates. New blank documents are based on the built-in Normal template, which defines paragraph styles for regular text paragraphs, a title, and different levels of headings. It also defines a few character styles that you can use to change the look of selected text. These styles appear in the Styles pane and are also available in the Style gallery on the Home tab. You can apply these template styles to format the content in the document.

> **SEE ALSO** For information about applying styles, see "Apply built-in styles to text" in Chapter 4.

Depending on the types of documents you create and the organization for which you create them, it might be realistic for you to work in the Normal template for the entire length of your word-processing career. If none of the templates that come with Word or that you download from Office.com meet your needs, you can create your own template. You can also distribute the custom template to other people. By doing so, you can ensure that documents you and your coworkers create adhere to a specific set of styles or are based on the same content.

In Chapter 4, we discuss how to assign formats and outline levels to content by applying styles, and how to change the appearance of styled content by using style sets. You can apply local character formatting to modify the appearance of text and change the paragraph spacing for an entire document. All these actions, however, are effective only in the document you're working on. If you want to consistently create coordinated documents, your most efficient option is to create a template that contains styles and colors specific to your purpose.

If you work for a company that has specific corporate fonts and colors, you can save a significant amount of time (and create very professional documents) by creating a corporate template.

Creating a custom template is easy: you simply create a document containing the content, styles, and settings that you want, and then save it as a document template (a .dotx file) rather than as a document (a .docx file). You can save a custom template with text in it, which is handy if you create many documents with only slight variations. Or you can delete the text so that a new document based on the template will open as a blank document with the set of predefined styles available to apply to whatever content you enter.

You can save a custom template anywhere and then browse to and double-click the file name to open a new document based on the template. However, if you save the template in your default Personal Templates folder, it will be available when you select the Personal heading on the New page of the Backstage view. If you want to make changes to the content or formatting that is part of an existing template, you must open the template file (by using the Open command) instead of creating a document based on the template.

> **TIP** As with themes, the default location for user templates is the hidden folder C:\ Users*<user name>*\AppData\Roaming\Microsoft\Templates. If you prefer, you can specify your own Personal Templates folder from the Save page of the Word Options dialog. If you create a lot of your own templates, you might consider organizing them in subfolders of your personal templates folder. Create subfolders either by browsing to your personal templates folder in File Explorer and selecting New Folder or by selecting New Folder in the Save As dialog.

If you're working with an existing document and want to convert it to your custom template, you can either attach the custom template to the existing document or create a new document based on the custom template and import or paste in the content of the existing document. You attach a template by using the Document Template command, which is located in the Templates group on the hidden Developer tab.

> **TIP** You can load additional templates as *global templates* to make their contents available in all documents that you work on. Two global templates are automatically loaded by Word—the Normal template and the Building Blocks template—but you can load others. For example, your organization might have a Custom Building Blocks template containing corporate-themed document parts that it wants you to use in all documents.

15

If you modify the Normal template, you can easily revert to the original by closing all open Word documents, deleting the Normal.dotx template file from the default template location, and then restarting Word. If Word doesn't find the Normal template, it automatically creates a new one for you with the default settings.

To save a document as a personal template

1. In the Backstage view, select the **Save As** page tab.

2. In the left pane of the **Save As** page, select the **Browse** button to open the Save As dialog.

3. In the **Save as type** list, select **Word Template**. The folder path in the Address bar changes to display your default personal templates folder.

4. In the **File name** box, enter a name for the template, such as Company Fax Template. Then select **Save**.

5. Close the template. It is now available from the Personal view of the New page of the Backstage view. (On the New page, select the *Office* and *Personal* headings above the lower template area to switch between templates that come with Word and custom templates.)

To create a document based on a personal template

1. On the **New** page of the **Backstage** view, below the search box, Featured and Personal appear above the thumbnails if custom templates are saved in the default personal templates location. Select **Personal** to display the contents of your personal templates folder.

2. In the **Personal** templates view, select a thumbnail. Word creates a new document based on your custom template.

To edit a personal template

1. Display your personal templates folder.

2. Right-click the template that you want to edit, and then select **Open**.

Or

1. On the **Open** page of the Backstage view, browse to your personal templates folder.

2. Set the file type to **Word Templates**, and then double-click the template you want to edit.

To access the Document Template command

- Do the following to display the Templates group on the Quick Access Toolbar:

    a. Display the **Quick Access Toolbar** page of the **Word Options** dialog.

    b. In the **Choose commands from** list, select **Developer Tab**.

    c. In the **Choose commands from** pane, select **Templates**.

    d. Select **Add,** and then select **OK**.

- Do the following to display the Developer tab on the ribbon:

    e. Display the **Customize Ribbon** page of the **Word Options** dialog.

    f. In the **Customize the Ribbon** pane displaying the main tabs, select the checkbox to the left of **Developer**, and then select **OK**.

> **SEE ALSO** For information about customizing the Quick Access Toolbar and ribbon, see Chapter 16.

To open the Templates And Add-ins dialog

1. Display the **Templates** group on the Quick Access Toolbar or display the **Developer** tab on the ribbon.

2. On the **Quick Access Toolbar** or **Developer** tab, in the **Templates** group, select **Document Template** to display the Templates page of the Templates And Add-ins dialog.

A document with the Normal template attached

To attach a different template to an open document

1. Open the **Templates and Add-ins** dialog.

2. On the **Templates** tab, in the **Document template** section, select **Attach** to open the Attach Template dialog. Until you navigate elsewhere, the dialog automatically opens to the Microsoft Templates folder.

3. Navigate to the template you want to attach, and then double-click it to enter the path to the template in the Document Template box.

4. In the **Templates and Add-ins** dialog, select the **Automatically update document styles** checkbox, and then select **OK** to attach the new template and update the document styles.

Attach a template from any location you can browse to

If the styles in the new template have the same names as the styles in the original template, the formatting associated with the styles changes when you attach the new template. If the styles have different names, you can quickly restyle the document content from the Styles pane by first selecting all the original style instances and then applying the new styles.

To replace the styles attached to content

- In the **Styles** pane, point to the old style name, select the arrow that appears, and select **Select All**. Then select the new style name.

To load a global template and make it available for use

1. Open the **Templates and Add-ins** dialog.

2. On the **Templates** page, in the **Global templates and add-ins** section, select **Add** to open the Add Template dialog.

3. In the **Add Template** dialog, navigate to the template you want to load, and then double-click it to enter the template name in the Global Templates And Add-Ins pane. A check mark indicates that the template is active.

4. In the **Templates and Add-ins** dialog, select **OK**.

> ✓ **TIP** Deactivate a global template (but keep it available for future use) by clearing its checkbox, and unload it by selecting it in the list and selecting Remove.

Create custom building blocks

A *building block* is a document element that is saved in the Building Blocks global template. A building block can be as straightforward as a single word or as complicated as a page full of formatted elements. Many building blocks are provided with Word 365, including professionally designed page elements such as cover pages, headers and footers, and sidebars; and content elements such as bibliographies, common equations, Quick Tables, and watermarks. You can use these building blocks to assemble or enhance a document.

> 🔍 **SEE ALSO** For information about working with building blocks to insert document elements such as cover pages, headers, footers, and page numbers, see Chapter 9, "Format document elements."

15

You can save information and document elements that you use frequently as custom building blocks so that you can easily insert them into documents. A custom building block can be a simple phrase or sentence that you use often, or it can include multiple paragraphs, formatting, graphics, and more.

You need to create the element exactly as you want it only one time; then you can save it as a building block and use it confidently wherever you need it. You insert a custom building block into a document from the Quick Parts gallery on the Quick Parts menu.

Custom building blocks make it easy to insert specific text and objects in any document

> **TIP** The Quick Parts gallery displays only the building blocks you create. The built-in building blocks are available from other galleries, such as the Cover Page gallery.

To save content as a building block

1. Select the content that you want to save as a building block.

2. On the **Insert** tab, in the **Text** group, select the **Quick Parts** button to display the Quick Parts menu.

3. Select **Save Selection to Quick Part Gallery** to open the Create New Building Block dialog.

Word suggests text from the selection as the building block name

4. In the **Name** box, enter a name for your new building block.

5. In the **Category** list, do either of the following:

   - Select the category you want to save the building block in. General is the default.

   - If you want to create a custom category, Select **Create New Category**, and in the **Create New Category** dialog, enter a new category name in the name box, and then select **OK**.

6. In the **Create New Building Block** dialog, add a description and make a selection in the **Options** box if you want, and then select **OK** to add the selected content to the **Quick Parts** gallery and the **Building Blocks** template.

> ⚠ **IMPORTANT** When you exit Word after saving a custom building block, Word prompts you to save changes to the Building Blocks template, which is a separate template from the document template. If you want the building block to be available for future documents, save the changes.

15

To insert a custom building block in a document

- Position the cursor in the document where you want to insert a building block. Then do any of the following:

  - In the **Quick Parts** gallery, select a building block.

  - In the **Quick Parts** gallery, select **Building Blocks Organizer**, and then, in the **Building Blocks Organizer** dialog, select the building block and then **Insert**.

  - In the document, enter the name of the building block, and then press **F3** to replace the building block name with the building block.

  The building block picks up the formatting information from the document into which you insert it.

> **SEE ALSO** For a comprehensive list of keyboard shortcuts in Word 365 and keyboard shortcuts common to all Office 365 apps, and instructions for creating custom keyboard shortcuts in Word, see the appendix, "Keyboard shortcuts."

Or

1. Position the cursor anywhere in the document.

2. In the **Quick Parts** gallery, right-click a building block, and then select one of the insertion options.

The custom building block insertion options

To change the content or formatting of a custom building block

1. Insert the building block in a document and make the modifications to it that you want to save.

2. Select the modified content and save it to the **Quick Parts Gallery** with the same name as the original building block, selecting **Yes** when asked whether you want to redefine the building block entry.

To change the properties of a custom building block

1. Display the **Quick Parts Gallery**.

2. Right-click the building block you want to modify, and then select **Edit Properties**.

3. In the **Modify Building Block** dialog, change the name, gallery, category, description, template, or insertion option. Then select **OK**.

To delete a custom building block

- In the **Building Blocks Organizer** dialog, select a building block, select **Delete**, and then select **Yes** when Word prompts you to indicate whether you want to delete the selected building block.

Key points

- Colors, fonts, and effects can be combined into a custom theme to consistently create the look you want. You can easily create styles that draw on thematic elements to format characters and paragraphs.

- You can create styles and templates to speed up the work of formatting a document and ensure that formatting is consistent within and between documents.

- If you frequently use the same text snippets or pages in your documents, you don't have to enter and proof it each time. Instead, save the text as a building block in your document template, insert it where you need it, and customize it as necessary.

15

Practice tasks

Before you can complete these tasks, you must copy the book's practice files to your computer. The practice files for these tasks are in the **Word365SBS\Ch15** folder. You can save the results of the tasks in the same folder.

The Introduction includes a complete list of practice files and download instructions.

Create and modify styles

Open the **CreateStyles** document in Word, and then perform the following tasks:

1. Open the **Styles** pane and review the styles that are part of the document template. Notice that they use fonts and colors that are different from those of the Normal template.

2. In the **Styles** pane, point to the **Heading 1** style to display its properties. Notice that it's based on the Normal style. Point to **Heading 2** and **Heading 3**, and notice that each is based on the previous heading level.

3. Change the font of the **Normal** style from Candara to **Franklin Gothic Book** and notice the effect on the document content.

4. Select the heading *America's Finest Publishing Team* and change the font color to **Green**.

5. With the heading still selected, update the **Heading 1** style to match the selection. Notice the effect on the Heading 2 and Heading 3 styles.

6. In the *Description of Services* section, under *Management*, select *Project Management*.

7. Change the font color to **Orange**. Remove the bold formatting and apply italic formatting.

8. Create a new character style based on the formatting, and name it ServiceName.

9. Apply the **ServiceName** style to the words *Document Management* at the beginning of the next paragraph. Then apply it to the other services in the *Description of Services* section of the document.

10. Save and close the document.

Create and manage custom themes

Open the **CreateThemes** document in Word, and then perform the following tasks:

1. Change the theme font set from Candara/Candara to a font set of your choice.

2. Change the theme colors to a color set of your choice.

3. Save the customized theme in the default theme location as MyTheme.

4. From the practice file folder, open the **ChangeTheme** document. Review the document content and note the fonts and colors.

5. Apply the **MyTheme** theme to the document. Then review the document and notice the changes.

6. Save and close the open documents.

Create and attach templates

Open the **CreateTemplates** document in Word, and then perform the following tasks:

1. Delete the content from the body of the document. (Do not delete the header or footer content.)

2. Open the **Styles** pane and display a preview of the styles in the document.

3. Save the blank document in the default template location, as a template named MyTemplate. Then close the file.

4. Start Word or switch to an open document and display the **New** page of the Backstage view.

5. Select the **Personal** link that is now available at the top of the page to display your personal templates.

6. Create a new document based on the **MyTemplate** template. Notice that the new document includes the header and footer.

7. In the **Style** gallery, notice that the styles in the new document are the same as those in the **CreateTemplates** document.

8. Close the open documents without saving changes.

9. If you want to delete your custom template, browse to the default template location and delete the **MyTemplate.dotx** file.

Create custom building blocks

Open the **CreateBuildingBlocks** document in Word, and then perform the following tasks:

1. Activate the footer and select all the footer content.

2. Save the selected content as a building block with the following properties:

   - Name: MyFooter
   - Gallery: **Footers**
   - Category: Create a new category named MyBlocks
   - Description: My custom footer
   - Save in: **Building Blocks**
   - Options: **Insert content only**

3. Create a new, blank document. On the **Insert** tab, display the **Footer** gallery, locate the **MyFooter** building block, and insert it in the document.

4. Open the **Building Blocks Organizer**. Locate the **MyFooter** building block and delete it.

5. Close the open documents without saving changes.

Customize options and the user interface

After you become accustomed to using Word 365, you might notice certain default functionality that doesn't fit the way you work. For example, you might retain the source formatting more often than not when you paste copied text. The default Word functionality is based on the way that most people work with documents, or in some cases, because one option had to be selected as the default. You can modify the default behavior of many functions so that you can work more efficiently. You can also change aspects of the program to make it more suitable for the kinds of documents you create.

When working in Word, you interact with commands (in the form of buttons, lists, and galleries) that are available on the various tabs of the ribbon. Many people use a few commands from each tab often and don't frequently use other commands. You can centralize and streamline your interactions by adding the commands you use most often to the optional Quick Access Toolbar. To gain vertical working space in Word, position the Quick Access Toolbar below the ribbon (closer to the document content) and then minimize the ribbon. It's also possible to modify the commands that appear on the ribbon, hide or show specific tabs, and create custom tabs.

This chapter guides you through procedures related to changing default Word options, displaying and customizing the Quick Access Toolbar, customizing the ribbon, and managing add-ins and security options.

In this chapter

- Change default Word options
- Display and customize the Quick Access Toolbar
- Customize the ribbon
- Manage add-ins and security options

Change default Word options

Many of the options available in the Word Options dialog are discussed in context in other chapters in this book. This topic includes information about all the available options, including a few that power users of Word might find particularly useful to modify.

The Word Options dialog includes options for Word and for all Microsoft 365 desktop apps (Word, Excel, PowerPoint, Outlook, and Access). The options are divided among pages (and in some cases, additional dialogs that you open from the pages). The pages are represented by page tabs in the left pane of the Word Options dialog.

Shading indicates the active page tab

The left pane of the Word Options dialog is divided into sections:

- **Functionality options** The first section contains the General, Display, Proofing, Save, Language, Accessibility, and Advanced page tabs. These are the pages of options that standard Word users will most commonly make changes to when customizing the app functionality.

- **User interface options** The second section contains the Customize Ribbon and Quick Access Toolbar page tabs. These are the pages on which you customize the presentation of commands in the user interface.

- **Security options** The third section contains the Add-ins and Trust Center page tabs. These pages are access points for higher-level customizations that can affect the security of your computer and are not often necessary to modify.

> **TIP** This topic discusses the options on the General, Display, Proofing, Save, Language, Accessibility, and Advanced pages. For information about customizing the ribbon and Quick Access Toolbar and managing add-ins and security options, see the related topics later in this chapter.

A brief description of the page content appears at the top of each page. Each page is further divided into sections of related options. The General page contains information that's shared among the Office apps. Other pages contain options that are specific to the app or to the file you're working in.

The images in this topic depict the default selections for each option. Many options have only On/Off settings as indicated by a selected or cleared checkbox. Options with settings other than On or Off are described in the content that follows the image.

Manage general Office and Word options

Options that affect the user interface and startup behavior of Word are available from the General page of the Word Options dialog.

Common configuration options on the General page

The options in the first four sections of the General page are shared among the Office apps installed on the computer you're working on, and include the following configuration options:

- When using multiple displays, you can choose whether to optimize for best appearance or for compatibility.

- You can turn off the Mini Toolbar, which by default appears when you select content. The Mini Toolbar displays common formatting commands and commands relevant to the selected content. Because the commands are contextual, the Mini Toolbar can't currently be customized.

- You can turn off the Live Preview feature if you find it distracting to have content formatting change when the pointer passes over a formatting command.

- You can minimize or turn off the display of ScreenTips when you point to buttons.

- You can specify the user name and initials you want to accompany your comments and tracked changes, and override the display of information from the account associated with your installation of Office.

- You can choose the background graphics (Office background) and color scheme (Office theme) for the Office app windows.

> ✓ **TIP** You can also set the Office background and theme on the Account page of the Backstage view. For information about Office backgrounds and themes, see "Manage Office and app settings" in Chapter 1, "Word basics."

I don't show two sections of the General page of the Word Options dialog here because they contain no configurable settings. Nevertheless, they provide access to useful features.

- **Privacy Settings.** A button provides direct access to the Privacy Settings window from which you can learn about and manage the collection of optional diagnostic and usage data and various "connected experiences" that enhance the capabilities of Microsoft 365 apps when you're online. Connected experiences are those that require online access, either to analyze content and return the results to you or to make content (stored on servers) available to you.

  In Word, online analysis features include Dictation, Read Aloud, Research, Smart Lookup, Microsoft Translator, and several others. It's important to note that

Microsoft *analyzes and then discards* any content sent to its analysis servers; it does not store your content or identify the content owner.

Online content features include the Stock Images library, the Online 3D Models library, and the Online Pictures feature (the latter two powered by Bing Search). The Stock Images library (in my opinion, one of the two greatest recent enhancements to Word) contains an incredibly rich collection of images, icons, cutout people, stickers, illustrations, and cartoon people available to Microsoft 365 subscribers for royalty-free use. Cloud fonts, online video connections, and the Researcher tool also download online content.

- **LinkedIn Options**. A checkbox provides access to LinkedIn features (if you have a LinkedIn account). In Word, LinkedIn provides the Résumé Assistant. (LinkedIn features also include profile cards in Outlook, SharePoint, and OneDrive for Business.)

Start up options

☐ Open e-mail attachments and other uneditable files in reading view ⓘ
☑ Show the Start screen when this application starts

Co-authoring options

☑ Allow co-authoring on files with macros ——————————— New in Word 365

Start up and co-authoring options

The last two sections of options on the General page of the Word Options dialog are specific to Word:

- The Start Up Options section contains options related to setting Word as the default document editor, and a couple of options that you might want to configure: one to open documents in Reading view if you can't edit them, and another to turn off the Home page (also called the Start screen) that appears when you start Word without opening a specific file. When the Home page is turned off, starting the app without opening a specific file automatically creates a new, blank document.

- The new Co-authoring Options section gives you the choice of allowing other people into macro-enabled documents at the same time as you.

> **SEE ALSO** For information about collaborative document development in Word 365, see Chapter 11, "Collaborate on documents."

16

To open the Word Options dialog

1. Select the **File** tab to display the Backstage view.

2. In the left pane, select **Options**.

To display a specific page of the Word Options dialog

1. Open the **Word Options** dialog.

2. In the left pane, select the tab of the page that you want to display.

To close the Word Options dialog

- To commit to any changes, select **OK**.

- To cancel any changes, select **Cancel** or select the **Close** button (**X**) in the upper-right corner of the dialog.

To enable or disable the Mini Toolbar

1. Open the **Word Options** dialog, and display the **General** page.

2. In the **User Interface options** section, select or clear the **Show Mini Toolbar on selection** checkbox.

To enable or disable the Live Preview feature

1. Display the **General** page of the **Word Options** dialog.

2. In the **User Interface options** section, select or clear the **Enable Live Preview** checkbox.

To control the display of ScreenTips

1. Display the **General** page of the **Word Options** dialog.

2. In the **User Interface options** section, display the **ScreenTip style** list, and then select any of the following:

   - **Show feature descriptions in ScreenTips**

   - **Don't show feature descriptions in ScreenTips**

   - **Don't show ScreenTips**

To change the user identification that appears in comments and tracked changes

> ⚠ **IMPORTANT** The User Name and Initials settings are shared by all the Office apps, so changing them in any one app immediately changes them in all the apps.

1. Display the **General** page of the **Word Options** dialog.

2. In the **Personalize your copy of Microsoft Office** section, do the following:

   - In the **User name** and **Initials** boxes, enter the information you want to use.

   - Select or clear the **Always use these values regardless of sign in to Office** checkbox.

To enable LinkedIn features

- Select the **Enable LinkedIn features in my Office applications** checkbox.

To enable or disable the Word Home page

1. Display the **General** page of the **Word Options** dialog.

2. In the **Start up options** section, select or clear the **Show the Start screen when this application starts** checkbox.

Manage display options

Options on the Display page control what is shown in the content pane and how documents are printed. The default settings on this page are appropriate for most types of documents. You can turn on and off the display of formatting marks from within the app window, and set many of the printing options when you print a document.

Change how document content is displayed on the screen and when printed.

Page display options

- ☑ Show white space between pages in Print Layout view ⓘ
- ☑ Show highlighter marks ⓘ
- ☑ Show document tooltips on hover

Always show these formatting marks on the screen

- ☐ Tab characters →
- ☐ Spaces ···
- ☐ Paragraph marks ¶
- ☐ Hidden text abc
- ☐ Optional hyphens ¬
- ☑ Object anchors ⚓
- ☐ Show all formatting marks

Printing options

- ☑ Print drawings created in Word ⓘ
- ☐ Print background colors and images
- ☐ Print document properties
- ☐ Print hidden text
- ☐ Update fields before printing
- ☐ Update linked data before printing

16

Options for displaying document content

Controlling connected experiences

Microsoft 365 desktop apps have access to several intelligent online services, which are referred to as "connected experiences." These cloud-enhanced features, which are available only with a Microsoft 365 subscription, help you to create the best possible content by interacting behind the scenes with online databases of content, information, and ideas.

Some connected experiences, such as Translator, upload your content to process it in the cloud and return the results to you. Others offer you online content options such as stock images that you download at will or the weather forecast that you can choose to automatically display on the Outlook calendar.

The connected experiences available in Word include Automatic Alt Text, Dictate Editor, Smart Lookup, Tell Me, Translator, file templates, Office help materials, and the stock image library of images, icons, illustrations, stickers, cutout people, and cartoon people. Other connected experiences include Analyze Data and rich data types in Excel; Calendar weather forecast in Outlook; Ink to Math, Ink to Shape, Ink to Text, PowerPoint Designer and QuickStarter in PowerPoint; and Presenter Coach in PowerPoint Online.

You're prompted to enable connected features the first time you open a Microsoft 365 desktop app. Thereafter, you can enable or disable these features for all apps from the Account page of the Backstage view of any app. (You can control some features, such as PowerPoint Designer, temporarily within the app.)

To control connected experiences:

1. On the **Account** page of the Backstage view, under **Account Privacy**, select **Manage Settings**.

2. In the **Connected experiences** section, do one of the following:

   - To enable or disable all cloud-enhanced features, select or clear the third checkbox: **Turn on all connected experiences**.

   - To enable or disable only the online analysis features, select or clear the first checkbox: **Turn on experiences that analyze your content**.

   - To enable or disable only the online content features, select or clear the second checkbox: **Turn on experiences that download online content**.

Manage proofing options

Options that affect the spelling and grammar-checking and automatic text replacement functions of Word are available from the Proofing page of the Word Options dialog.

abc ✓ Change how Word corrects and formats your text.

AutoCorrect options

Change how Word corrects and formats text as you type: [AutoCorrect Options...]

When correcting spelling in Microsoft Office programs

☑ Ignore words in UPPERCASE
☑ Ignore words that contain numbers
☑ Ignore Internet and file addresses
☑ Flag repeated words
☑ German: Use post-reform rules
☐ Enforce accented uppercase in French
☐ Suggest from main dictionary only

[Custom Dictionaries...]

French modes: [Traditional and new spellings ⌄]
Spanish modes: [Tuteo verb forms only ⌄]
☐ Russian: Enforce strict ë

When correcting spelling and grammar in Word

☑ Check spelling as you type
☑ Mark grammar errors as you type
☑ Frequently confused words
☐ Show readability statistics

Choose the checks Editor will perform for Grammar and Refinements

Writing Style: [Grammar & Refinements ⌄]   [Settings...]

[Recheck Document]

Exceptions for: [📄 Legal Contract.docx ⌄]

☐ Hide spelling errors in this document only
☐ Hide grammar errors in this document only

Editorial options for working with document content .

You might find that you want to modify the spelling and grammar correction options in the When Correcting Spelling And Grammar In Word section of the page. These options control whether Word automatically checks for spelling errors, grammar errors, and writing style issues. When automatic checking is turned on, Word displays red wavy lines under words it thinks are spelled wrong, blue double lines under words that don't meet its grammar guidelines, and gold dotted lines under words or phrases that could be rephrased for clarity or conciseness. If you find those lines distracting, you can turn off the automatic checking, modify the grammar and style issues Word checks for, or turn off the display of the lines for the current document (or for all documents).

When reviewing spelling in a document, you have options to ignore one or all instances of suspected spelling errors. You choose to ignore all instances of a flagged spelling error in a document either from the shortcut menu or from the Spelling pane. Word remembers your selection and removes the squiggly underlines from all instances of that word. If you want Word to forget those settings and conduct a fresh spelling check, you can do that from this page.

16

> **SEE ALSO** For information about configuring the spelling and grammar-checking options in Word, see "Locate and correct text errors" in Chapter 12, "Finalize and distribute documents."

The AutoCorrect settings affect the way Word processes specific text and character combinations that you enter, so it's good to be familiar with them.

Reasons to modify the AutoCorrect settings include:

- If you find that Word is consistently changing text that you enter, in a way that you don't want it to.

- If you consistently make a spelling mistake that you would like Word to correct for you.

- If you want to create a shortcut for entering longer text segments. (For example, if you want Word to enter *Wide World Importers* whenever you type *WW*.)

- If you want suggestions to improve your choice of words.

To stop Word from automatically correcting a specific type of text entry

1. Display the **Proofing** page of the **Word Options** dialog.

2. In the **AutoCorrect options** section, select the **AutoCorrect Options** button.

3. In the **AutoCorrect** dialog, display the **AutoCorrect** or **Math AutoCorrect** tab.

Automatic text correction options

4. For each correction that you want to turn off, locate the correction and clear its checkbox. Then select **OK**.

To automatically change a specific text entry to another

1. Display the **Proofing** page of the **Word Options** dialog.

2. In the **AutoCorrect options** section, select the **AutoCorrect Options** button.

3. In the **AutoCorrect** dialog, on the **AutoCorrect** tab, do the following, and then select **OK**:

   a. In the **Replace** box, enter the misspelling or abbreviated text. The list scrolls to display the closest entries.

   b. In the **With** box, enter the corrected spelling or full-length text you want Word to replace the original entry with.

To stop Word from automatically applying formatting

1. Display the **Proofing** page of the **Word Options** dialog.

2. In the **AutoCorrect options** section, select the **AutoCorrect Options** button.

3. In the **AutoCorrect** dialog, display the **AutoFormat** or **AutoFormat As You Type** tab.

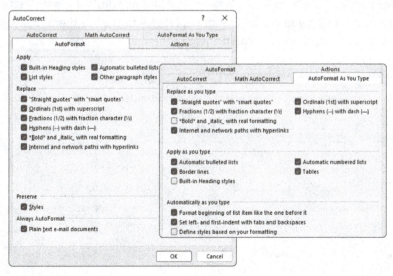

Automatic formatting options

4. For each formatting option that you want to turn off, locate the option and clear its checkbox. Then select **OK**.

16

Manage file saving options

The Save page of the Word Options dialog contains two sections of options that control the behavior of the app, and one section that's specific to the document you're working in.

Manage where and how frequently Word saves various types of files

Options that affect where and when Word saves and looks for documents and templates are available in the Save Documents and Offline Editing Options sections. These options can be rather important—not necessarily to change them, but to know where Word stores files so that you can browse to them if necessary.

Manage cached document settings from within Office apps

Options that you might find useful include:

- **AutoSave files stored in the Cloud by default in Word**   This setting previously referenced only OneDrive and SharePoint. When you're working on documents that you've opened from a cloud storage location, this option ensures that Word automatically saves changes as you make them. This option is on by default to ensure that you don't lose changes and to support coauthoring. (When multiple people are editing a document, each person sees the changes of other editors only when they save the document.)

- **Save AutoRecover information every**   If you're making a lot of changes that you don't want to lose, or feel that your system might run into trouble (for example, if you're in a location that experiences frequent power outages and you don't have battery backup), you can automatically save drafts more frequently than the default of every 10 minutes.

- **Default local file location**   You can specify the folder that Word displays in the Save As dialog when you select This PC in the Other Locations list. The default is your Documents folder, but if you routinely save in another location, you can save yourself a few steps by choosing that instead. (Or you can add the location to the Other Locations list.)

- **Default personal templates location**   This is the folder to which Word saves templates by default. When you create a new document, templates in this folder are available from the Personal tab of the New page of the Word Options dialog.

The server draft location specified in the Offline Editing section has been retired in Microsoft 365, and not officially supported since Office 2013. I assume Microsoft will remove this section from the page in a future update.

Options for saving fonts with the current document are available in the Preserve Fidelity section. When you distribute a Word document electronically (as a .docx file), the fonts in the document render correctly on-screen only if they are installed on the computer that's displaying the document. If you use fonts in your document other than those that come with Office, or if you have reason to believe that the fonts you use won't be available on a computer or device that displays the document, you can embed the fonts in the document.

16

Preserve fidelity when sharing this document: Legal Contract.docx

☑ Embed fonts in the file ①
  ☑ Embed only the characters used in the document (best for reducing file size)
  ☑ Do not embed common system fonts

Embed nonstandard fonts in documents so they display correctly on other computers

Embedding fonts in a document increases the size of the file. You can minimize the size increase by embedding only the characters that are used in the document. Letters, numbers, and symbols that aren't in the document when you embed the fonts will not be available. Embedding all the characters of a font requires more storage space, especially if you use multiple fonts in the document, but makes the characters available on other systems so the document content can be edited gracefully.

To turn off the AutoSave feature when working with online files

- Clear the **AutoSave files stored in the Cloud by default in Word** checkbox.

- On the Quick Access Toolbar, toggle AutoSave to Off.

To change the automatic draft saving frequency

1. Display the **Save** page of the **Word Options** dialog.

2. In the **Save documents** section, set the saving frequency in the **Save AutoRecover information every** box.

To change the default local folder

1. Start File Explorer and browse to the folder you want to set as the default.

2. Do either of the following to copy the folder path to the Clipboard:

   - Select the folder icon at the left end of the **Address** box to display the folder path. Then press **Ctrl+C**.

   - Right-click or long-press (tap and hold) the **Address** box, and then select **Copy address as text**.

3. Display the **Save** page of the **Word Options** dialog.

4. In the **Save documents** section, select the content of the **Default local file location** box.

5. Do either of the following to paste the folder path into the box:

   - Press **Ctrl+V**.

   - Right-click the selection, and then select **Paste**.

> **SEE ALSO** For a comprehensive list of keyboard shortcuts in Word 365 and keyboard shortcuts common to all Microsoft 365 apps, and instructions for creating custom keyboard shortcuts in Word, see the appendix, "Keyboard shortcuts."

To embed fonts in a document

1. Display the **Save** page of the **Word Options** dialog.

2. In the **Preserve fidelity when sharing this document** section, select the **Embed fonts in the file** checkbox.

3. If you don't want to embed the entire character set of all fonts used in the document, select **Embed only the characters used in the document (best for reducing file size)** checkbox.

> ✓ **TIP** Additional fidelity-related options are in the Preserve Fidelity When Sharing This Document section of the Advanced page of the Word Options dialog. For information about those settings, see "Manage advanced options" later in this topic.

Manage language options

Most people use only one editing and display language when working in documents, but people who work or collaborate in a multilingual environment use additional languages. The Language page of the Word Options dialog contains options for adding, removing, and prioritizing language options in all the installed Office apps.

Set the Office Language Preferences

Office display language

Buttons, menus, and other controls will show in the first available language on this list. ⓘ

1. **Match Microsoft Windows [English] <preferred>**	Add a Language...
2. English	Move Up
3. German [Deutsch]	Move Down
4. Ukrainian [українська]	Set as Preferred

Office authoring languages and proofing

Manage languages used for creating and editing documents, including proofing tools such as spelling and grammar check. ⓘ

English (United States) <preferred>	Proofing installed	Add a Language...
French (France)	Proofing installed	Remove
German (Germany)	Proofing installed	Set as Preferred
Ukrainian	Proofing installed	

☑ Store my authoring languages in the cloud for my account. ⓘ

Install additional keyboards from Windows Settings

Install alternative display, authoring, and proofing languages

16

From the Language page of the Word Options dialog, you can install languages for two distinct purposes:

- Display languages, which control the language of user interface labels (such as the names of ribbon tabs and buttons) and built-in user assistance features (such as ScreenTips)

- Editing languages, which control the authoring and proofing settings

Installing a display language also installs the associated editing language.

To install a display language

1. Display the **Language** page of the **Word Options** dialog.

2. In the **Office display language** section, select **Add a Language**.

3. In the **Install a display language** dialog, select the language you want to add.

Install a display language	✕
Select the language you want to install.	
Afrikaans [Afrikaans]	
Albanian [shqip]	
Amharic [አማርኛ]	
Arabic [العربية]	
Armenian [Հայերեն]	
Assamese [অসমীয়া]	
Azerbaijani (Latin) [azərbaycan]	
Bangla (Bangladesh) [বাংলা (বাংলাদেশ)]	
Basque [euskara]	
Belarusian [Беларуская]	
Bengali (India) [বাংলা (ভারত)]	
Bosnian (Latin) [bosanski]	
Bulgarian [български]	
Catalan [català]	
Chinese (Simplified) [中文(简体)]	
Chinese (Traditional) [中文(繁體)]	
Croatian [hrvatski]	
Czech [čeština]	
Danish [dansk]	
Dari [دری]	
Dutch [Nederlands]	
English (United Kingdom)	
English (United States)	
Estonian [eesti]	
☑ Set as Office display language	
Install Cancel	

Approximately 100 languages are available

4. If you do NOT want to change the Word user interface language immediately, clear the **Set as Office display language** checkbox.

5. Select **Install** to begin the installation.

   After the language installation pack downloads, you must restart. The Office installer will prompt you to save changes and close Word and other Microsoft 365 Apps to complete the installation. After the installation completes, a notification will appear to tell you that you can use the apps again. You're usually unable to interact with the apps for only a minute or two.

To set the Word user interface language

1. Display the **Language** page of the **Word Options** dialog.

2. In the **Office display language** section, select the language in which you want the Word and other Microsoft 365 Apps user interface elements.

3. To the right of the language list, select **Set as Preferred**.

To add an editing language to Office

1. Display the **Language** page of the **Word Options** dialog.

2. In the **Office authoring languages and proofing** section, select **Add a Language**.

3. In the **Add an authoring language** dialog, select the language you want to add.

Add an authoring language	✕
Select the language you want to add.	

Lithuanian
Lower Sorbian
Lule Sami (Norway)
Lule Sami (Sweden)
Luxembourgish
Macedonian
Malagasy
Malay (Brunei Darussalam)
Malay (Malaysia)
Malayalam
Maltese
Manipuri
Māori
Mapuche
Marathi
Mohawk
Mongolian (Mongolia)
Mongolian (Traditional Mongolian, China)
Mongolian (Traditional Mongolian, Mongolia)

☐ Get proofing tools

[Add] [Cancel]

Proofing tools may be included or separate

16

4. If the **Get proofing tools** checkbox is unavailable (grayed out), the proofing tools are installed by default with the authoring language. If the checkbox is available and you want to install the proofing tools in the selected language, select the **Get proofing tools** checkbox.

5. Select **Add** to begin the installation.

6. When a dialog informs you that it is necessary to restart Word so that the language changes can take effect, select **OK** and then restart Word when it's convenient.

To install proofing tools after installing an authoring language

1. Display the **Language** page of the **Word Options** dialog.

2. In the **Office authoring languages and proofing** section, to the right of the installed authoring language, select **Proofing available**.

3. Office downloads the proofing tools, prompts you to exit running Office apps, completes the installation, and then notifies you that you can restart the Office apps.

To set a default editing language

1. Display the **Language** page of the **Word Options** dialog.

2. In the **Office authoring languages and proofing** section, select the language you want to set as the default.

3. To the right of the language list, select **Set as Preferred**.

To remove an editing language

1. Display the **Language** page of the **Word Options** dialog.

2. In the **Office authoring languages and proofing** section, select the language you want to remove.

3. To the right of the language list, select **Remove**.

Manage advanced options

The most interesting and useful options are on the Advanced page of the Word Options dialog. Some of the settings on the Advanced page are for Word, and others are specific to the document you're working in.

App setting sections:

- Editing options
- Cut, copy, and paste
- Link handling
- Pen
- Show document content
- Display
- Print
- Save
- General

Document setting sections:

- Image Size and Quality
- Chart
- When printing this document
- Preserve fidelity when sharing this document
- Layout options
- Compatibility options

Document-specific settings are indicated by a dropdown file list in the section header. Select the document to which you want to apply the settings before saving your changes in the Word Options dialog.

16

Editing options

The first section of advanced options are the Editing options. These settings are reasonably self-explanatory.

Manage the ways you edit content

There are two settings here to be particularly aware of:

- **Keep track of formatting** has been associated for many years with an issue in long, complex documents where Word freezes, the computer whirs madly, and the message "Word is finishing analyzing your document" appears on the status bar. You can wait this out without losing your progress on the document, but the process will reoccur. Turning off the Keep Track Of Formatting setting (and AutoSave, if the document is saved in the cloud) should resolve the issue.

- **Show text predictions while typing** is a new Microsoft 365 feature that suggests words and phrases to complete the phrase you're typing in a Word document or Outlook email message. You can press Tab to accept the suggestion or continue typing to remove it.

> Dear Mr. Putnam,
>
> I recently attended your lecture about Dynamic Conversations. Thank you for taking the time to
>
> I recently attended your lecture about Dynamic Conversations. Thank you for taking the time to put together this information
>
> I recently attended your lecture about Dynamic Conversations. Thank you for taking the time to put together this information in support of
>
> I recently attended your lecture about Dynamic Conversations. Thank you for taking the time to put together this information in such a clear and accessible
>
> I recently attended your lecture about Dynamic Conversations. Thank you for taking the time to put together this information in such a clear and accessible format. I learned a lot and will share my newfound knowledge
>
> I recently attended your lecture about Dynamic Conversations. Thank you for taking the time to put together this information in such a clear and accessible format. I learned a lot and will share my newfound knowledge with my classmates in an upcoming presentation.

Word correctly predicting upcoming text four out of five times

Having words appear and disappear while you're working can be somewhat nerve wracking. If you don't find the suggestions helpful, you can turn off the feature here.

> ✓ **TIP** When the Text Predictions command is displayed on the Word status bar, you can jump directly to the Editing options section of the Advanced page of the Word Options dialog by selecting it. For more information, see the "Work with the ribbon and status bar" section of "Work in the Word user interface" in Chapter 1.

16

Cut, Copy, and Paste options

The options in the Cut, Copy, And Paste section are also self-explanatory, other than the Use Smart Cut And Paste option. This option is very useful when working with text in a Word document because it controls whether the app tries to merge content into adjacent lists when you cut it from one location and paste it in another.

Manage the ways Word pastes content

Link, Pen, Image, and Chart options

Next come the Link Handling, Pen, Image Size And Quality, and Chart sections. The file lists in the headers of the Image Size And Quality and Chart sections indicate that the options in those sections apply to the scope selected in the list, which is either All New Documents or a specific document that is currently open.

Manage the impact of images on file size

The two image-related options can be useful when you're finalizing a file for distribution.

- **Discard editing data**   When you insert images in a document and then edit them by using the tools on the Format tab for pictures, Word saves the editing data so you can undo your changes. You can decrease the file size of a document by discarding the editing data.

- **Do not compress images in file**   When you're finalizing a document for distribution, you have the option to compress the media within the file. This results in a smaller file size but also a lower quality. You also have the option to exclude images from the media compression.

The option in the Chart section controls whether custom data labels and formatting stay with data points in charts. It seems likely that this would always be the better option, but if you find that it presents a problem, you can turn it off here.

Show Document Content options

The options in the Show Document Content section enable you to control the display of document structural elements that aren't affected by the Show/Hide Formatting Marks button.

Display hidden structural markings

Display options

Options in the Display section are among those that you might want to configure for the way you work.

Display

Show this number of Recent Documents: `20`

☐ Quickly access this number of Recent Documents: `4`

Show this number of unpinned Recent Folders: `1`

Show measurements in units of: `Inches`

Style area pane width in Draft and Outline views: `0"`

☐ Show pixels for HTML features

☑ Show shortcut keys in ScreenTips

☑ Show horizontal scroll bar

☑ Show vertical scroll bar

☑ Show vertical ruler in Print Layout view

☐ Optimize character positioning for layout rather than readability

☑ Update document content while dragging ⓘ

☑ Use subpixel positioning to smooth fonts on screen

☑ Show pop-up buttons for adding rows and columns in tables

Configure the display of information in the Backstage view and in the app window

The first three settings are particularly useful:

- You can change the number of recent documents and folders that appear in the right pane of the Open page of the Backstage view.

- You can also display your most recently edited documents directly in the left pane of the Backstage view, below the Options button, for easy access. This can be very convenient, but the option isn't turned on by default, probably because it introduces user-specific content into an area that otherwise contains Word commands.

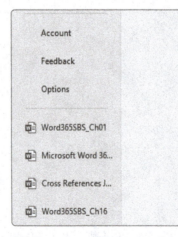

Account

Feedback

Options

📄 Word365SBS_Ch01

📄 Microsoft Word 36...

📄 Cross References J...

📄 Word365SBS_Ch16

Quickly access recent documents from the left pane of the Backstage view

You configure the display of ScreenTips and whether they include feature descriptions on the General page of the Word Options dialog. (Not to be confused with the General section of the Advanced page, discussed later in this section.) However, the option to display keyboard shortcuts within ScreenTips is here in the Display section of the Advanced page. If you like to work from the keyboard and don't have the full list of keyboard shortcuts memorized, you can learn them by including them in ScreenTips.

Printing options

There are two sections of printing options. The options in the Print section are general printing options that you can also configure on the Print page of the Backstage view. The options in the When Printing This Document section are specific to the document you select in the list and will travel with the document.

Save specific print options with the current document

16

Saving and Sharing options

The options in the Save section of the Advanced page are important to consider. The first option, which is *not* selected by default, prevents Word from overwriting the Normal template without your permission. The option to allow background saves, which *is* on by default, is important for the saving of recovery versions.

Save

☐ Prompt before saving Normal template ⓘ
☐ Always create backup copy
☐ Copy remotely stored files onto your computer, and update the remote file when saving
☑ Allow background saves

Preserve fidelity when sharing this document: [▥ Legal Contract.docx ⌄]

☐ Save form data as delimited text file
☑ Embed linguistic data

Advanced options related to saving documents

The first option in the Preserve Fidelity When Sharing This Document section can be useful if you're having people fill out a Word form (for example, on a tablet at your daughter's high school color guard registration), and you want the data each person enters to save to a text file. However, be aware that the setting works only with legacy form controls in a restricted-editing document.

> 🔍 **SEE ALSO** Additional fidelity-related options are in the Preserve Fidelity When Sharing This Document section of the Save page of the Word Options dialog. For information about those settings, see "Manage file saving options" earlier in this topic.

General options

The General section of the Advanced page includes options that don't fit elsewhere. One item of note here is the Mailing Address box. If you enter your name and address in this box, Word automatically fills it in for you when you create envelopes and mailing labels.

Provide your address to Word for use in mail merge documents

> **SEE ALSO** For information about creating envelopes and mailing labels, see Chapter 14, "Merge data with documents and labels."

The document-specific options in the Layout Options section of the Advanced page are reasonably specialized. Few Word users will need to modify these settings; if you publish a newsletter or other communication that you create in Word and want to fine-tune the layout, consider these options.

Layout options modify the positioning of content

16

Display and customize the Quick Access Toolbar

The Quick Access Toolbar is a customizable toolbar that you can display above or below the ribbon. If you regularly use a few commands that are scattered on various tabs of the ribbon and you don't want to switch between tabs to access the commands, add them to the Quick Access Toolbar so that they're always available to you.

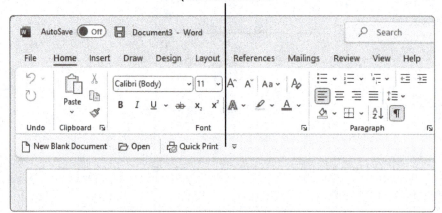

The Quick Access Toolbar positioned below the ribbon

You can configure a separate Quick Access Toolbar for each Office app. By default, the Quick Access Toolbar is available in all files that you open in that app. You can also create a Quick Access Toolbar that is specific to a file and travels with it, so the commands are available to anyone who opens that file. When a file has a file-specific custom toolbar, Word displays it to the right of the primary Quick Access Toolbar so no one loses access to their own customizations.

You can add commands to the Quick Access Toolbar from a menu on the toolbar, directly from the ribbon, or from the Quick Access Toolbar page of the app-specific Options dialog.

> **TIP** You can display a list of commands that do not appear on the ribbon by selecting Commands Not In The Ribbon in the Choose Commands From list on the Quick Access Toolbar or on the Customize Ribbon page of the app-specific Options dialog.

Add any Word command to the Quick Access Toolbar

You can customize the Quick Access Toolbar in the following ways:

- Define a custom Quick Access Toolbar for all files opened in the app or for a specific file.

- Add any command from any group of any tab, including tool tabs, to the toolbar.

- Display a separator between different types of buttons.

- Move commands around on the toolbar until they are in the order you want.

- Reset everything back to the default Quick Access Toolbar configuration.

After you add commands to the Quick Access Toolbar, you can reorganize them and divide them into groups (using lines called separators) to simplify the process of locating the command you want.

As you add commands to the Quick Access Toolbar, it expands to accommodate them. If you add a lot of commands, it might become difficult to view the text in

16

the title bar, or all the commands on the Quick Access Toolbar might not be visible, defeating the purpose of adding them. To resolve this problem (and to position the Quick Access Toolbar closer to the file content), you can move the Quick Access Toolbar below the ribbon.

To display the Quick Access Toolbar

- Right-click any ribbon tab and then select **Show Quick Access Toolbar**.

- Right-click any command on the ribbon, and then select **Show Quick Access Toolbar**.

- In the left pane of the **Options** dialog, select **Quick Access Toolbar**. On the **Customize the Quick Access Toolbar** page, select the **Show Quick Access Toolbar** checkbox, and then select **OK**.

To add a popular command to the Quick Access Toolbar

1. At the right end of the Quick Access Toolbar, select the **Customize Quick Access Toolbar** button.

2. On the menu of commonly used commands, select a command you want to add.

Popular commands are available directly from the Toolbar

To add a command to the Quick Access Toolbar from the ribbon

- Right-click a command on the ribbon, and then select **Add to Quick Access Toolbar**. You can add any type of command this way; you can even add a drop-down list of options or gallery of thumbnails.

To display the Quick Access Toolbar page of the Options dialog

- At the right end of the Quick Access Toolbar, select the **Customize Quick Access Toolbar** button, and then select **More Commands**.

- Select the **File** tab and then, in the left pane of the Backstage view, select **Options**. In the left pane of the **Word Options** dialog, select **Quick Access Toolbar**.

To add a command to the Quick Access Toolbar from the Options dialog

1. Display the **Quick Access Toolbar** page of the **Word Options** dialog.

2. In the **Choose commands from** list, select the tab the command appears on, or select **Popular Commands**, **Commands Not in the Ribbon**, **All Commands**, or **Macros**.

3. In the left list, locate and select the command you want to add to the Quick Access Toolbar. Then select the **Add** button.

4. Make any other changes, and then select **OK** in the **Word Options** dialog.

To move the Quick Access Toolbar

- At the right end of the Quick Access Toolbar, select the Customize Quick Access Toolbar button, and then select **Show Above the Ribbon** or **Show Below the Ribbon**.

- Display the **Quick Access Toolbar** page of the **Word Options** dialog. In the **Toolbar Position** list below the **Choose Commands From** pane, select **Above Ribbon** or **Below Ribbon**.

To define a custom Quick Access Toolbar for a specific file

1. Display the **Quick Access Toolbar** page of the **Word Options** dialog.

2. In the **Customize Quick Access Toolbar** list (above the right pane) select **For** *file name*.

3. Add the commands to the toolbar that you want to make available to anyone who edits the file, and then select **OK**.

16

The app displays the file-specific Quick Access Toolbar to the right of the user's own Quick Access Toolbar.

> ✓ **TIP** If a command is on a user's Quick Access Toolbar and on a file-specific Quick Access Toolbar, it will be shown in both toolbars.

To display a separator on the Quick Access Toolbar

1. Display the **Quick Access Toolbar** page of the **Word Options** dialog.

2. In the right pane, select the command after which you want to insert the separator.

3. Do either of the following:

   - In the left pane, double-click **<Separator>**.

   - Select **<Separator>** in the left pane, and then select the **Add** button.

4. Make any other changes you want, and then select **OK**.

To move buttons on the Quick Access Toolbar

1. Display the **Quick Access Toolbar** page of the **Word Options** dialog.

2. In the right pane, select the button you want to move. Then select the **Move Up** or **Move Down** arrow until the button reaches the position you want.

To reset the Quick Access Toolbar to its default configuration

1. Display the **Quick Access Toolbar** page of the **Word Options** dialog.

2. In the lower-right corner of the page, select **Reset**, and then select either of the following:

   - Reset only Quick Access Toolbar

   - Reset all customizations

3. In the Microsoft Office message box verifying the change, select **Yes**.

> ⚠ **IMPORTANT** Resetting the Quick Access Toolbar doesn't change its location. You must manually move the Quick Access Toolbar by using either of the procedures described earlier.

Transfer user interface customizations to another Word installation

You can easily transfer Quick Access Toolbar and ribbon customizations to another computer so you can use the toolset you're familiar with, without having to rebuild the environment.

IMPORTANT This process replaces any existing Quick Access Toolbar and ribbon customizations on the destination computer.

Follow these steps:

1. Open a Word document that has the custom Quick Access Toolbar. (Ribbon customizations are present in all Word documents, whereas a Quick Access Toolbar can be specific to one document.)

2. Display the **Quick Access Toolbar** or **Customize Ribbon** page of the **Word Options** dialog. In the lower-right corner of the page, select **Import/Export**, and then select **Export all customizations**.

3. In the **File Save** dialog, navigate to the location where you want to save the customization file; preferably one from which you can share the file with the destination computer such as a USB flash drive, network folder, or online folder. Accept the default file name (*Word Customizations*) or give the file a name that has specific meaning to you. Then select **Save** to export the settings to an *exportedUI* file.

4. In the **Word Options** dialog, select **OK**.

5. Ensure that the *exportedUI* file is available to the destination computer. (Email or otherwise transfer it if necessary.)

6. On the destination computer, start Word.

7. Display the **Quick Access Toolbar** page of the **Word Options** dialog. In the lower-right corner of the page, select **Import/Export**, and then select **Import customization file**.

8. In the **File Open** dialog, navigate to the *exportedUI* file. Select the file, and then select **Open**.

9. In the **Microsoft Office** dialog prompting you to replace customizations, select **Yes**.

10. In the **Word Options** dialog, select **OK**.

16

Customize the ribbon

The ribbon was designed to make all the commonly used commands visible so that people can more easily discover the full potential of an Office app. But many Word users perform the same set of tasks all the time, and for them, seeing buttons (or even entire groups of buttons) that they never use is just another form of clutter.

Would you prefer to display fewer commands, not more? Or would you prefer to display more-specialized groups of commands? You can! From the Customize Ribbon page of the Word Options dialog, you can control the tabs that appear on the ribbon, and the groups of commands that appear on the tabs.

Control the display of individual ribbon tabs

On this page, you can customize the ribbon in the following ways:

- Hide an entire tab.

- Remove a group of commands from a tab. (The group is not removed from the app, only from the tab.)

- Move or copy a group of commands to another tab.

- Create a custom group on any tab and then add commands to it. (You cannot add commands to a predefined group.)

- Create a custom tab. For example, you might want to do this if you use only a few commands from each tab and you find it inefficient to flip between them.

Don't be afraid to experiment with the ribbon to create the configuration that best suits the way you work. If at any point you find that your new ribbon is harder to work with rather than easier, you can easily reset everything back to the default configuration.

> ⚠️ **IMPORTANT** Although customizing the default ribbon content might seem like a great way of making the app yours, it isn't recommended that you do so. A great deal of research has been done about the way that people use the commands in each app, and the ribbon has been organized to reflect the results of that research. If you modify the default ribbon settings, you might end up inadvertently hiding or moving commands that you need. Instead, consider the Quick Access Toolbar as the command area that you customize and make your own. If you add all the commands you use frequently to the Quick Access Toolbar, you can hide the ribbon and have extra vertical space for document display (this is very convenient when working on a smaller device). Or, if you really want to customize the ribbon, gather your most frequently used commands on a custom tab and leave the others alone.

To display the Customize Ribbon page of the Options dialog

- Display the **Word Options** dialog. In the left pane, select **Customize Ribbon**.

- Right-click any ribbon tab or empty area of the ribbon, and then select **Customize the Ribbon**.

To permit or prevent the display of a tab

1. Display the **Customize Ribbon** page of the **Word Options** dialog.

2. In the **Customize the Ribbon** list, select the tab set you want to manage:

   - All Tabs

   - Main Tabs

   - Tool Tabs

3. In the right pane, select or clear the checkbox of any tab other than the File tab. (You can't hide the File tab.)

16

To remove a group of commands from a tab

1. Display the **Customize Ribbon** page of the **Word Options** dialog.

2. In the **Customize the Ribbon** list, select the tab set you want to manage.

3. In the right pane, select the **Expand** button (>) to the left of the tab you want to modify.

4. Select the group you want to remove, and then in the center pane, select the **Remove** button.

To create a custom tab

1. Display the **Customize Ribbon** page of the **Word Options** dialog.

2. Near the lower-right corner, select the **New Tab** button to insert a new custom tab below the active tab in the right pane. The new tab includes an empty custom group.

Creating a new tab and group

To rename a custom tab

1. Select the custom tab, and then select the **Rename** button.

2. In the **Rename** dialog, replace the existing tab name with the tab name you want, and then select **OK**.

To rename a custom group

1. Select the custom group, and then select the **Rename** button to open a Rename dialog that includes hundreds of symbol options.

You can assign an icon to appear when the group is minimized

> **TIP** You can scroll through the available symbols or resize the dialog by dragging the dotted triangular handle in the lower-right corner to display all the symbols at one time, as shown.

2. In the **Rename** dialog, change the display name, select the symbol you want to display when the ribbon is too narrow to display the group's commands, and then select **OK**.

To create a custom group

1. Display the **Customize Ribbon** page of the **Word Options** dialog.

2. In the right pane, select the tab you want to add the group to. Then select the **New Group** button to add an empty custom group.

To add commands to a custom group

1. Display the **Customize Ribbon** page of the **Word Options** dialog.

2. In the **Customize the Ribbon** list, expand the tab set you want to manage, and then select the group you want to add the commands to.

3. In the **Choose commands from** list, select the tab the command appears on, or select **Popular Commands**, **Commands Not in the Ribbon**, **All Commands**, or **Macros**.

16

4. In the left list, locate and select the command you want to add to the group. Then select the **Add** button.

5. Make any other changes, and then select **OK**.

To reset the ribbon to its default configuration

1. Display the **Customize Ribbon** page of the **Word Options** dialog.

2. In the lower-right corner of the page, select **Reset**, and then select either of the following:

   - Reset only selected Ribbon tab

   - Reset all customizations

Manage add-ins and security options

The final section of pages in the Word Options dialog contains the settings that you should think carefully about before changing, because they can affect the security of your system.

Manage add-ins

Add-ins are utilities that add specialized functionality to a program but aren't full-fledged programs themselves. Word includes two primary types of add-ins: COM add-ins (which use the Component Object Model) and Word add-ins.

There are several sources of add-ins:

- You can purchase add-ins from third-party vendors. For example, you can purchase an add-in that allows you to assign keyboard shortcuts to Word commands that don't already have them.

- You can download free add-ins from the Microsoft website or other websites.

- Third-party applications such as Adobe Acrobat and Intuit QuickBooks might install add-ins so you can interact with them from within Microsoft 365 desktop apps.

> **TIP** Be careful when downloading add-ins from websites other than those you know and trust. Add-ins are executable files that can easily be used to spread viruses and otherwise wreak havoc on your computer. For this reason, the Microsoft Office Trust Center might disable the installation of add-ins or require your permission to install or run them.

You can locate information about the add-ins on your computer and manage the add-ins from the Add-ins page of the Word Options dialog.

The Add-ins page displays installed add-ins of all types

Each type of add-in has its own management interface. You can add and remove add-ins, turn off installed add-ins, and enable add-ins that have been disabled.

Display and manage active and disabled add-ins

Many add-ins install themselves, but to use some add-ins, you must first install them on your computer and then load them into your computer's memory.

> **SEE ALSO** For information about third-party Office add-ins you can install from the Add-ins group on the Insert tab, see the sidebar "Install Office tools" in Chapter 3, "Enter and edit text."

To display management options for a type of add-in

1. Display the **Add-Ins** page of the **Word Options** dialog.

2. In the **Manage** list at the bottom of the page, select the type of add-in you want to manage. Then select the adjacent **Go** button.

To install an add-in

1. Display the dialog for the type of add-in you want to manage.

2. In the dialog, select **Add** or **Add New**.

3. In the **Add Add-In** dialog, navigate to the folder where the add-in you want to install is stored, and double-click its name.

4. In the list of available add-ins in the **Add-In** dialog, select the checkbox of the new add-in, and then select **OK** or **Load** to make the add-in available for use in Word.

Configure Trust Center options

The Trust Center is a separate multipage dialog in which you can configure security and privacy settings. You open the Trust Center from the Trust Center page of the Word Options dialog. The Trust Center settings aren't exposed directly on the page; you must select a button next to a warning recommending that you do not change any of the settings.

> Help keep your documents safe and your computer secure and healthy.
>
> **Security & more**
>
> Visit Office.com to learn more about protecting your privacy and security.
>
> Microsoft Trust Center
>
> **Microsoft Word Trust Center**
>
> The Trust Center contains security and privacy settings. These settings help keep your computer secure. We recommend that you do not change these settings.
>
> [Trust Center Settings...]

You can configure security and privacy settings in the Trust Center

If you don't take care when modifying the Trust Center settings, you could expose Word, your computer, and your network to malicious software. Depending on the type of files you work with and the breadth of your work network, you might find it appropriate to modify some of these settings in Word. Review the available settings so you can evaluate whether any of them would be appropriate to change in your specific situation.

The Trust Center has 12 pages of options that you can configure. When you first open the Trust Center from the Backstage view, the Macro Settings page is active. As in the Word Options dialog, you select a page tab name in the left pane to display that page in the right pane.

It's safest to run macros only from trusted sources

Most pages display options that are very specific to the page name. When you're working in Word, some circumstances will send you directly to this dialog—for example, if you open a document that contains macros, and then select the info bar to enable them, Word takes you to this page.

Many of the Trust Center options are beyond the scope of any needs that you'd usually have when creating documents. Some options that might be of interest are those that make it easier to work in documents that you trust, but that Word might not know are safe.

When you open a document from an online location (such as a cloud storage location or email message) or from a location that has been deemed unsafe, Word opens

16

the file in Protected View, with most editing functions disabled. This prevents any malicious code embedded in the file from gaining access to your computer. If you're uncertain about the origin of a file that you're opening, you can choose to open the file in Protected View.

In Protected View, the title bar displays *Read-Only* in brackets to the right of the file name, and a yellow banner at the top of the content pane provides information about why the file has been opened in Protected View. If you know that the document is from a safe location or sender, and you want to edit the file content, you can choose to enable editing.

If the documents you edit frequently open in Protected View and you don't want them to, change this behavior by modifying options in the Trust Center.

- If you want to open a document from a specific storage location without going into Protected View, you can add that folder (and its subfolders, if you want) to your Trusted Locations list.

Trust the contents of specific storage folders

If you want to trust folders on other computers on your network, you must first specifically choose that option. Otherwise, when you try to add a network folder as a trusted location, the Trust Center displays a message that it is not permitted by your current security settings. Before selecting the option to allow network locations, consider who or what has access to the network locations you intend to allow, and whether the locations are secure or could host malicious content.

- If you want to be able to edit all files of a specific type (based on the file extension) you can modify the File Block settings.

File Block Settings

For each file type, you can select the Open and Save check boxes. By selecting Open, Word blocks this file type, or opens it in Protected View. By selecting Save, Word prevents saving in this file type.

File Type	Open	Save
Word 2007 and later Documents and Templates	☐	☐
OpenDocument Text Files	☐	☐
Word 2007 and later Binary Documents and Templates	☐	☐
Word 2003 Binary Documents and Templates	☐	
Word 2003 and Plain XML Documents	☐	☐
Word XP Binary Documents and Templates	☐	
Word 2000 Binary Documents and Templates	☐	
Word 97 Binary Documents and Templates	☐	
Word 95 Binary Documents and Templates	☑	
Word 6.0 Binary Documents and Templates	☑	
Word 2 and earlier Binary Documents and Templates	☑	
Web Pages	☐	☐
RTF Files	☐	☐
Plain Text Files	☐	☐
Legacy Converters for Word	☐	☐
Office Open XML Converters for Word	☐	☐
PDF Files	☐	

Open behavior for selected file types:
- ○ Do not open selected file types
- ● Open selected file types in Protected View
- ○ Open selected file types in Protected View and allow editing

[Restore Defaults]

Block specific file types or permit editing in Protected View

- You can exclude an entire class of files (files originating from the internet, stored in unsafe locations, or received as email attachments) from Protected View.

Protected View

Protected View opens potentially dangerous files, without any security prompts, in a restricted mode to help minimize harm to your computer. By disabling Protected View you could be exposing your computer to possible security threats.
- ☑ Enable Protected View for files originating from the Internet
- ☑ Enable Protected View for files located in potentially unsafe locations ⓘ
- ☑ Enable Protected View for Outlook attachments ⓘ

Protect your computer and network from security threats in files

16

Before doing any of these things, you should carefully consider whether the "rule" you're making will always yield the results you want.

If you frequently work with a specific Word document that contains active content, and you feel that the security prompts are unnecessarily slowing you down, you can choose to trust the document. When you do so, it is added to the Trusted Documents list. You can manage the Trusted Documents list from the Trusted Documents page of the Trust Center. You can stipulate whether to trust documents that aren't stored locally, turn off the Trusted Documents function completely (to stop trusting all documents), or clear the Trusted Documents list to start over.

Trusted Documents

Warning: Trusted Documents may open without any security prompts for macros, ActiveX controls and other types of active content in the document, and the document will no longer open in Protected View or Application Guard. For a Trusted Document, you may not be prompted the next time you open the document, even if new active content was added to the document or changes were made to existing active content. Therefore, you should only trust documents if you trust the source.

Exception: If an IT administrator blocks active content by setting a policy, or if you set a Trust Center setting blocking active content, the active content will remain blocked.

☑ Allow documents on a network to be trusted

☐ Disable Trusted Documents

Clear all Trusted Documents so that they are no longer trusted   [Clear]

If you experience trouble with a trusted document, you can reset the list here

If you track changes and insert comments in documents, you might run into this surprising behavior: Word changing your user information to "Author" when you save the document. To correct that problem, clear the Remove Personal Information From File Properties On Save checkbox in the Document-specific Settings section of the Privacy Options page.

Privacy Options

[Privacy Settings...]
Read our privacy statement
[View Diagnostic Data...]

Document-specific settings

☐ Warn before printing, saving or sending a file that contains tracked changes or comments

☑ Make hidden markup visible when opening or saving

☐ Remove personal information from file properties on save ⓘ

[Document Inspector...]

Research & Reference

[Translation Options...]
[Research Options...]

Privacy options are important to manage if you use collaboration features

From the Research & Reference section of this page, you can configure translation options and manage the reference books and research sites available in Word.

Add reference services to your available resources

Some, but not all, of the Trust Center pages include buttons that you can select to reset that set of options to the defaults, so take care when making changes; if you're uncertain whether you should invoke a change, select Cancel to close the Trust Center without committing to the changes.

As with options in the Word Options dialog, you should take the time to familiarize yourself with the Trust Center settings so you know what changes are possible to make, in the event that it is appropriate to do so in your computing environment.

To open the Trust Center

1. Open the Word Options dialog.

2. In the left pane, select the **Trust Center** page tab.

3. On the **Trust Center** page, select the **Trust Center Settings** button.

To stop Word from attributing your comments to Author when you save files

1. Open the **Trust Center** and display the **Privacy Options** page.

2. In the **Document-specific settings** section of the Privacy Options page, clear the **Remove personal information from file properties on save** checkbox.

16

Key points

- Most of the settings that control the Word environment are available from the pages of the Word Options dialog. From this dialog, you also have access to security and privacy settings.

- The Quick Access Toolbar is an optional toolbar that you can display above or below the ribbon. Add almost any Word command to the Quick Access Toolbar so you can access it directly without navigating through ribbon tabs and menus. You can customize the Quick Access Toolbar for all documents, and create custom Quick Access Toolbars for specific documents or templates.

- You can customize the ribbon to display precisely the development tools you want.

Practice tasks

No practice files are necessary to complete the practice tasks in this chapter.

The introduction includes a complete list of practice files and download instructions.

Change default Word options

Start Word, display any document, and then perform the following tasks:

1. Open the **Word Options** dialog.

2. Explore each page of the dialog.

3. On the **General**, **Display**, **Proofing**, **Save**, **Language**, and **Advanced** pages, do the following:

   - Notice the sections and the options in each section.

   - Note the options that apply only to the current file.

   - Modify the options on each page as necessary to fit the way you work.

4. Close the **Word Options** dialog.

Display and customize the Quick Access Toolbar

Start Word, display any document, and then perform the following tasks:

1. Display the Quick Access Toolbar below the ribbon. Consider the merits of this location versus above the ribbon.

2. From the **Customize Quick Access Toolbar** menu, add the **Print Preview and Print** command to the Quick Access Toolbar.

3. From the **Design** tab of the ribbon, add the following commands to the Quick Access Toolbar:

   - From the **Document Formatting** group, add the **Paragraph Spacing** command.

   - From the **Page Background** group, add the **Watermark** command.

   - Notice that each of the commands is represented on the Quick Access Toolbar exactly as it is on the ribbon. Selecting the Paragraph Spacing arrow displays a list, and selecting Watermark displays a gallery.

4. From the **Show** group on the **View** tab, add the **Ruler** command and the **Gridlines** command to the Quick Access Toolbar. Notice that the commands are represented on the Quick Access Toolbar as checkboxes.

5. Point to the commands you added to the Quick Access Toolbar and then to the same commands on the View tab. Notice that ScreenTips for commands on the Quick Access Toolbar are identical to those for commands on the ribbon.

6. Display the **Quick Access Toolbar** page of the **Word Options** dialog, and then do the following:

   - In the left pane, display the commands that appear on the **Layout** tab.

   - Add the **Grid Settings** button from the Layout tab to the Quick Access Toolbar.

   - In the right pane, move the **Paragraph Spacing** button to the bottom of the list so that it will be the rightmost button on the Quick Access Toolbar (immediately to the left of the Customize Quick Access Toolbar button).

   - Insert a separator between the original commands and the commands you added in this task set.

   - Insert two separators between the **Watermark** and **Ruler** commands.

7. Close the **Word Options** dialog and observe your customized Quick Access Toolbar. Note the way that a single separator sets off commands, and the way that a double separator sets off commands.

8. Redisplay the **Quick Access Toolbar** page of the **Word Options** dialog.

9. Reset the Quick Access Toolbar to its default configuration, and then close the dialog. Notice that resetting the Quick Access Toolbar doesn't change its location.

10. Close the document without saving it.

Customize the ribbon

Start Word, display any document, and then perform the following tasks:

1. Display the **Customize Ribbon** page of the **Word Options** dialog.

2. Remove the **Mailings** tab from the ribbon and add the **Developer** tab (if it isn't already shown).

3. Create a custom tab and name it MyShapes.

4. Move the **MyShapes** tab to the top of the right pane so that it will be the left-most optional ribbon tab (immediately to the right of the File tab).

5. Change the name of the custom group on the **MyShapes** tab to Curved Shapes and select a curved or circular icon to represent the group.

6. Create another custom group on the **MyShapes** tab. Name the group Angular Shapes and select a square or triangular icon to represent the group.

7. In the **Choose commands from** list, select **Commands Not in the Ribbon**. From the list, add the **Arc** and **Oval** commands to the **Curved Shapes** group. Then add the **Isosceles Triangle** and **Rectangle** commands to the **Angular Shapes** group.

8. Close the **Word Options** dialog and display your custom tab. Select the **Arc** command, and then drag on the page to draw an arc.

9. Change the width of the app window to collapse at least one custom group. Verify that the group button displays the icon you selected.

10. Restore the app window to its original width and redisplay the **Customize Ribbon** page of the **Word Options** dialog.

11. Reset the ribbon to its default configuration, and then close the dialog.

12. Close the document without saving it.

Manage add-ins and security options

Start Word, display any document, and then perform the following tasks:

1. Open the **Word Options** dialog.

2. Display the **Add-ins** page, and then do the following:

   - Review the add-ins installed on your computer.

   - Notice the types of add-ins that are active, and display the dialog for that type of add-in.

   - Notice add-ins that are turned on or off. Modify these settings if you know what the add-ins do and want to.

   - Close the dialog.

Chapter 16

3. Display the **Trust Center** page, and then do the following:

   - Open the Trust Center.

   - Review the settings therein, but don't make any changes.

   - Close the Trust Center.

4. Close the **Word Options** dialog.

Keyboard shortcuts

Throughout this book, we provide information about how to perform tasks quickly and efficiently by using keyboard shortcuts. You can use the following keyboard shortcuts when working in Word, and you can create your own shortcuts for use in Word.

In this appendix

- Word 365 keyboard shortcuts

- Office 365 keyboard shortcuts

- Create custom keyboard shortcuts

> ✓ **TIP** In the keyboard shortcut tables, keys you press at the same time are separated by a plus sign (+), and keys you press sequentially are separated by a comma (,).

Word 365 keyboard shortcuts

This section provides a comprehensive list of keyboard shortcuts built into Word 365. You can use these keyboard shortcuts to:

- Perform common tasks

- Work with documents and webpages

- Edit and move text and graphics

- Apply character and paragraph formatting

- Work with mail merge and fields

- Use the Language bar

- Perform function key tasks

Perform common tasks

Action	Keyboard shortcut
Create a nonbreaking space	Ctrl+Shift+Spacebar
Create a nonbreaking hyphen	Ctrl+Shift+Hyphen
Apply bold formatting	Ctrl+B
Apply italic formatting	Ctrl+I
Apply underline formatting	Ctrl+U
Decrease font size one value	Ctrl+<
Increase font size one value	Ctrl+>
Decrease font size 1 point	Ctrl+[
Increase font size 1 point	Ctrl+]
Remove paragraph or character formatting	Ctrl+Spacebar
Copy the selected text or object	Ctrl+C
Cut the selected text or object	Ctrl+X
Paste text or an object	Ctrl+V
Refine paste action (Paste Special)	Ctrl+Alt+V
Paste formatting only	Ctrl+Shift+V
Undo the last action	Ctrl+Z
Redo the last action	Ctrl+Y
Open the Word Count dialog	Ctrl+Shift+G

Work with documents and webpages

Create, view, and save documents

Action	Keyboard shortcut
Create a new document	Ctrl+N
Open a document	Ctrl+O
Close a document	Ctrl+W
Split the document window	Alt+Ctrl+S
Remove the document window split	Alt+Shift+C or Alt+Ctrl+S
Save a document	Ctrl+S

Find, replace, and browse through text

Action	Keyboard shortcut
Open the Navigation pane (to search the document)	Ctrl+F
Repeat a Find action (after closing the Find And Replace dialog)	Alt+Ctrl+Y
Replace text, specific formatting, and special items	Ctrl+H
Go to a page, bookmark, footnote, table, comment, graphic, or other location	Ctrl+G
Switch between the last four places you edited	Alt+Ctrl+Z
Open a list of browse options	Alt+Ctrl+Home
Move to the previous browse object (set in browse options)	Ctrl+Page Up
Move to the next browse object (set in browse options)	Ctrl+Page Down

Switch to another view

Action	Keyboard shortcut
Switch to Print Layout view	Alt+Ctrl+P
Switch to Outline view	Alt+Ctrl+O
Switch to Draft view	Alt+Ctrl+N

Work in Outline view

Action	Keyboard shortcut
Promote a paragraph	Alt+Shift+Left Arrow
Demote a paragraph	Alt+Shift+Right Arrow
Demote to body text	Ctrl+Shift+N
Move selected paragraphs up	Alt+Shift+Up Arrow
Move selected paragraphs down	Alt+Shift+Down Arrow
Expand text under a heading	Alt+Shift+Plus sign
Collapse text under a heading	Alt+Shift+Minus sign
Expand or collapse all text or headings	Alt+Shift+A
Hide or display character formatting	/ (slash) on the numeric keypad
Show the first line of body text or all body text	Alt+Shift+L
Show all headings with the Heading 1 style	Alt+Shift+1
Show all headings up to the Heading n style	Alt+Shift+n
Insert a tab character	Ctrl+Tab

Work in Read Mode

Action	Keyboard shortcut
Go to the beginning of the document	Home
Go to the end of the document	End
Go to page n	n, Enter
Exit Read Mode	Esc

Print and preview documents

Action	Keyboard shortcut
Print a document	Ctrl+P
Display the Print page of the Backstage view	Alt+Ctrl+I
Move around the preview page when zoomed in	Arrow keys
Move by one preview page when zoomed out	Page Up or Page Down
Move to the first preview page when zoomed out	Ctrl+Home
Move to the last preview page when zoomed out	Ctrl+End

Review documents

Action	Keyboard shortcut
Insert a comment	Alt+Ctrl+M
Turn change tracking on or off	Ctrl+Shift+E
Close the Reviewing pane if it's open	Alt+Shift+C

Work with references, footnotes, and endnotes

Action	Keyboard shortcut
Mark a table of contents entry	Alt+Shift+O
Mark a table of authorities entry (citation)	Alt+Shift+I
Mark an index entry	Alt+Shift+X
Insert a footnote	Alt+Ctrl+F
Insert an endnote	Alt+Ctrl+D

Work with webpages

Action	Keyboard shortcut
Insert a hyperlink	Ctrl+K
Go back one page	Alt+Left Arrow
Go forward one page	Alt+Right Arrow
Refresh	F9

Edit and move text and graphics

Delete text and graphics

Action	Keyboard shortcut
Delete one character to the left	Backspace
Delete one word to the left	Ctrl+Backspace
Delete one character to the right	Delete
Delete one word to the right	Ctrl+Delete
Cut selected content to the Clipboard	Ctrl+X
Undo the last action	Ctrl+Z
Cut selected content to the Spike (single-use Clipboard instance)	Ctrl+F3

Copy and move text and graphics

Action	Keyboard shortcut
Open the Clipboard	Press Alt+H to move to the Home tab, and then press F,O
Copy selected text or graphics to the Clipboard	Ctrl+C
Cut selected text or graphics to the Clipboard	Ctrl+X
Paste the most recent addition or pasted item from the Clipboard	Ctrl+V

Action	Keyboard shortcut
Move text or graphics once	F2 (then move the cursor and press Enter)
Copy text or graphics once	Shift+F2 (then move the cursor and press Enter)
When text or an object is selected, open the Create New Building Block dialog	Alt+F3
Display the shortcut menu associated with the selected building block	Shift+F10
Copy the header or footer used in the previous section of the document	Alt+Shift+R

Insert special characters

Action	Keyboard shortcut
A field	Ctrl+F9
A line break	Shift+Enter
A page break	Ctrl+Enter
A column break	Ctrl+Shift+Enter
An em dash	Alt+Ctrl+Minus sign
An en dash	Ctrl+Minus sign
An optional hyphen	Ctrl+Hyphen
A nonbreaking hyphen	Ctrl+Shift+Hyphen
A nonbreaking space	Ctrl+Shift+Spacebar
The copyright symbol	Alt+Ctrl+C
The registered trademark symbol	Alt+Ctrl+R
The trademark symbol	Alt+Ctrl+T
An ellipsis	Alt+Ctrl+Period
An AutoText entry	Enter (after the ScreenTip appears)

Insert characters by using character codes

Action	Keyboard shortcut
Insert the Unicode character for the specified Unicode (hexadecimal) character code. For example, to insert the euro currency symbol (€), enter 20AC, and then hold down Alt and press X.	The character code, Alt+X
Find out the Unicode character code for the selected character	Alt+X
Insert the ANSI character for the specified ANSI (decimal) character code. For example, to insert the euro currency symbol, hold down Alt and press 0128 on the numeric keypad.	Alt+the character code (on the numeric keypad)

Select text and graphics outside of a table

Action	Keyboard shortcut
Select text and graphics	Hold down Shift and use the arrow keys to move the cursor
Turn on Extend mode	F8 (press Esc to cancel)
Select the nearest character	F8+Left Arrow or Right Arrow
Increase the size of a selection	F8 (press once to turn on Extend mode, twice to select a word, three times to select a sentence, four times to select a paragraph, and so on; press Esc to cancel Extend mode)

Action	Keyboard shortcut
Reduce the size of a selection	Shift+F8
Turn off Extend mode	Esc
Extend a selection one character to the right	Shift+Right Arrow
Extend a selection one character to the left	Shift+Left Arrow
Extend a selection to the end of a word	Ctrl+Shift+Right Arrow
Extend a selection to the beginning of a word	Ctrl+Shift+Left Arrow
Extend a selection to the end of a line	Shift+End
Extend a selection to the beginning of a line	Shift+Home
Extend a selection one line down	Shift+Down Arrow
Extend a selection one line up	Shift+Up Arrow
Extend a selection to the end of a paragraph	Ctrl+Shift+Down Arrow
Extend a selection to the beginning of a paragraph	Ctrl+Shift+Up Arrow
Extend a selection one screen down	Shift+Page Down
Extend a selection one screen up	Shift+Page Up
Extend a selection to the beginning of a document	Ctrl+Shift+Home
Extend a selection to the end of a document	Ctrl+Shift+End
Extend a selection to the end of a window	Alt+Ctrl+Shift+Page Down
Extend a selection to include the entire document	Ctrl+A
Select a vertical block of text	Ctrl+Shift+F8, and then use the arrow keys; press Esc to cancel
Extend a selection to a specific location in a document	F8+arrow keys; press Esc to cancel

Select text and graphics in a table

Action	Keyboard shortcut
Select the next cell's contents	Tab
Select the preceding cell's contents	Shift+Tab
Extend a selection to adjacent cells	Hold down Shift and press an arrow key repeatedly
Select a column	Use the arrow keys to move to the column's top or bottom cell, and then do either of the following: Press Shift+Alt+Page Down to select the column from top to bottom Press Shift+Alt+Page Up to select the column from bottom to top
Extend a selection (or block)	Ctrl+Shift+F8, and then use the arrow keys; press Esc to cancel selection mode
Select an entire table	Alt+5 on the numeric keypad

Move through documents

Action	Keyboard shortcut
One character to the left	Left Arrow
One character to the right	Right Arrow
One word to the left	Ctrl+Left Arrow
One word to the right	Ctrl+Right Arrow
One paragraph up	Ctrl+Up Arrow
One paragraph down	Ctrl+Down Arrow
One cell to the left (in a table)	Shift+Tab
One cell to the right (in a table)	Tab
Up one line	Up Arrow
Down one line	Down Arrow

Action	Keyboard shortcut
To the end of a line	End
To the beginning of a line	Home
To the top of the window	Alt+Ctrl+Page Up
To the end of the window	Alt+Ctrl+Page Down
Up one screen (scrolling)	Page Up
Down one screen (scrolling)	Page Down
To the top of the next page	Ctrl+Page Down
To the top of the previous page	Ctrl+Page Up
To the end of a document	Ctrl+End
To the beginning of a document	Ctrl+Home
To a previous revision	Shift+F5
Immediately after opening a document, go to the location you were working in when the document was last closed	Shift+F5

Move around in a table

Action	Keyboard shortcut
To the next cell in a row	Tab
To the previous cell in a row	Shift+Tab
To the first cell in a row	Alt+Home
To the last cell in a row	Alt+End
To the first cell in a column	Alt+Page Up
To the last cell in a column	Alt+Page Down
To the previous row	Up Arrow
To the next row	Down Arrow

Insert characters and move content in tables

Action	Keyboard shortcut
Insert a new paragraph in a cell	Enter
Insert a tab character in a cell	Ctrl+Tab
Move content up one row	Alt+Shift+Up Arrow
Move content down one row	Alt+Shift+Down Arrow

Apply character and paragraph formatting

Copy formatting

Action	Keyboard shortcut
Copy formatting from text	Ctrl+Shift+C
Apply copied formatting to text	Ctrl+Shift+V

Change or resize the font

> **TIP** The following keyboard shortcuts do not work when Word is in Read mode.

Action	Keyboard shortcut
Open the Font dialog to change the font	Ctrl+Shift+F
Increase the font size	Ctrl+>
Decrease the font size	Ctrl+<
Increase the font size by 1 point	Ctrl+]
Decrease the font size by 1 point	Ctrl+[

Apply character formatting

Action	Keyboard shortcut
Open the Font dialog to change the formatting of characters	Ctrl+D
Change the case of letters	Shift+F3
Format all letters as capitals	Ctrl+Shift+A
Apply bold formatting	Ctrl+B
Apply an underline	Ctrl+U
Underline words but not spaces	Ctrl+Shift+W
Double-underline text	Ctrl+Shift+D
Apply hidden text formatting	Ctrl+Shift+H
Apply italic formatting	Ctrl+I
Format letters as small capitals	Ctrl+Shift+K
Apply subscript formatting (automatic spacing)	Ctrl+Equal sign
Apply superscript formatting (automatic spacing)	Ctrl+Shift+Plus sign
Remove manual character formatting	Ctrl+Spacebar
Change the selection to the Symbol font	Ctrl+Shift+Q

View and copy text formats

Action	Keyboard shortcut
Display nonprinting characters	Ctrl+Shift+8
Review text formatting	Shift+F1 (then select the text with the formatting you want to review)
Copy formats	Ctrl+Shift+C
Paste formats	Ctrl+Shift+V

Set the line spacing

Action	Keyboard shortcut
Single-space lines	Ctrl+1
Double-space lines	Ctrl+2
Set 1.5-line spacing	Ctrl+5
Add or remove one line space preceding a paragraph	Ctrl+0 (zero)

Align paragraphs

Action	Keyboard shortcut
Switch a paragraph between centered and left-aligned	Ctrl+E
Switch a paragraph between justified and left-aligned	Ctrl+J
Switch a paragraph between right-aligned and left-aligned	Ctrl+R
Left align a paragraph	Ctrl+L
Indent a paragraph from the left	Ctrl+M
Remove a paragraph indent from the left	Ctrl+Shift+M
Create a hanging indent	Ctrl+T
Reduce a hanging indent	Ctrl+Shift+T
Remove paragraph formatting	Ctrl+Q

Apply paragraph styles

Action	Keyboard shortcut
Open the Apply Styles pane	Ctrl+Shift+S
Open the Styles pane	Alt+Ctrl+Shift+S
Start AutoFormat	Alt+Ctrl+K
Apply the Normal style	Ctrl+Shift+N
Apply the Heading 1 style	Alt+Ctrl+1
Apply the Heading 2 style	Alt+Ctrl+2
Apply the Heading 3 style	Alt+Ctrl+3
Close the active Styles pane	Ctrl+Spacebar, C

Work with mail merge and fields

Perform mail merges

Action	Keyboard shortcut
Preview a mail merge	Alt+Shift+K
Merge a document	Alt+Shift+N
Print the merged document	Alt+Shift+M
Edit a mail-merge data document	Alt+Shift+E
Insert a merge field	Alt+Shift+F

Work with fields

Action	Keyboard shortcut
Insert a Date field	Alt+Shift+D
Insert a ListNum field	Alt+Ctrl+L
Insert a Page field	Alt+Shift+P
Insert a Time field	Alt+Shift+T
Insert an empty field	Ctrl+F9
Update linked information in a Word source document	Ctrl+Shift+F7
Update selected fields	F9
Unlink a field	Ctrl+Shift+F9
Switch between a selected field code and its result	Shift+F9
Switch between all field codes and their results	Alt+F9
Run GoToButton or MacroButton from the field that displays the field results	Alt+Shift+F9
Go to the next field	F11
Go to the previous field	Shift+F11
Lock a field	Ctrl+F11
Unlock a field	Ctrl+Shift+F11

Use the Language bar

Action	Keyboard shortcut
Switch between languages or keyboard layouts	Left Alt+Shift (Alt+Shift on the left side of the keyboard)
Display a list of correction alternatives	Windows logo key+C
Turn handwriting on or off	Windows logo key+H
Turn Japanese Input Method Editor (IME) on 101 keyboard on or off	Alt+~
Turn Korean IME on 101 keyboard on or off	Right Alt
Turn Chinese IME on 101 keyboard on or off	Ctrl+Spacebar

> ✓ **TIP** The Windows logo key is available on the bottom row of keys on most keyboards.

Perform function key tasks

Function keys

Action	Keyboard shortcut
Get Help or visit Office.com	F1
Move text or graphics	F2
Repeat the last action	F4
Choose the Go To command (Home tab)	F5
Go to the next pane or frame	F6
Choose the Spelling command (Review tab)	F7
Extend a selection	F8 (press once to turn on Extend mode, twice to select a word, three times to select a sentence, four times to select a paragraph, and so on; press Esc to cancel Extend mode)

Action	Keyboard shortcut
Update the selected fields	F9
Show KeyTips	F10
Go to the next field	F11
Choose the Save As command	F12

Shift+function key

Action	Keyboard shortcut
Start context-sensitive Help or reveal formatting	Shift+F1
Copy text	Shift+F2
Change the case of letters	Shift+F3
Repeat a Find or Go To action	Shift+F4
Move to the last change	Shift+F5
Go to the previous pane or frame (after pressing F6)	Shift+F6
Choose the Thesaurus command (Review tab, Proofing group)	Shift+F7
Reduce the size of a selection	Shift+F8
Switch between a field code and its result	Shift+F9
Display a shortcut menu	Shift+F10
Go to the previous field	Shift+F11
Choose the Save command	Shift+F12

Ctrl+function key

Action	Keyboard shortcut
Expand or collapse the ribbon	Ctrl+F1
Choose the Print Preview command	Ctrl+F2
Close the window	Ctrl+F4
Go to the next window	Ctrl+F6
Insert an empty field	Ctrl+F9
Maximize the document window	Ctrl+F10
Lock a field	Ctrl+F11
Choose the Open command	Ctrl+F12

Ctrl+Shift+function key

Action	Keyboard shortcut
Insert the contents of the Spike	Ctrl+Shift+F3
Edit a bookmark	Ctrl+Shift+F5
Go to the previous window	Ctrl+Shift+F6
Update linked information in a Word source document	Ctrl+Shift+F7
Extend a selection or block	Ctrl+Shift+F8, and then press an arrow key
Unlink a field	Ctrl+Shift+F9
Unlock a field	Ctrl+Shift+F11
Choose the Print command	Ctrl+Shift+F12

Alt+function key

Action	Keyboard shortcut
Go to the next field	Alt+F1
Create a new building block	Alt+F3

Action	Keyboard shortcut
Exit Word	Alt+F4
Restore the app window size	Alt+F5
Move from an open dialog back to the document, for dialogs that support this behavior	Alt+F6
Find the next misspelling or grammatical error	Alt+F7
Run a macro	Alt+F8
Switch between all field codes and their results	Alt+F9
Display the Selection And Visibility pane	Alt+F10
Display Microsoft Visual Basic code	Alt+F11

Alt+Shift+function key

Action	Keyboard shortcut
Go to the previous field	Alt+Shift+F1
Choose the Save command	Alt+Shift+F2
Display the Research pane	Alt+Shift+F7
Run GoToButton or MacroButton from the field that displays the field results	Alt+Shift+F9
Display a menu or message for an available action	Alt+Shift+F10
Select the Table Of Contents button when the table of contents is active	Alt+Shift+F12

Ctrl+Alt+function key

Action	Keyboard shortcut
Display Microsoft System Information	Ctrl+Alt+F1
Choose the Open command	Ctrl+Alt+F2

Office 365 keyboard shortcuts

The following keyboard shortcuts are available in all the primary Office 365 apps, including Word. You can use these keyboard shortcuts to:

- Display and use windows

- Work in dialogs

- Use the Backstage view

- Navigate the ribbon

- Change the keyboard focus without using the mouse

- Move around in and work in tables

- Access and use panes and galleries

- Access and use available actions

- Find and replace content

- Get Help

Display and use windows

Action	Keyboard shortcut
Switch to the next window	Alt+Tab
Switch to the previous window	Alt+Shift+Tab
Close the active window	Ctrl+W or Ctrl+F4
Restore the size of the active window after you maximize it	Alt+F5
Move to a pane from another pane in the app window (clockwise direction) If pressing F6 does not display the pane that you want, press Alt to put the focus on the ribbon, and then press Ctrl+Tab to move to the pane	F6 or Shift+F6

Action	Keyboard shortcut
Switch to the next open window	Ctrl+F6
Switch to the previous window	Ctrl+Shift+F6
Maximize or restore a selected window	Ctrl+F10
Copy a picture of the screen to the Clipboard	Print Screen (or PrtScn)
Copy a picture of the selected window to the Clipboard	Alt+Print Screen

Work in dialogs

Action	Keyboard shortcut
Move to the next option or option group	Tab
Move to the previous option or option group	Shift+Tab
Switch to the next tab in a dialog	Ctrl+Tab
Switch to the previous tab in a dialog	Ctrl+Shift+Tab
Move between options in an open dropdown list, or between options in a group of options	Arrow keys
Perform the action assigned to the selected button; select or clear the selected checkbox	Spacebar
Select an option; select or clear a checkbox	Alt+the underlined letter
Open a selected dropdown list	Alt+Down Arrow
Select an option from a dropdown list	First letter of the list option
Close a selected dropdown list; cancel a command and close a dialog	Esc
Run the selected command	Enter

Use edit boxes within dialogs

An edit box is a blank box in which you enter or paste an entry.

Action	Keyboard shortcut
Move to the beginning of the entry	Home
Move to the end of the entry	End
Move one character to the left or right	Left Arrow or Right Arrow
Move one word to the left	Ctrl+Left Arrow
Move one word to the right	Ctrl+Right Arrow
Select or unselect one character to the left	Shift+Left Arrow
Select or unselect one character to the right	Shift+Right Arrow
Select or unselect one word to the left	Ctrl+Shift+Left Arrow
Select or unselect one word to the right	Ctrl+Shift+Right Arrow
Select from the insertion point to the beginning of the entry	Shift+Home
Select from the insertion point to the end of the entry	Shift+End

Use the Open and Save As dialogs

Action	Keyboard shortcut
Open the Open dialog	Ctrl+F12 or Ctrl+O
Open the Save As dialog	F12
Open the selected folder or file	Enter
Open the folder one level above the selected folder	Backspace
Delete the selected folder or file	Delete
Display a shortcut menu for a selected item such as a folder or file	Shift+F10
Move forward through options	Tab
Move back through options	Shift+Tab
Open the Look In list	F4 or Alt+I
Refresh the file list	F5

Use the Backstage view

Action	Keyboard shortcut
Display the Open page of the Backstage view	Ctrl+O
Display the Save As page of the Backstage view (when saving a file for the first time)	Ctrl+S
Continue saving an Office file (after giving the file a name and location)	Ctrl+S
Display the Save As page of the Backstage view (after initially saving a file)	Alt+F+S
Close the Backstage view	Esc

 TIP You can use dialogs instead of Backstage view pages by selecting the Don't Show The Backstage When Opening Or Saving Files With Keyboard Shortcuts checkbox on the Save page of the Word Options dialog. Set this option in any Office app to enable it in all Office apps.

Navigate the ribbon

Follow these steps:

1. Press **Alt** to display the KeyTips over each feature in the current view.

2. Press the character(s) shown in the KeyTip over the feature that you want to use.

TIP To cancel the action and hide the KeyTips, press Alt.

Change the keyboard focus without using the mouse

Action	Keyboard shortcut
Select the active tab of the ribbon and activate the access keys	Alt or F10 (press either key again to return to the document and cancel the access keys)
Move to another tab of the ribbon	F10 to select the active tab, and then Left Arrow or Right Arrow
Expand or collapse the ribbon	Ctrl+F1
Display the shortcut menu for the selected item	Shift+F10
Move the focus to select each of the following areas of the window: ■ Active tab of the ribbon ■ Any open panes ■ Status bar at the bottom of the window ■ Your document	F6
Move the focus to each command on the ribbon, forward or backward, respectively	Tab or Shift+Tab
Move among the items on the ribbon	Arrow keys
Activate the selected command or control on the ribbon	Spacebar or Enter
Display the selected menu or gallery on the ribbon	Spacebar or Enter
Activate a command or control on the ribbon so that you can modify a value	Enter
Finish modifying a value in a control on the ribbon, and move focus back to the document	Enter
Get help on the selected command or control on the ribbon	F1

Move around in and work in tables

Action	Keyboard shortcut
Move to the next cell	Tab
Move to the preceding cell	Shift+Tab
Move to the next row	Down Arrow
Move to the preceding row	Up Arrow
Insert a tab in a cell	Ctrl+Tab
Start a new paragraph	Enter
Add a new row at the bottom of the table	Tab at the end of the last row

Access and use panes and galleries

Action	Keyboard shortcut
Move to a pane from another pane in the app window	F6
When a menu is active, move to a pane	Ctrl+Tab
When a pane is active, select the next or previous option in the pane	Tab or Shift+Tab
Display the full set of commands on the pane menu	Ctrl+Spacebar
Perform the action assigned to the selected button	Spacebar or Enter
Open a dropdown menu for the selected gallery item	Shift+F10
Select the first or last item in a gallery	Home or End
Scroll up or down in the selected gallery list	Page Up or Page Down
Close a pane	Ctrl+Spacebar, C
Open the Clipboard	Alt+H, F, O

Access and use available actions

Action	Keyboard shortcut
Display the shortcut menu for the selected item	Shift+F10
Display the menu or message for an available action or for the AutoCorrect Options button or the Paste Options button	Alt+Shift+F10
Move between options in a menu of available actions	Arrow keys
Perform the action for the selected item on a menu of available actions	Enter
Close the available actions menu or message	Esc

Find and replace content

Action	Keyboard shortcut
Open the Find dialog	Ctrl+F
Open the Replace dialog	Ctrl+H
Repeat the last Find action	Shift+F4

Get Help

Action	Keyboard shortcut
Open the Help window	F1
Close the Help window	Alt+F4
Switch between the Help window and the active app	Alt+Tab
Return to the Help table of contents	Alt+Home
Select the next item in the Help window	Tab
Select the previous item in the Help window	Shift+Tab
Perform the action for the selected item	Enter
Select the next hidden text or hyperlink, including Show All or Hide All at the top of a Help topic	Tab

Action	Keyboard shortcut
Select the previous hidden text or hyperlink	Shift+Tab
Perform the action for the selected Show All, Hide All, hidden text, or hyperlink	Enter
Move back to the previous Help topic (Back button)	Alt+Left Arrow or Backspace
Move forward to the next Help topic (Forward button)	Alt+Right Arrow
Scroll small amounts up or down, respectively, within the currently displayed Help topic	Up Arrow, Down Arrow
Scroll larger amounts up or down, respectively, within the currently displayed Help topic	Page Up, Page Down
When in the Help window, display a menu of commands for the Help window	Shift+F10
Stop the last action (Stop button)	Esc
Print the current Help topic If the cursor is not in the current Help topic, press F6 and then press Ctrl+P	Ctrl+P
In a table of contents in tree view, select the next or previous item, respectively	Up Arrow, Down Arrow
In a table of contents in tree view, expand or collapse the selected item, respectively	Left Arrow, Right Arrow

Create custom keyboard shortcuts

If a command you use frequently doesn't have a built-in keyboard shortcut, or if you don't like the keyboard shortcut assigned to a command, you can create one either in a specific document or in a template. You can also modify the built-in keyboard shortcuts.

To manage keyboard shortcuts

1. Display the **Customize Ribbon** page of the **Word Options** dialog.

2. Below the **Choose commands from** pane, to the right of **Keyboard shortcuts**, select the **Customize** button.

609

3. In the **Customize Keyboard** dialog, select the category containing the command for which you want to create a keyboard shortcut, and then select the command.

   The Current Keys box displays any keyboard shortcut already assigned to the command.

4. Position the cursor in the **Press new shortcut key** box, and then press the key combination you want to use as a keyboard shortcut for the selected command.

   In the area below the Current Keys box, Word tells you whether the keyboard shortcut is currently assigned to a command or unassigned.

5. To delete an existing keyboard shortcut to make it available for reassignment, select it in the **Current keys** box, and then select the **Remove** button.

6. To assign an available keyboard shortcut to the selected command, do either of the following:

   • To save the keyboard shortcut in all documents based on the current template, verify that the template name is selected in the **Save changes in** list, and then select **Assign**.

   • To save the keyboard shortcut only in the current document, select the document name in the **Save changes in** list, and then select **Assign**.

7. To delete all custom keyboard shortcuts, select **Reset All**.

8. Close the **Customize Keyboard** dialog and the **Word Options** dialog.

Glossary

Accessibility Checker A feature of the Microsoft 365 desktop apps that detects common accessibility issues such as missing alternative text, improperly structured tables, illogical heading order, and insufficient color contrast.

accessible content Content that is created, packaged, and delivered in a way that supports equitable access by all people, including people with vision or mobility issues and people using assistive technology such as screen magnifiers and screen readers.

add-in A utility that adds specialized functionality to an app such as Word but does not operate as an independent app.

All Markup view A view that displays all tracked changes, including formatting, text edits, and comments.

alt text A descriptive text alternative for an image or object as required for accessibility.

aspect ratio The relationship between an image's width and height.

attribute An individual item of character formatting, such as size or color, that determines how text looks.

AutoCorrect A feature that automatically detects and corrects misspelled words and incorrect capitalization. You can add your own AutoCorrect entries.

AutoShape One of an array of ready-made shapes provided by Word to assist you with creating more complex pictures.

background The colors, shading, texture, and graphics that appear behind the text and objects in a document.

balloon In Print Layout view or Web Layout view, a box that shows comments and tracked changes in the margins of a document, making it easy to review and respond to them.

bar chart A chart with bars that compares the quantities of two or more items.

bibliography A listing of reference sources for information in a report or other publication.

blog A frequently updated online journal or column. Blogs are often used to publish personal or company information in an informal way. Short for *web log*. See also *vlog*.

bookmark A location or section of text that is electronically marked so it can be returned to later. Like a physical bookmark, a Word bookmark marks a specific location in a document. You can display a specific bookmark from the Go To page of the Find And Replace dialog or from the Insert Bookmark dialog.

border A visible outline applied to a paragraph, page, picture, table, table cell, or other document element. You can specify the color, pattern, and weight or width of a border. See also *gridlines*.

building block Frequently used text or image elements saved in a gallery, from which it can be inserted quickly into a document.

caption Descriptive text associated with a figure, photo, illustration, or screenshot.

category axis The horizontal reference line of a chart or graph, which usually depicts category or time data. Also called the *x-axis*.

cell A box formed by the intersection of a row and column in a worksheet or a table, in which you enter information.

cell address The location of a cell, expressed as its column letter and row number, as in A1.

character formatting Formatting such as bold and italic that affects the appearance of characters rather than of an entire paragraph.

character spacing The distance between characters in a line of text. (In typography, also referred to as kerning.) Can be adjusted by pushing characters apart (expanding) or squeezing them together (condensing).

character style A combination of character formatting options identified by a style name. See also *paragraph style; table style.*

chart area A chart region in which you position chart elements, render axes, and plot data.

chevron The « and » characters that enclose each merge field in a main document. Also known as *merge field characters* or *guillemet characters.*

citation A reference within a document to the source of the information, the details of which are given in a bibliography.

Click and Type A feature that allows you to double-click a blank area of a document to position the cursor in that location, with the appropriate paragraph alignment already in place. You can turn this feature on or off in Advanced Options.

clip art A piece of free, ready-made art distributed without copyright. Usually cartoons, sketches, illustrations, or photographs.

Clipboard A storage area shared by all Microsoft 365 apps, where cut or copied items are temporarily stored so they can be pasted elsewhere.

coauthor To collaborate with other people on the development of a document.

collaborate To work with other people to update or interact with content.

column The vertical arrangement of text into one or more side-by-side sections; vertically aligned table cells.

column break A break inserted in the text of a column to force the text below it to move to the next column.

column chart A chart that displays data in vertical bars to facilitate data comparison.

comment A note or annotation an author or reviewer adds to a document. Word displays the comment in a balloon in the right margin of the document or in the Comments pane.

Compatibility Checker A feature of the Microsoft 365 desktop apps that detects formatting and features in a file that aren't supported by older versions of the application.

contextual tab See *tool tab.*

cross-reference entry An entry in an index that refers readers to a related entry.

cursor A representation on the screen of the input device pointer location.

cycle diagram A diagram that shows a continuous process.

data marker A customizable symbol or shape that identifies a data point on a chart. Data markers can be bars, columns, pie or doughnut slices, dots, and various other shapes and can be various sizes and colors.

data point An individual value plotted in a chart.

data series Related data points plotted in a chart. Most charts can display multiple data series. A pie chart has only one data series.

data source A file containing variable information, such as names and addresses, that is merged with a main document containing static information.

demoting In an outline, changing a heading to a lower heading level or body text; for example, changing from Heading 5 to Heading 6. See also *promoting*.

desktop publishing A process that creates pages by combining text and objects, such as tables and graphics, in a visually appealing way.

destination file The file into which a linked or embedded object or mail merge data is inserted. When you change information in a destination file, the information is not updated in the source file. See also *source file*.

diagram A graphic in which shapes, text, and pictures are used to illustrate a process, cycle, or relationship.

dialog box launcher On the ribbon, a button in the lower-right corner of some groups that opens a dialog or pane in which you can configure additional features related to the group.

digital certificate A file that contains a unique string of characters that can be combined with another file, such as a Word document, to create a verifiable signature for that file.

digital signature An electronic, encrypted stamp of authentication that verifies the authorship and integrity of the content of a file, such as a Word document.

Display For Review options The four options for displaying comments in a Word document. The options are All Markup, Simple Markup, No Markup, and Original.

Document Inspector A feature of the Microsoft 365 desktop apps that detects and optionally removes hidden properties and personal information from a document.

Draft view A document view that displays the content of a document with a simplified layout.

drag-and-drop editing A way of moving or copying selected text by dragging it from one location to another.

dragging A way of moving objects by selecting them and then, while the selection device is active (for example, while you're holding down the mouse button), moving the selection to the new location.

drawing canvas A work area for creating pictures in Word. The drawing canvas keeps the parts of the picture together, helps you position the picture, and provides a frame-like boundary between your picture and the text on the page.

drawing object Any graphic you draw or insert that can be changed and enhanced. Drawing objects include AutoShapes, curves, lines, and WordArt.

drop cap An enlarged, decorative capital letter that appears at the beginning of a paragraph.

embedded object An object that is wholly inserted into a file. Embedding the object, rather than simply inserting or pasting its contents, ensures that the object retains its original format. If you open the embedded object, you can edit it with the toolbars and menus from the app used to create it.

endnote A note at the end of a section or document that is referenced by text in the main body of the document. An endnote consists of two linked parts: a reference mark within the main body of text, and the corresponding text of the note. See also *footnote*.

Extensible Markup Language See *XML*.

field A placeholder that tells Word to supply the specified information in the specified way. Also, the set of information of a specific type in a data source, such as all the last names in a contacts list.

field name A first-row cell in a data source that identifies data in the column below.

file format The structure or organization of data in a file. The file format of a document is usually indicated by the file name extension.

filtering Displaying files or records in a data source that meet certain criteria—for example, filtering a data source to display only the records for people who live in a particular state. Filtering doesn't delete files; it simply changes the view so you display only the files that meet your criteria.

font A graphic design applied to a collection of numbers, symbols, and characters. A font describes a certain typeface, which can have qualities such as size, spacing, and pitch.

font effect An attribute, such as superscript, small capital letters, or shadow, that can be applied to a font.

font size The height (in points) of a collection of characters, where one point is equal to approximately 1/72 of an inch.

font style The emphasis placed on a font by using formatting such as bold, italic, underline, or color.

footer An area at the bottom of a document page that typically contains elements such as the page number and file name. See also *header*.

footnote A note at the end of a page that explains, comments on, or provides references for text in the main body of a document. A footnote consists of two linked parts: a reference mark within the main body of the document, and the corresponding text of the note. See also *endnote*.

formatting See *character formatting; paragraph formatting*.

formula A sequence of values, cell references, names, functions, or operators in a cell of a table or worksheet that together produce a new value. A formula always begins with an equal sign (=).

gallery A grouping of thumbnails that display options visually.

graphic Any piece of art used to illustrate or convey information or to add visual interest to a document.

grayscale The range of shades of black in an image.

gridlines In a table, thin lines that indicate the cell boundaries. Table gridlines do not print when you print a document. In a chart, lines that visually carry the y-axis values across the plot area. See also *border*.

group On a ribbon tab, an area containing buttons related to a specific document element or function.

grouping Assembling several objects, such as shapes, into a single unit so they act as one object. Grouped objects can easily be moved, sized, and formatted.

hands-free typing The ability to use your voice to enter text by using the Office Dictation feature.

hard copy Printed output on paper, film, or another permanent medium.

header An area at the top of a document page that typically contains elements such as the title, page number, or author's name. See also *footer*.

hierarchy diagram A diagram that illustrates the structure of an organization or entity.

HTML *Hypertext Markup Language* is a markup language that uses tags to mark elements in a document to indicate how web browsers, such as Microsoft Edge, should display these elements to the user and how they should respond to user actions.

hyperlink A connection from an anchor, such as text or a graphic, to a target such as a file, a location in a file, or a website. By default, text hyperlinks in Word documents are formatted as colored and underlined text. When you point to a hyperlink, the pointer shape changes to a hand.

Hypertext Markup Language See *HTML*.

hyphenating Separating syllables of a word that would otherwise extend beyond the right margin of the page, by using a hyphen.

icon A small picture or symbol representing a command, file type, function, app, or tool.

indent marker A marker on the horizontal ruler that controls the indentation of text from the left or right margin of a document.

index A list of the words and phrases discussed in a printed document and the page numbers they appear on.

index entry A field code that marks specific text for inclusion in an index. When you mark text as an index entry, Word inserts an XE (index entry) field formatted as hidden text.

index entry field The XE field, including the braces ({ }), that defines an index entry.

inking Entering content in a document through a touchscreen or touchpad.

justifying Making all lines of text in a paragraph or column fit the width of the document or column, with even margins on each side.

keyboard shortcut Any combination of keystrokes that can be used to perform a task that would otherwise require a mouse or other pointing device.

landscape The orientation of a picture or page where the width is greater than the height. See also *portrait*.

legend A key in a chart that identifies the colors and names of the data series or categories in the chart.

line break A manual break that forces the text that follows it to the next line. Also called a *text wrapping break*.

line graph or line chart A type of chart in which data points in a series are connected by a line.

link See *hyperlink*; *linked object*.

linked object An object that is inserted into a document but still exists in the source file. When information is linked, the document can be updated automatically if the information in the original document changes.

LinkedIn A social networking website used by business professionals.

list diagram A diagram in which lists of related or independent information are visually represented.

Live Preview A Microsoft 365 feature that temporarily displays the effect of applying a specific format to a selected document element, without implementing the change.

macro A recording of a series of commands performed in a Microsoft 365 file that can be run with a selection or keyboard shortcut.

mail merge The process of merging information into a main document from a data source, such as an email address book or database, to create customized documents, such as form letters or mailing labels.

main document In a mail merge operation in Word, the document that contains the static text and graphics that are the same for each version of the merged document.

manual page break A page break inserted to force subsequent information to appear on the next page.

margin The blank space outside the printing area on a page.

markup Comments and tracked changes such as insertions, deletions, and formatting changes.

markup views Views that display tracked changes such as insertions, deletions, and formatting changes.

matrix diagram A diagram that shows the relationship of components to a whole.

merge field A placeholder in a document that is replaced with variable information from a data source during the merge process.

Microsoft 365 Clipboard See *Clipboard*.

Navigation pane A pane that displays an outline of a document's headings, or thumbnails of a document's pages, and allows you to jump to a heading or page in the document by selecting it. Also provides content search capabilities.

nested table A table inserted into a cell of another table.

No Markup view A document view that hides all tracked changes and comments.

object An item, such as a graphic, video clip, sound file, or worksheet, that can be inserted into a document and then selected and modified.

OneDrive Part of Microsoft 365, OneDrive is a cloud storage and file sharing solution available to individual, business, and enterprise Microsoft 365 subscribers.

orientation The direction (horizontal or vertical) in which a page is laid out.

Original view A document view that displays all content as it was originally entered in the document, with any tracked changes and comments hidden.

orphan The first line of a paragraph printed by itself at the bottom of a page.

Outline view A view that shows the headings of a document indented to represent their level in the document's structure.

palette A collection of color swatches that you can apply to the selected text or object.

paragraph In word processing, a block of text that ends when you press the Enter key.

paragraph formatting Formatting that controls the appearance of a paragraph. Examples include indentation, alignment, line spacing, and pagination.

paragraph style A combination of character formatting and paragraph formatting that is named and stored as a set. Applying the style to a paragraph applies all the formatting characteristics at one time.

path A sequence of folders that leads to a specific file or folder. A backslash is used to separate each folder in a Windows path, and a forward slash is used to separate each directory in an internet path.

PDF (Portable Document Format) A fixed-layout file format in which the formatting of the document appears the same regardless of the computer on which it is displayed.

pen A customizable tool used for inking.

picture A photograph, clip art image, illustration, or another type of image created with an app other than Word.

picture diagram A diagram that uses pictures to convey information, rather than or in addition to text.

pie chart A round chart that shows the proportion of items in a single data series to the sum of the items. The pie chart represents each data set as a wedge of the round pie.

plot area In a two-dimensional chart, the area bounded by the axes, including all data series. In a three-dimensional chart, the area bounded by the axes, including the data series, category names, tick-mark labels, and axis titles.

point The unit of measure for expressing the size of characters in a font, where 72 points equals approximately 1 inch.

pointing to Pausing the mouse pointer or other pointing device over an on-screen element.

Portable Document Format See *PDF*.

portrait The orientation of a picture or page where the page is taller than it is wide. See also *landscape.*

post A message published on a blog, discussion board, or message board.

Print Layout view A view of a document as it will appear when printed—for example, items such as headers, footnotes, columns, and text boxes appear in their actual positions.

process diagram A diagram that visually represents the ordered set of steps required to complete a task.

promoting In an outline, changing body text to a heading, or changing a heading to a higher-level heading. See also *demoting.*

pull quote Text taken from the body of a document and showcased in a text box to create visual interest.

pyramid diagram A diagram that shows foundation-based relationships.

Query Selection criteria for extracting information from a data source.

quick Access Toolbar A customizable toolbar that displays commands of your choice above or below the ribbon.

Quick Table A table with sample data you can customize.

Read Mode A document view that displays a document in a simplified window with minimal controls, at a size optimized for reading documents on a computer screen. Previously referred to as Full Screen Reading view or Reading Layout view.

read-only A setting that allows a file to be read or copied but not changed or saved. If you change a read-only file, you can save your changes only if you give the document a new name.

record A collection of data about a person, a place, an event, or some other item. Records are the logical equivalents of rows in a table.

reference mark The number or symbol displayed in the body of a document when you insert a footnote or endnote.

relationship diagram A diagram that shows convergent, divergent, overlapping, merging, or containment elements.

revision A change in a document.

ribbon A user interface design introduced in Microsoft Office 2007 that organizes commands into logical groups on separate tabs.

row Horizontally aligned table cells.

saturation In color management, the purity of a color's hue, moving from gray to the pure color.

scalable vector graphic (SVG) A graphic format that stores image data in XML format instead of pixels. See also *vector graphic.*

screen clipping An image of all or part of the content displayed on a computer screen. Screen clippings can be captured by using a graphics capture tool such as the Screen Clipping tool included with Microsoft 365 apps and the Snipping Tool built into the Windows operating system.

ScreenTip A note that appears on the screen to provide information about the app interface or certain types of document content, such as proofing marks and hyperlinks within a document.

section break A mark you insert to show the end of a section. A section break stores the section formatting elements, such as the margins, page orientation, headers and footers, and sequence of page numbers.

selecting Highlighting text or activating an object so you can manipulate or edit it in some way.

selection area An area in a document's left margin in which you can drag to select blocks of text.

series axis The third axis in a three-dimensional coordinate system, used in charts or graphs to represent depth. Also called the *z-axis*.

SharePoint Part of Microsoft 365, SharePoint is an enterprise-level commercial productivity solution for communication, content and information management, collaboration, reporting, and more. By linking to and leveraging other Microsoft 365 apps and services such as Power Apps, Power Automate, Microsoft Forms, Microsoft Lists, and Yammer, enterprise customers can create powerful intranet sites, dashboards, and productivity tools that are available on desktop and mobile devices.

SharePoint library A file storage unit on a SharePoint site.

shortcut See *hyperlink; keyboard shortcut.*

Simple Markup view A document view that identifies the location of tracked changes in a document by an indicator in the margin. You can select the indicator to toggle the display of the changes.

sizing handle A small circle, square, or set of dots at the corner or on the side of a selected object. You drag these handles to change the size of the object horizontally, vertically, or proportionally.

SmartArt graphic A predefined set of shapes and text used as a basis for creating a diagram.

soft page break A page break Word inserts when the text reaches the bottom margin of a page.

source file A file that contains information that is linked, embedded, or merged into a destination file. Updates to source file content are reflected in the destination file when the data connection is refreshed. See also *destination file.*

Spike Similar to the Clipboard, the Spike is a building block in which you can collect content. You cut content to the Spike by pressing Ctrl+F3. You paste content from the Spike by pressing Ctrl+Shift+F3, by typing spike and then pressing F3, or from the Building Blocks gallery, where you can also view the current Spike content.

stack A set of graphics that overlap each other.

status bar An app window element, located at the bottom of the app window, that displays indicators and controls.

status bar indicator A notification on the status bar that displays information related to the current app.

style Any kind of formatting that is named and stored as a set. See also *character style; paragraph style; table style.*

style area pane An optional pane that displays the assigned paragraph style of the adjacent paragraph in Draft or Outline view. The style area pane width is set in the Display section of the Advanced page of the Outlook Options dialog. To display the pane, specify a width greater than 0.

subentry An index entry that falls under a more general heading; for example, *Mars* and *Venus* might be subentries of the index entry *planets*.

SVG See *scalable vector graphic.*

tab A tabbed page on the ribbon that contains buttons organized in groups.

tab leader An optional repeating character (usually a dot or dash) that separates the text before a tab stop from the text after the tab stop.

tab stop A location on the horizontal ruler that indicates how far to indent text or where to begin a column of text.

tabbed list A list that arranges text in simple columns separated by left, right, centered, or decimal tab stops.

table One or more rows of cells commonly used to display numbers and other items for quick reference and analysis. Items in a table are organized in rows and columns.

table of authorities A list of the references in a legal document, such as references to cases, statutes, and rules, along with the numbers of the pages on which the references appear.

table of contents A list of the headings in a document, along with the numbers of the pages on which the headings appear.

table of figures A list of the captions for pictures, charts, graphs, slides, or other illustrations in a document, along with the numbers of the pages on which the captions appear.

table style A set of formatting options, such as font, border style, and row banding, applied to a table. The regions of a table, such as the header row, header column, and data area, can be variously formatted.

target A file, location, object, or webpage displayed from a link or hyperlink.

template A file that can contain a predefined layout, text, graphics, and formatting, and that serves as the basis for new documents.

text box A container object that contains content separate from other document content.

text wrapping The way text wraps around an object on the page.

text wrapping break A manual break that forces the text that follows it to the next line. Also known as a *line break*.

theme A set of unified design elements that combine color, fonts, and effects, and that can be applied to a document or saved as part of a template.

thesaurus A reference tool that groups words and their synonyms.

thumbnail A small representation of an item, such as an image, a page of content, or a set of formatting, usually obtained by scaling a snapshot of it. Thumbnails are typically used to provide visual identifiers for related items.

tick-mark A small line of measurement, similar to a division line on a ruler, that intersects an axis in a chart.

tool tab A ribbon tab containing groups of commands that are pertinent only to a specific type of document element such as a picture, table, or text box. Tool tabs appear only when relevant content is selected.

value axis The vertical reference line of a chart or graph, which usually depicts value data. Also called the *y-axis*.

vector graphic A category of images that are composed of shapes instead of pixels, which means that as you increase or decrease their size, their edges remain smooth instead of becoming pixelated.

View Shortcuts toolbar A toolbar located at the right end of the status bar that contains tools for switching between views of document content and changing the display magnification.

view A common menu item that enables the user to select how the contents of the current app are displayed.

vlog A video blog or video log. See *blog*.

watermark A text or graphic image on the page behind the main content of a document.

web app See *Word for the web*.

web browser Software that interprets HTML files, formats them into webpages, and displays them. A web browser, such as Microsoft Edge, can follow hyperlinks, respond to requests to download files, and play sound or video files embedded in webpages.

Web Layout view A view of a document as it will appear in a web browser. In this view, a document appears as one page (without page breaks); text and tables wrap to fit the window.

web log See *blog*.

webpage A World Wide Web document. A webpage typically consists of an HTML file, with associated files for graphics and scripts, in a specific folder on a specific computer. It is identified by a Uniform Resource Locator (URL).

widow The last line of a paragraph printed by itself at the top of a page.

wildcard character A keyboard character that can be used to represent one or many characters when conducting a search. The question mark (?) represents a single character, and the asterisk (*) represents one or more characters.

Word for the web A Microsoft 365 online app that enables users to upload, view (in full fidelity), share, and edit Word files in a web browser. Users can create and edit new Word files directly from the web app, and these files can be saved, viewed, edited, and opened in the desktop Word app.

word processing The writing, editing, and formatting of documents in an app designed for working primarily with text.

word wrap The process of breaking lines of text automatically to stay within the page margins of a document or within window boundaries.

WordArt A group of text effects that incorporate qualities such as shadows, reflections, edge glow, beveled edges, 3D rotation, and transforms.

x-axis The horizontal reference line of a chart or graph, which usually depicts category or time data. Also called the *category axis*.

XML *eXtensible Markup Language* is a format for delivering rich, structured data in a standard, consistent way. XML tags describe a document's content, whereas HTML tags describe a document's appearance. XML is *extensible* because it allows designers to create their own customized tags. See also *HTML*.

y-axis The vertical reference line of a chart or graph, which usually depicts value data. Also called the *value axis*.

z-axis The third axis in a three-dimensional coordinate system, used in computer graphics to represent depth. Also called the *series axis*.

Index

0